Norihiro Yagi won the 32nd Akatsuka Award for his debut work, *UNDEADMAN*, which appeared in *Monthly Shonen Jump* magazine. His first serialized manga was his comedy *Angel Densetsu* (Angel Legend), which appeared in *Monthly Shonen Jump* from 1993 to 2000. His epic saga, *Claymore*, ran from 2001 to 2014 and was adapted into a television anime series and a video game.

In his spare time, Yagi enjoys things like the Japanese comedic duo Downtown, martial arts, games, driving, and hard rock music, but he doesn't consider these actual hobbies.

CLAYMORE VOL. 27
SHONEN JUMP ADVANCED Manga Edition

STORY AND ART BY
NORIHIRO YAGI

English Adaptation & Translation/John Werry
Touch-up Art & Lettering/Sabrina Heep
Design/Stacie Yamaki
Editor/Megan Bates

Printed in the U.S.A.

Published by VIZ Media, LLC
P.O. Box 77010
San Francisco, CA 94107

10 9 8 7 6 5 4 3 2 1
First printing, October 2015

PARENTAL ADVISORY
CLAYMORE is rated T+ for Older Teen
and is recommended for ages 16 and up.
This volume contains nudity and realistic
violence.
ratings.viz.com

SHONEN JUMP ADVANCED Manga Edition

Claymore
クレイモア

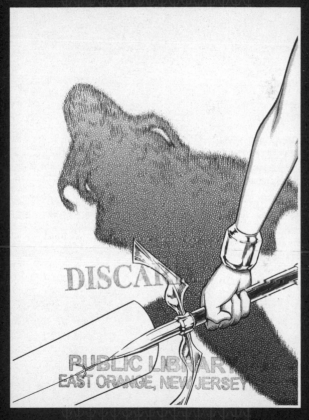

Vol. 27
Silver-Eyed Warriors

Story and Art by **Norihiro Yagi**

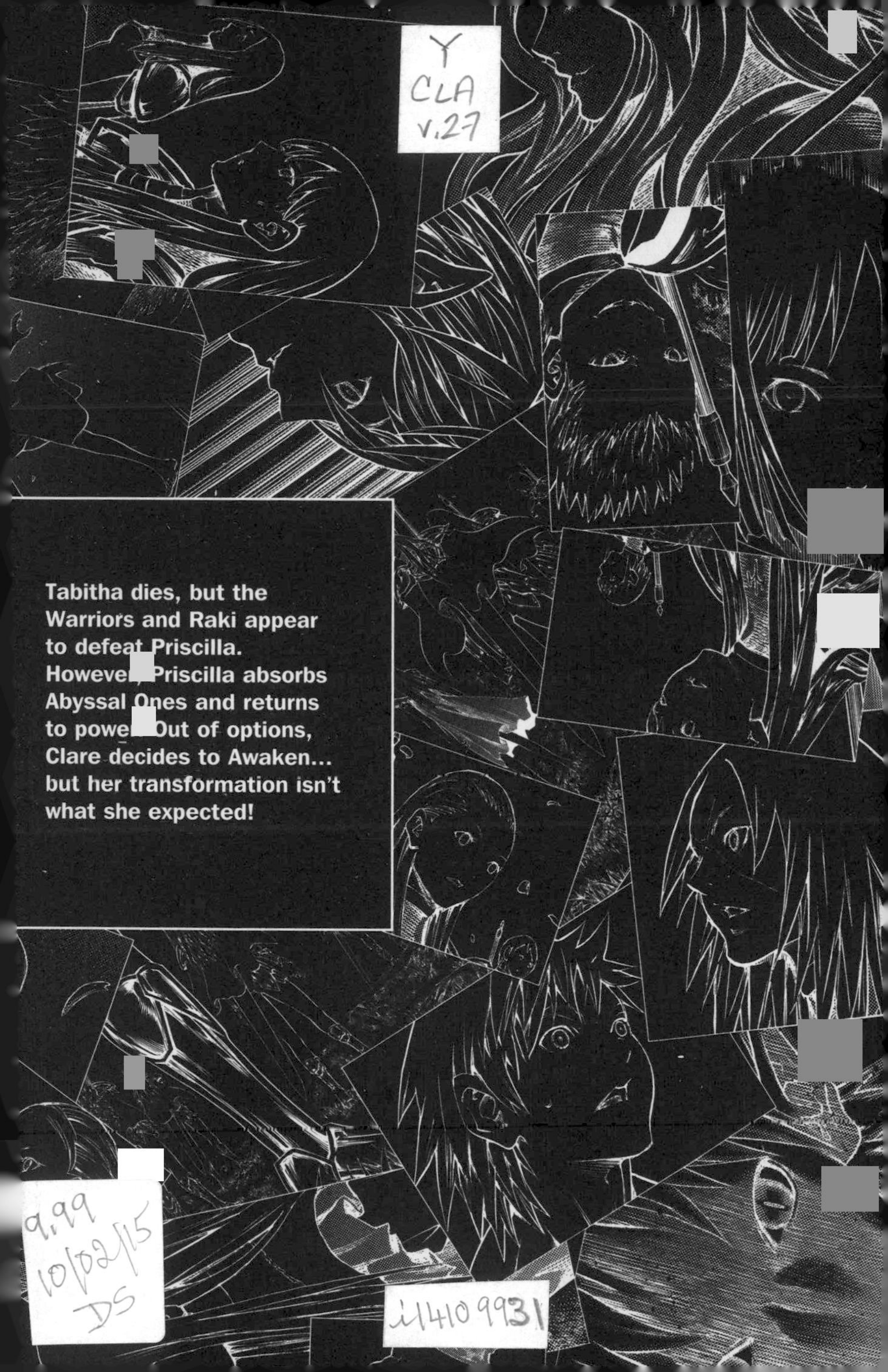

Tabitha dies, but the Warriors and Raki appear to defeat Priscilla. However, Priscilla absorbs Abyssal Ones and returns to power. Out of options, Clare decides to Awaken... but her transformation isn't what she expected!

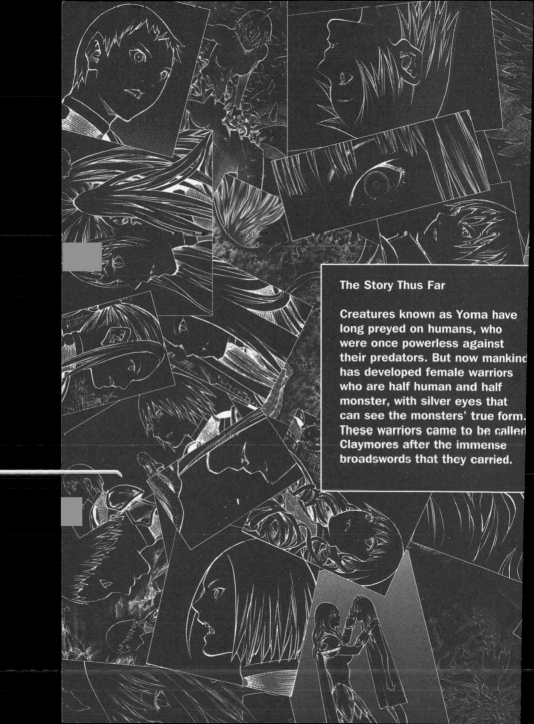

The Story Thus Far

Creatures known as Yoma have
long preyed on humans, who
were once powerless against
their predators. But now mankind
has developed female warriors
who are half human and half
monster, with silver eyes that
can see the monsters' true form.
These warriors came to be called
Claymores after the immense
broadswords that they carried.

Claymore

クレイモア

Vol. 27

CONTENTS

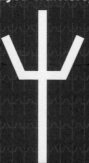

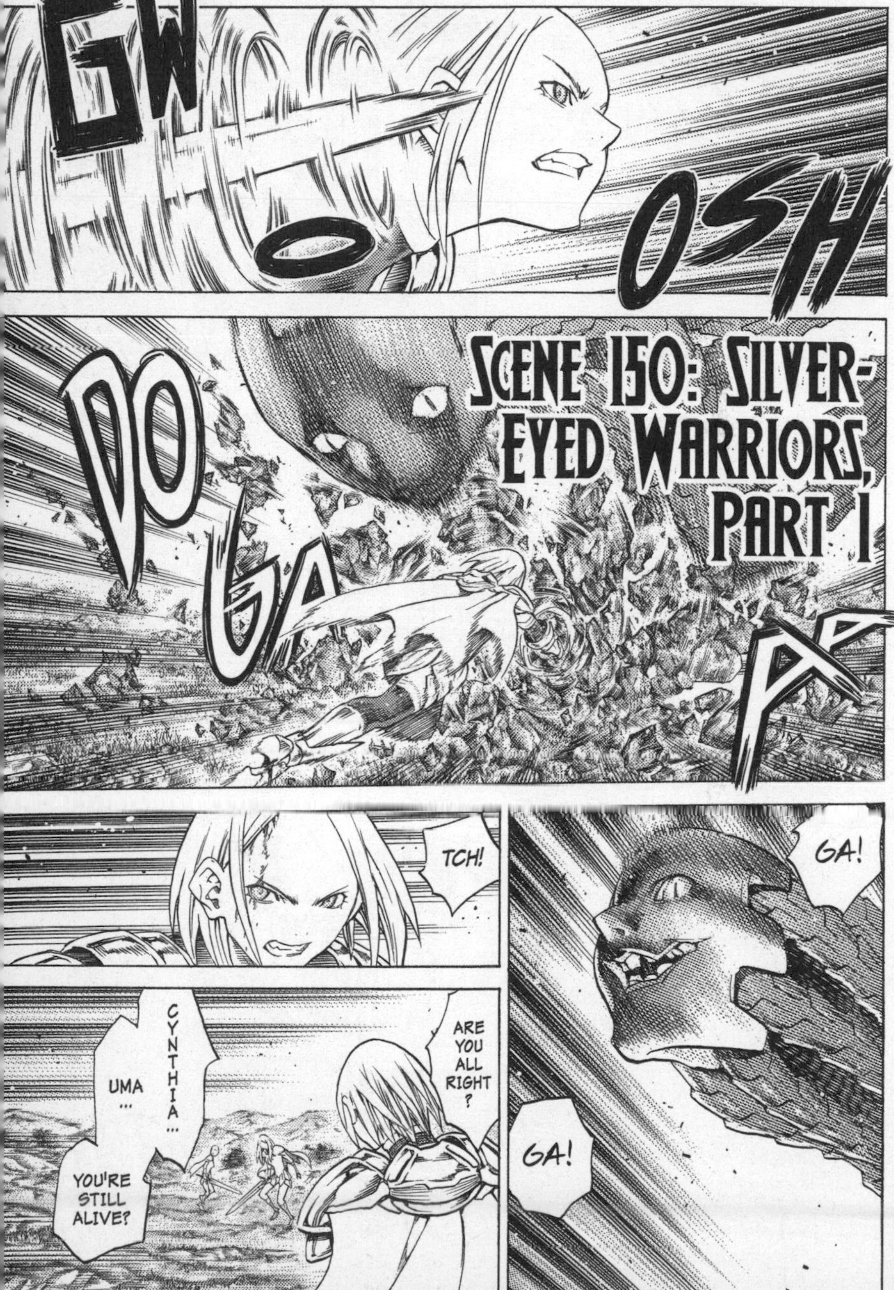
GWOOSH
SCENE 150: SILVER-EYED WARRIORS, PART 1
DOGA
GA!
GA!
TCH!
ARE YOU ALL RIGHT?
CYNTHIA...
UMA...
YOU'RE STILL ALIVE?

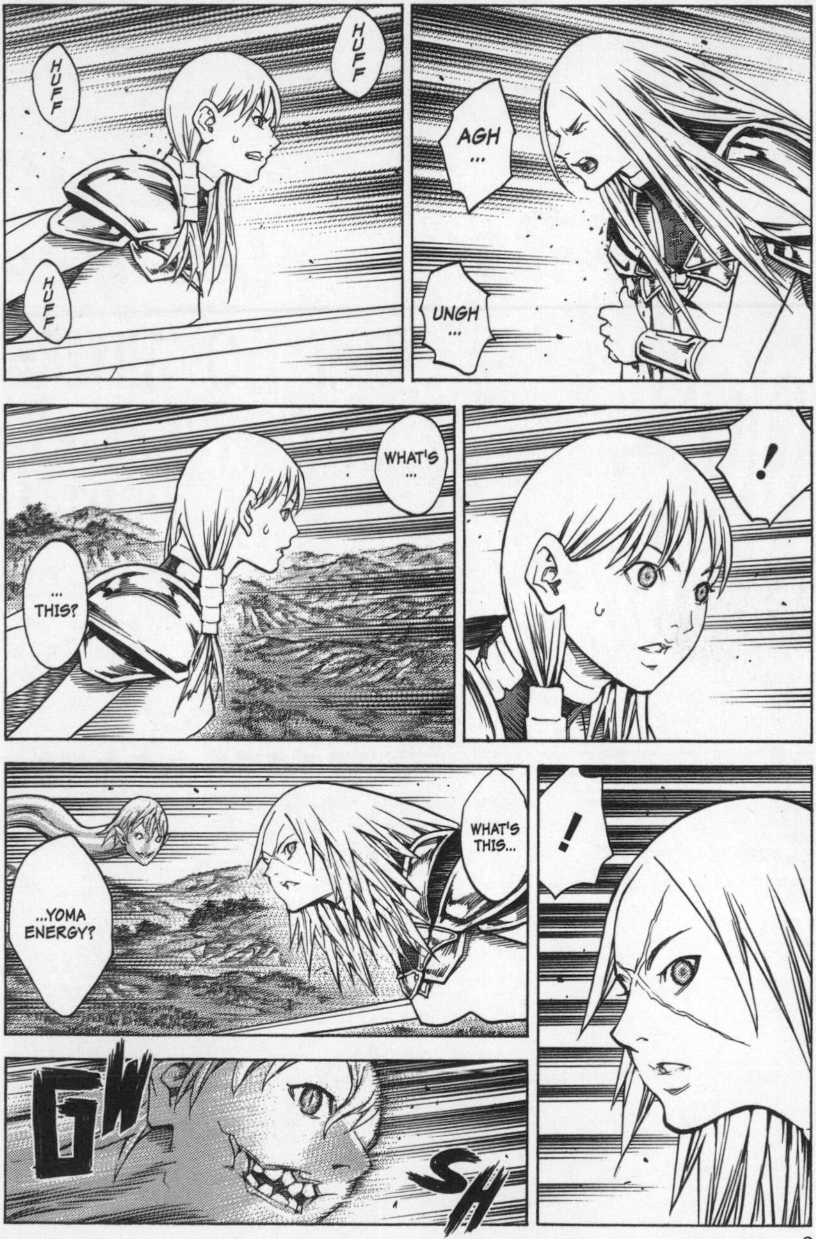
AGH ...
UNGH ...
HUFF
HUFF
HUFF
!
WHAT'S ...
... THIS?
!
WHAT'S THIS...
...YOMA ENERGY?
GW
SH

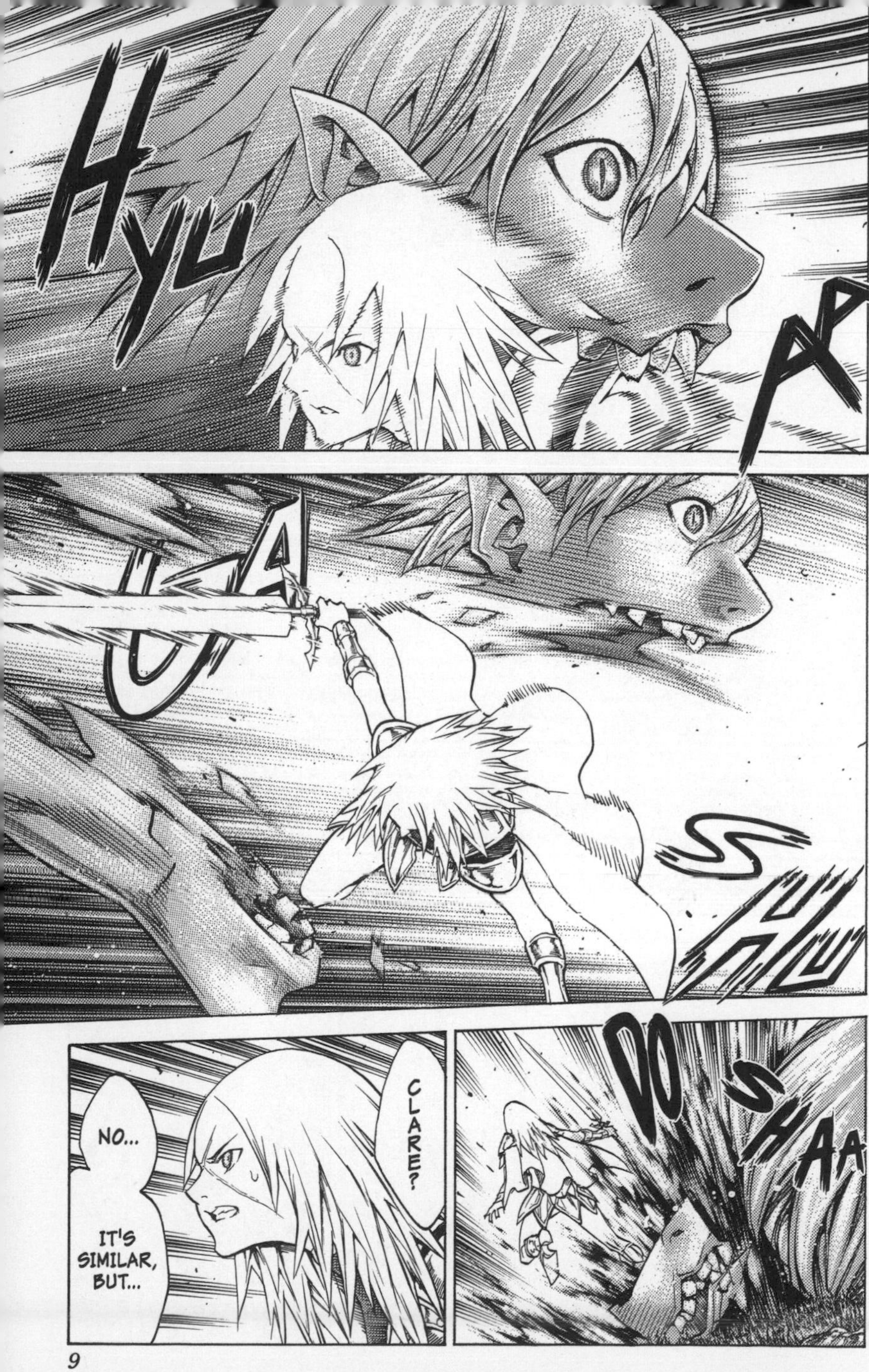
Hyu
GA
DOSHAA
CLARE?
NO...
IT'S SIMILAR, BUT...

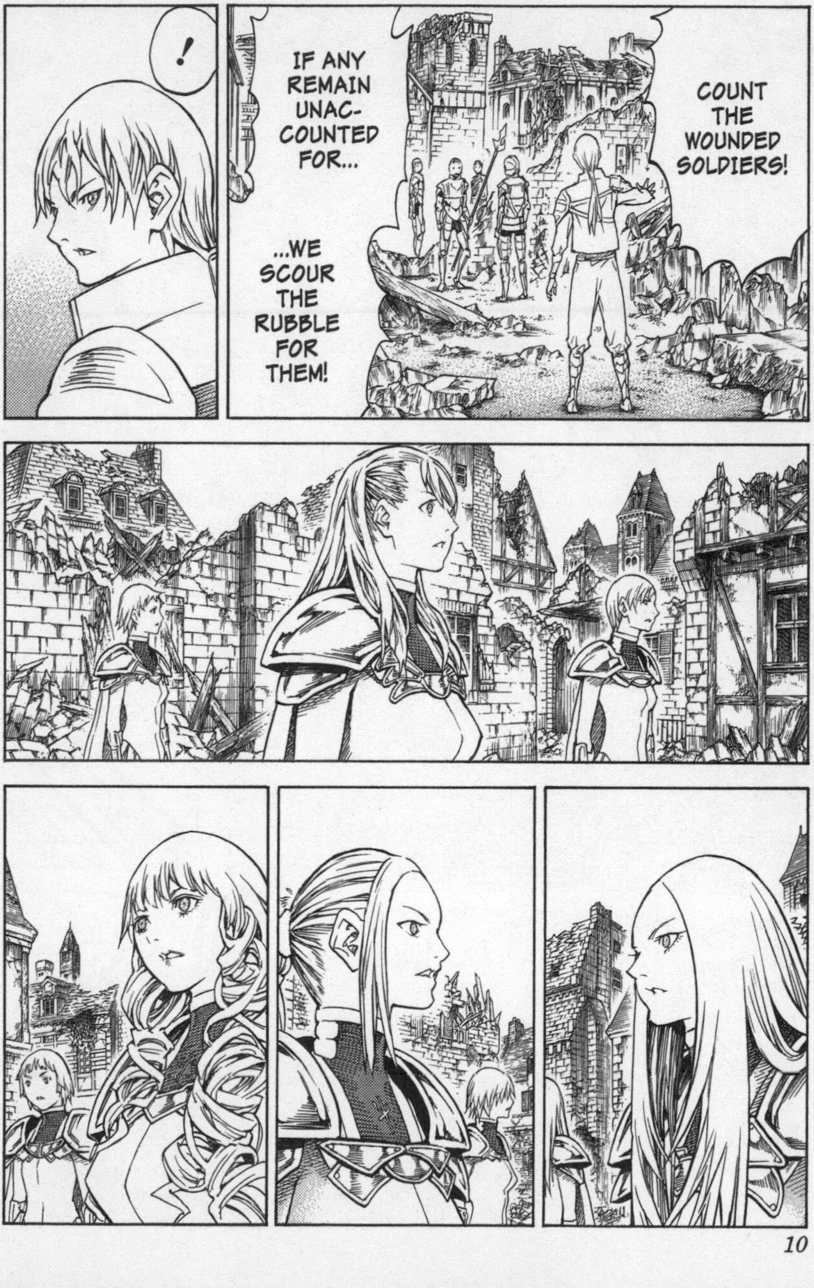
COUNT THE WOUNDED SOLDIERS!
IF ANY REMAIN UNAC-COUNTED FOR...
...WE SCOUR THE RUBBLE FOR THEM!
!

READ THIS WAY

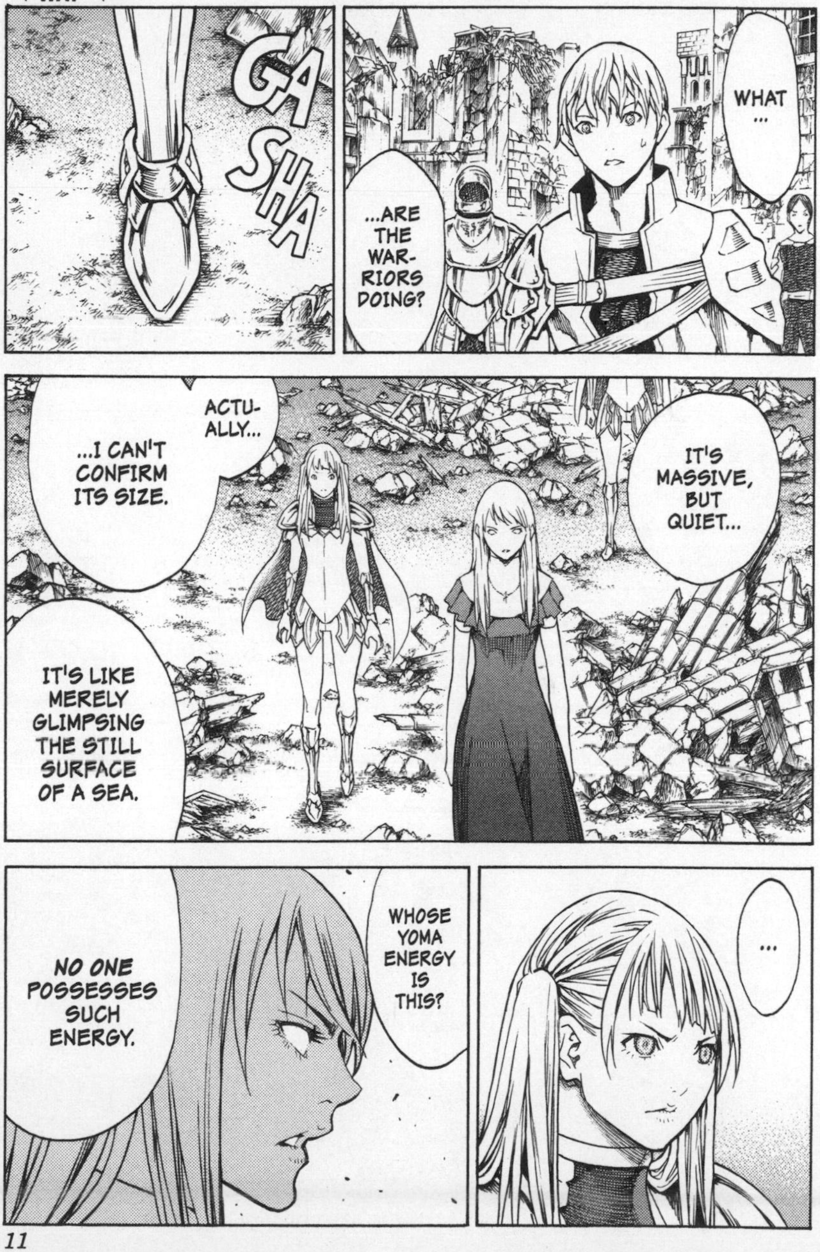
WHAT...
...ARE THE WARRIORS DOING?
GA SHA
IT'S MASSIVE, BUT QUIET...
ACTUALLY...
...I CAN'T CONFIRM ITS SIZE.
IT'S LIKE MERELY GLIMPSING THE STILL SURFACE OF A SEA.
...
WHOSE YOMA ENERGY IS THIS?
NO ONE POSSESSES SUCH ENERGY.

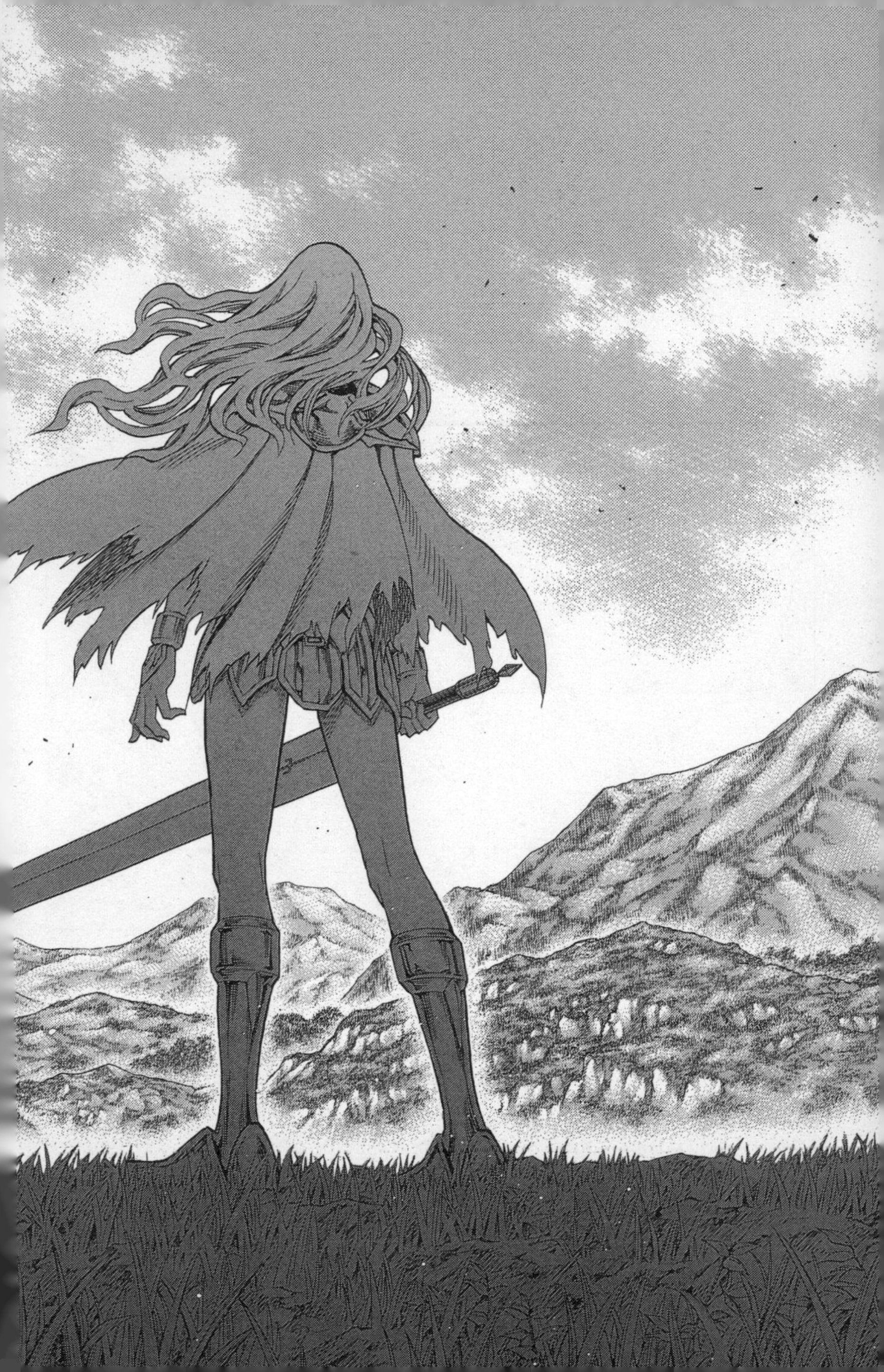

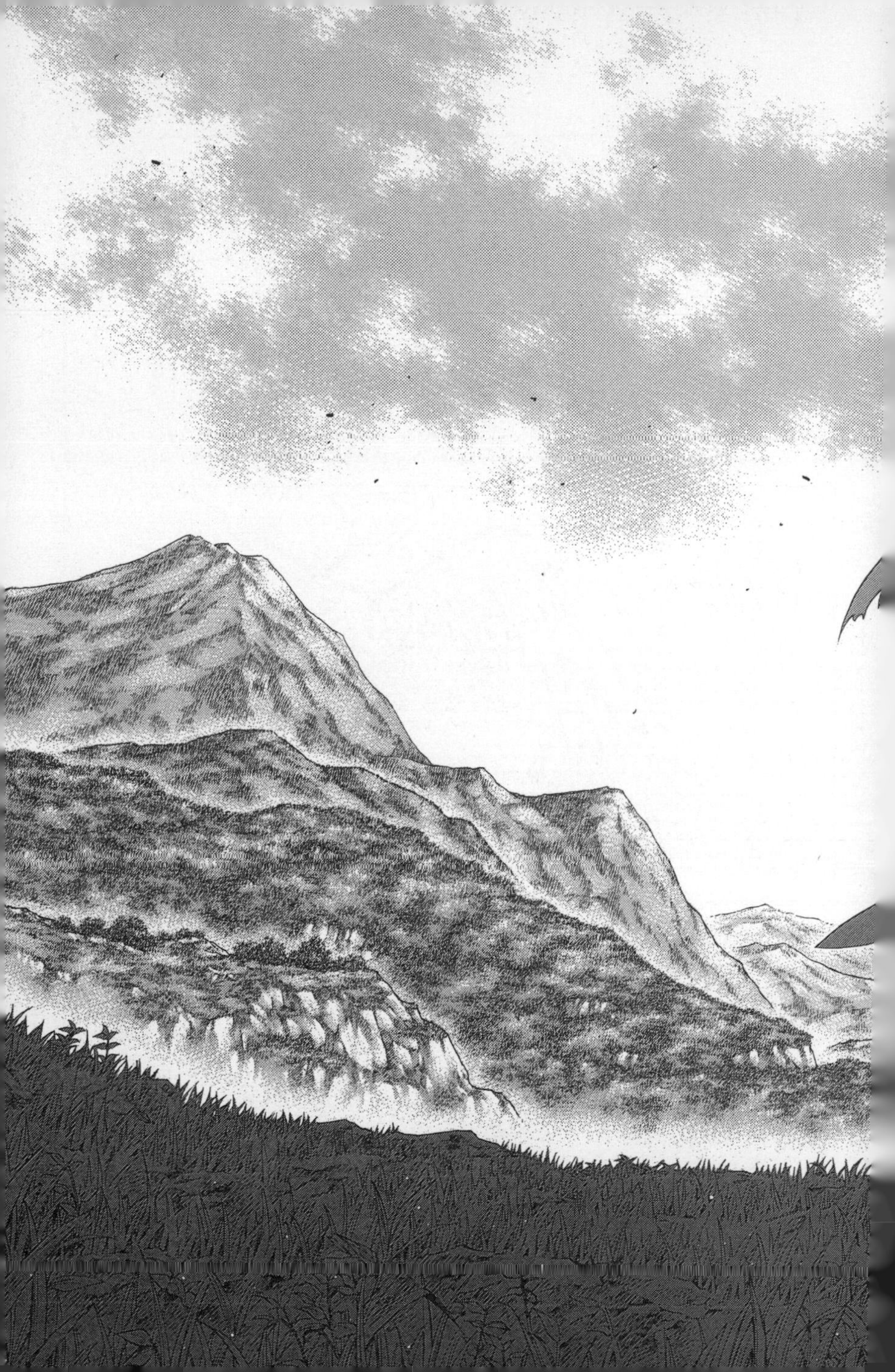

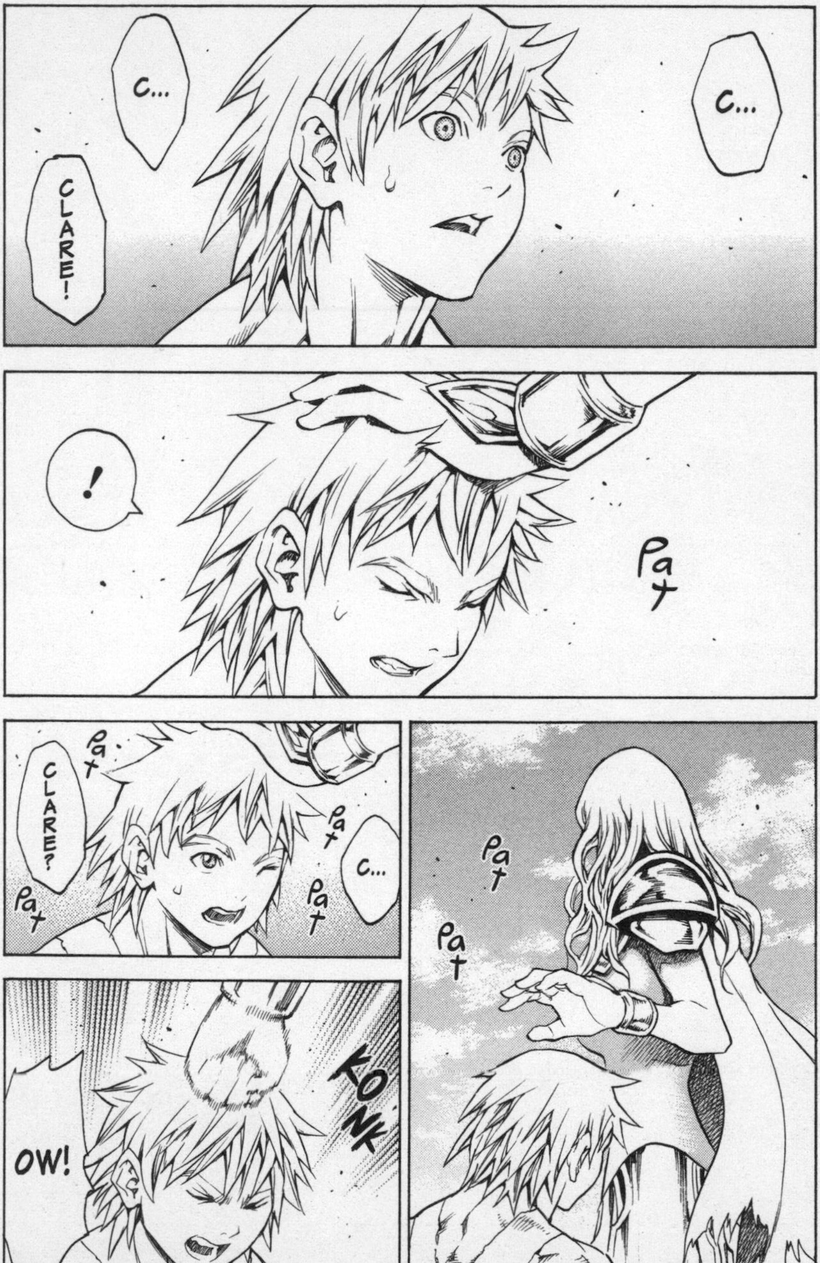
C...
C...
CLARE!
!
Pat
Pat
Pat
Pat
C...
Pat
Pat
CLARE?
Pat
KONK
OW!

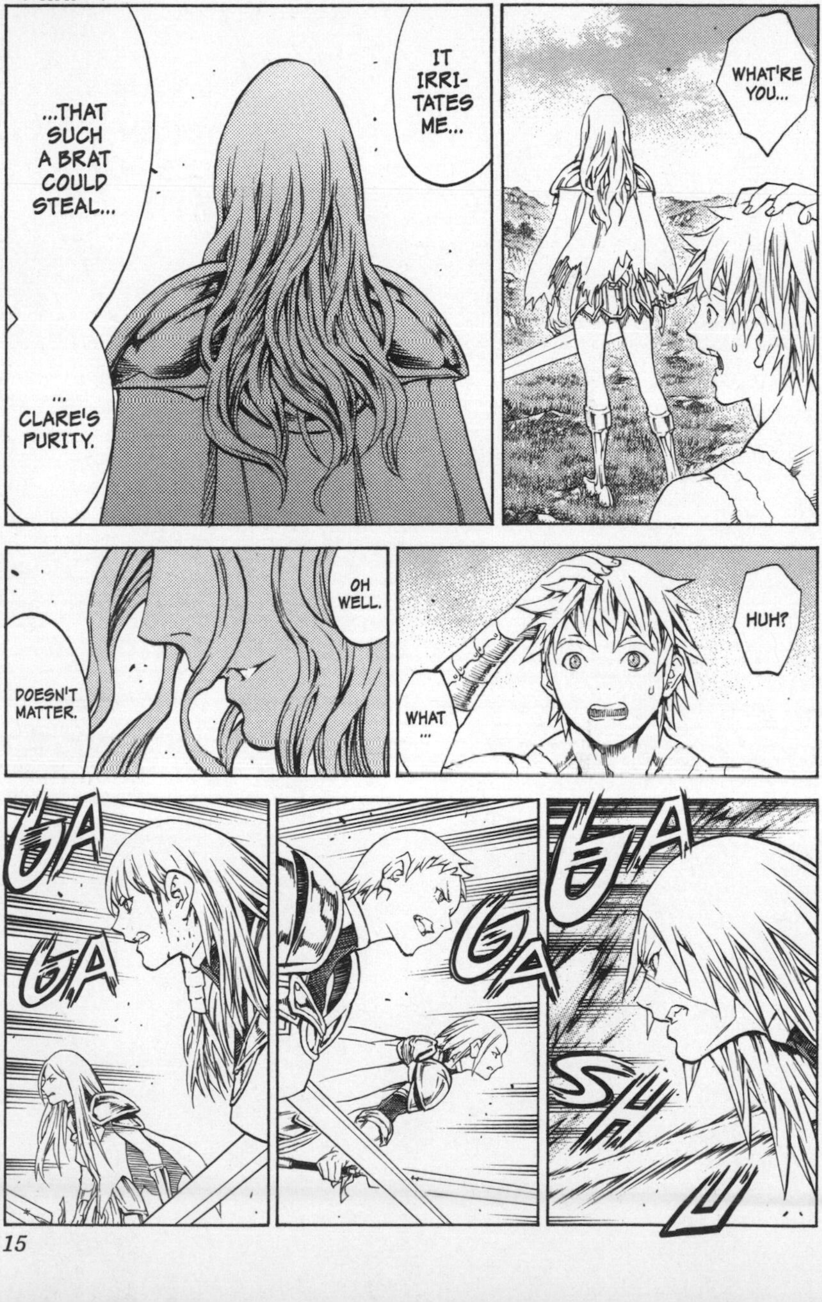
READ THIS WAY
WHAT'RE YOU...
IT IRRITATES ME...
...THAT SUCH A BRAT COULD STEAL...
...CLARE'S PURITY.
HUH?
WHAT...
OH WELL.
DOESN'T MATTER.
GA GA GASHU
GA GA

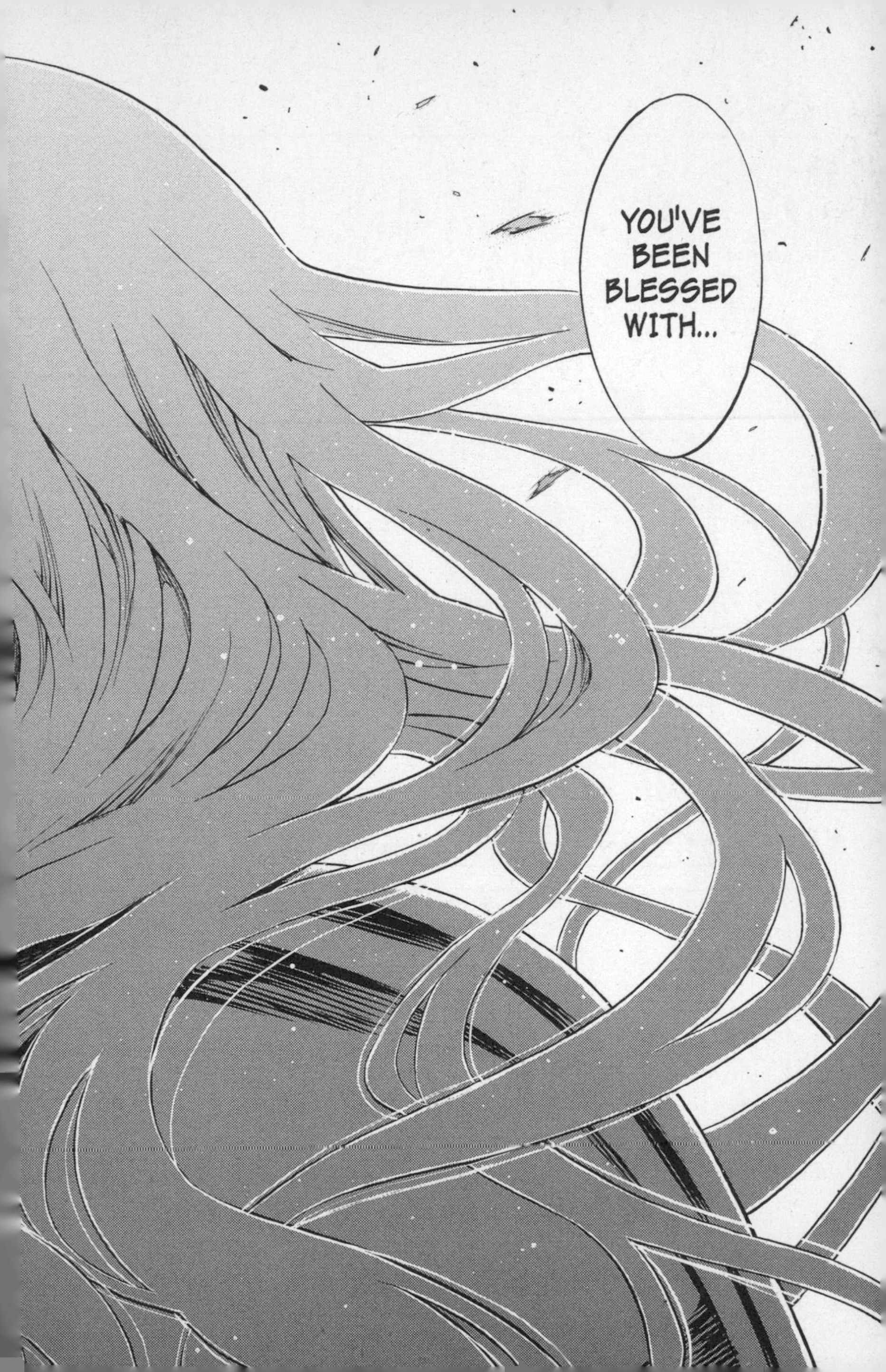
YOU'VE BEEN BLESSED WITH...

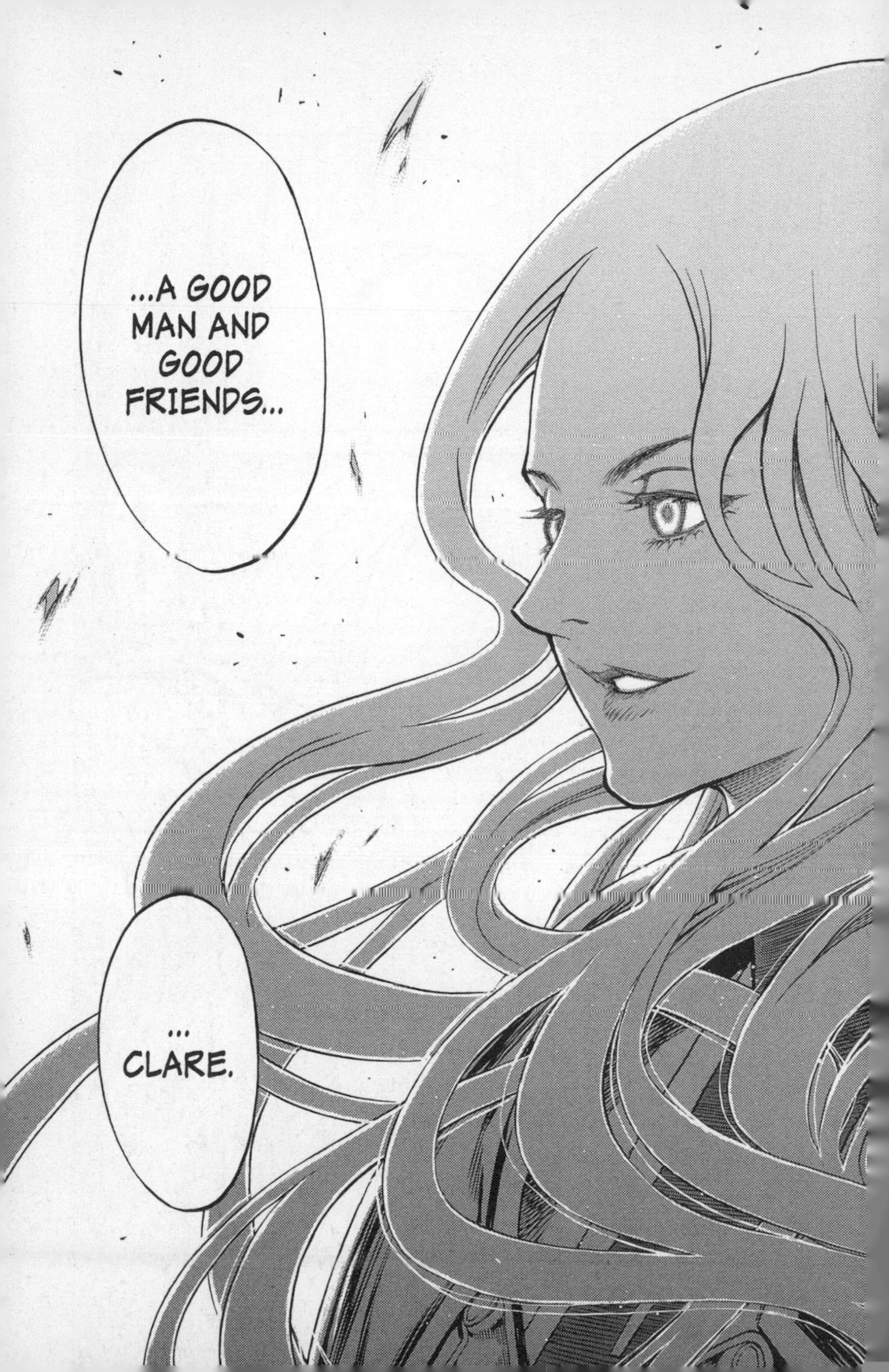
...A GOOD MAN AND GOOD FRIENDS...
... CLARE.

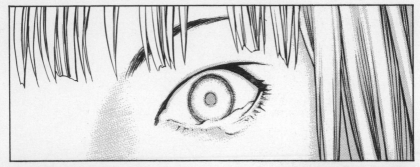

....?

TERESA...

TERESA...

TERESA...

TERESA...

TERESA...

TERESA...

READ THIS WAY

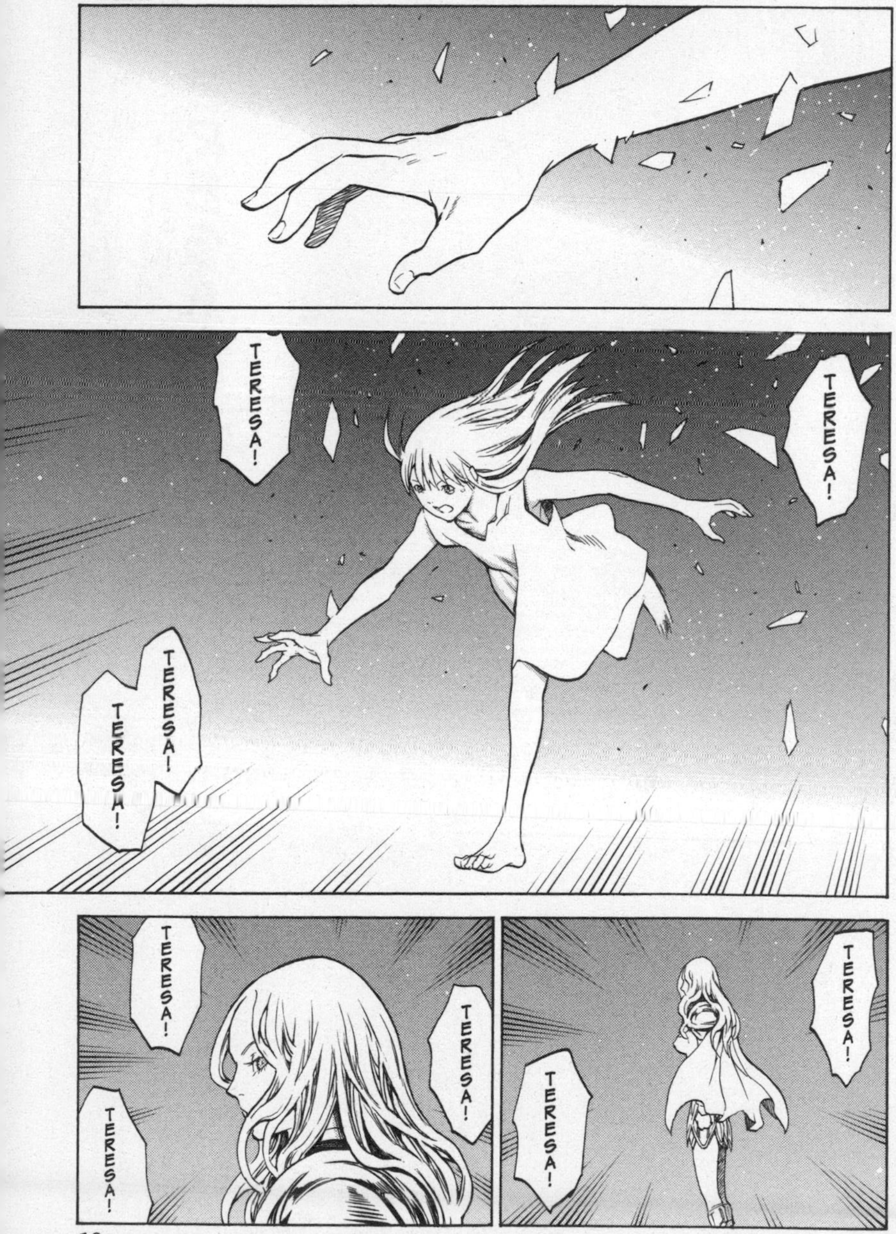
TERESA!
TERESA!
TERESA!
TERESA!
TERESA!
TERESA!
TERESA!
TERESA!
TERESA!

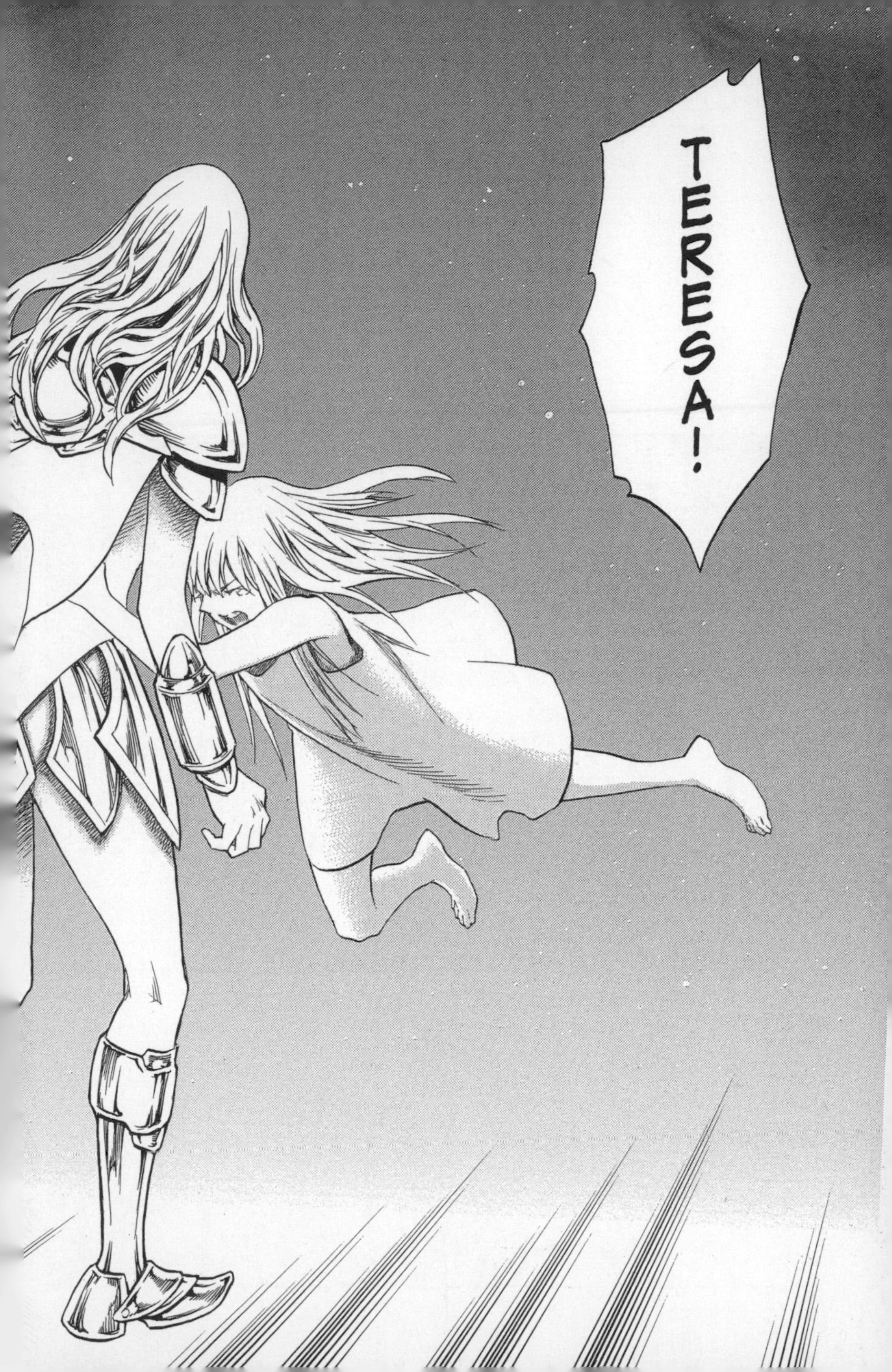
TERESA!

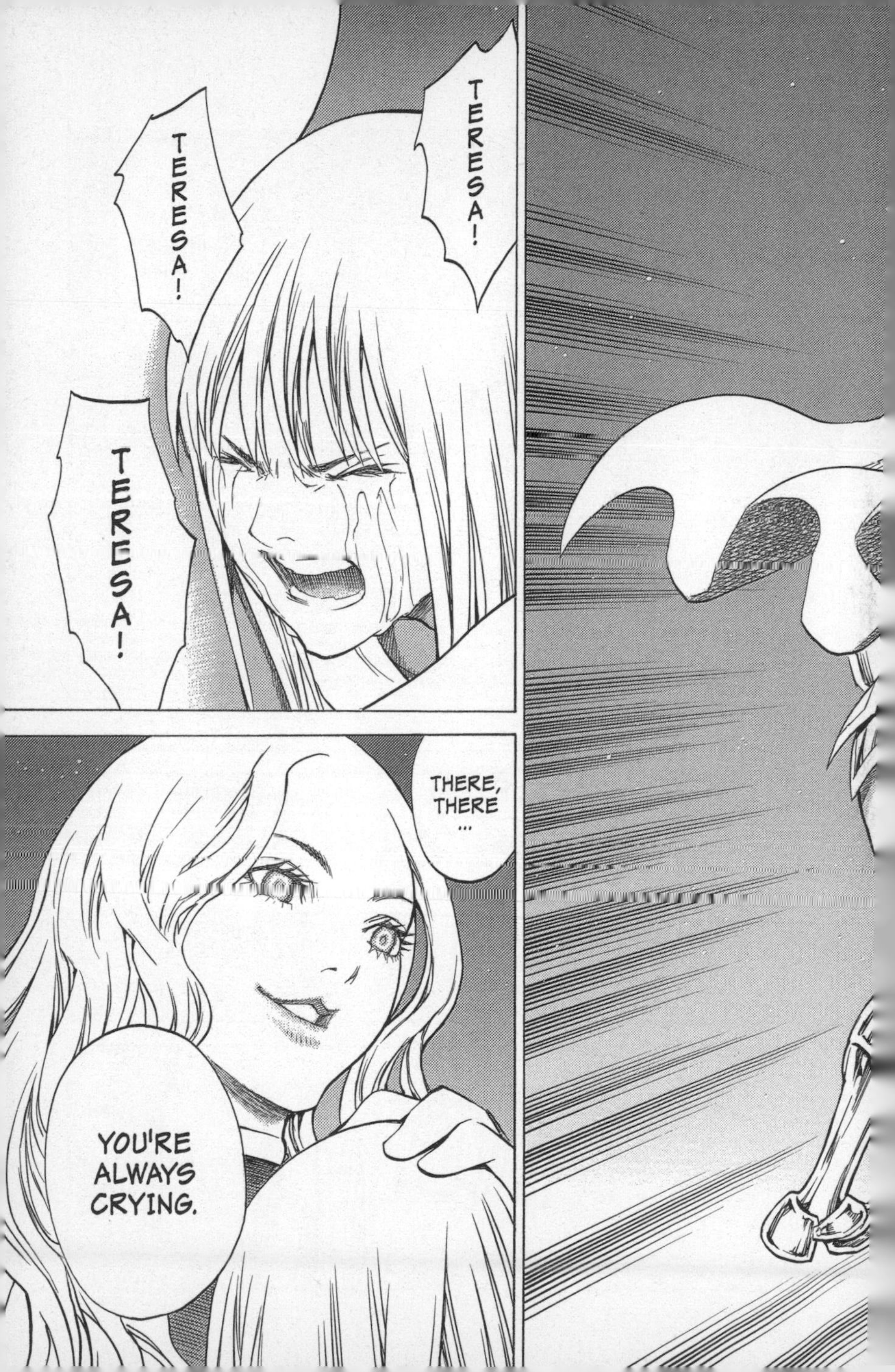
TERESA!
TERESA!
TERESA!
THERE, THERE ...
YOU'RE ALWAYS CRYING.

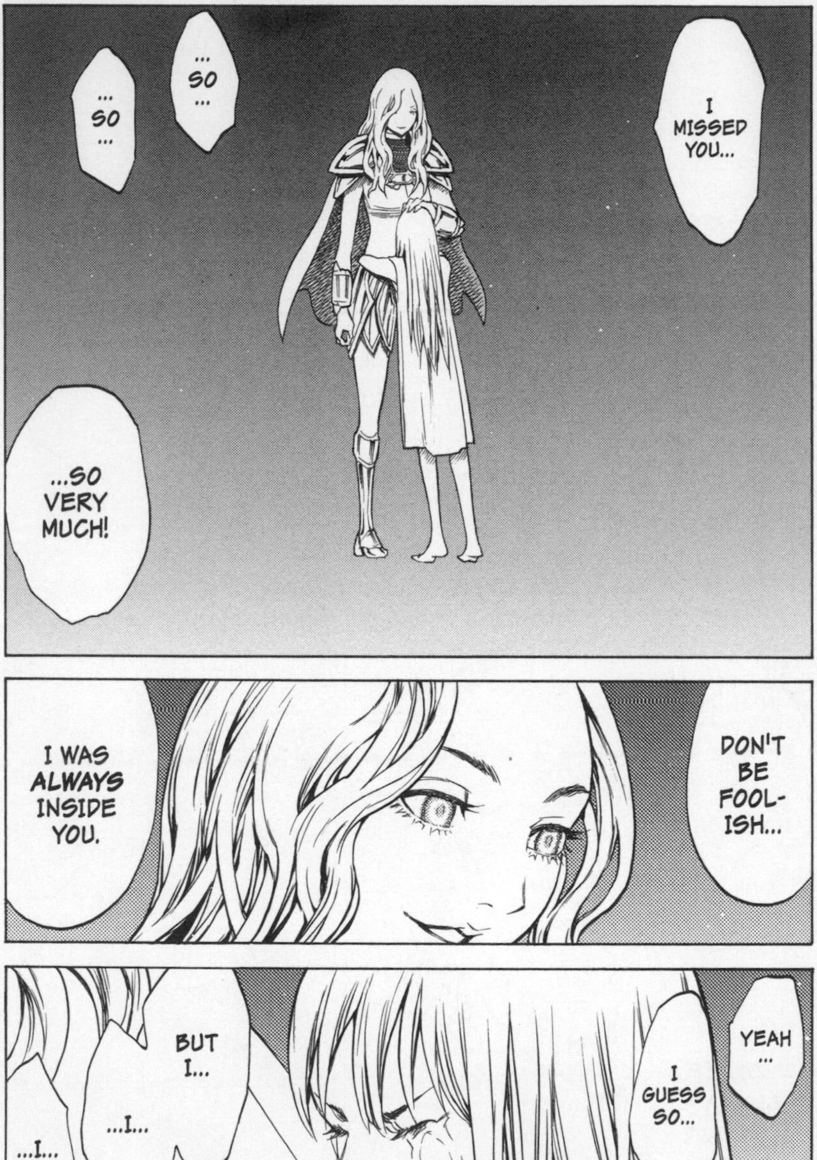
I MISSED YOU...
...SO...
...SO...
...SO VERY MUCH!
DON'T BE FOOL-ISH...
I WAS ALWAYS INSIDE YOU.
YEAH...
I GUESS SO...
BUT I...
...I...
...I...

READ THIS WAY

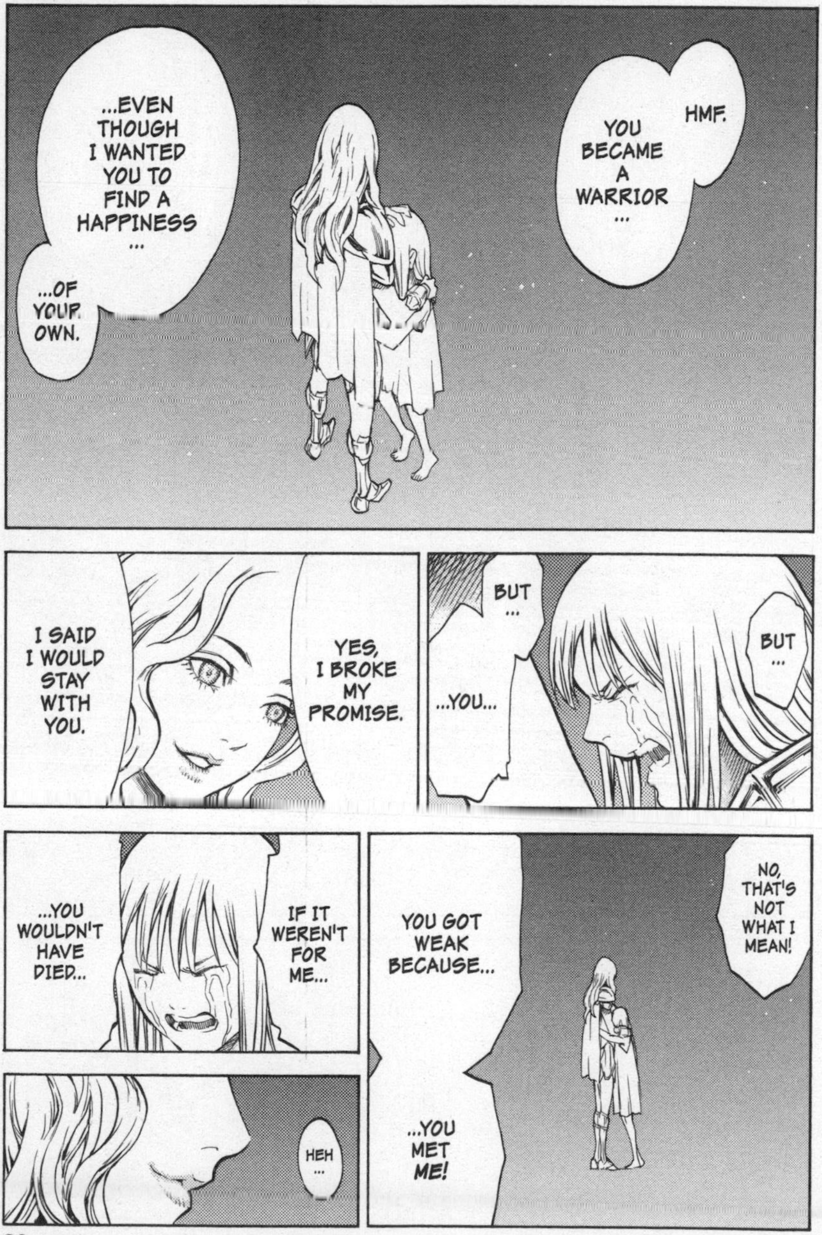
HMF.
YOU BECAME A WARRIOR ...
...EVEN THOUGH I WANTED YOU TO FIND A HAPPINESS ...
...OF YOUR OWN.
BUT ...
BUT ...
...YOU...
YES, I BROKE MY PROMISE.
I SAID I WOULD STAY WITH YOU.
NO, THAT'S NOT WHAT I MEAN!
IF IT WEREN'T FOR ME...
...YOU WOULDN'T HAVE DIED...
YOU GOT WEAK BECAUSE...
...YOU MET ME!
HEH ...

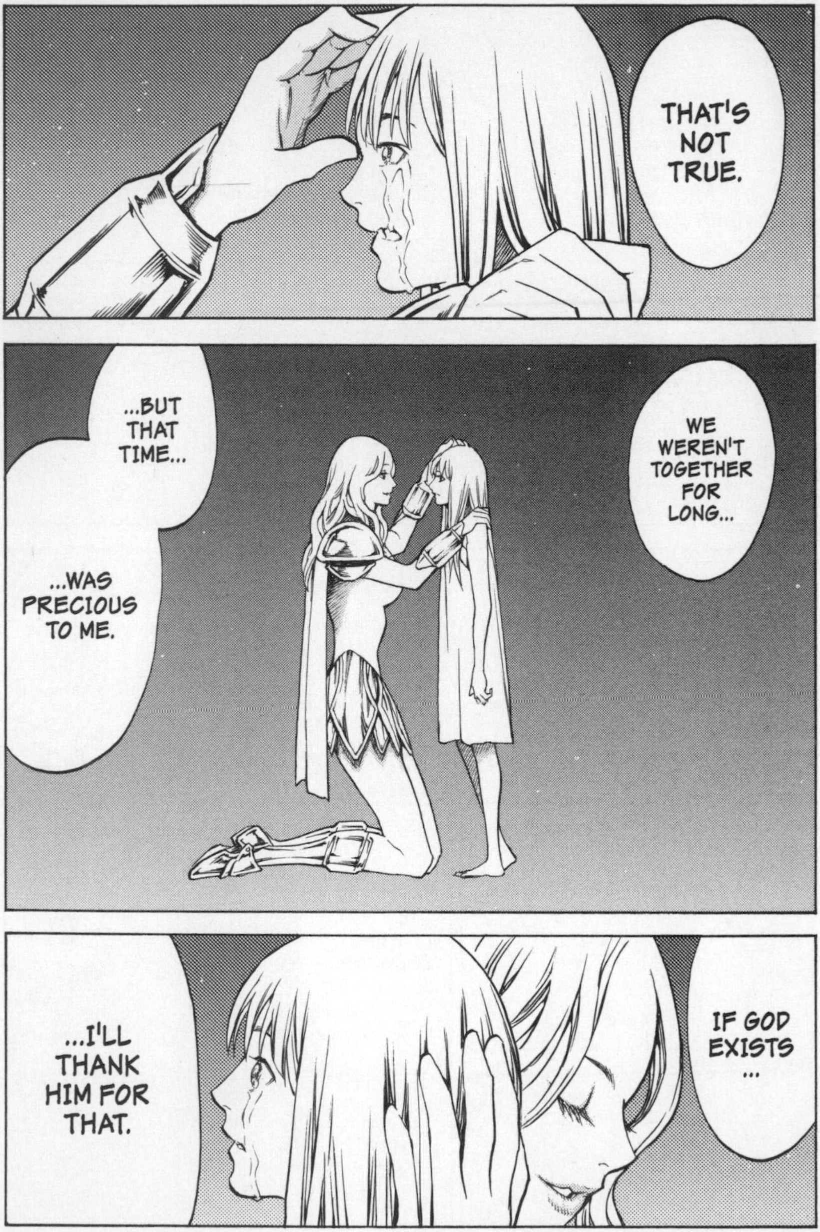
THAT'S NOT TRUE.
WE WEREN'T TOGETHER FOR LONG...
...BUT THAT TIME...
...WAS PRECIOUS TO ME.
IF GOD EXISTS ...
...I'LL THANK HIM FOR THAT.

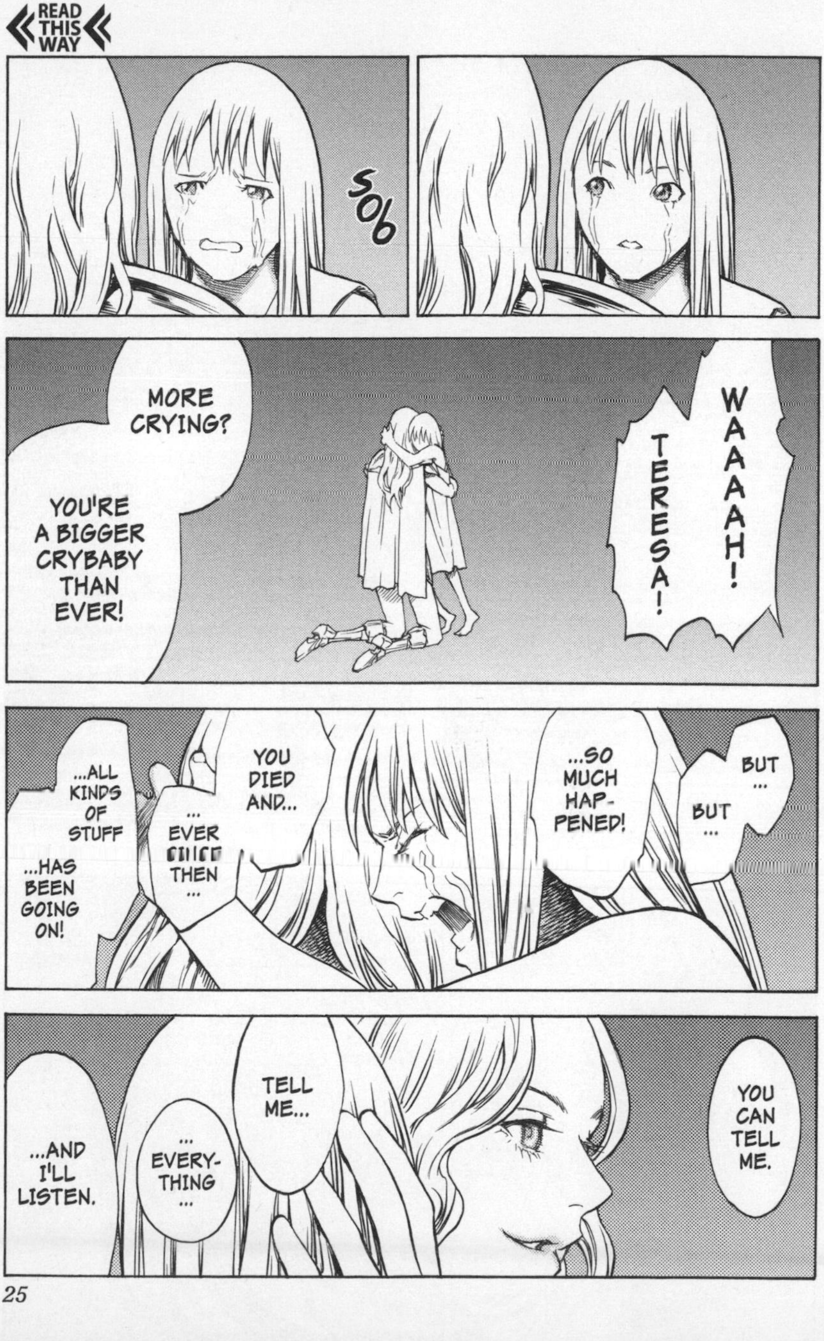
READ THIS WAY
SOB
WAAAAH! TERESA!
MORE CRYING?
YOU'RE A BIGGER CRYBABY THAN EVER!
BUT ...
BUT ...
...SO MUCH HAP-PENED!
YOU DIED AND...
... EVER SINCE THEN ...
...ALL KINDS OF STUFF
...HAS BEEN GOING ON!
YOU CAN TELL ME.
TELL ME...
... EVERY-THING ...
...AND I'LL LISTEN.

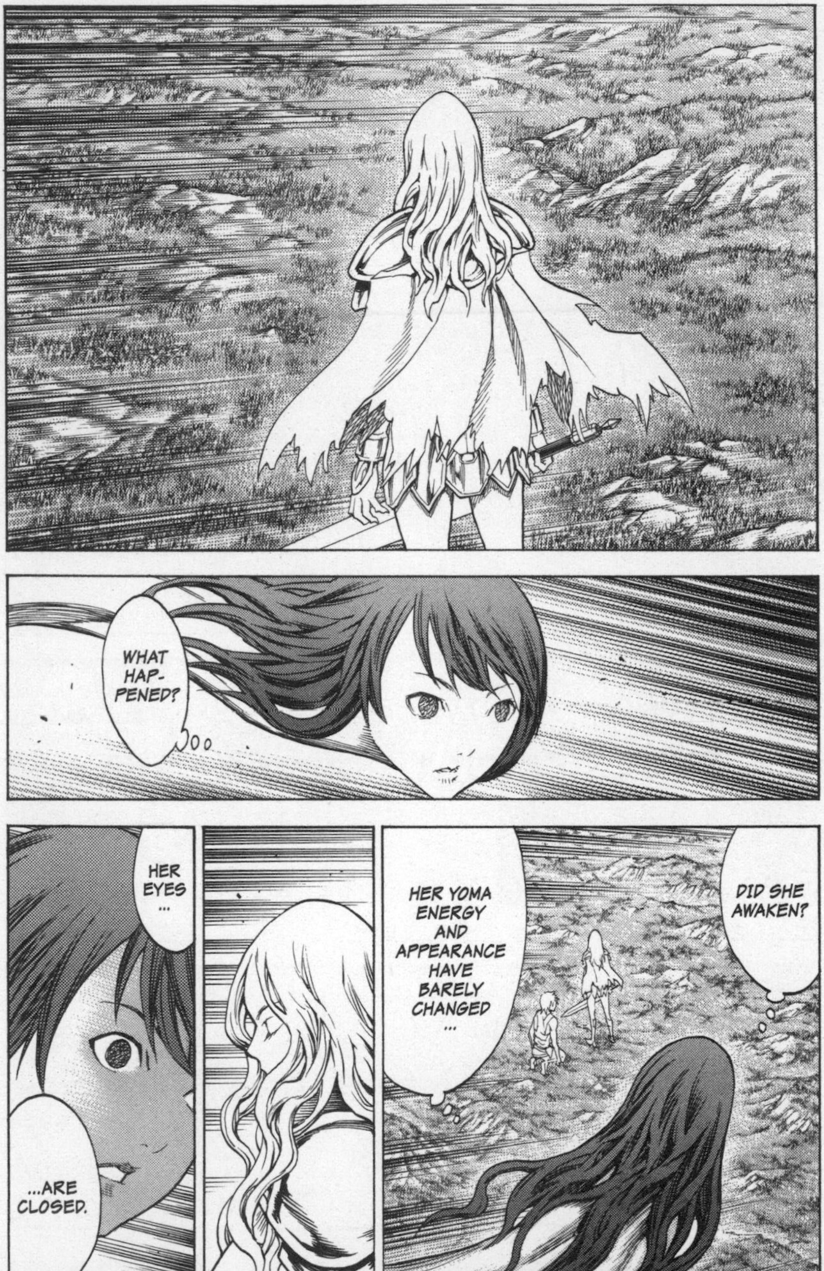
WHAT HAP-PENED?
DID SHE AWAKEN?
HER YOMA ENERGY AND APPEARANCE HAVE BARELY CHANGED...
HER EYES...
...ARE CLOSED.

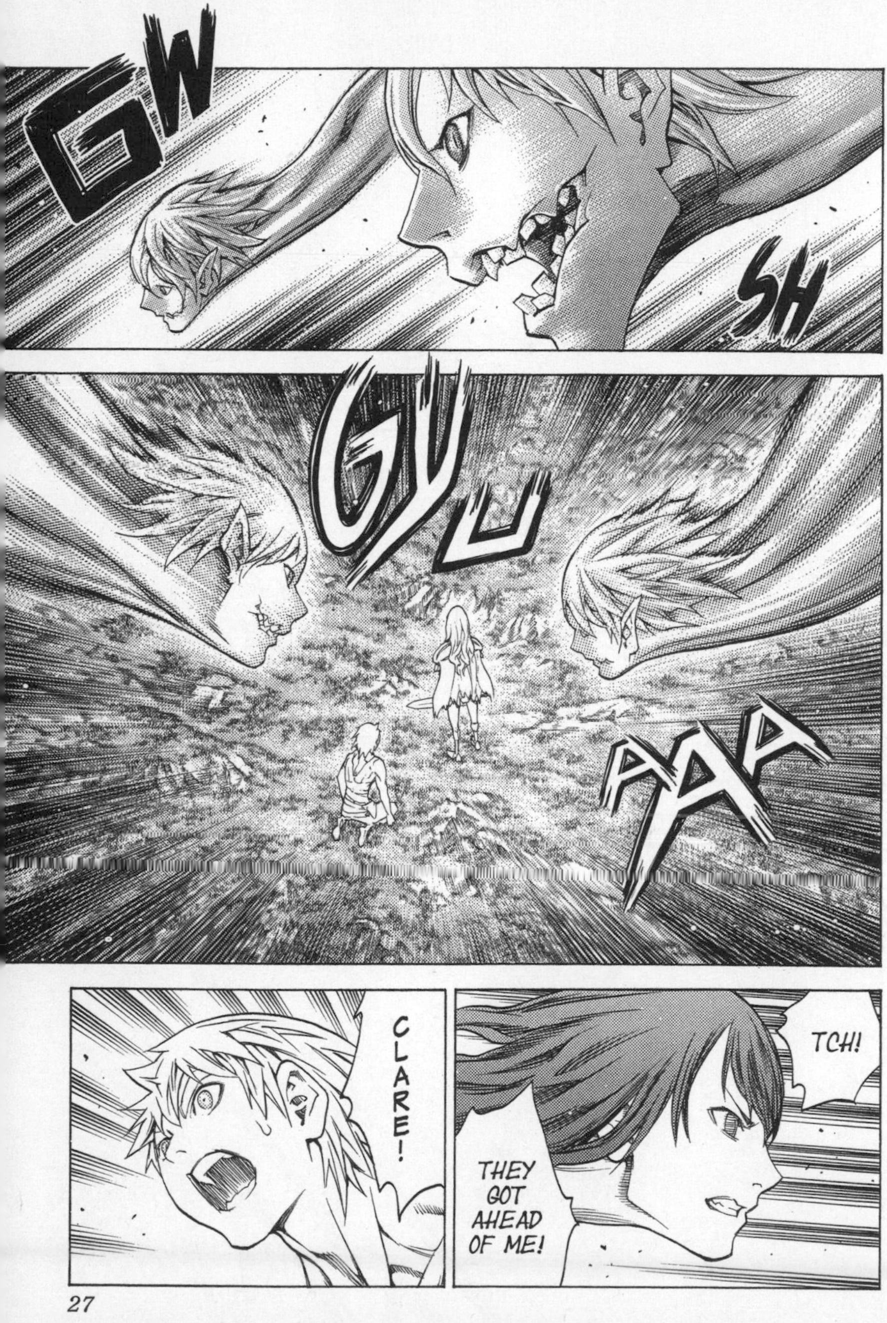
GW
SH
GYU
AAA
TCH!
THEY GOT AHEAD OF ME!
CLARE!

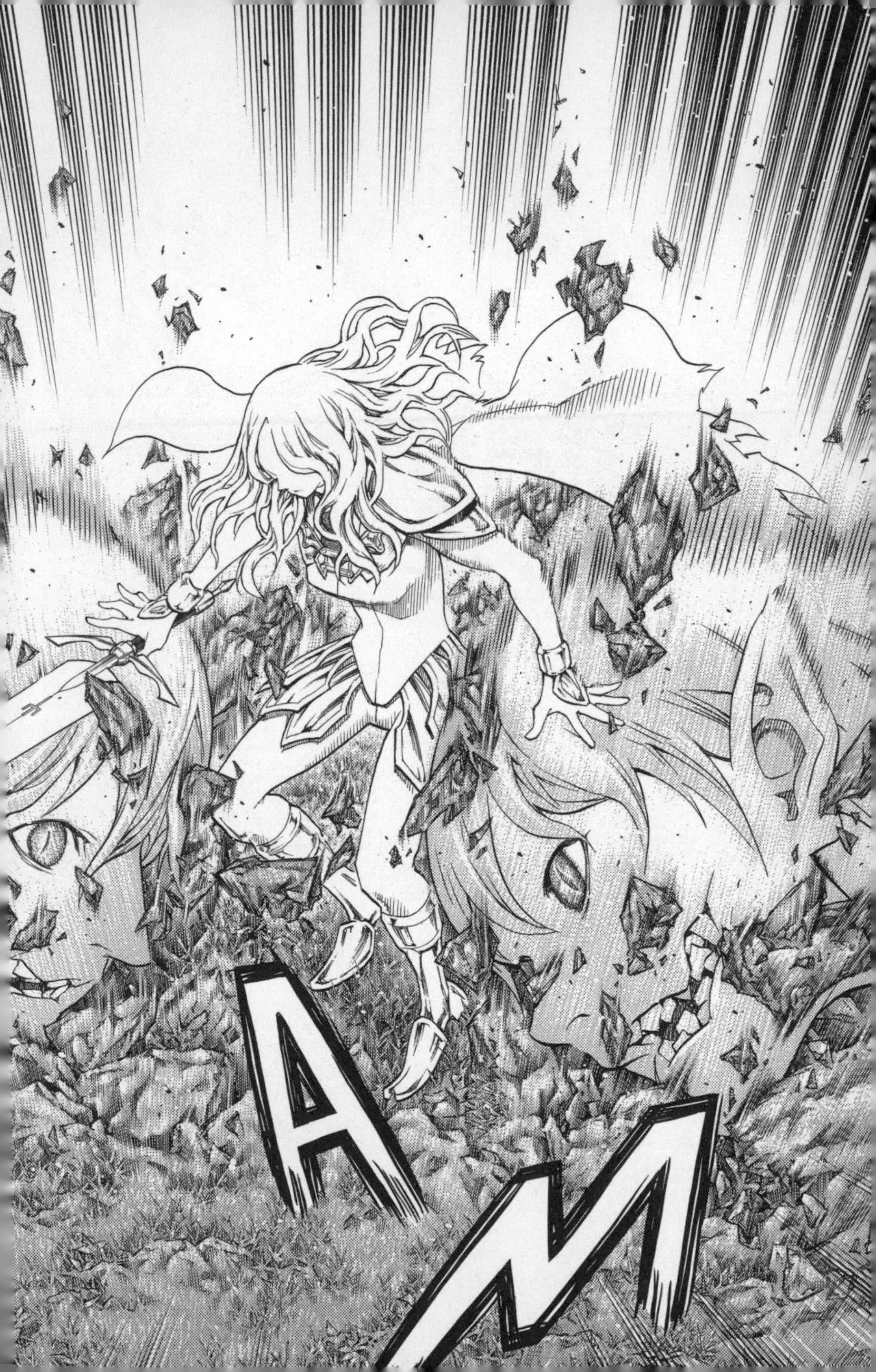
AM

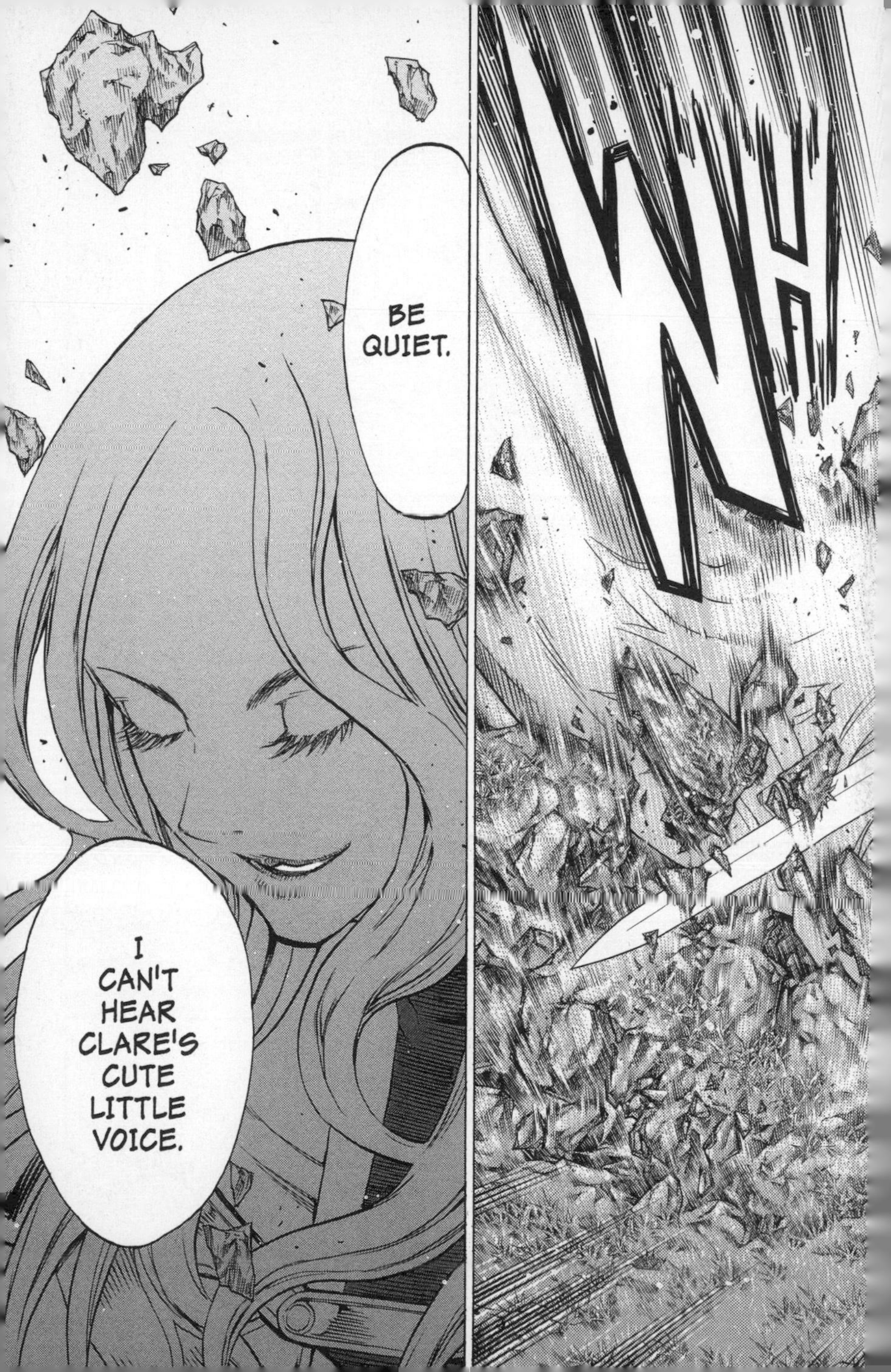
BE QUIET.
I CAN'T HEAR CLARE'S CUTE LITTLE VOICE.

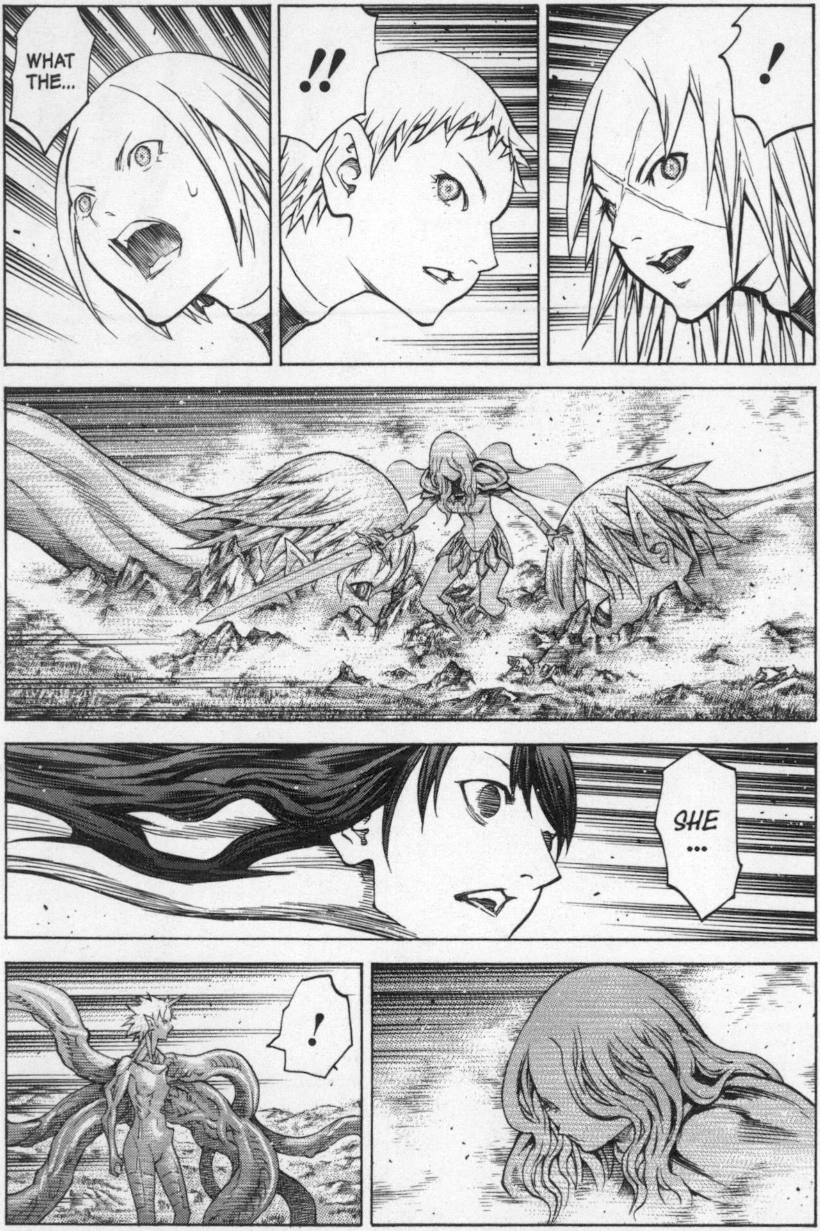
!
!!
WHAT THE...
SHE ...
!

READ THIS WAY

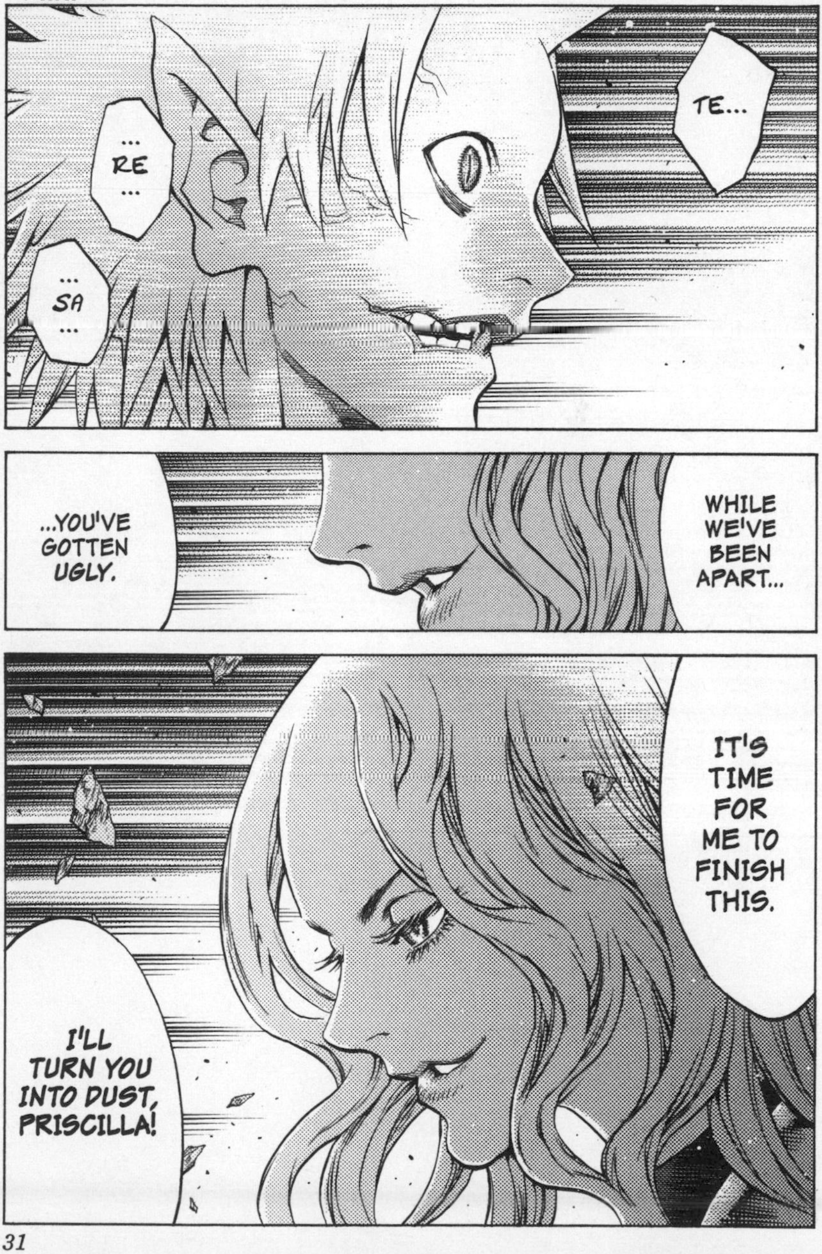

TE...
... RE ...
... SA ...
WHILE WE'VE BEEN APART...
...YOU'VE GOTTEN UGLY.
IT'S TIME FOR ME TO FINISH THIS.
I'LL TURN YOU INTO DUST, PRISCILLA!

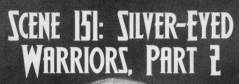

Scene 151: Silver-Eyed Warriors, Part 2

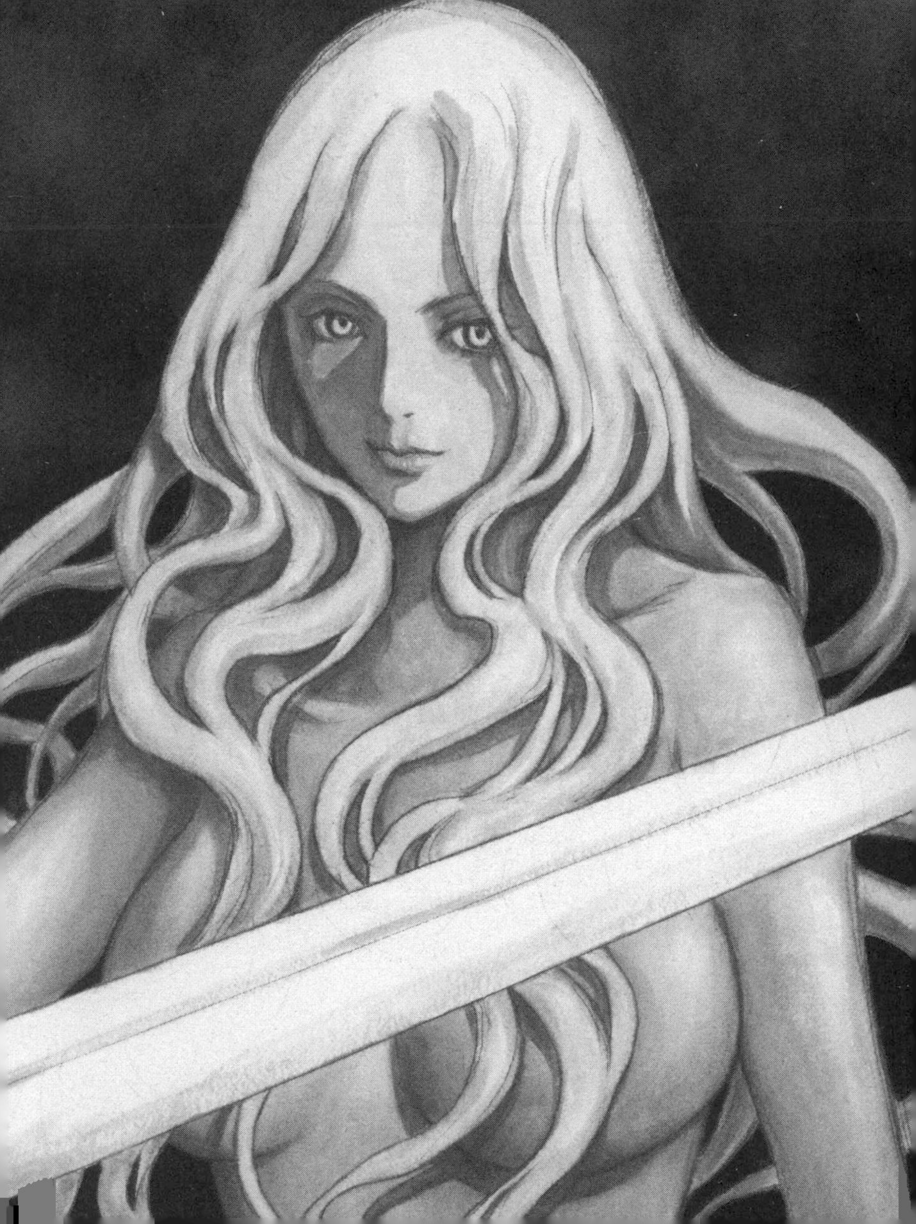

READ THIS WAY

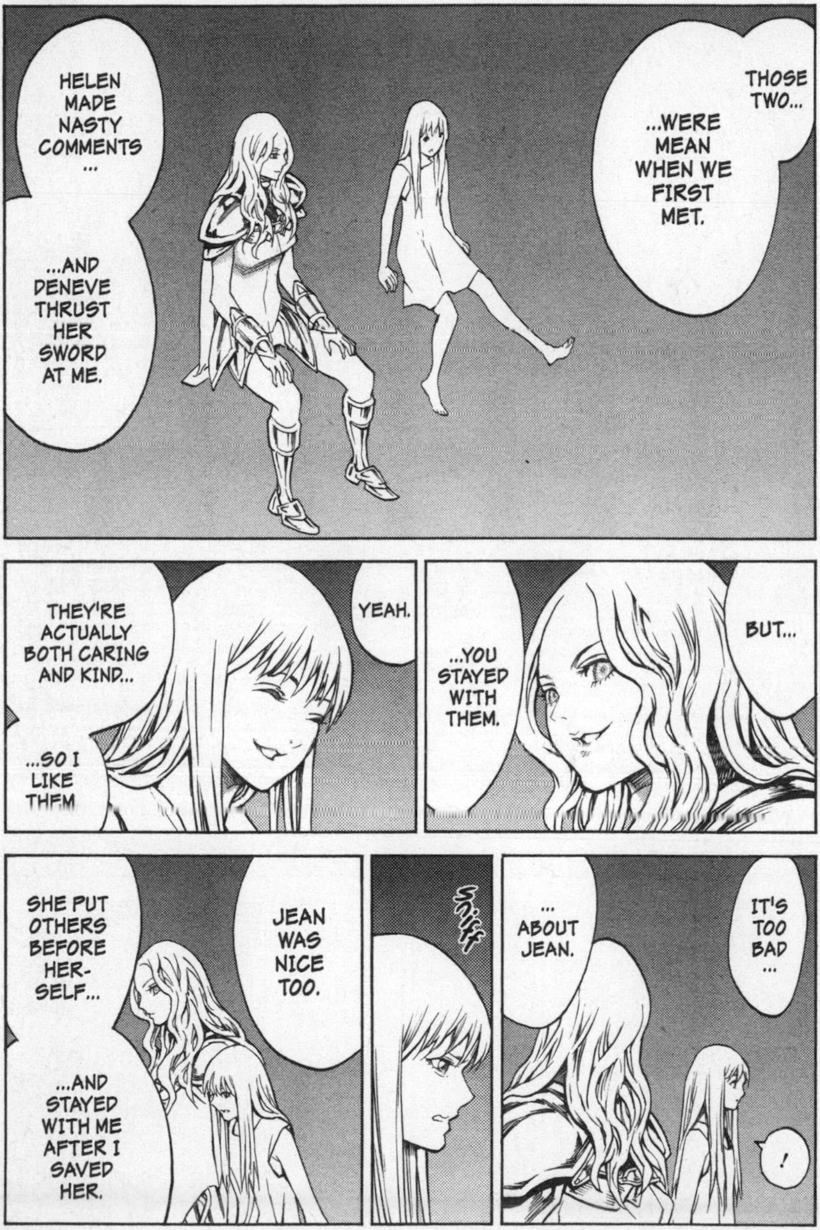
THOSE TWO...
...WERE MEAN WHEN WE FIRST MET.
HELEN MADE NASTY COMMENTS...
...AND DENEVE THRUST HER SWORD AT ME.
BUT...
...YOU STAYED WITH THEM.
YEAH.
THEY'RE ACTUALLY BOTH CARING AND KIND...
...SO I LIKE THEM
IT'S TOO BAD...
...ABOUT JEAN.
!
Sniff
JEAN WAS NICE TOO.
SHE PUT OTHERS BEFORE HER-SELF...
...AND STAYED WITH ME AFTER I SAVED HER.

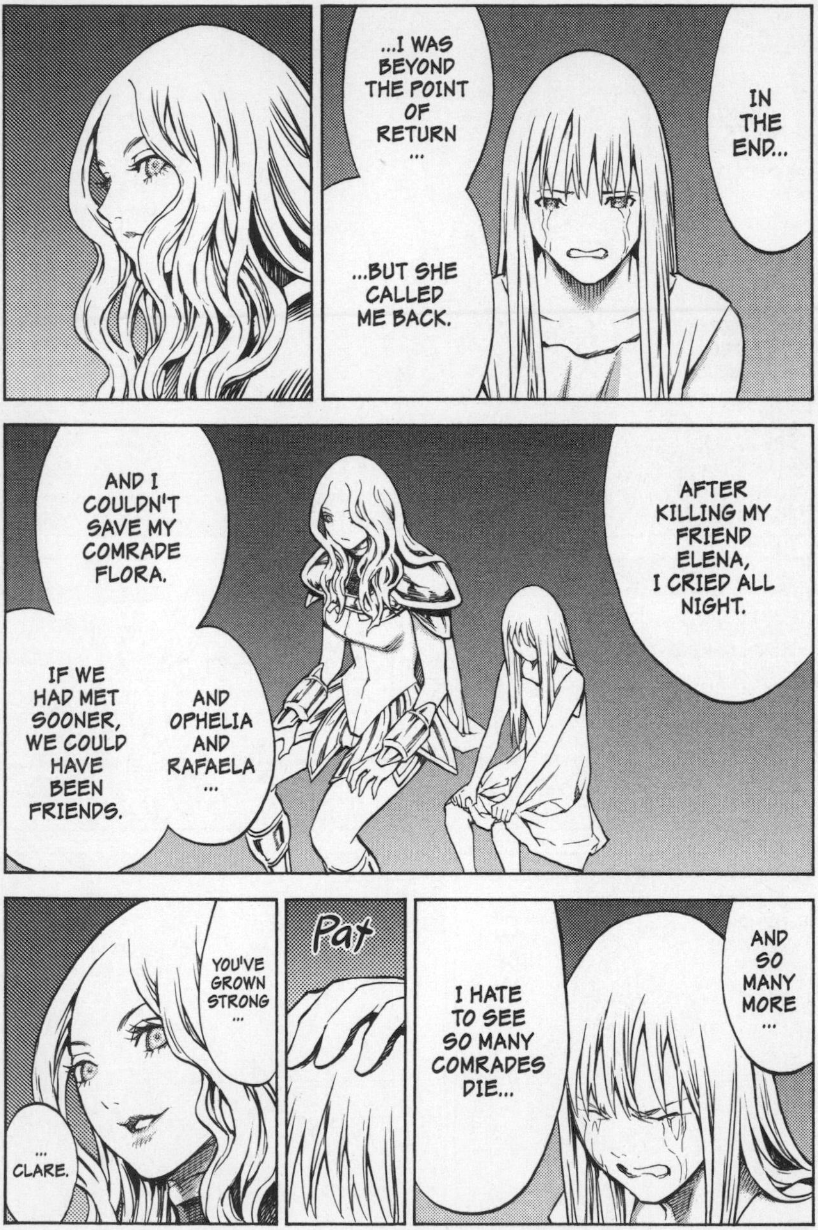
IN THE END...
...I WAS BEYOND THE POINT OF RETURN ...
...BUT SHE CALLED ME BACK.
AFTER KILLING MY FRIEND ELENA, I CRIED ALL NIGHT.
AND I COULDN'T SAVE MY COMRADE FLORA.
AND OPHELIA AND RAFAELA ...
IF WE HAD MET SOONER, WE COULD HAVE BEEN FRIENDS.
AND SO MANY MORE ...
I HATE TO SEE SO MANY COMRADES DIE...
Pat
YOU'VE GROWN STRONG ...
... CLARE.

READ THIS WAY

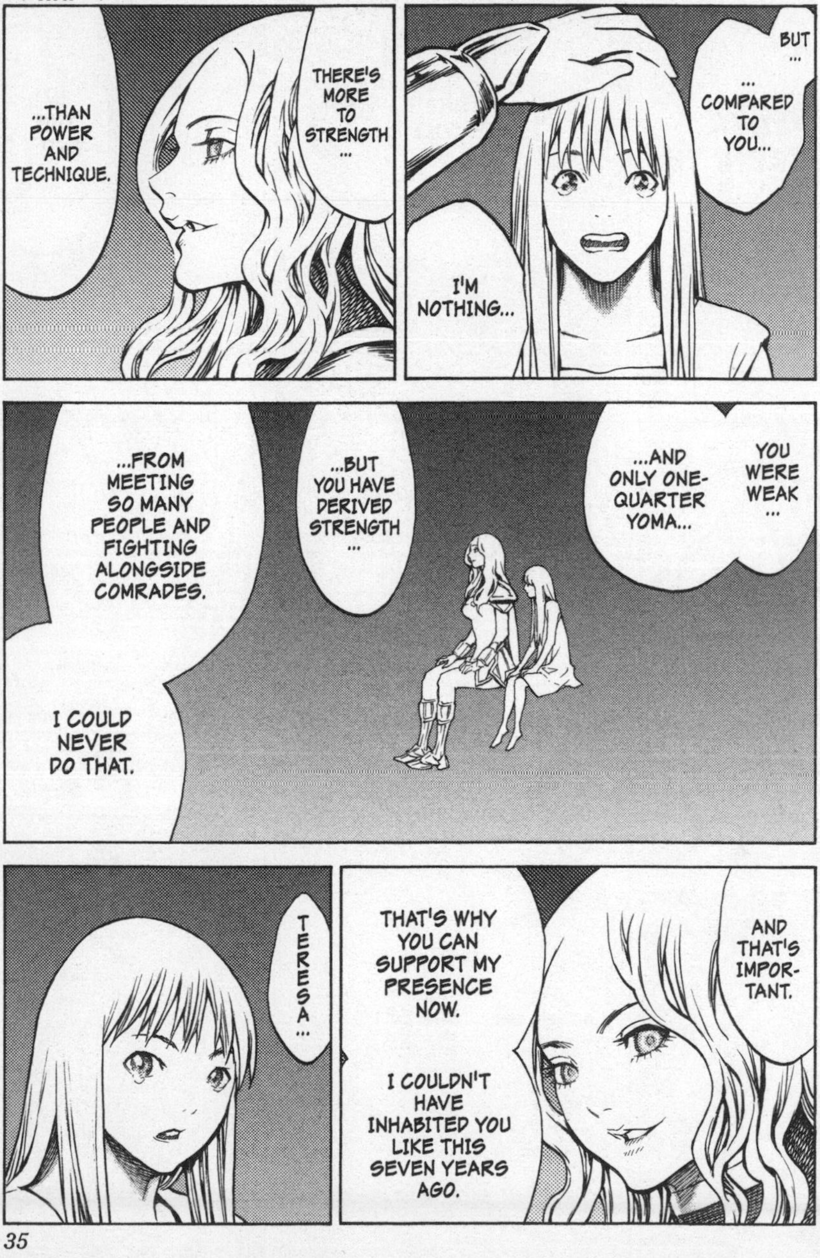
BUT ...
... COMPARED TO YOU...
I'M NOTHING...
THERE'S MORE TO STRENGTH ...
...THAN POWER AND TECHNIQUE.
YOU WERE WEAK ...
...AND ONLY ONE-QUARTER YOMA...
...BUT YOU HAVE DERIVED STRENGTH ...
...FROM MEETING SO MANY PEOPLE AND FIGHTING ALONGSIDE COMRADES.
I COULD NEVER DO THAT.
AND THAT'S IMPORTANT.
THAT'S WHY YOU CAN SUPPORT MY PRESENCE NOW.
I COULDN'T HAVE INHABITED YOU LIKE THIS SEVEN YEARS AGO.
TERESA...

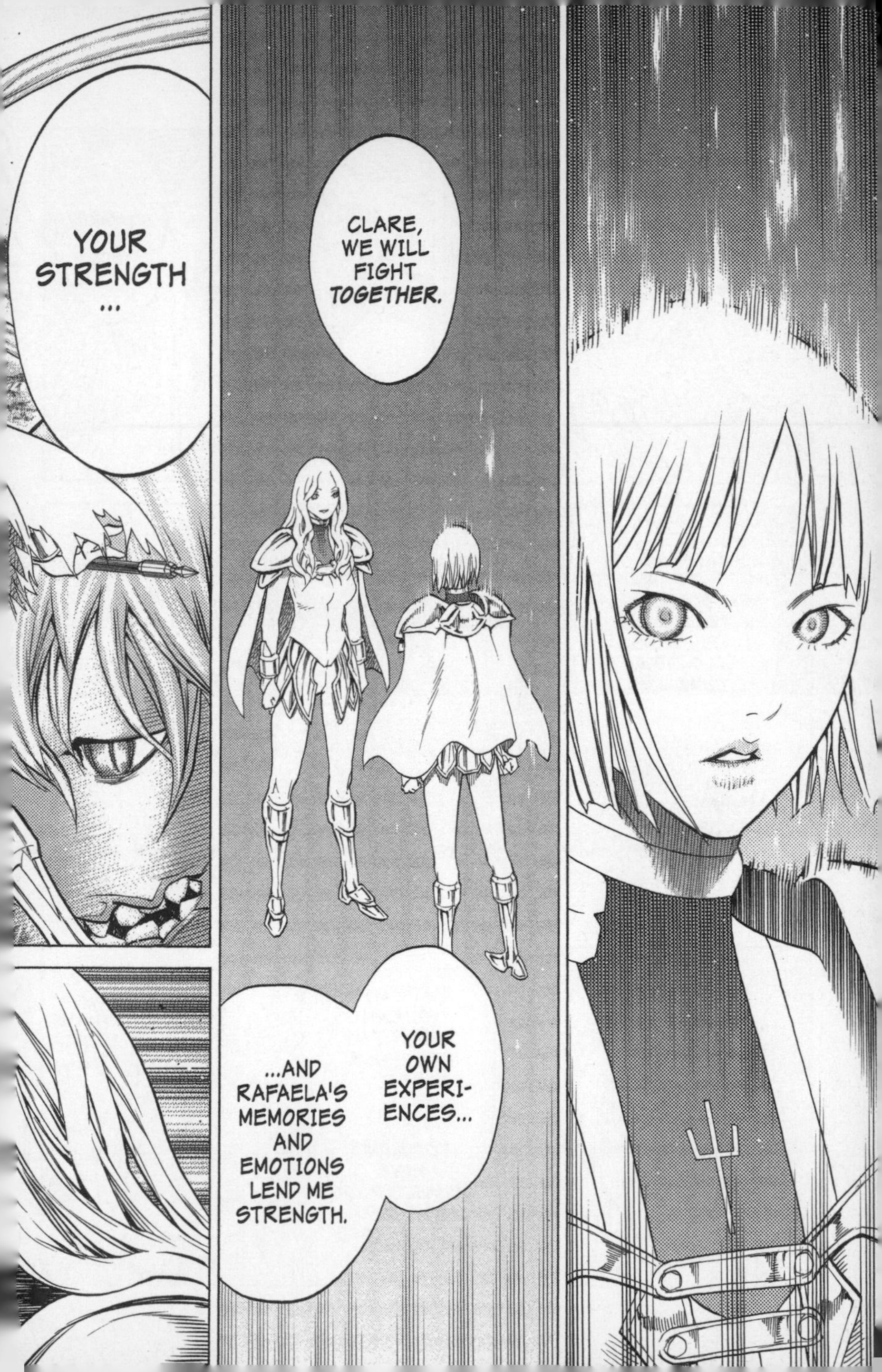
CLARE, WE WILL FIGHT TOGETHER.
YOUR OWN EXPERIENCES...
...AND RAFAELA'S MEMORIES AND EMOTIONS LEND ME STRENGTH.
YOUR STRENGTH ...

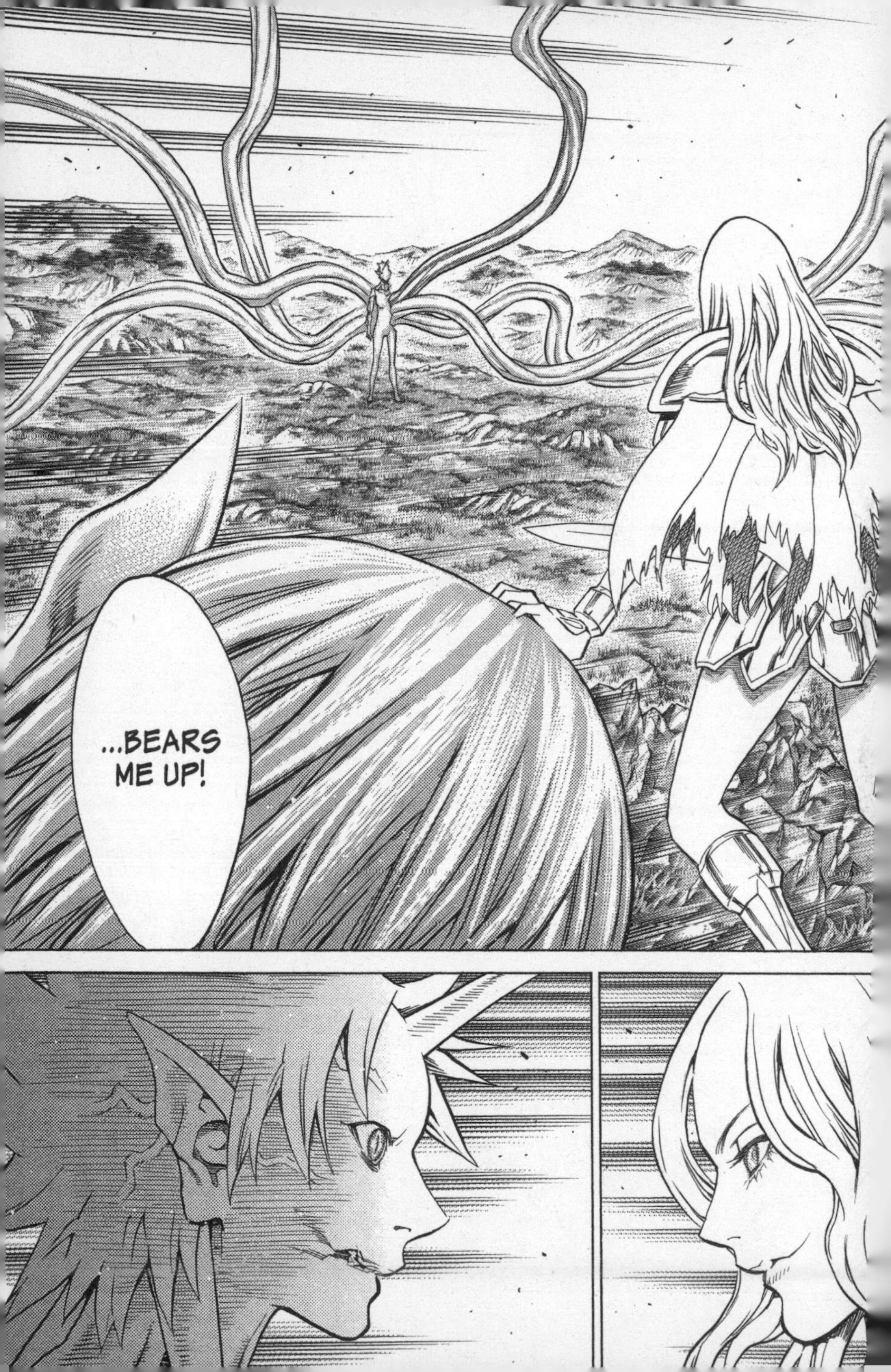
...BEARS
ME UP!

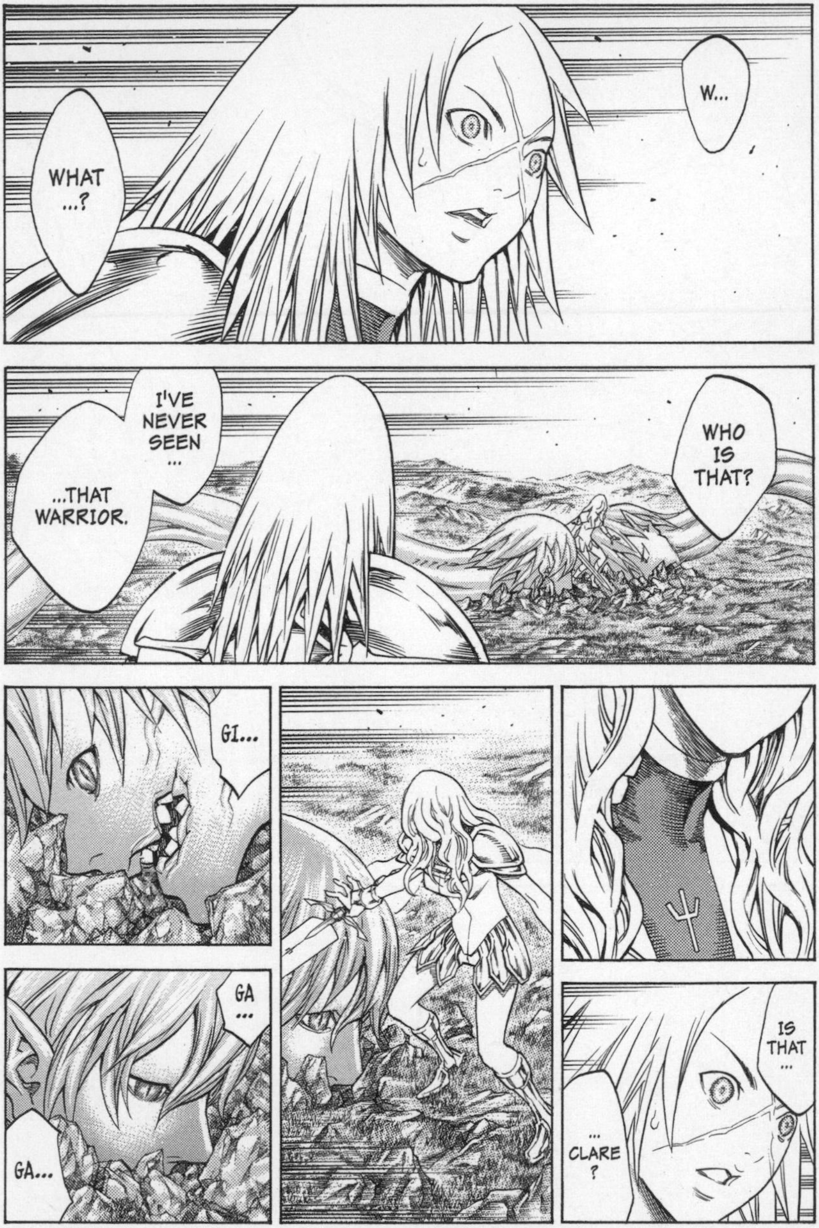
W...
WHAT ...?
WHO IS THAT?
I'VE NEVER SEEN ...
...THAT WARRIOR.
IS THAT ...
... CLARE ?
GI...
GA ...
GA...

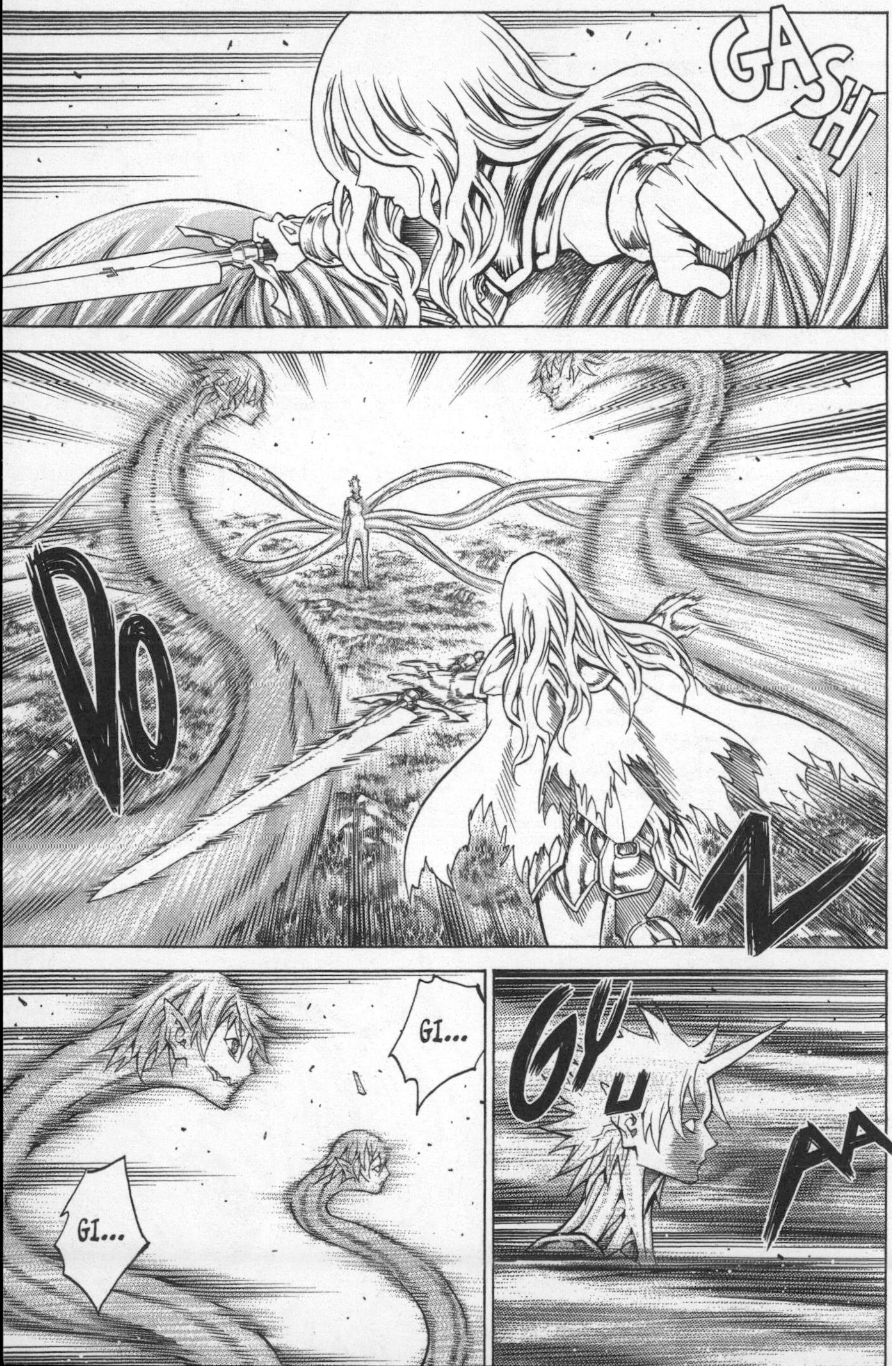
GASHI
DO
N
GI...
GI...
GYU
AA

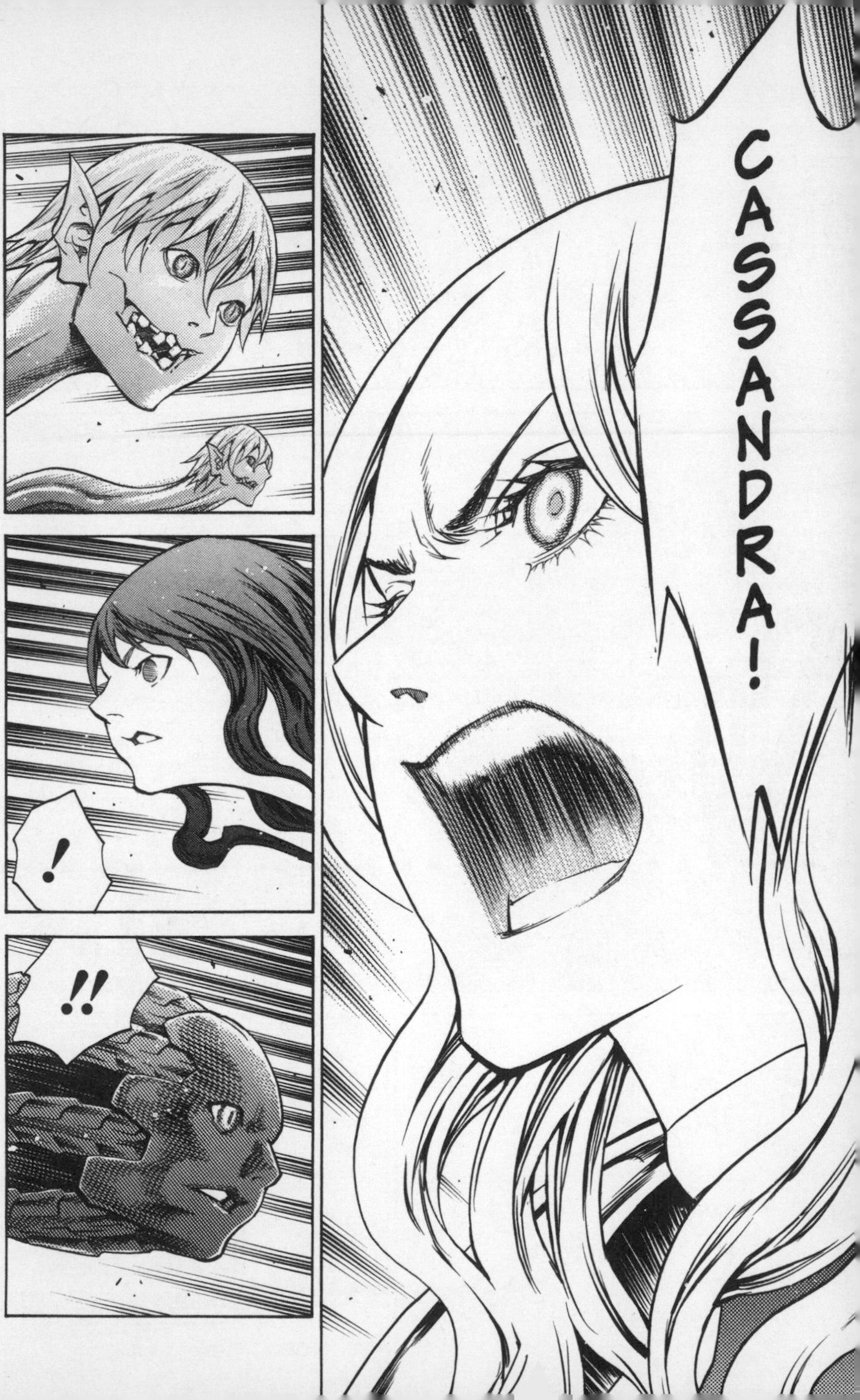

CASSANDRA!
!
!!

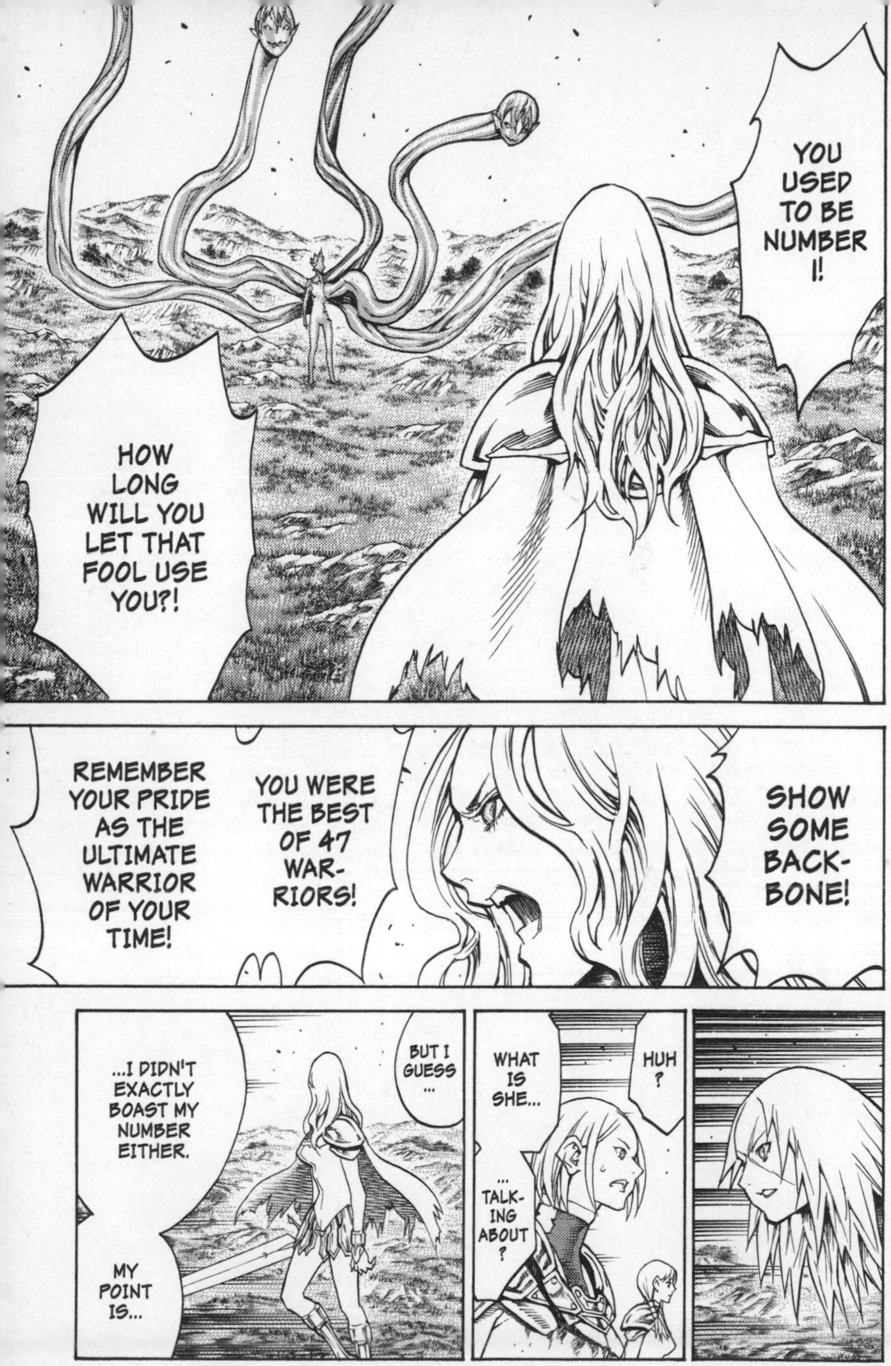
YOU USED TO BE NUMBER 1!
HOW LONG WILL YOU LET THAT FOOL USE YOU?!
SHOW SOME BACK-BONE!
YOU WERE THE BEST OF 47 WAR-RIORS!
REMEMBER YOUR PRIDE AS THE ULTIMATE WARRIOR OF YOUR TIME!
HUH?
WHAT IS SHE...
...TALK-ING ABOUT?
BUT I GUESS...
...I DIDN'T EXACTLY BOAST MY NUMBER EITHER.
MY POINT IS...

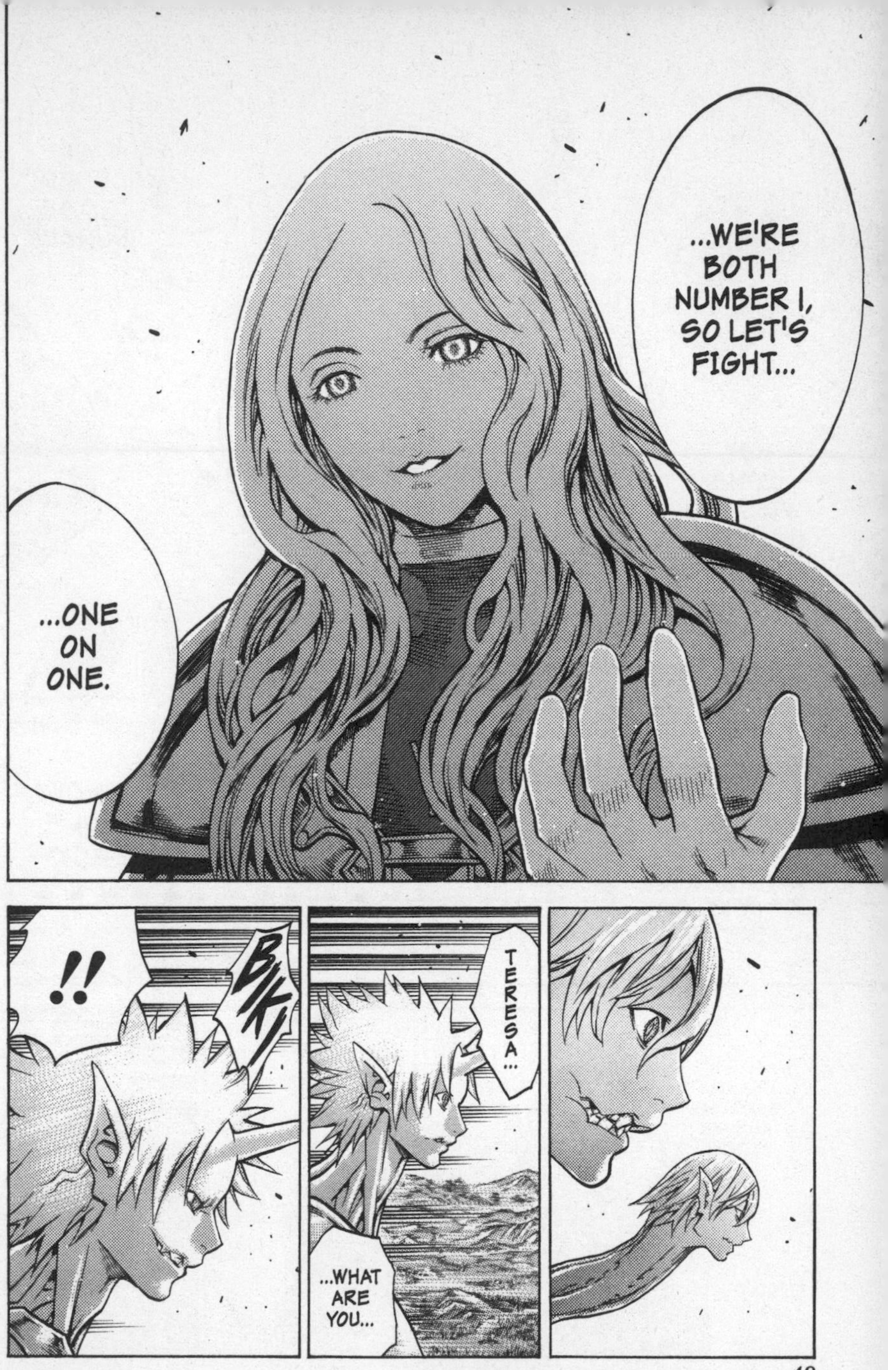
...WE'RE BOTH NUMBER 1, SO LET'S FIGHT...
...ONE ON ONE.
TERESA...
...WHAT ARE YOU...
BIK
!!

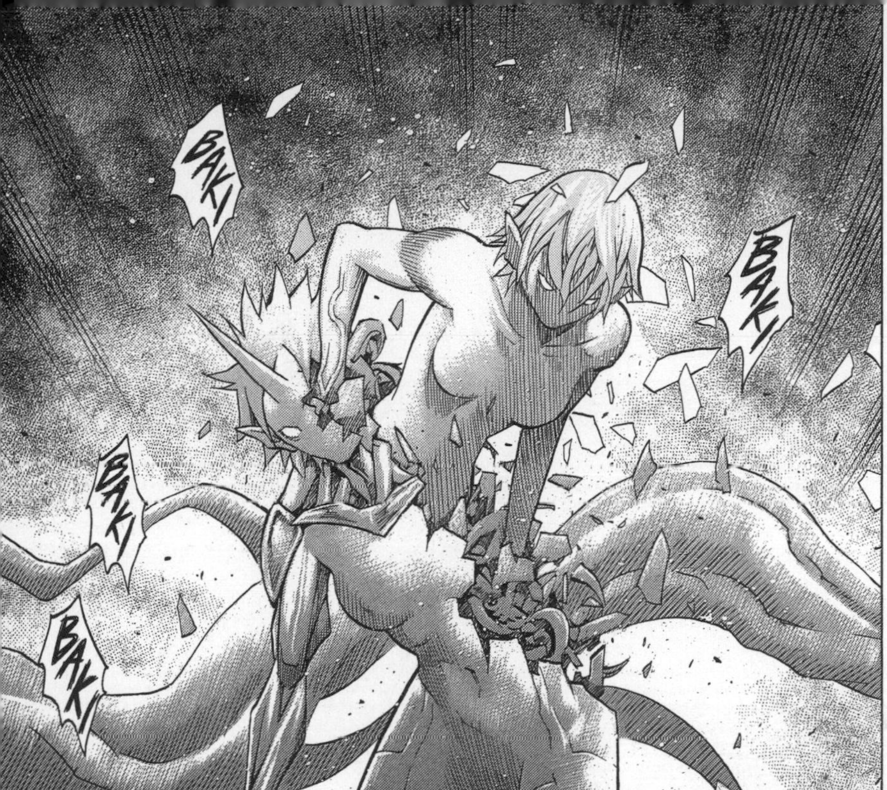
BAKI
BAKI
BAKI
BAKI
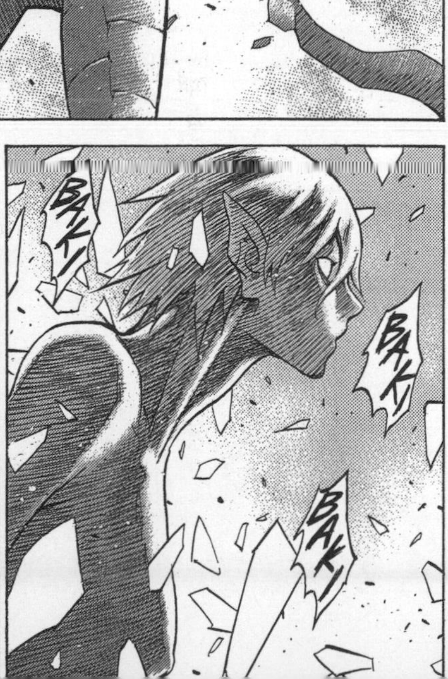
BAKI
BAKI
BAKI
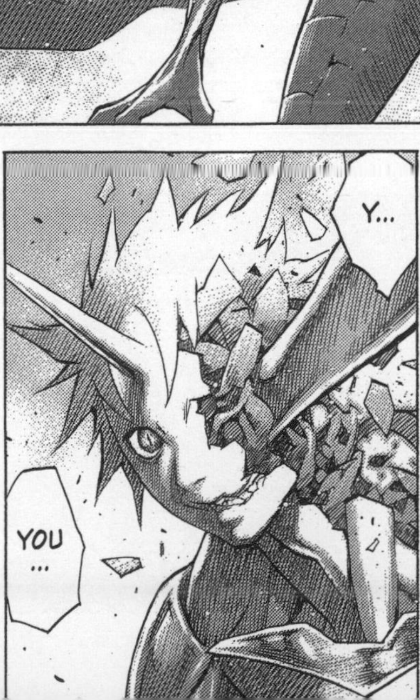
Y...
YOU ...

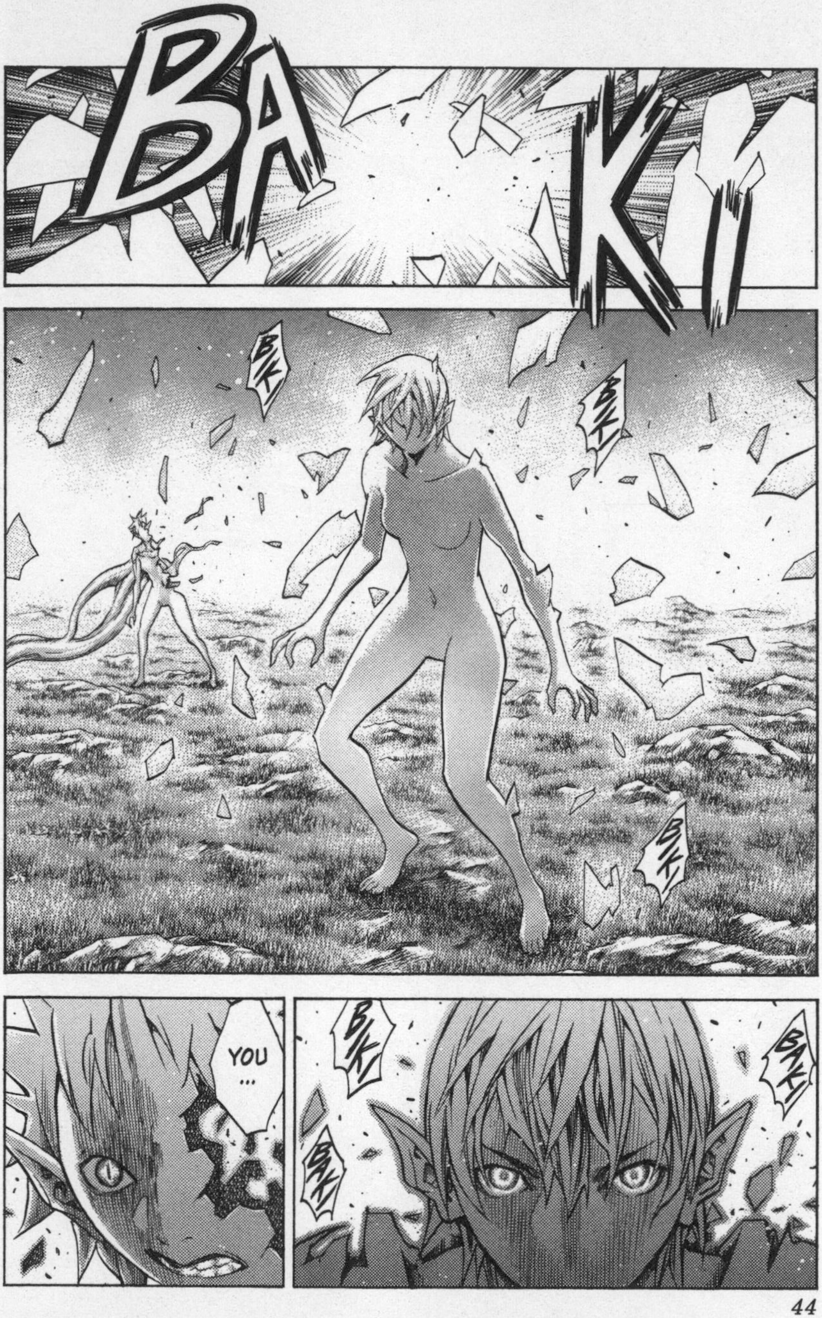
BAKI
BAK!
BAK!
BAK!
BAK!
BAK!
BAK!
YOU ...

READ THIS WAY

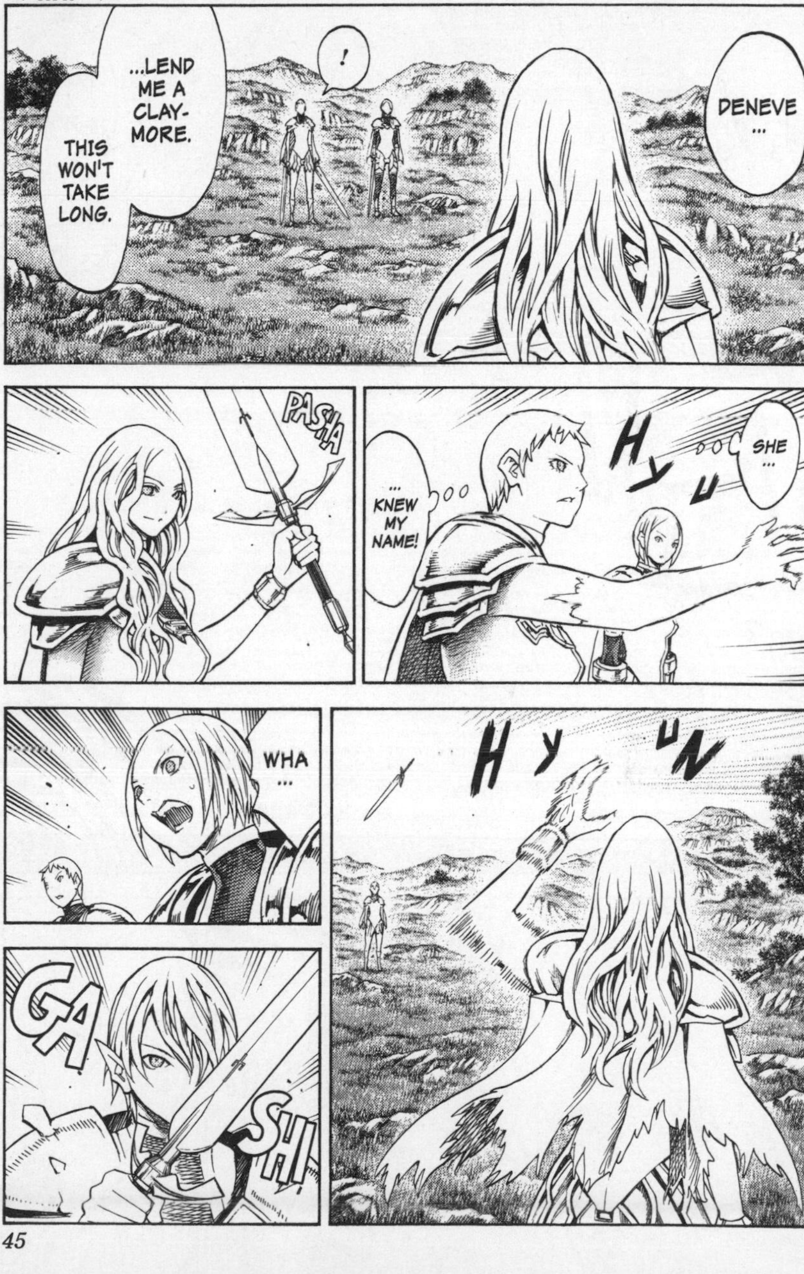

DENEVE ...
!
...LEND ME A CLAY-MORE.
THIS WON'T TAKE LONG.
SHE ...
HYU
... KNEW MY NAME!
PASHA
HYUN
WHA ...
GASHI!

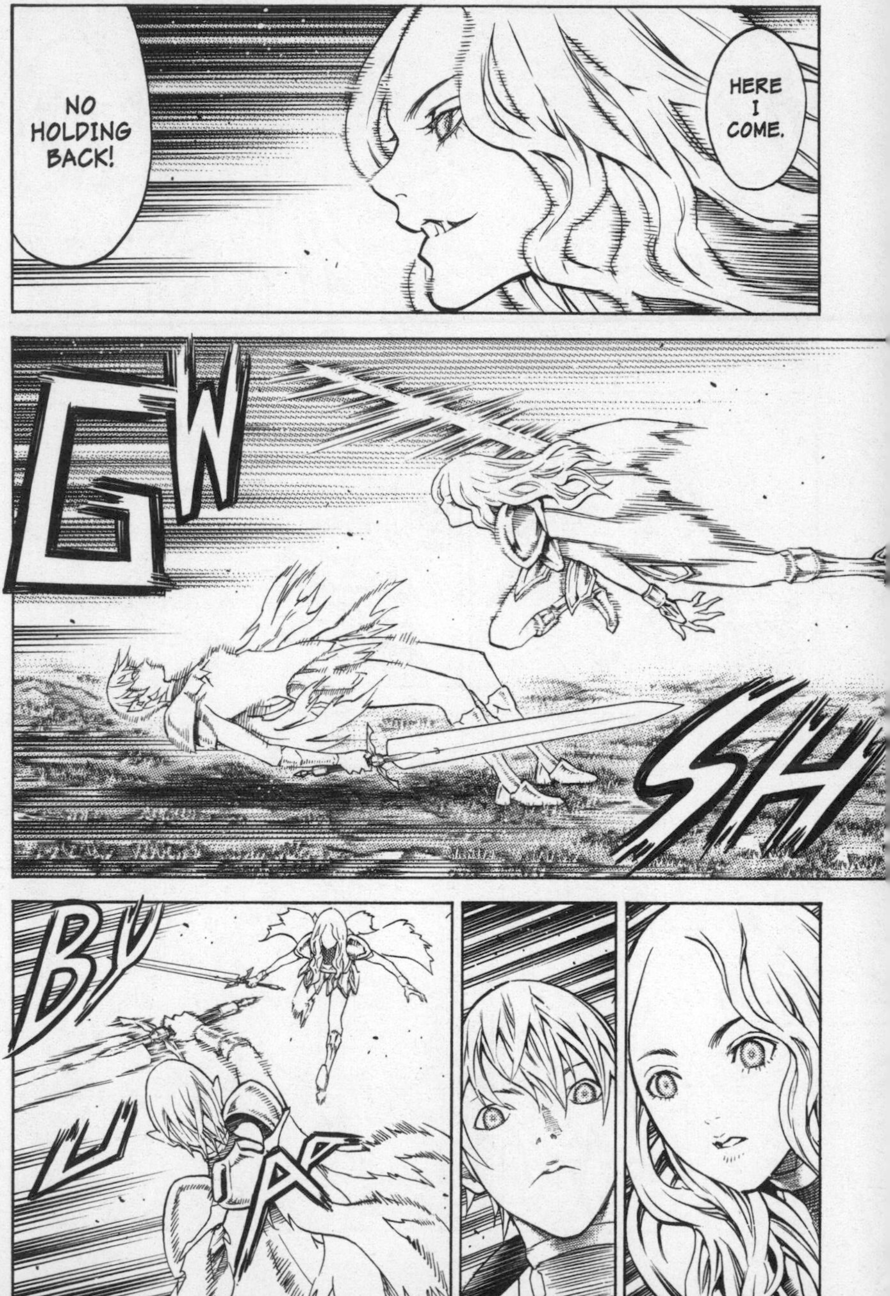
HERE I COME.
NO HOLDING BACK!
GW
SH
BY
U
A

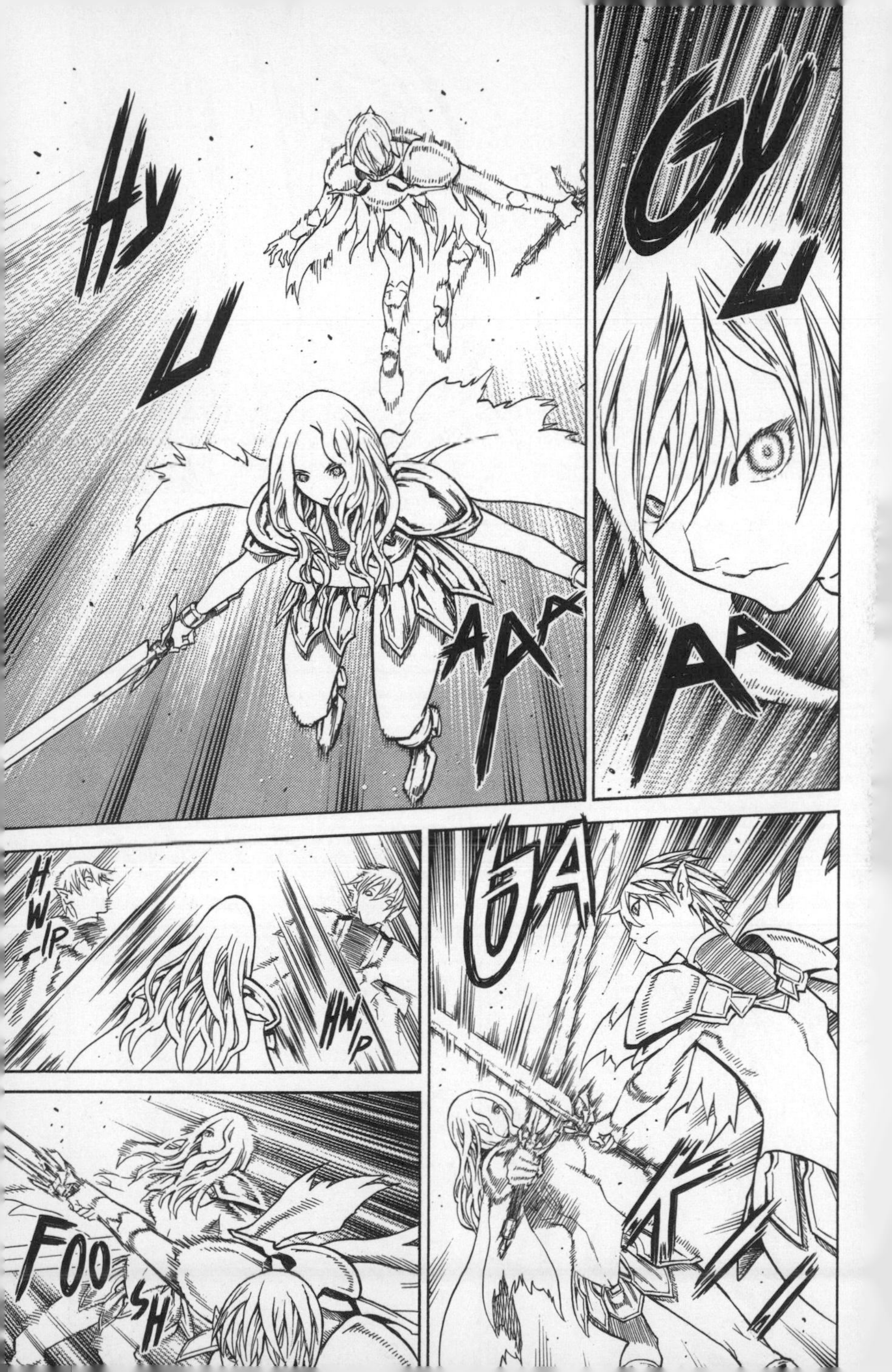
GYU
AA
HYU
AA
GAKIN
HWIP
HWIP
FOOSH

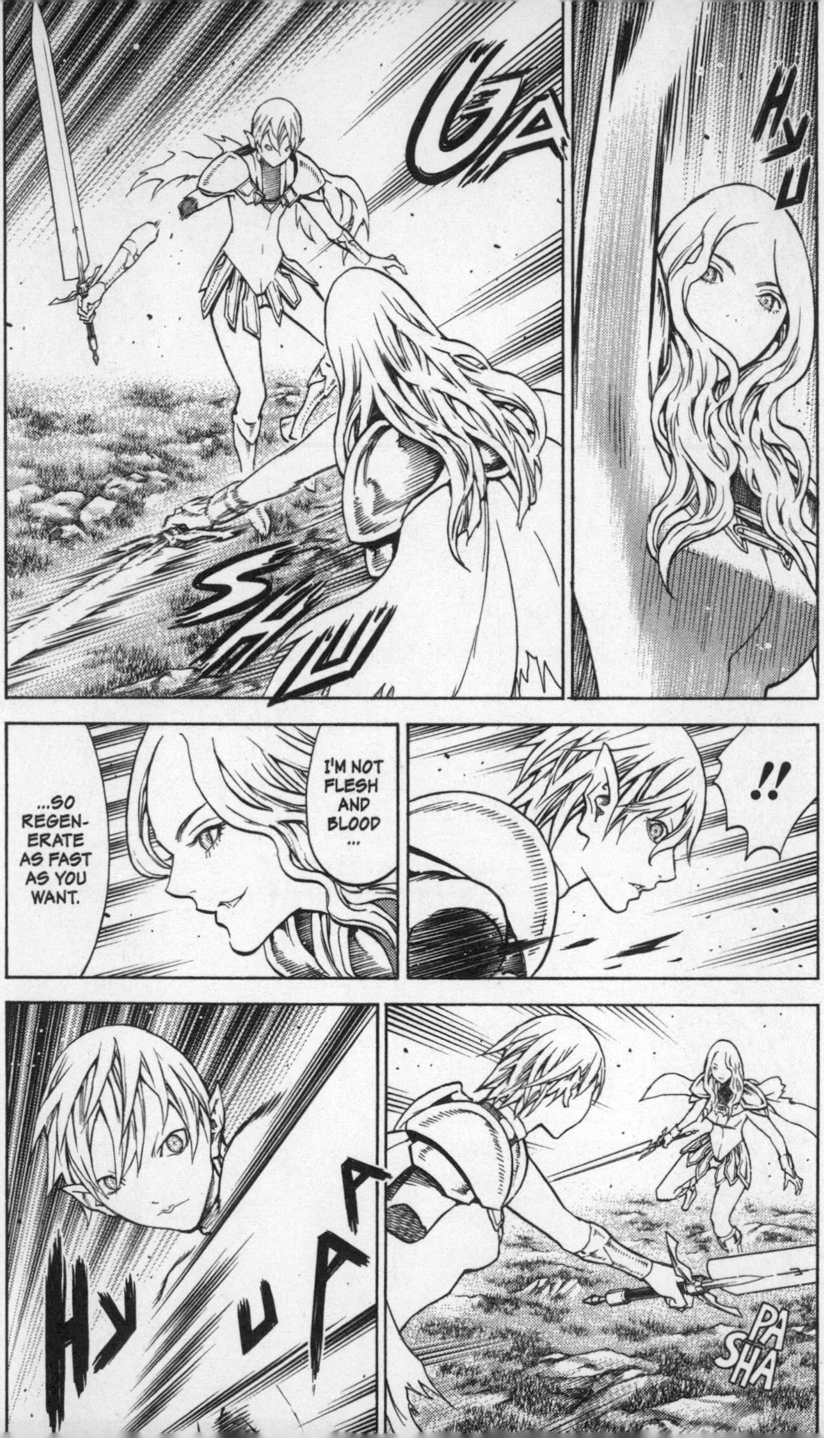

HYU
GA
SHU
!!
I'M NOT FLESH AND BLOOD ...
...SO REGEN-ERATE AS FAST AS YOU WANT.
PASHA
HYUPA

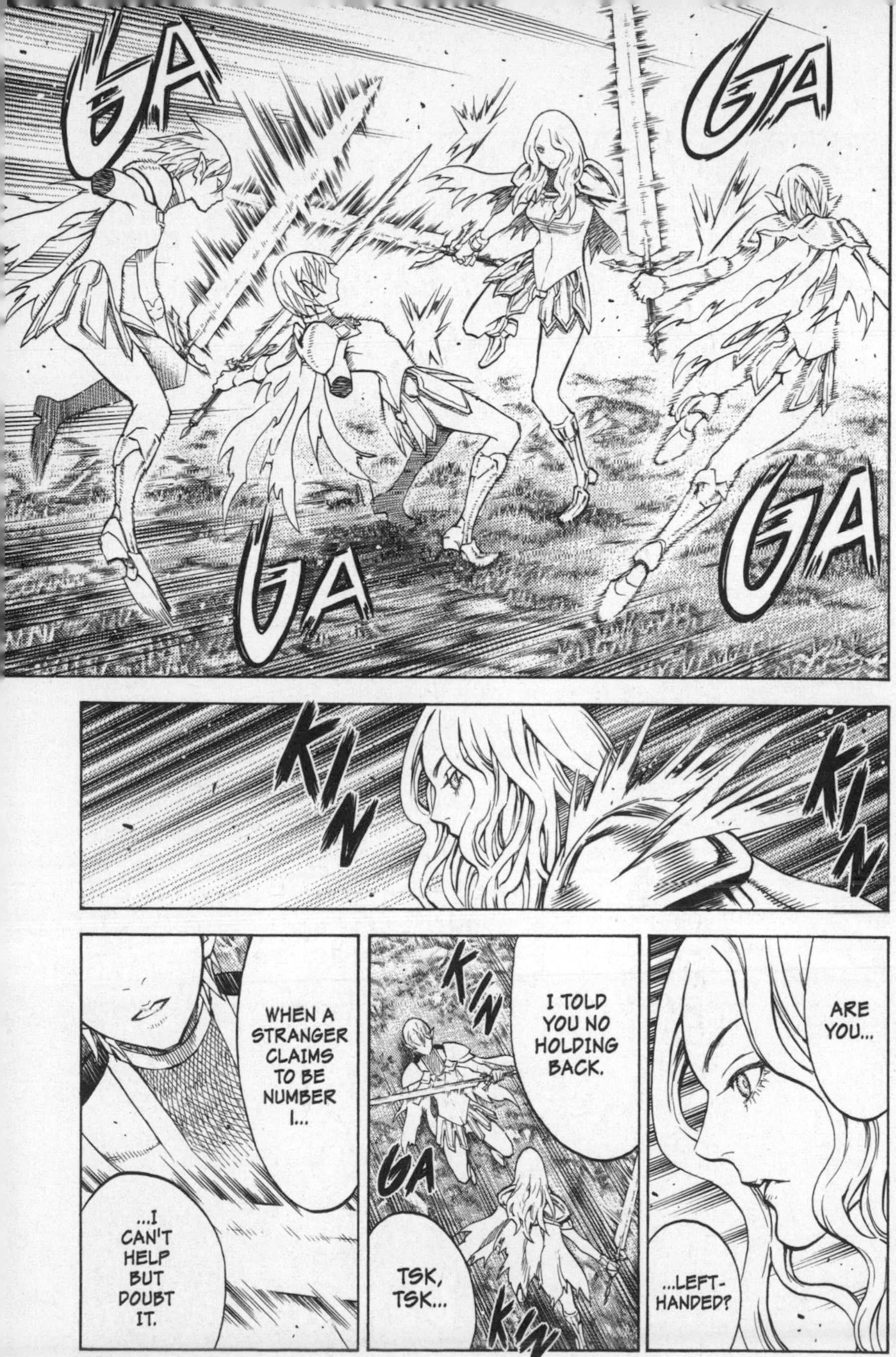
GA
GA
GA
GA
KIN
KIN
KIN
KIN
ARE YOU...
...LEFT-HANDED?
I TOLD YOU NO HOLDING BACK.
KIN
GA
TSK, TSK...
KIN
WHEN A STRANGER CLAIMS TO BE NUMBER 1...
...I CAN'T HELP BUT DOUBT IT.

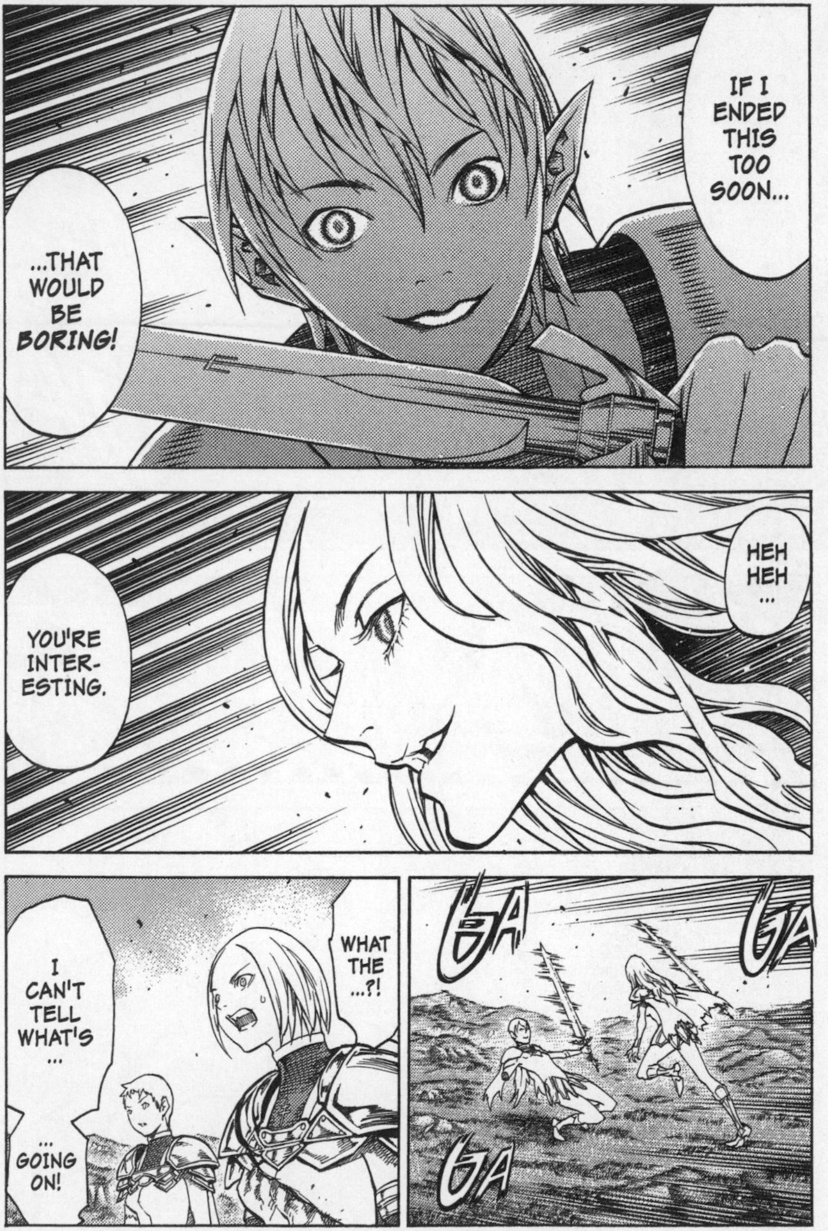
IF I ENDED THIS TOO SOON...
...THAT WOULD BE BORING!
HEH HEH ...
YOU'RE INTER-ESTING.
GA
GA
GA
WHAT THE ...?!
I CAN'T TELL WHAT'S ...
... GOING ON!

READ THIS WAY

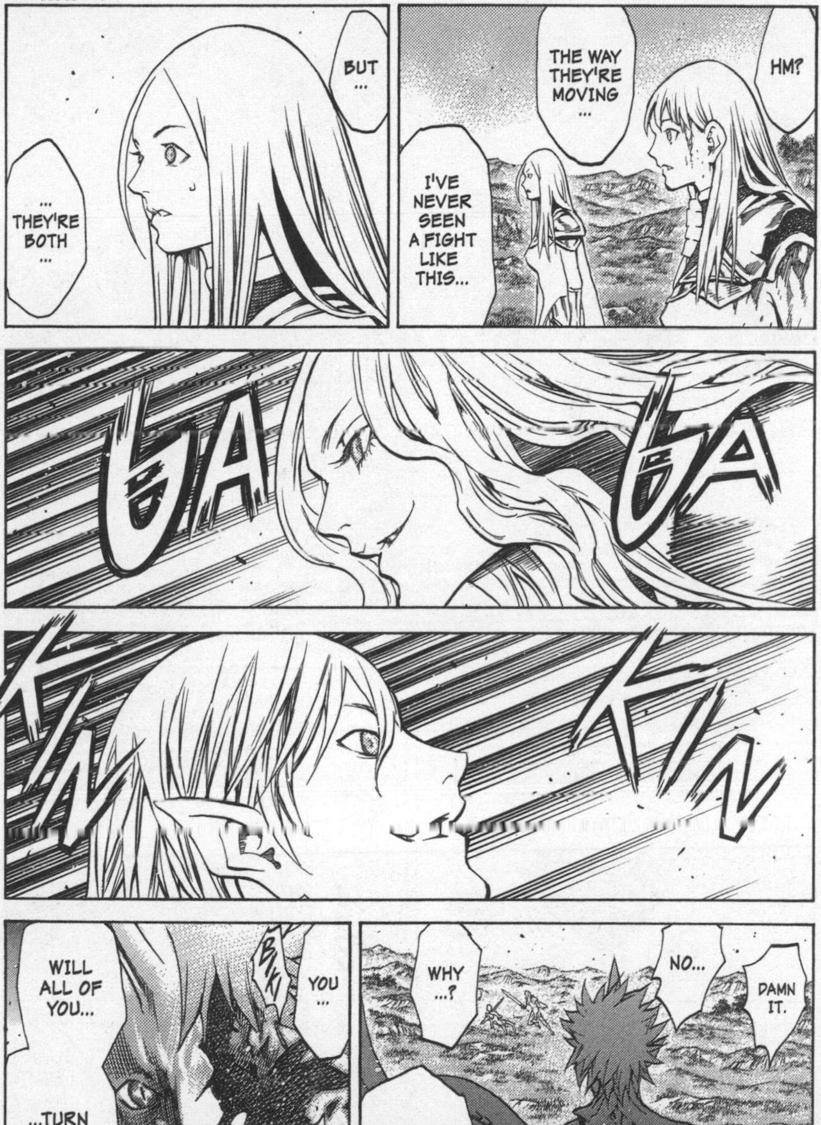
HM?
THE WAY THEY'RE MOVING ...
I'VE NEVER SEEN A FIGHT LIKE THIS...
BUT ...
... THEY'RE BOTH ...
BA
BA
KIN
KIN
NO...
DAMN IT.
WHY ...?
WHAT IS TERESA DOING?!
YOU ...
WILL ALL OF YOU...
...TURN ON ME TOO?!

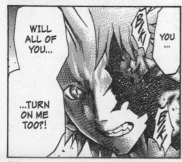

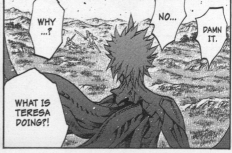

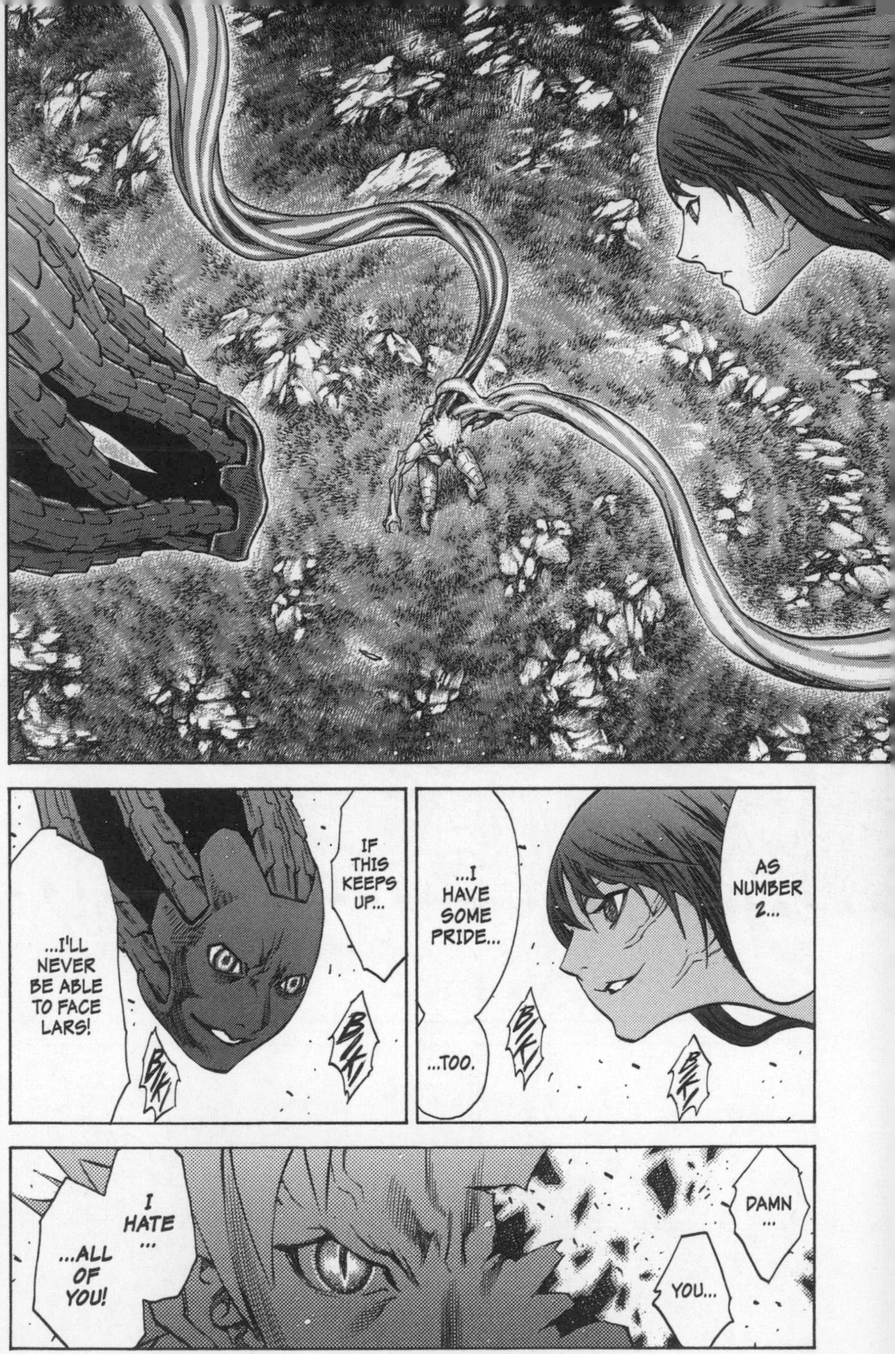
AS NUMBER 2...
...I HAVE SOME PRIDE...
BIKI
BIKI
...TOO.
IF THIS KEEPS UP...
BIKI
...I'LL NEVER BE ABLE TO FACE LARS!
BIKI
DAMN ...
YOU...
I HATE ...
...ALL OF YOU!

READ THIS WAY

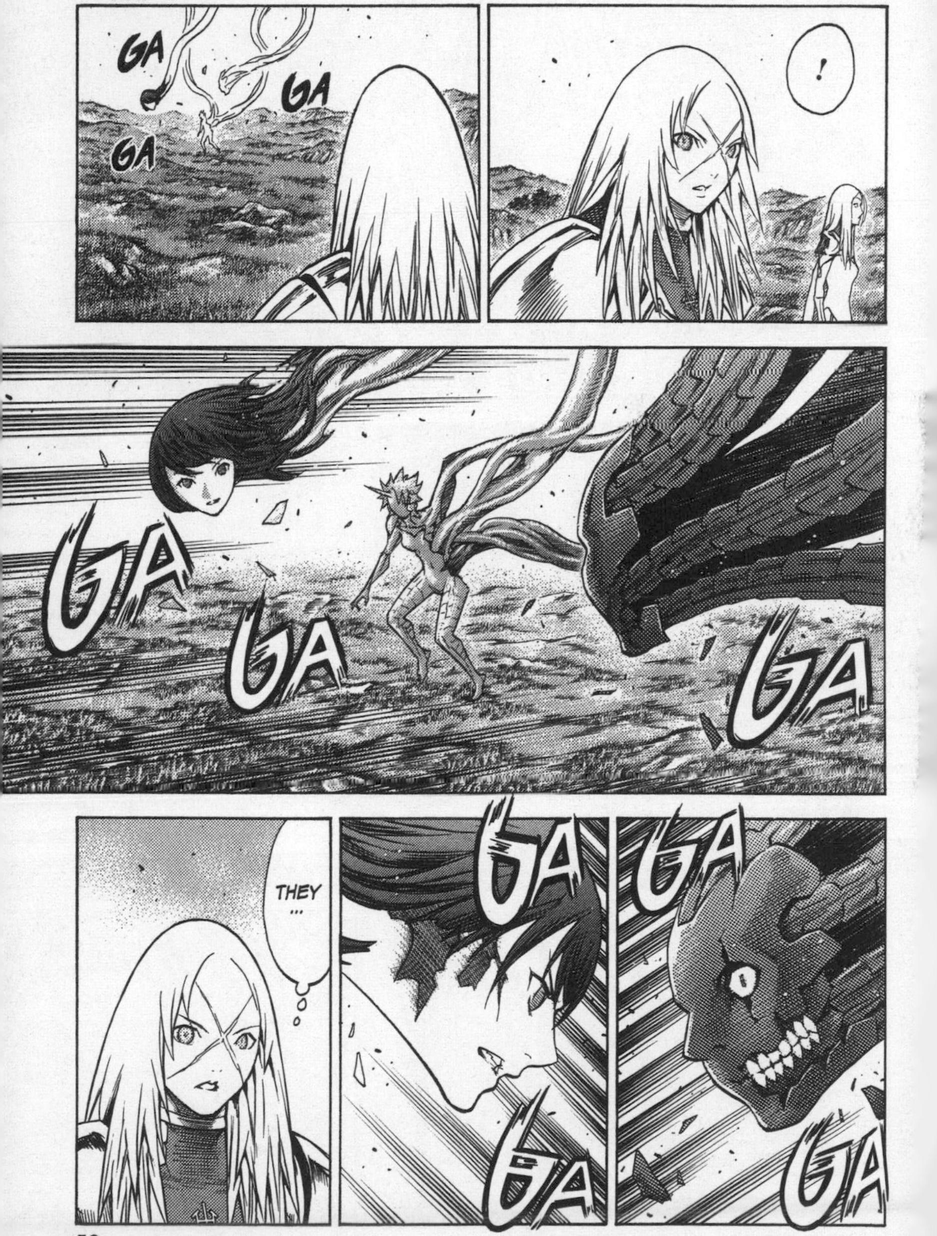
!
GA
GA
GA
GA
GA
GA
GA
GA
GA
GA
THEY ...

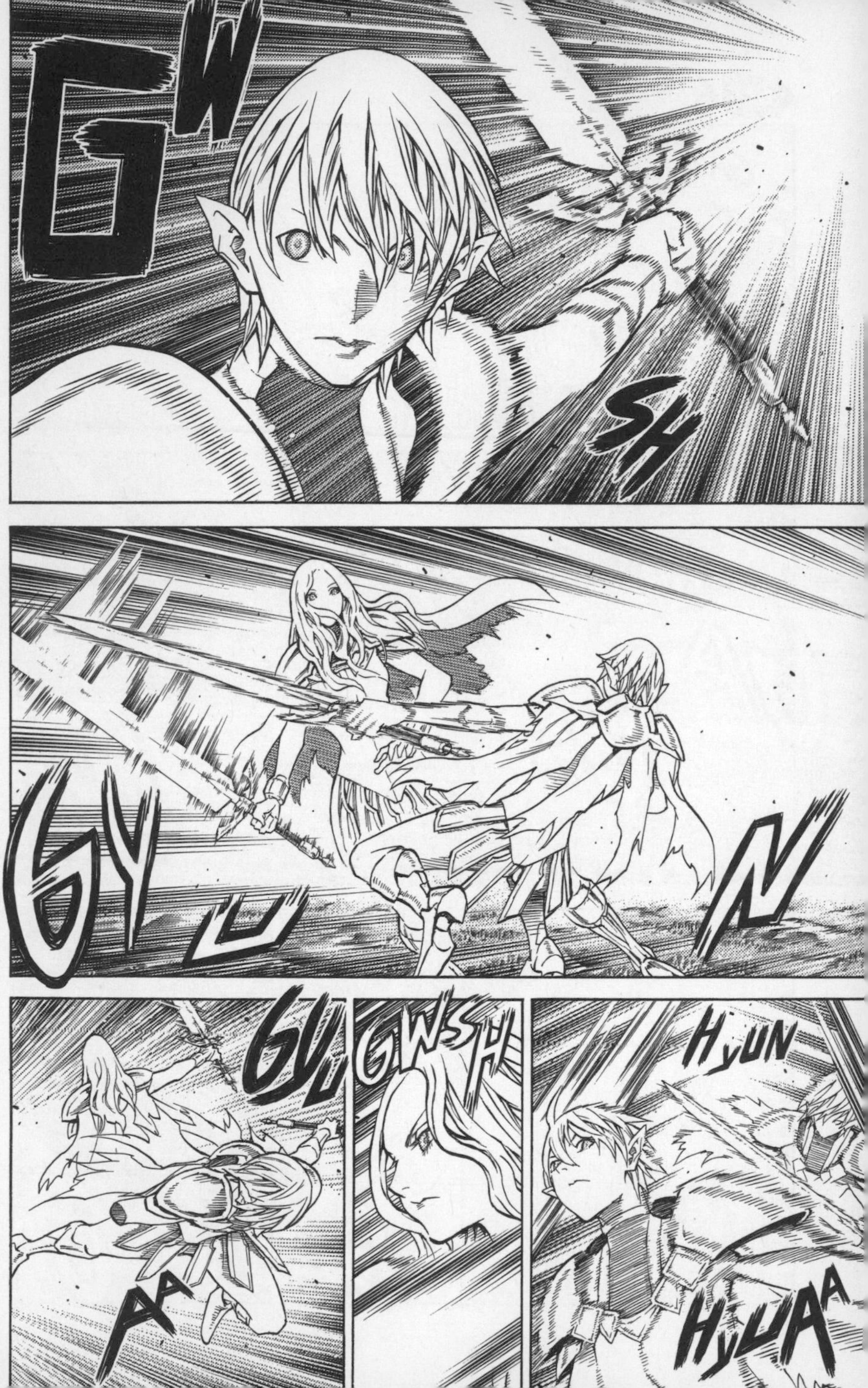
SH
GYUN
HyUN
HyUAA
GWSH
GU
AA

READ THIS WAY

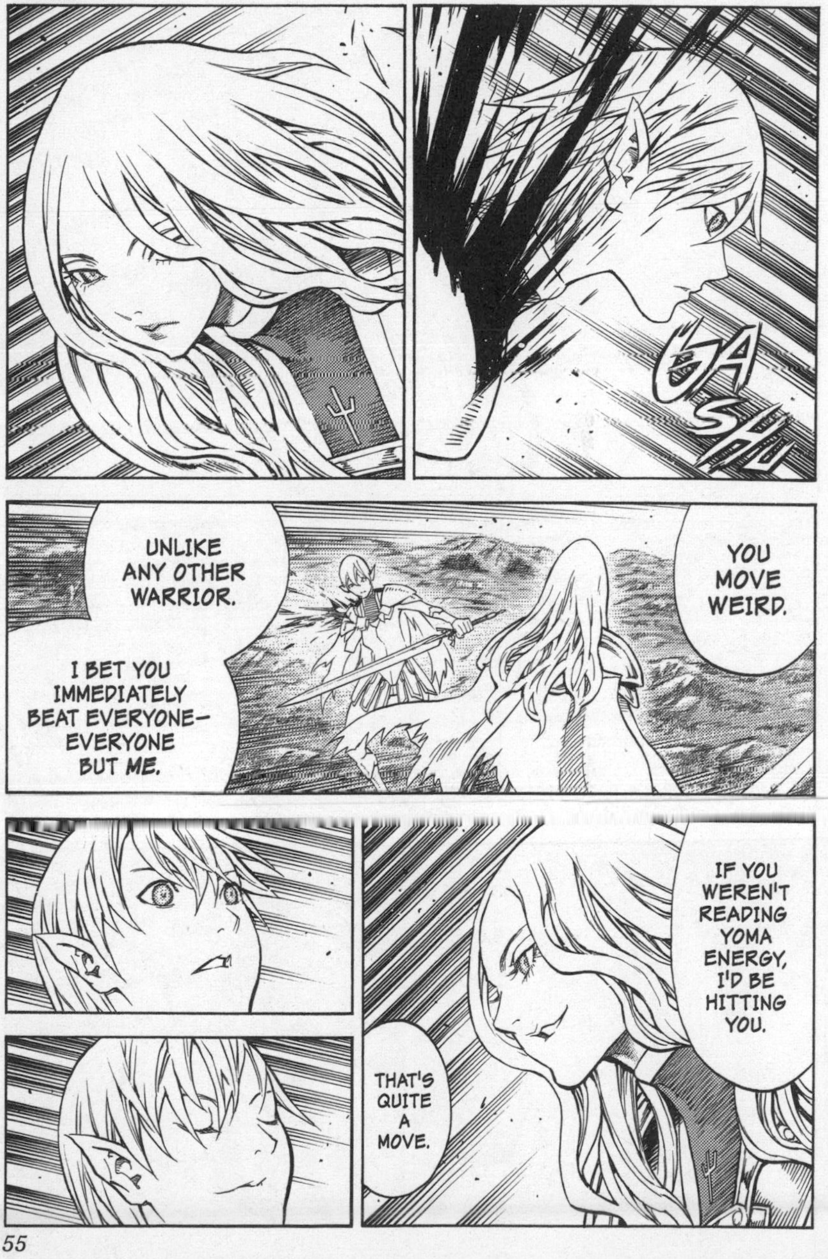
GASHU
YOU MOVE WEIRD.
UNLIKE ANY OTHER WARRIOR.
I BET YOU IMMEDIATELY BEAT EVERYONE— EVERYONE BUT ME.
IF YOU WEREN'T READING YOMA ENERGY, I'D BE HITTING YOU.
THAT'S QUITE A MOVE.

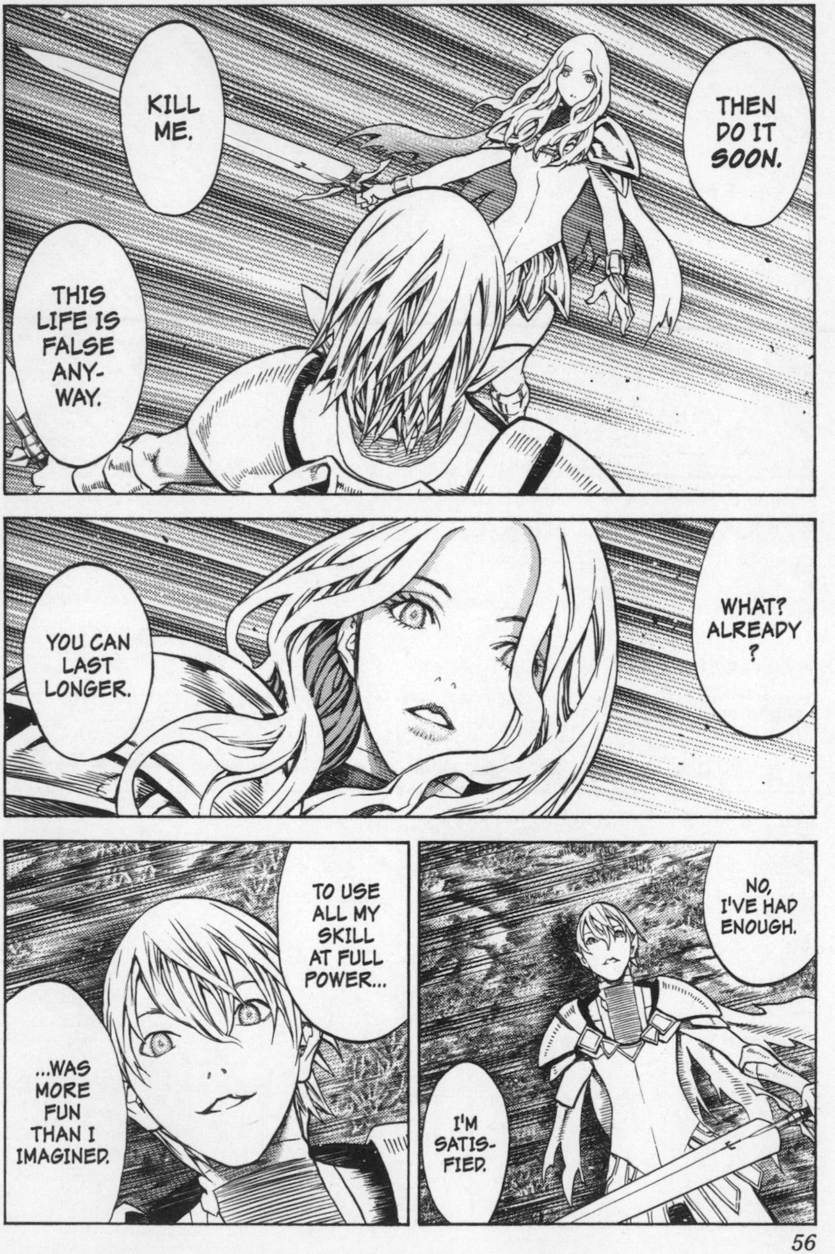
THEN DO IT SOON.
KILL ME.
THIS LIFE IS FALSE ANY-WAY.
WHAT? ALREADY?
YOU CAN LAST LONGER.
NO, I'VE HAD ENOUGH.
I'M SATIS-FIED.
TO USE ALL MY SKILL AT FULL POWER...
...WAS MORE FUN THAN I IMAGINED.

READ THIS WAY

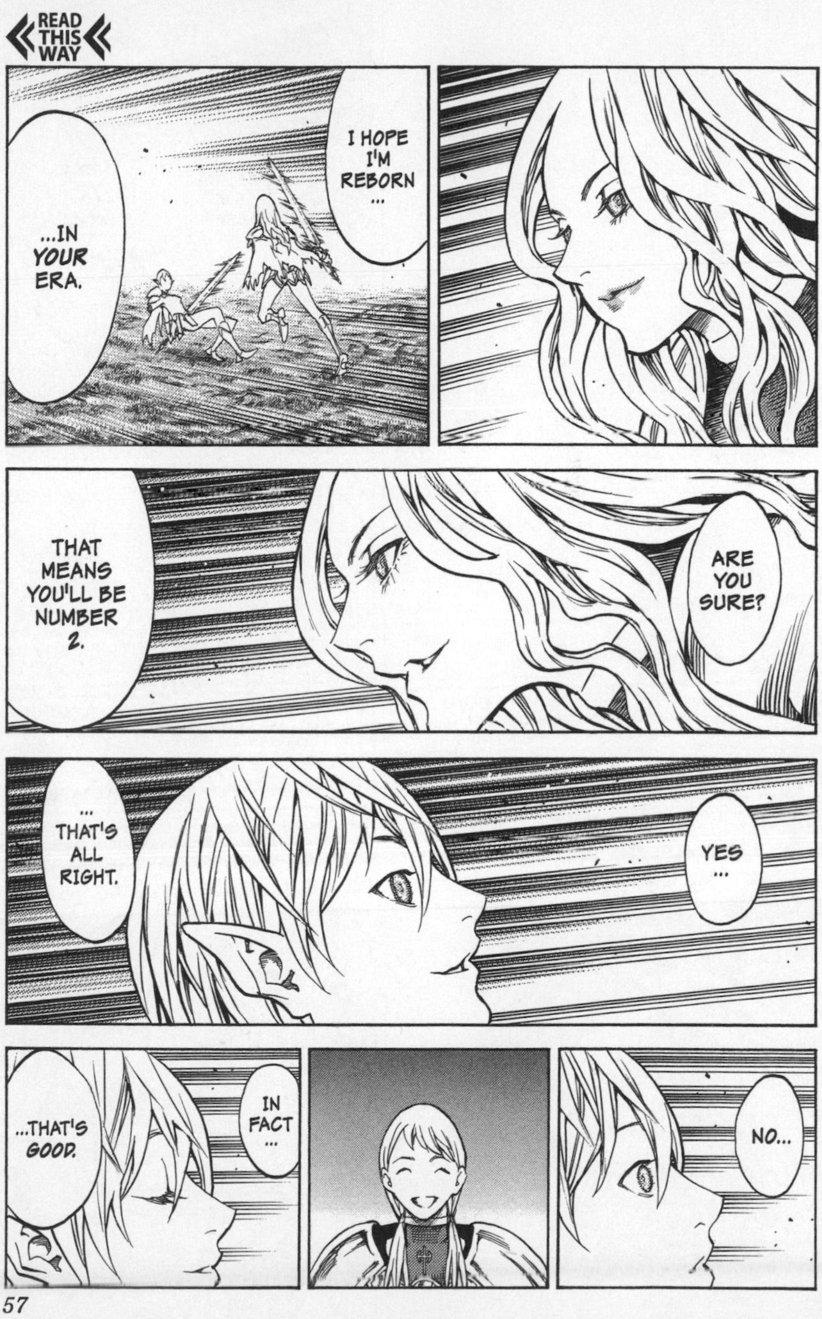
I HOPE I'M REBORN ...
...IN *YOUR* ERA.
ARE YOU SURE?
THAT MEANS YOU'LL BE NUMBER 2.
YES ...
... THAT'S ALL RIGHT.
NO...
IN FACT ...
...THAT'S *GOOD.*

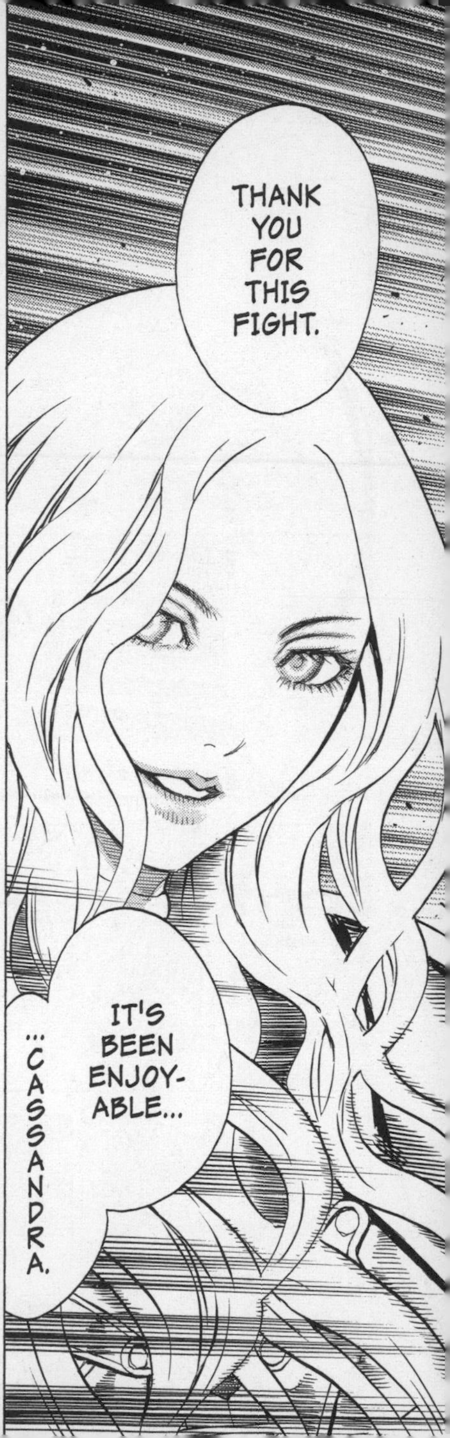
THANK YOU FOR THIS FIGHT.
IT'S BEEN ENJOY-ABLE...
...CASSANDRA.
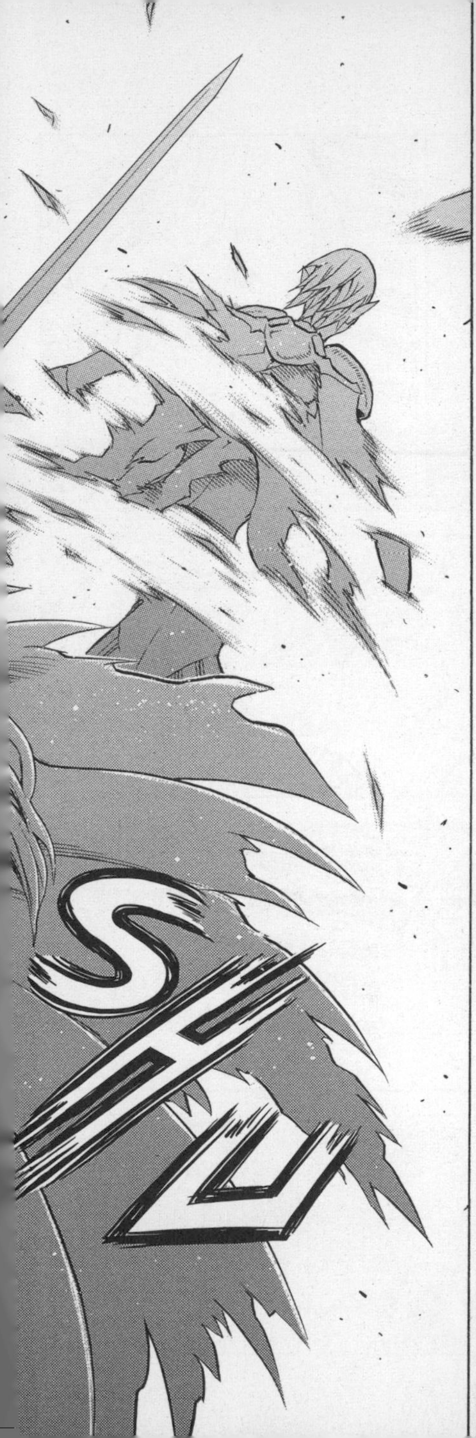
SHU

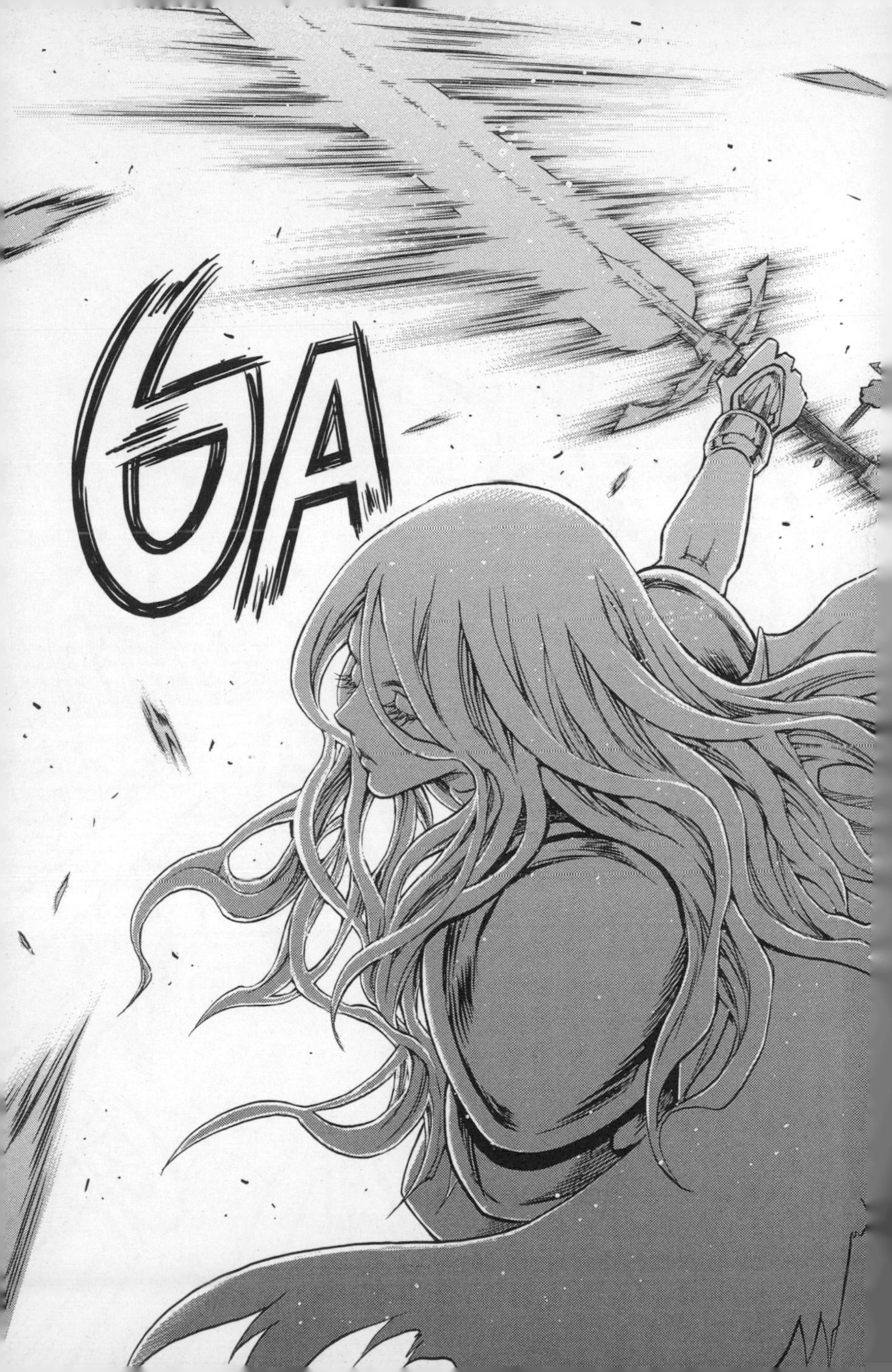
GA

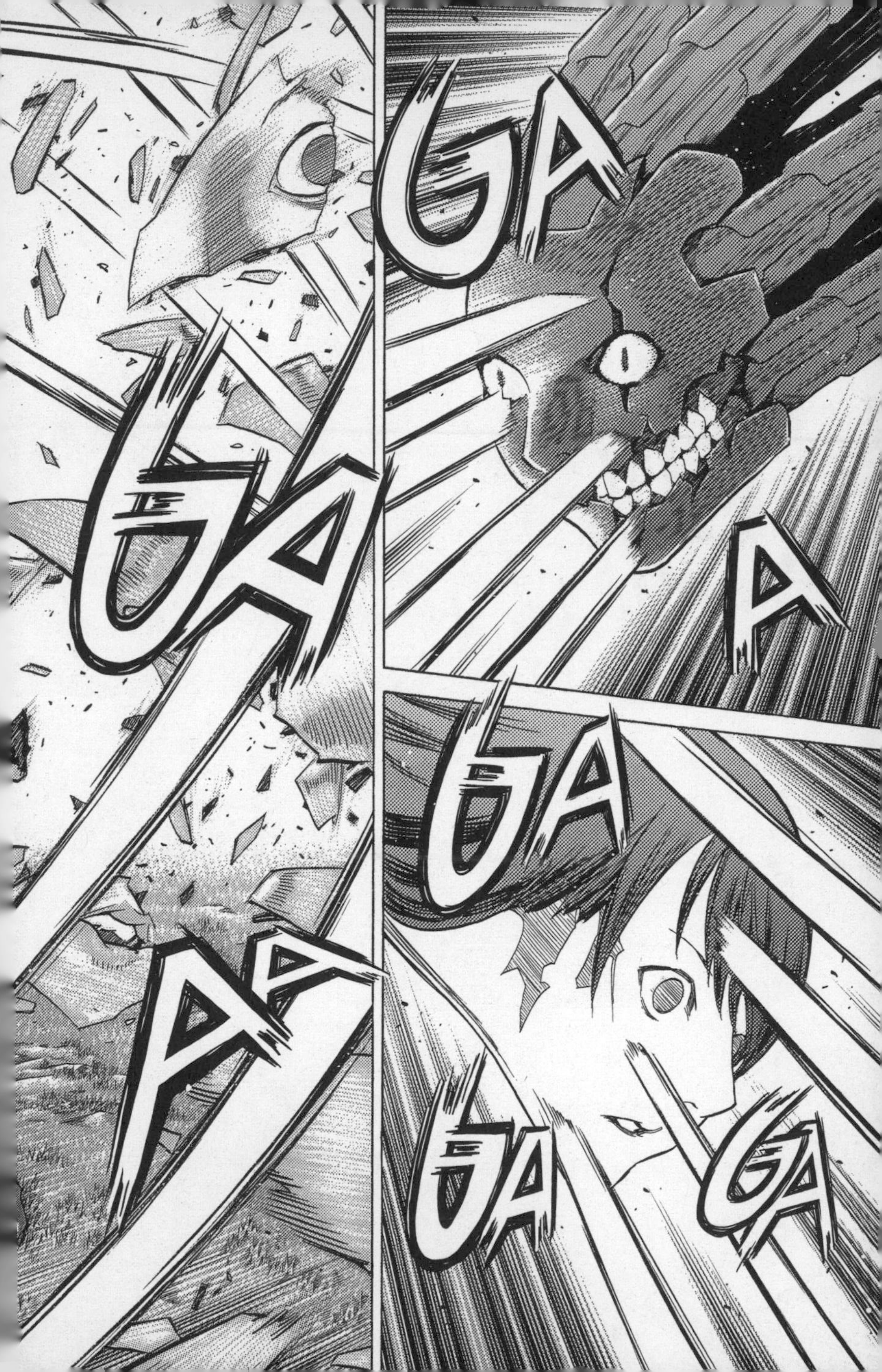
GA
A
GA
GA
GA
GA
AA

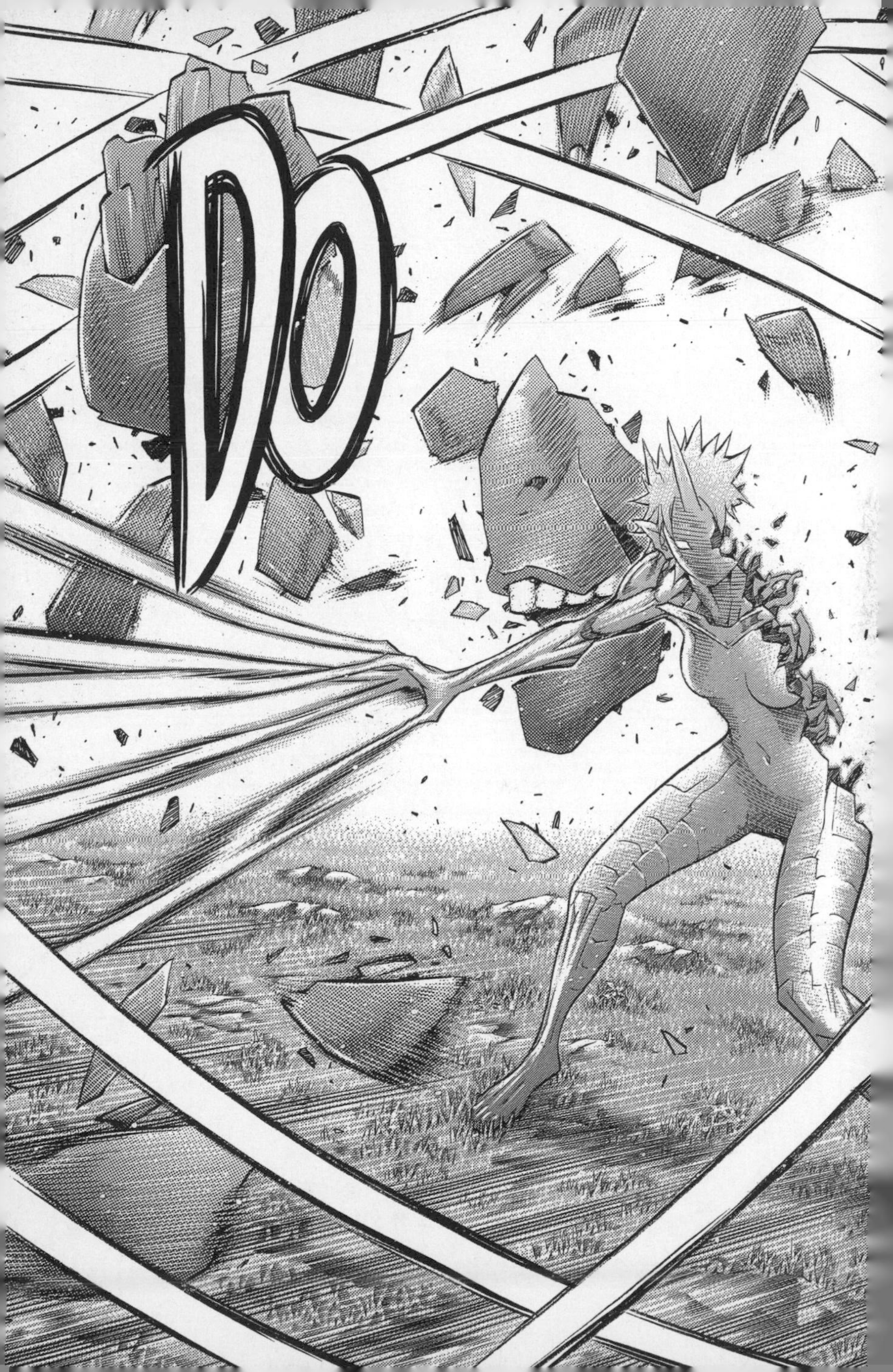
DO

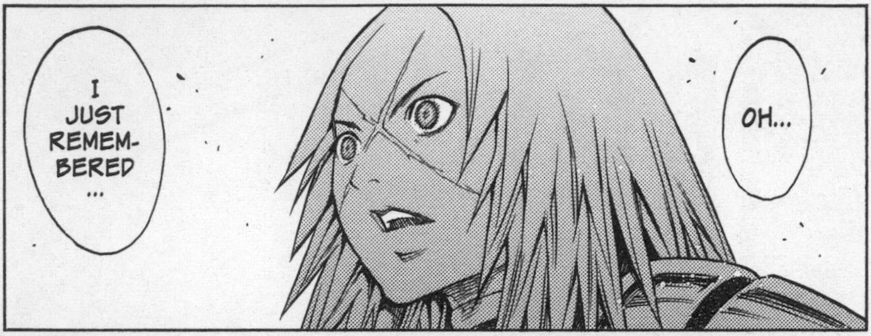
OH...
I JUST REMEMBERED...

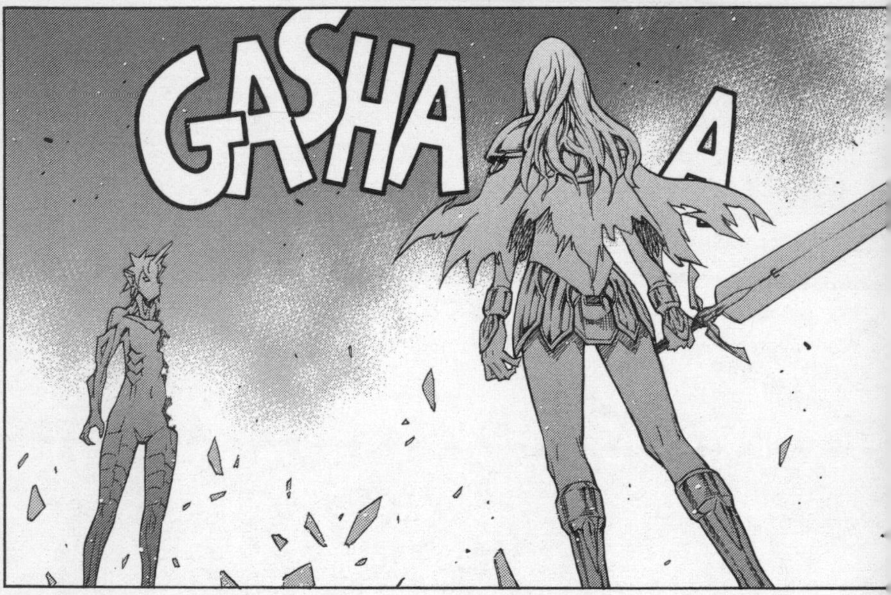
GASHA A

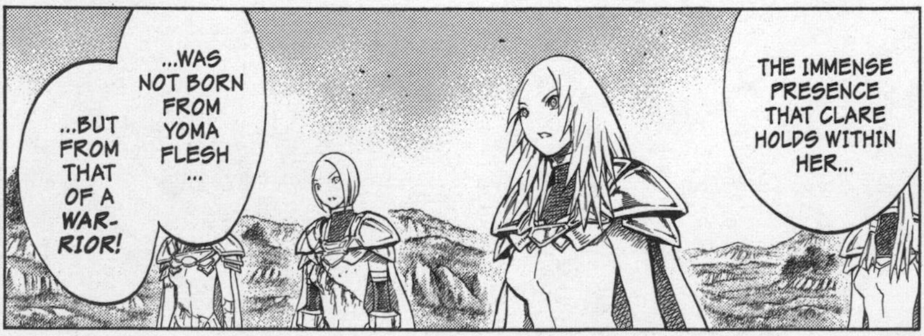
THE IMMENSE PRESENCE THAT CLARE HOLDS WITHIN HER...
...WAS NOT BORN FROM YOMA FLESH...
...BUT FROM THAT OF A WARRIOR!

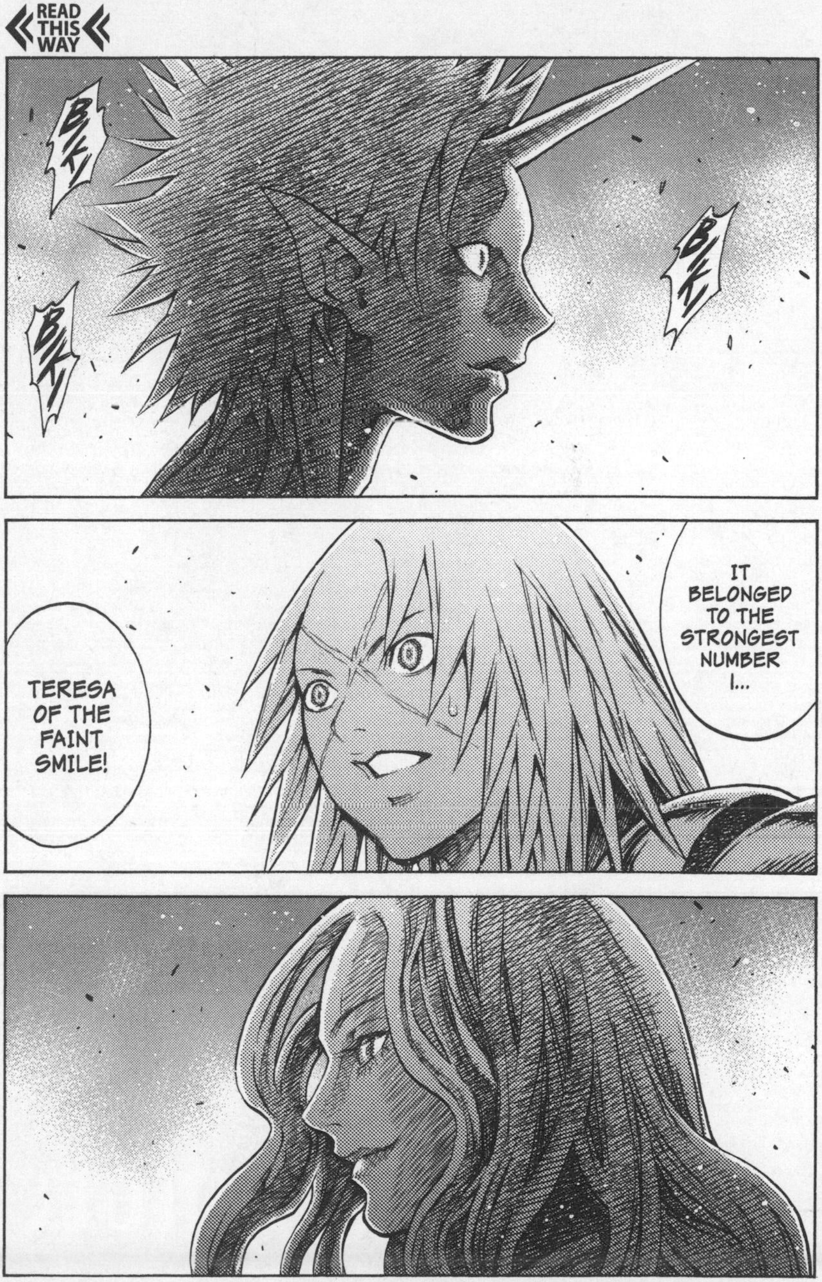
READ THIS WAY
BIKI
BIKI
BIKI
IT BELONGED TO THE STRONGEST NUMBER I...
TERESA OF THE FAINT SMILE!

クレイモア
Claymore

Scene 152: Silver-Eyed Warriors, Part 3

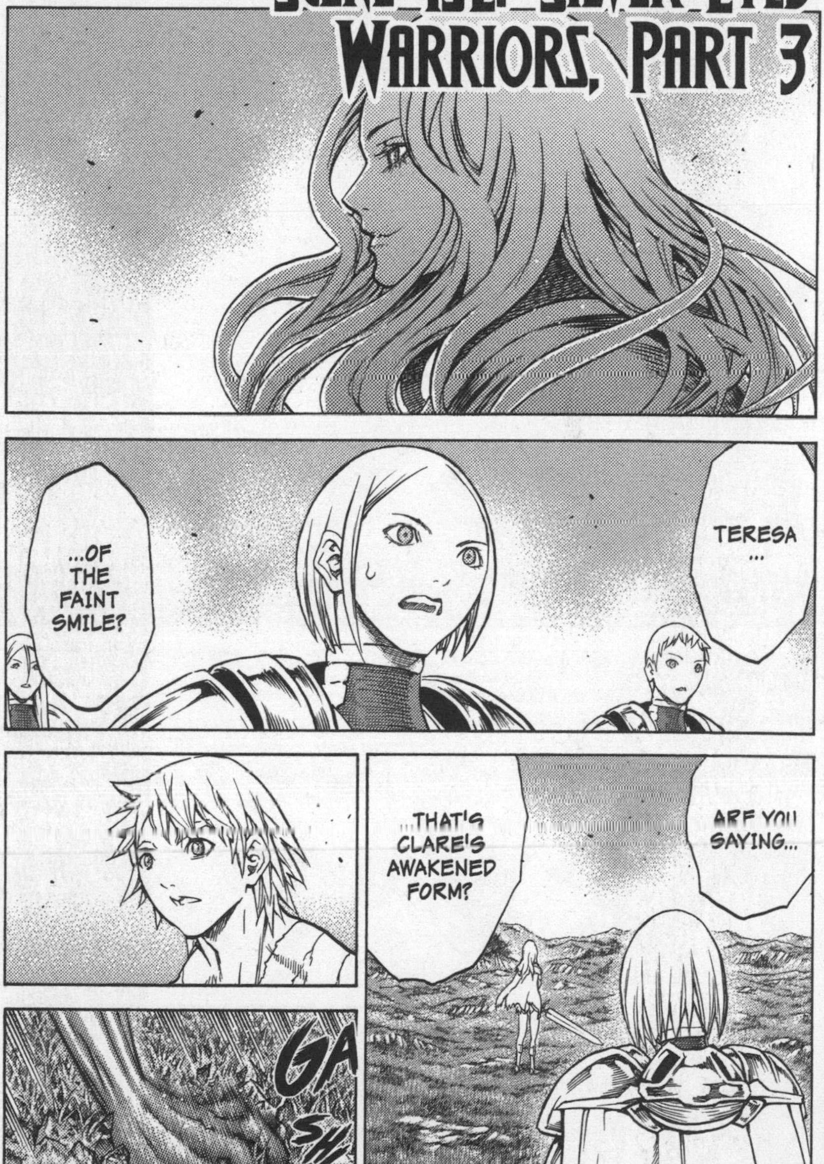
TERESA ...
...OF THE FAINT SMILE?
ARE YOU SAYING...
...THAT'S CLARE'S AWAKENED FORM?
GASH

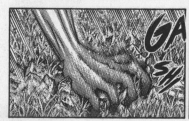

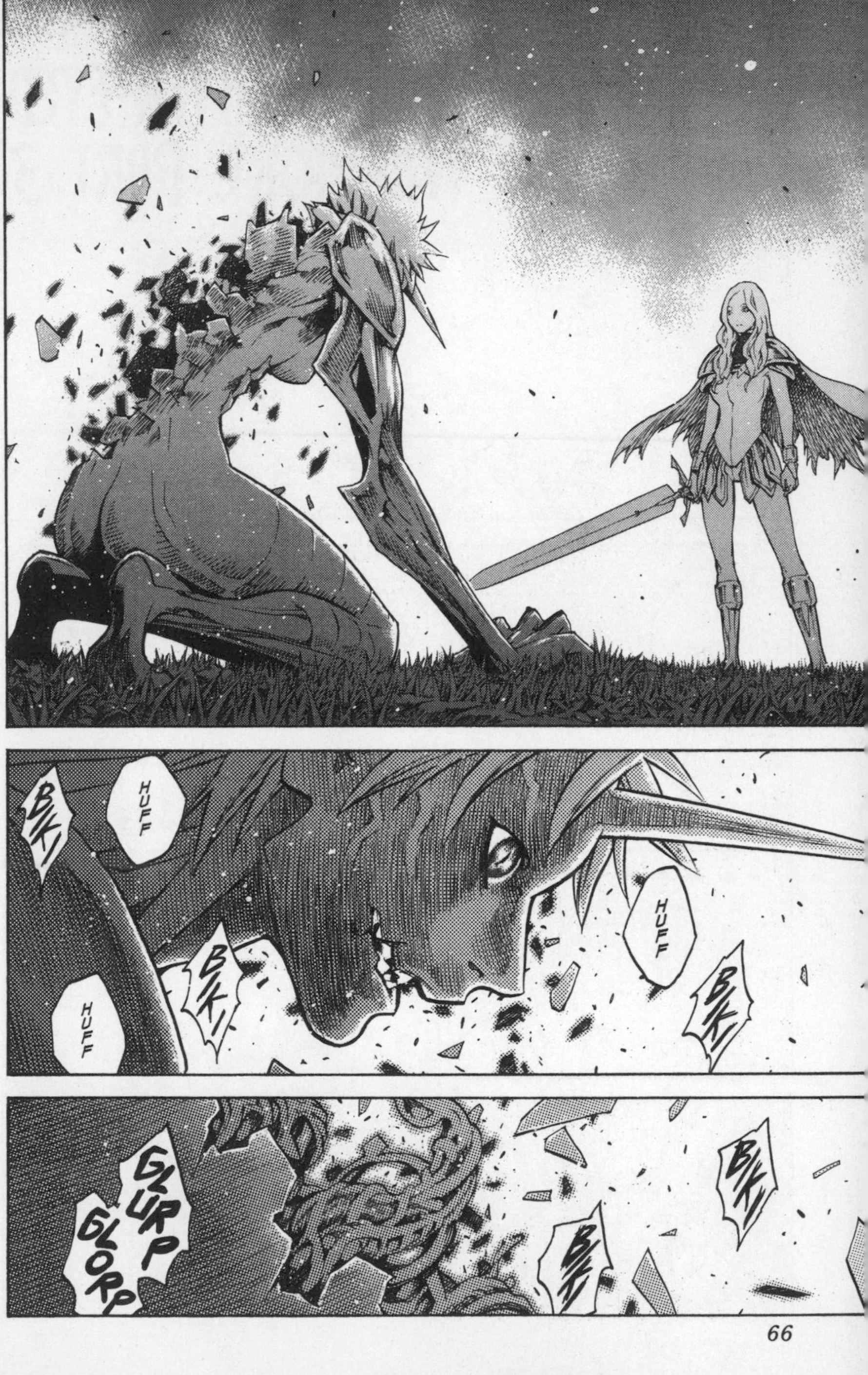
HUFF
BIKI
HUFF
BIKI
BIKI
HUFF
BIKI
BIKI
GLURP GLORP

READ THIS WAY

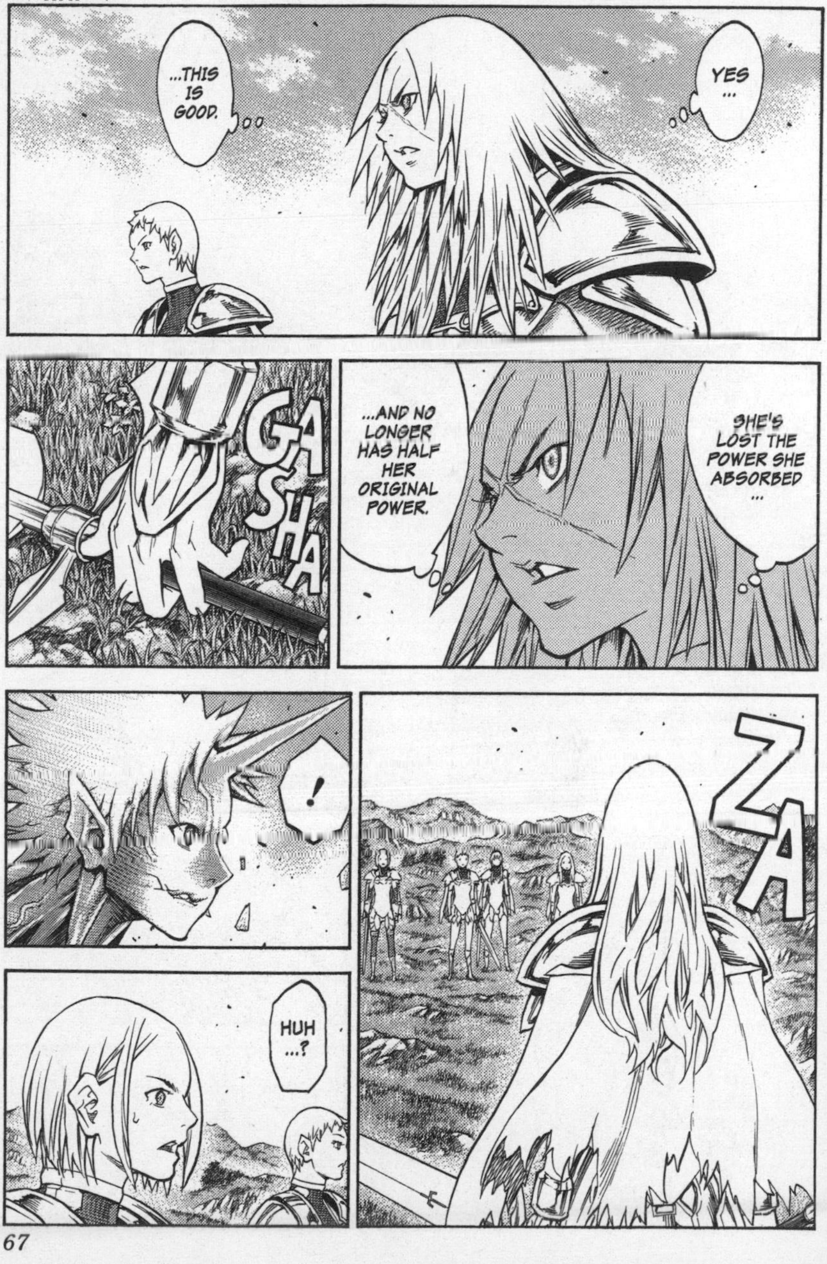
YES ...
...THIS IS GOOD.
SHE'S LOST THE POWER SHE ABSORBED ...
...AND NO LONGER HAS HALF HER ORIGINAL POWER.
GASHA
ZA
!
HUH ...?

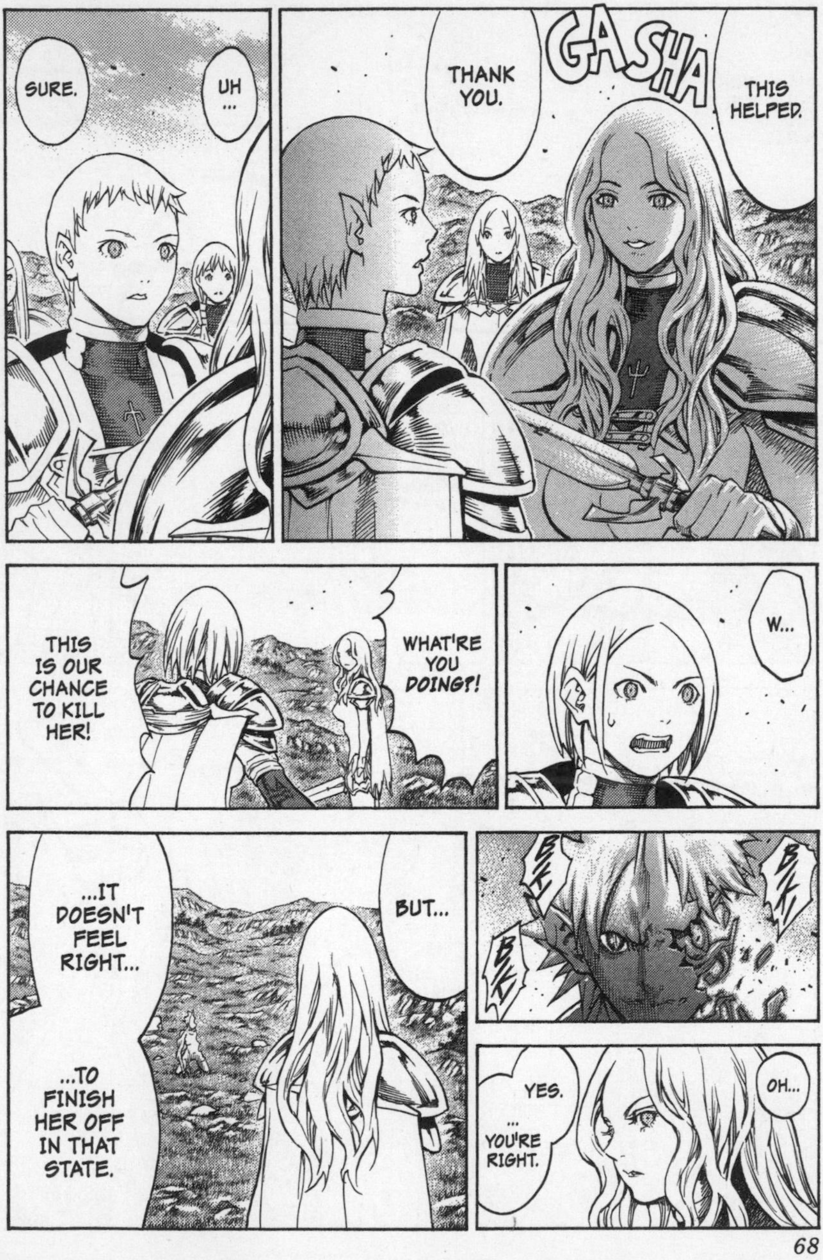
THIS HELPED.
GASHA
THANK YOU.
UH ...
SURE.
W...
WHAT'RE YOU DOING?!
THIS IS OUR CHANCE TO KILL HER!
BKI
BKI
BKI
OH...
YES.
... YOU'RE RIGHT.
BUT...
...IT DOESN'T FEEL RIGHT...
...TO FINISH HER OFF IN THAT STATE.

«READ THIS WAY«

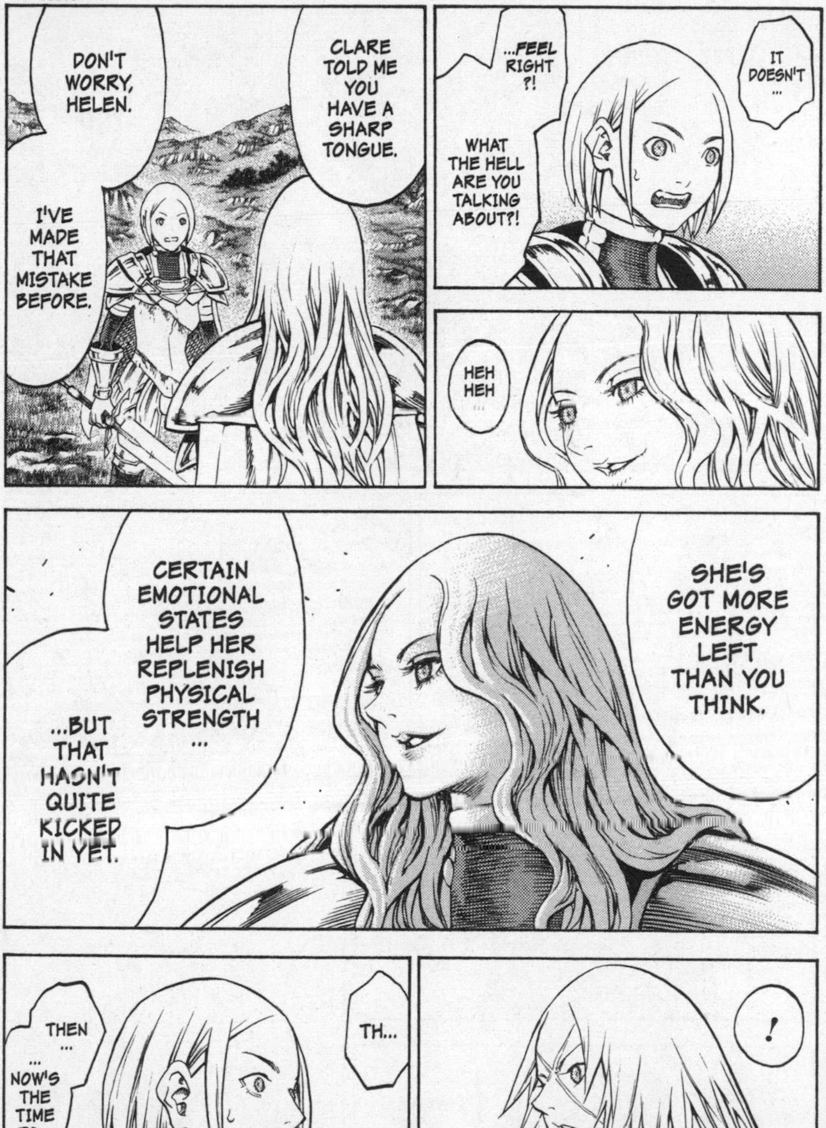
IT DOESN'T ...
...FEEL RIGHT ?!
WHAT THE HELL ARE YOU TALKING ABOUT?!
HEH HEH ...
CLARE TOLD ME YOU HAVE A SHARP TONGUE.
DON'T WORRY, HELEN.
I'VE MADE THAT MISTAKE BEFORE.
SHE'S GOT MORE ENERGY LEFT THAN YOU THINK.
CERTAIN EMOTIONAL STATES HELP HER REPLENISH PHYSICAL STRENGTH ...
...BUT THAT HASN'T QUITE KICKED IN YET.
!
TH...
THEN ... NOW'S THE TIME TO—

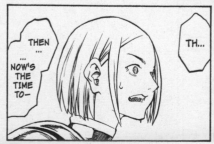

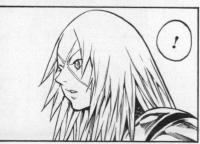

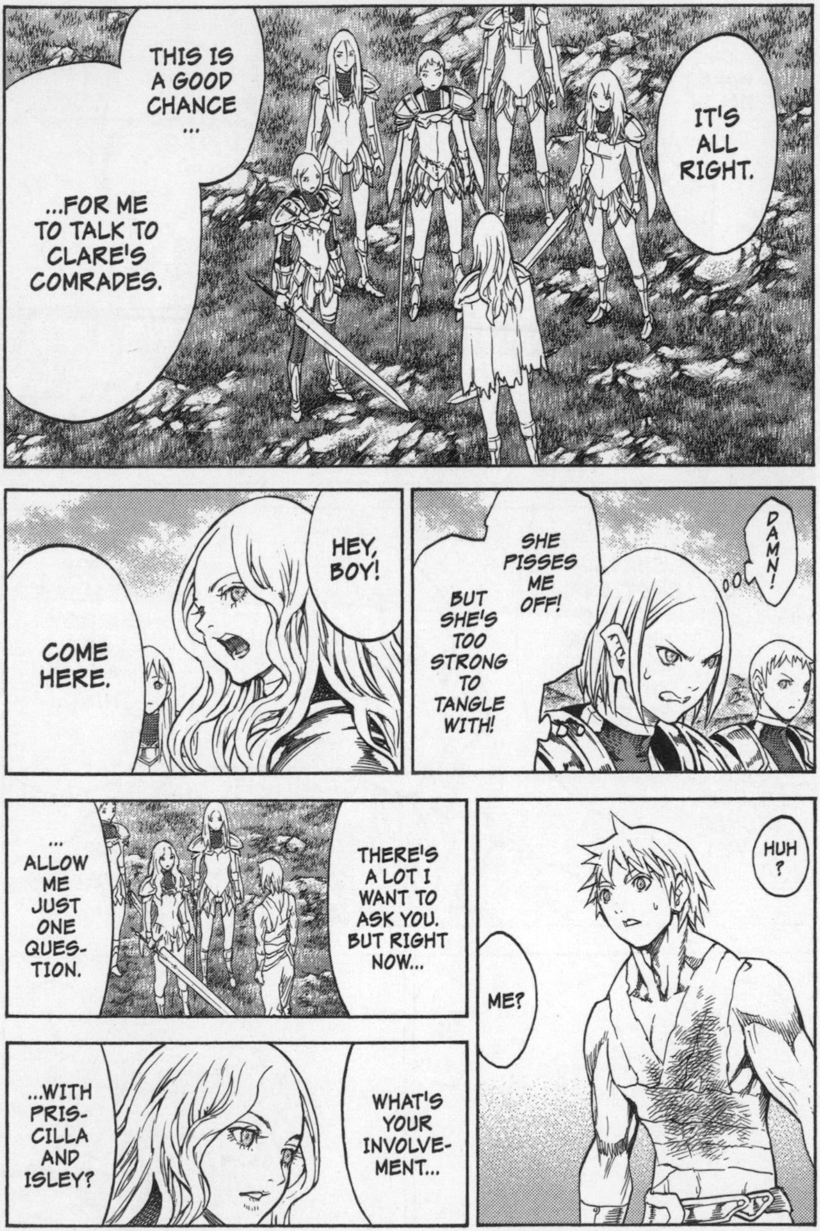
IT'S ALL RIGHT.
THIS IS A GOOD CHANCE ...
...FOR ME TO TALK TO CLARE'S COMRADES.
DAMN!
SHE PISSES ME OFF!
BUT SHE'S TOO STRONG TO TANGLE WITH!
HEY, BOY!
COME HERE.
HUH?
ME?
THERE'S A LOT I WANT TO ASK YOU. BUT RIGHT NOW...
... ALLOW ME JUST ONE QUES-TION.
WHAT'S YOUR INVOLVE-MENT...
...WITH PRIS-CILLA AND ISLEY?

READ THIS WAY

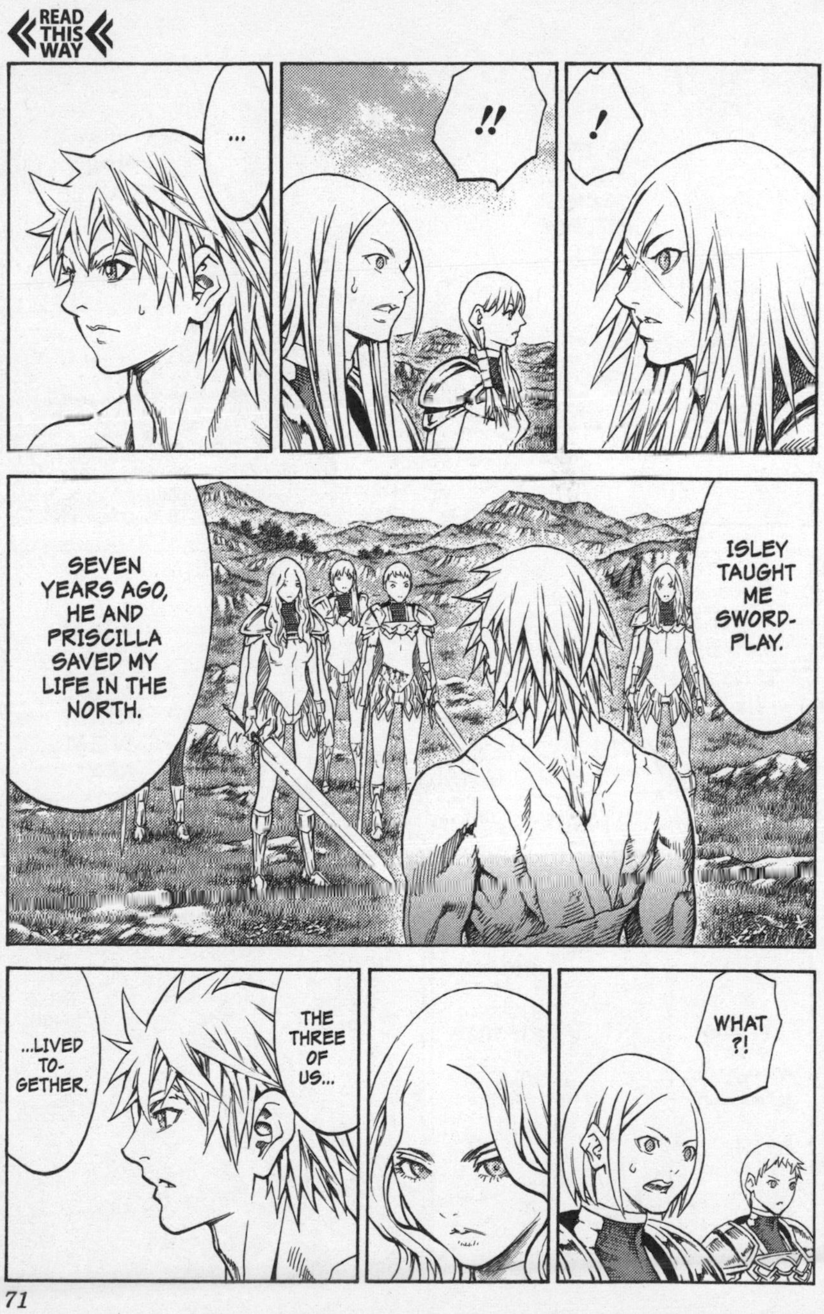
!
!!
...
ISLEY TAUGHT ME SWORD-PLAY.
SEVEN YEARS AGO, HE AND PRISCILLA SAVED MY LIFE IN THE NORTH.
WHAT ?!
THE THREE OF US...
...LIVED TO-GETHER.

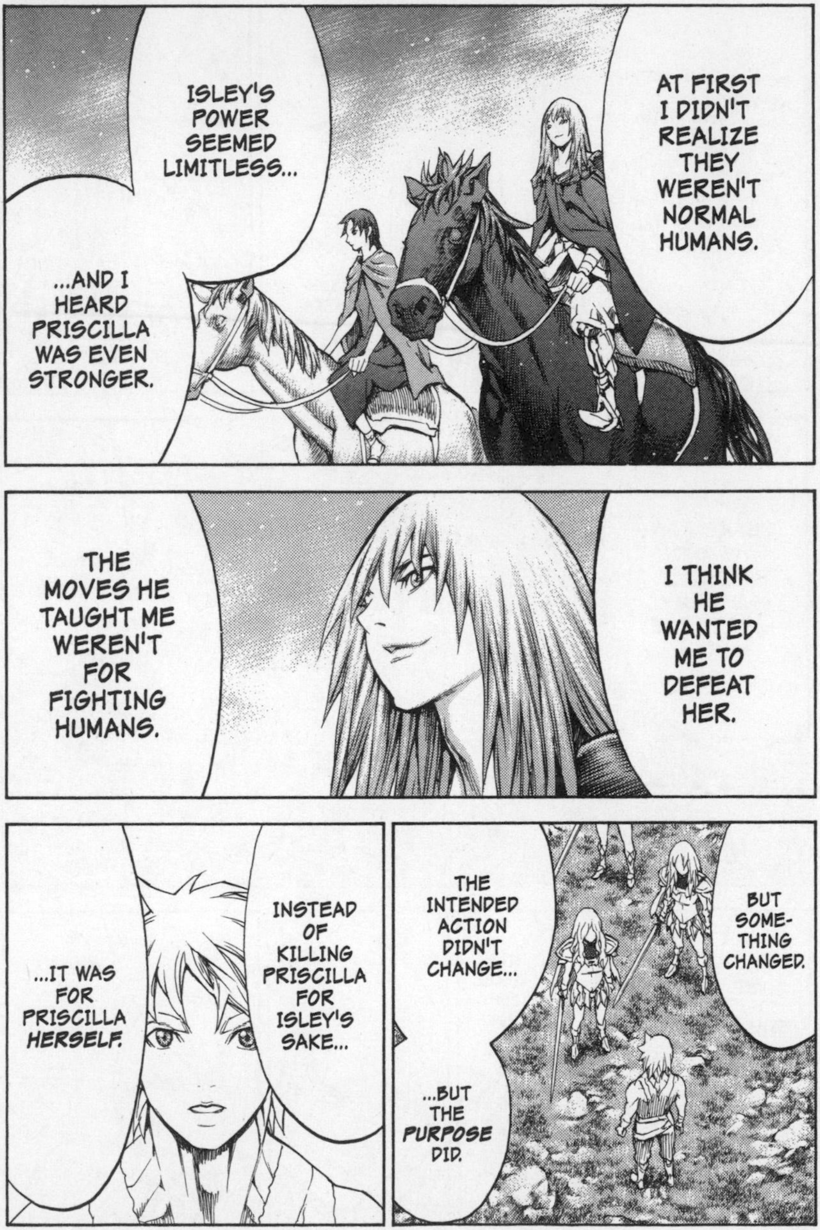
AT FIRST I DIDN'T REALIZE THEY WEREN'T NORMAL HUMANS.
ISLEY'S POWER SEEMED LIMITLESS...
...AND I HEARD PRISCILLA WAS EVEN STRONGER.
I THINK HE WANTED ME TO DEFEAT HER.
THE MOVES HE TAUGHT ME WEREN'T FOR FIGHTING HUMANS.
BUT SOME-THING CHANGED.
THE INTENDED ACTION DIDN'T CHANGE...
...BUT THE *PURPOSE* DID.
INSTEAD OF KILLING PRISCILLA FOR ISLEY'S SAKE...
...IT WAS FOR PRISCILLA HERSELF.

READ THIS WAY

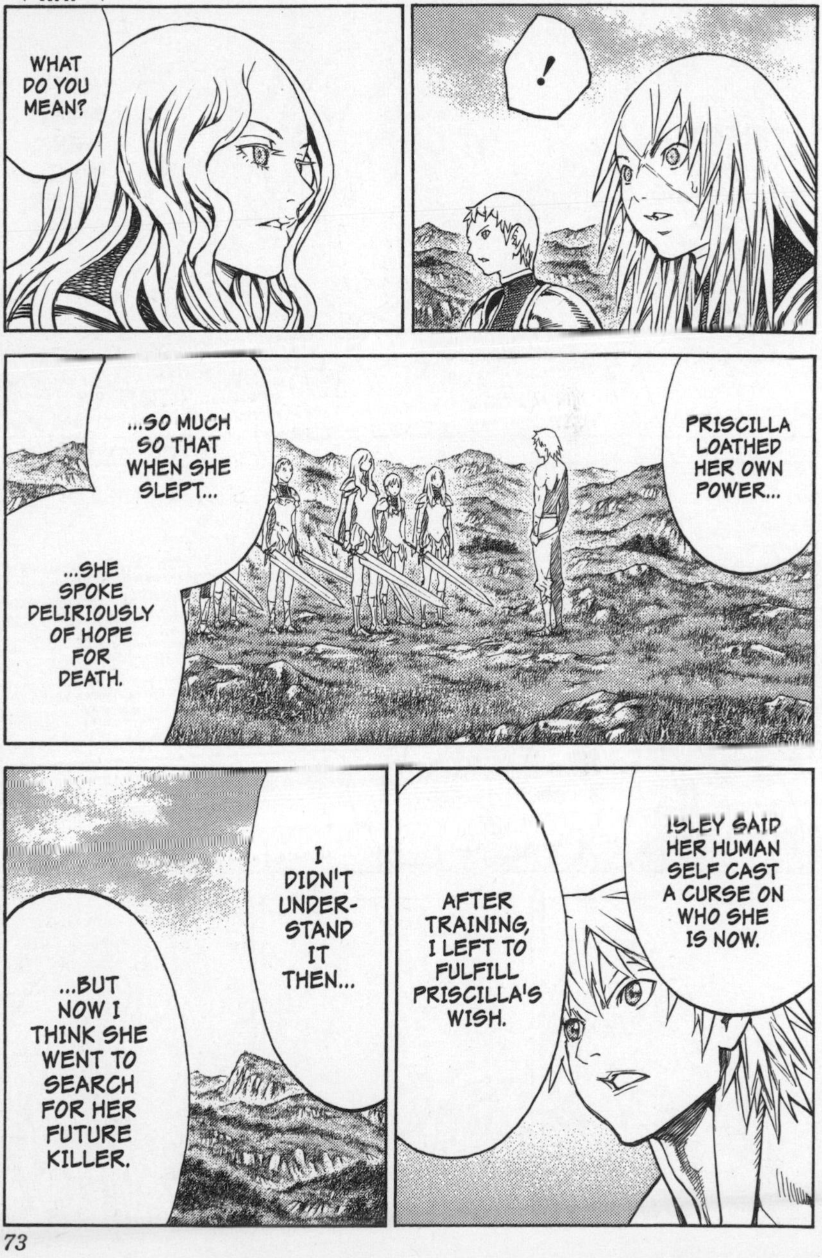
!
WHAT DO YOU MEAN?
PRISCILLA LOATHED HER OWN POWER...
...SO MUCH SO THAT WHEN SHE SLEPT...
...SHE SPOKE DELIRIOUSLY OF HOPE FOR DEATH.
ISLEY SAID HER HUMAN SELF CAST A CURSE ON WHO SHE IS NOW.
AFTER TRAINING, I LEFT TO FULFILL PRISCILLA'S WISH.
I DIDN'T UNDER-STAND IT THEN...
...BUT NOW I THINK SHE WENT TO SEARCH FOR HER FUTURE KILLER.

READ THIS WAY

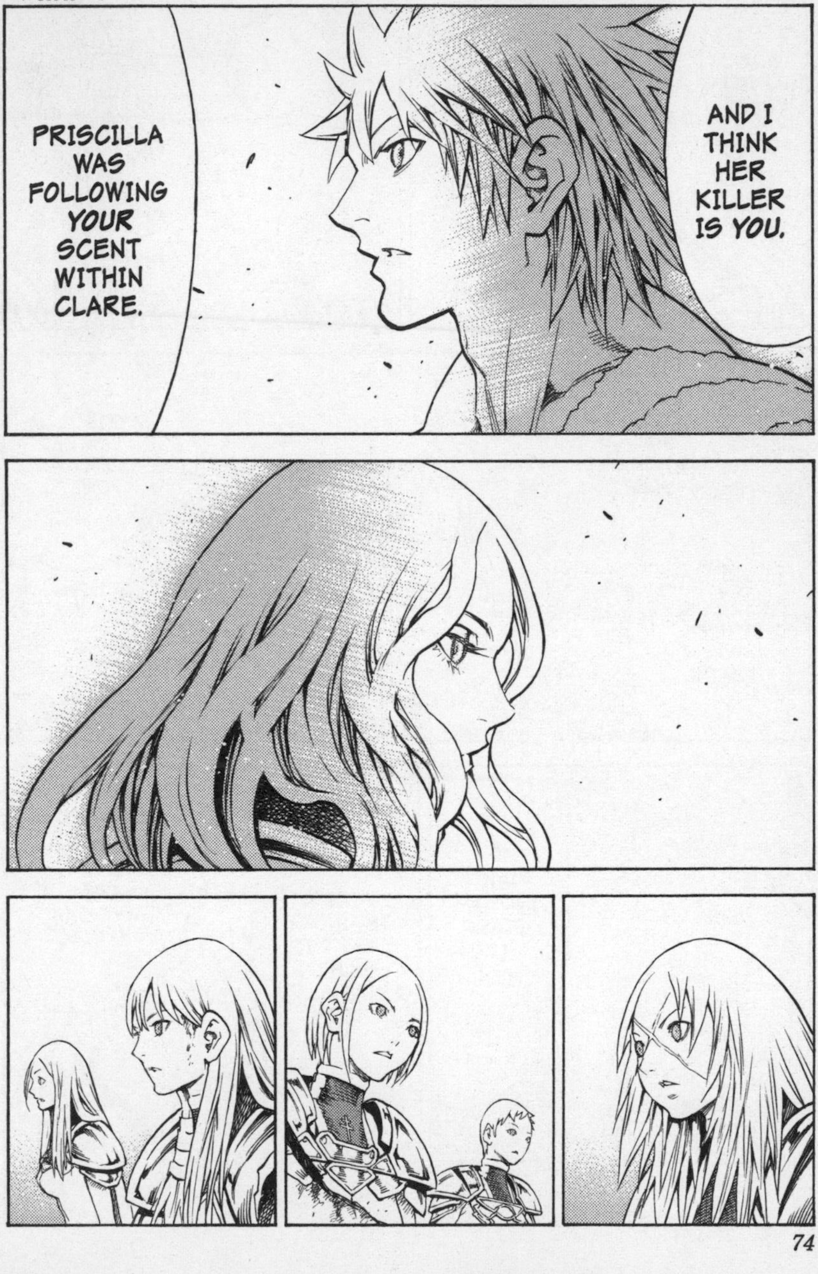

PRISCILLA WAS FOLLOWING YOUR SCENT WITHIN CLARE.
AND I THINK HER KILLER IS YOU.

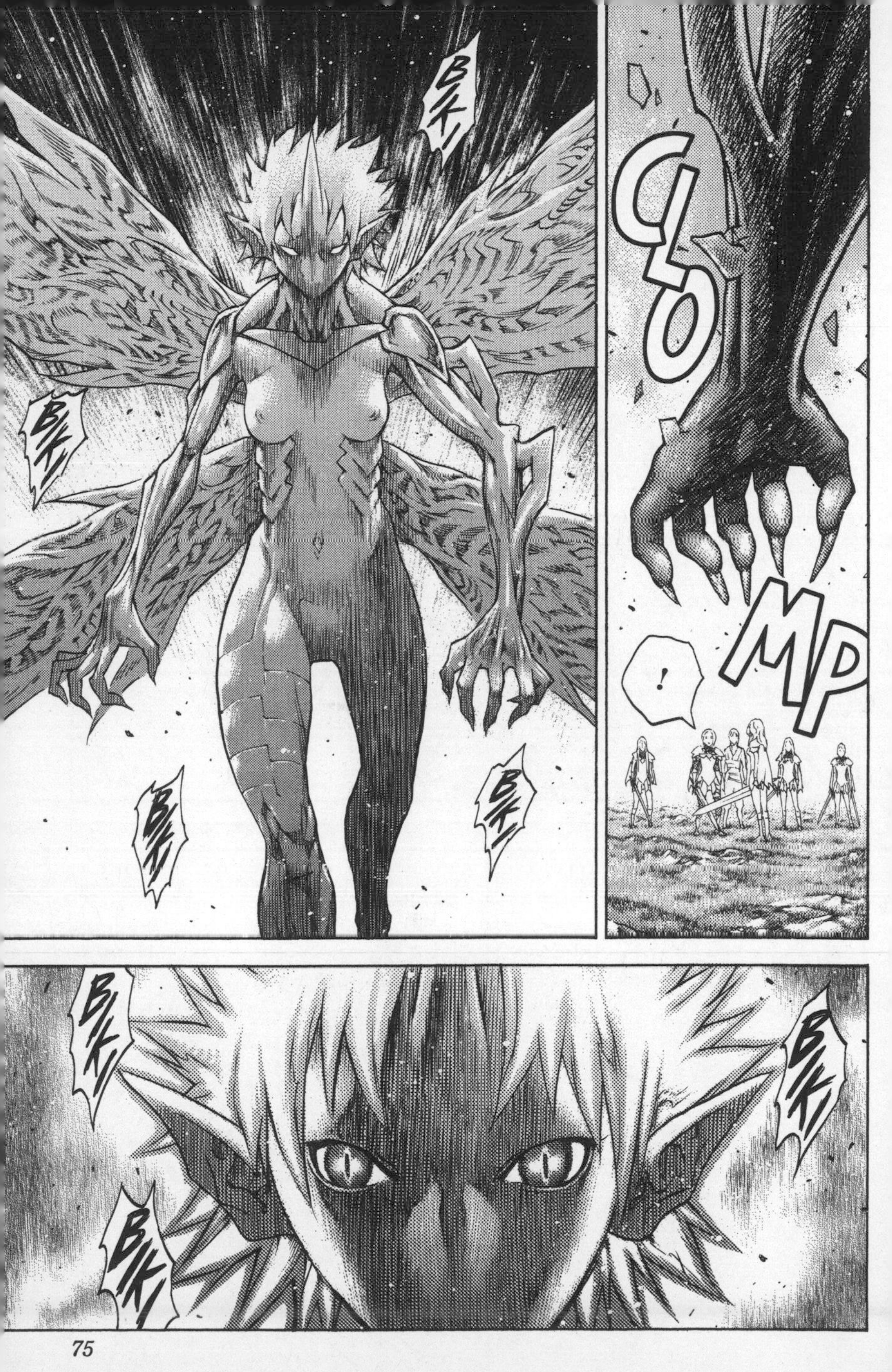
CLOMP
!
BIKI
BIKI
BIKI
BIKI
BIKI
BIKI
BIKI

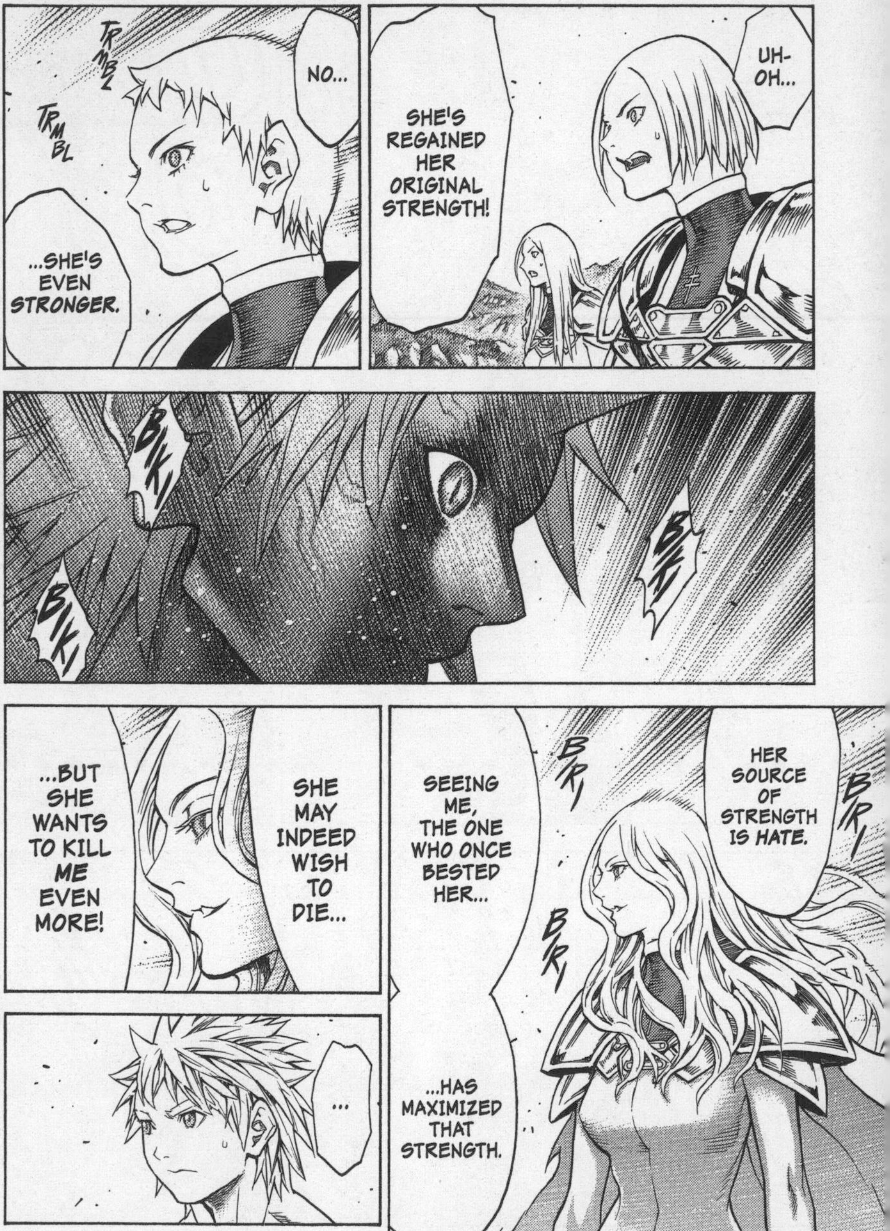
UH-OH...
SHE'S REGAINED HER ORIGINAL STRENGTH!
NO...
TRMBL
TRMBL
...SHE'S EVEN STRONGER.
BIKI
BIKI
BIKI
HER SOURCE OF STRENGTH IS HATE.
BRI
BRI
BRI
SEEING ME, THE ONE WHO ONCE BESTED HER...
...HAS MAXIMIZED THAT STRENGTH.
SHE MAY INDEED WISH TO DIE...
...BUT SHE WANTS TO KILL ME EVEN MORE!
...

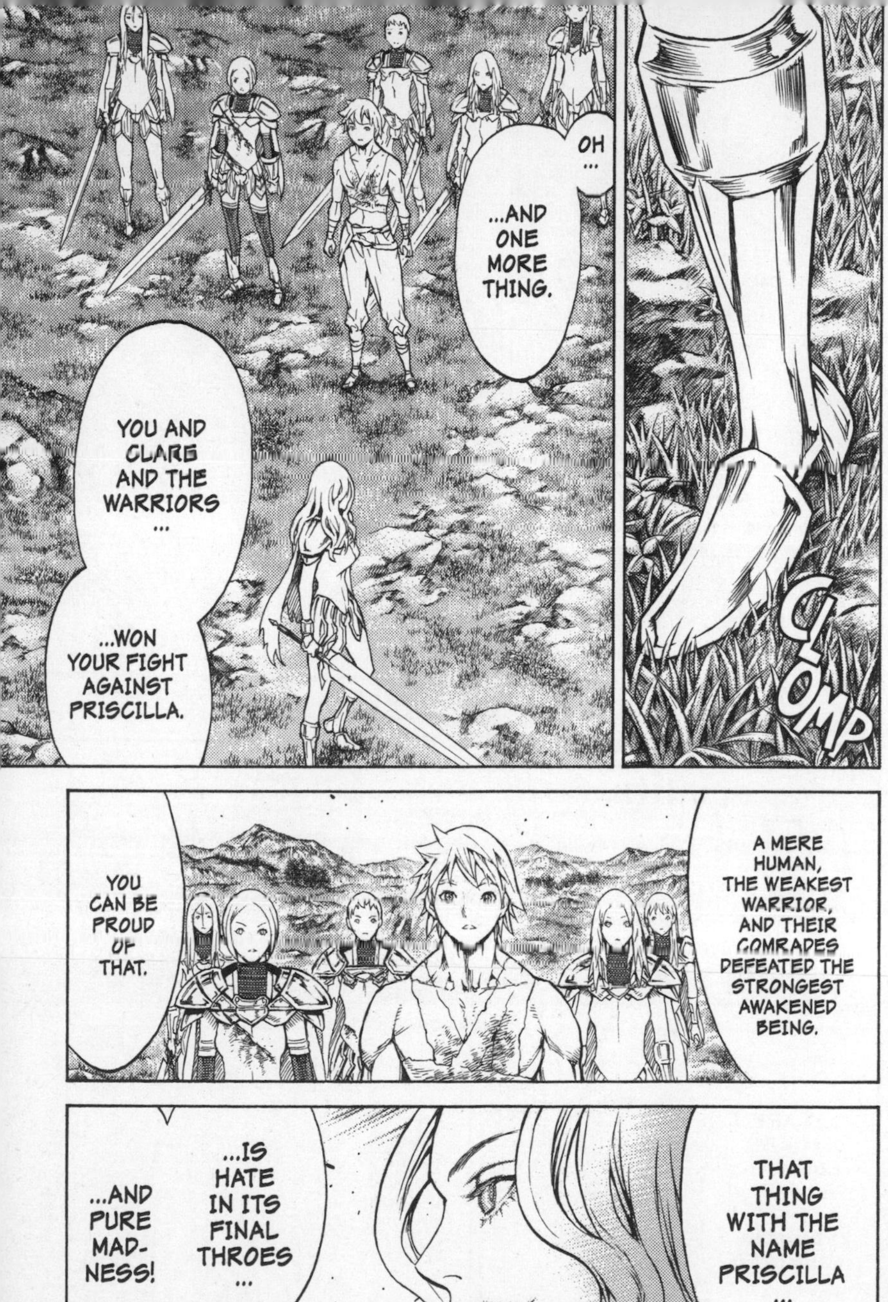
CLOMP
OH ...
...AND ONE MORE THING.
YOU AND CLARE AND THE WARRIORS ...
...WON YOUR FIGHT AGAINST PRISCILLA.
A MERE HUMAN, THE WEAKEST WARRIOR, AND THEIR COMRADES DEFEATED THE STRONGEST AWAKENED BEING.
YOU CAN BE PROUD OF THAT.
THAT THING WITH THE NAME PRISCILLA ...
...IS HATE IN ITS FINAL THROES ...
...AND PURE MAD-NESS!

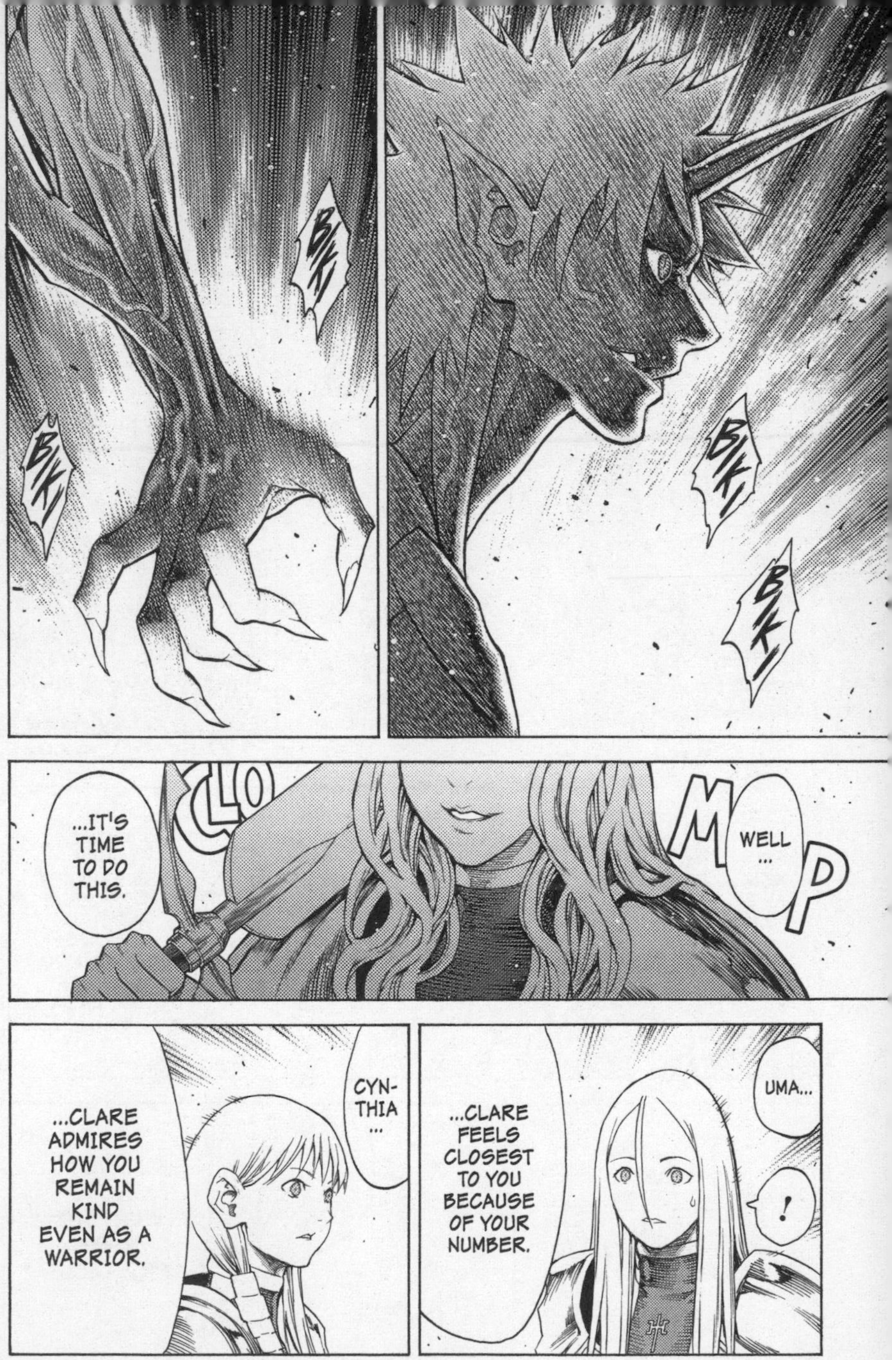
BIKI
BIKI
BIKI
BIKI
WELL ...
...IT'S TIME TO DO THIS.
UMA...
!
...CLARE FEELS CLOSEST TO YOU BECAUSE OF YOUR NUMBER.
CYN-THIA ...
...CLARE ADMIRES HOW YOU REMAIN KIND EVEN AS A WARRIOR.

READ THIS WAY

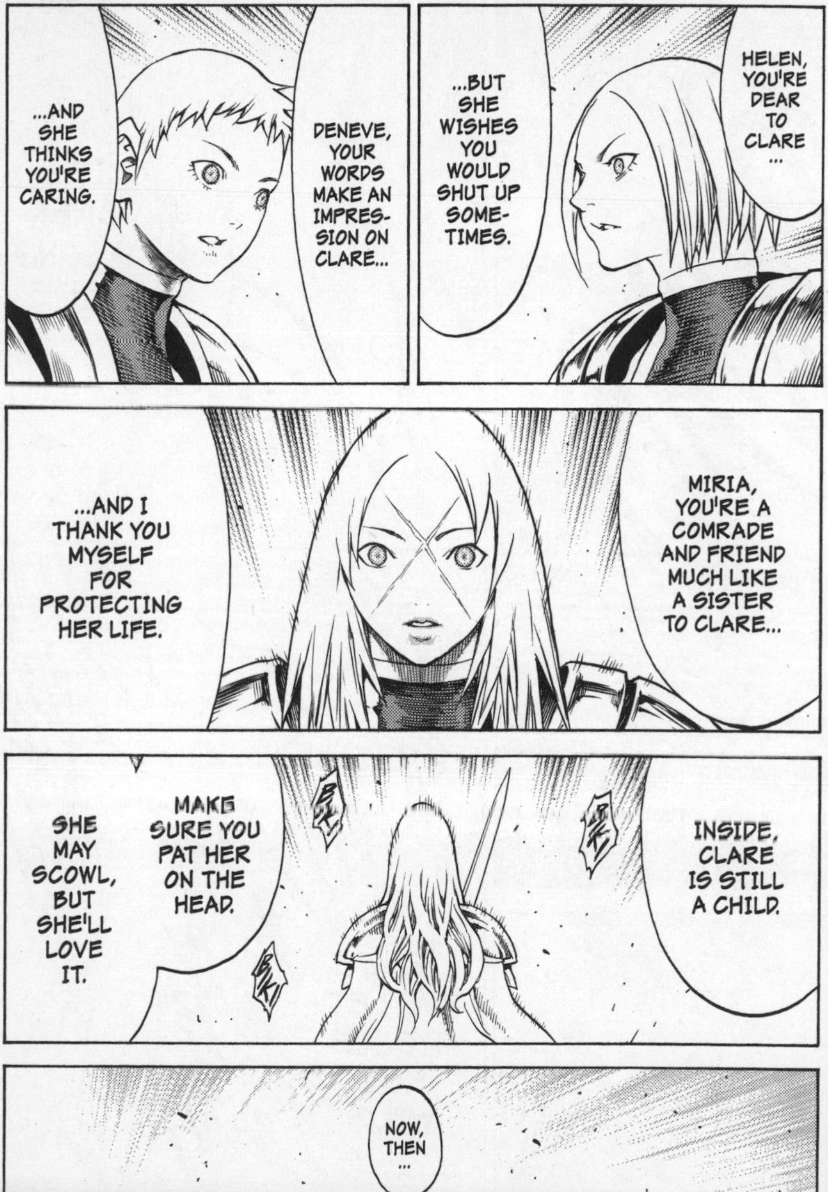
HELEN, YOU'RE DEAR TO CLARE ...
...BUT SHE WISHES YOU WOULD SHUT UP SOMETIMES.
DENEVE, YOUR WORDS MAKE AN IMPRESSION ON CLARE...
...AND SHE THINKS YOU'RE CARING.
MIRIA, YOU'RE A COMRADE AND FRIEND MUCH LIKE A SISTER TO CLARE...
...AND I THANK YOU MYSELF FOR PROTECTING HER LIFE.
BIK
BIK
INSIDE, CLARE IS STILL A CHILD.
MAKE SURE YOU PAT HER ON THE HEAD.
SHE MAY SCOWL, BUT SHE'LL LOVE IT.
BIK
NOW, THEN ...

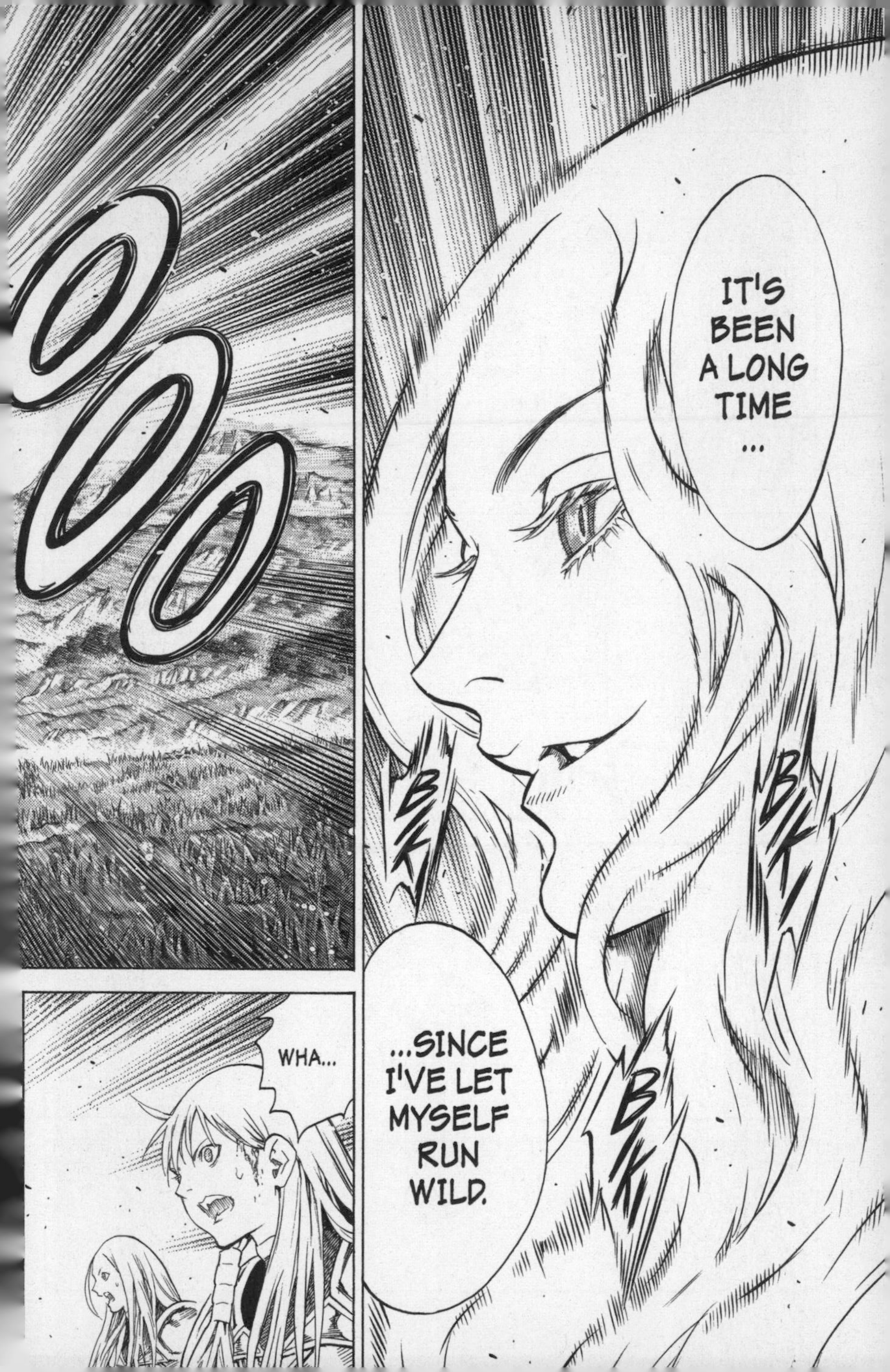
IT'S BEEN A LONG TIME ...
...SINCE I'VE LET MYSELF RUN WILD.
WHA...

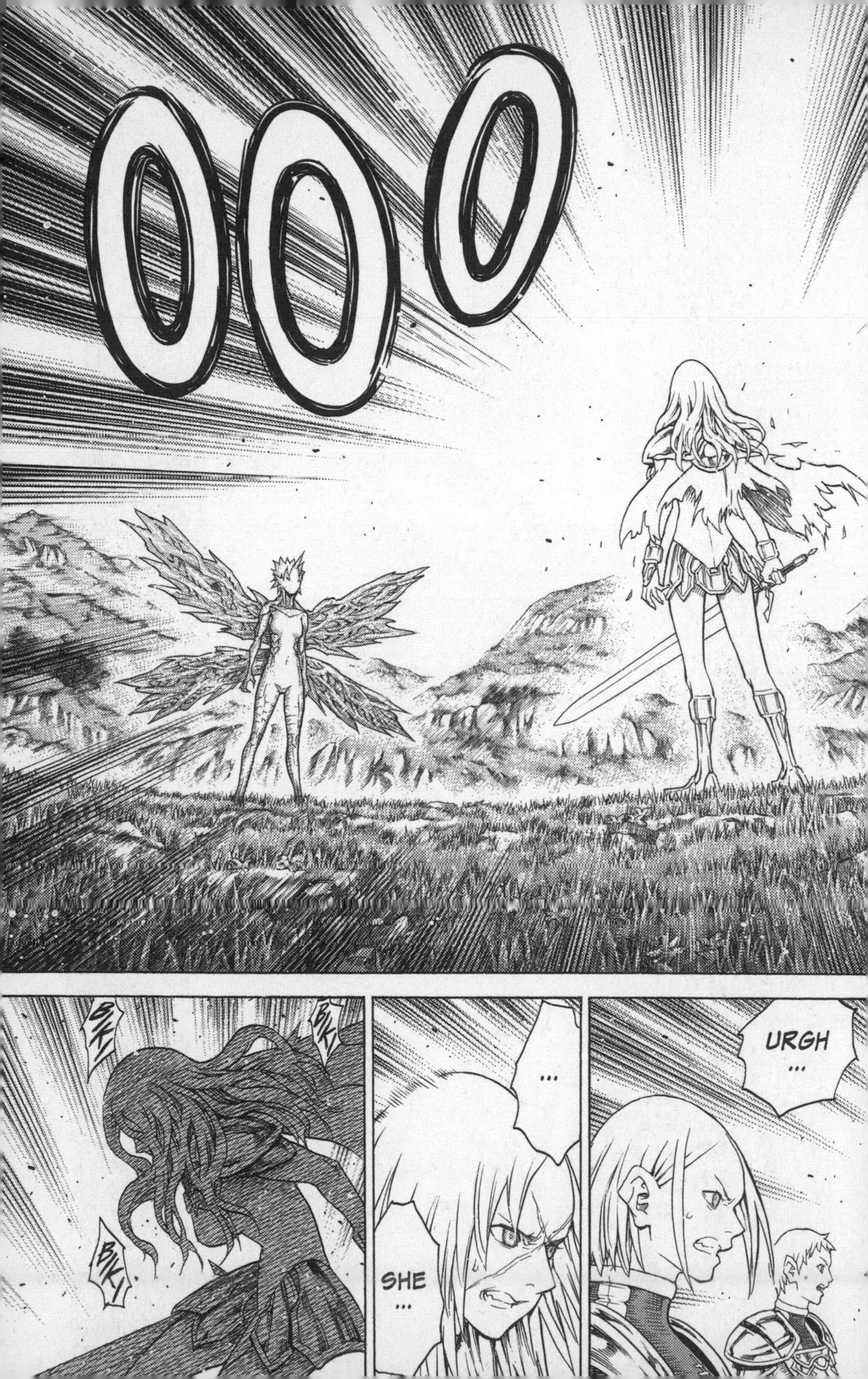
OOO
URGH ...
...
SHE ...
BIKI
BIKI
BIKI

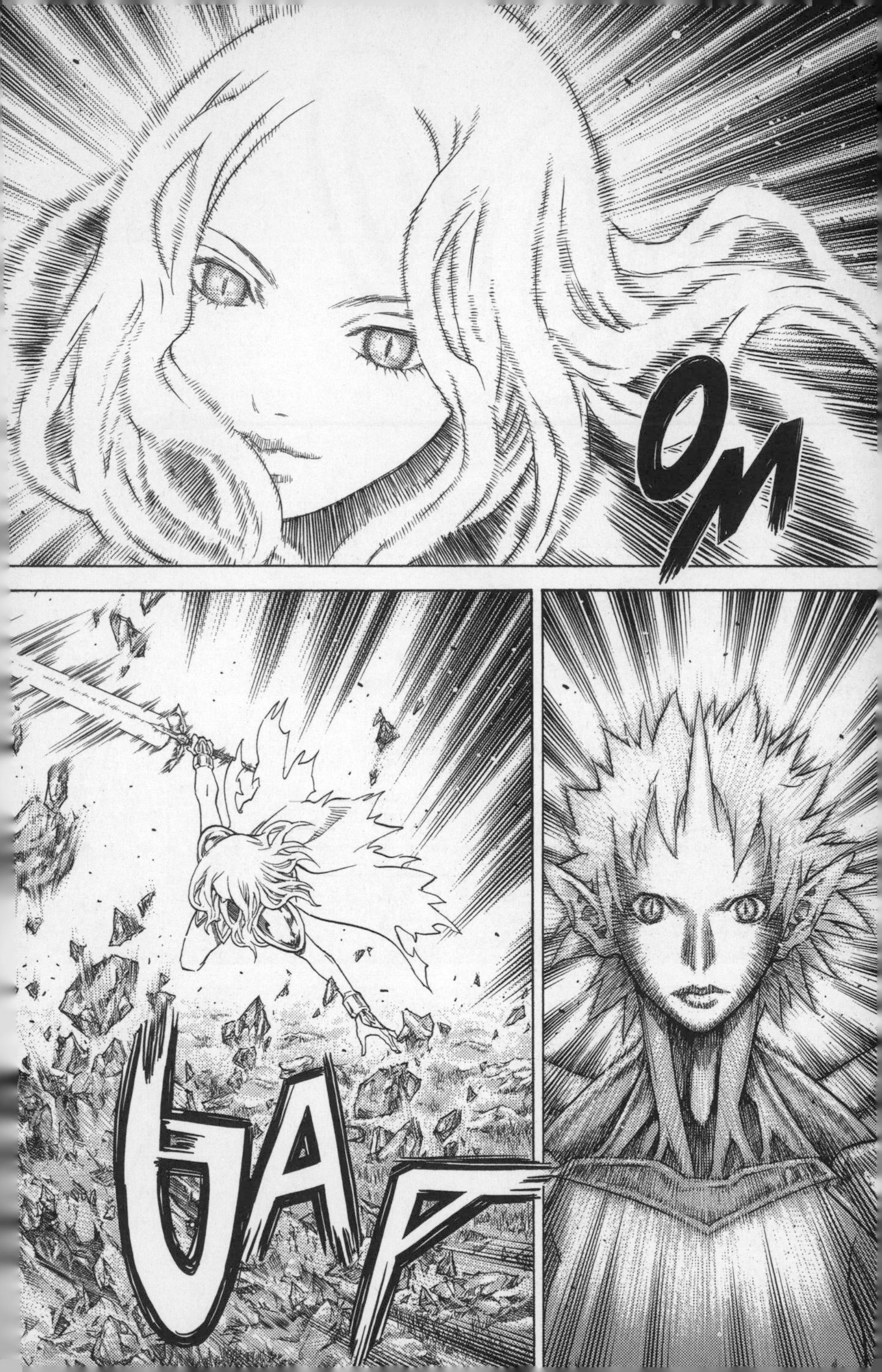
OM
GAP

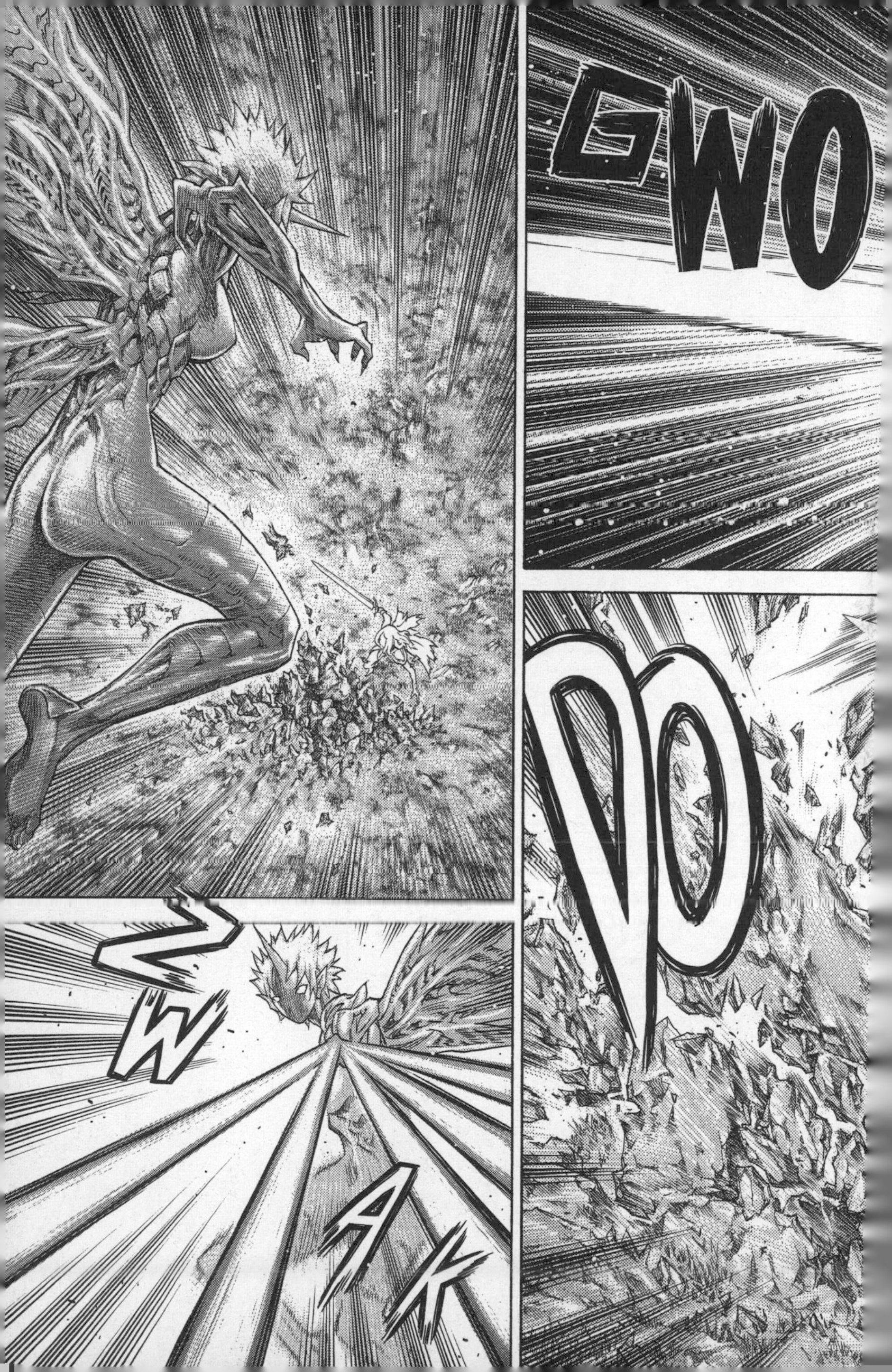
GWO
DO
ZWAK

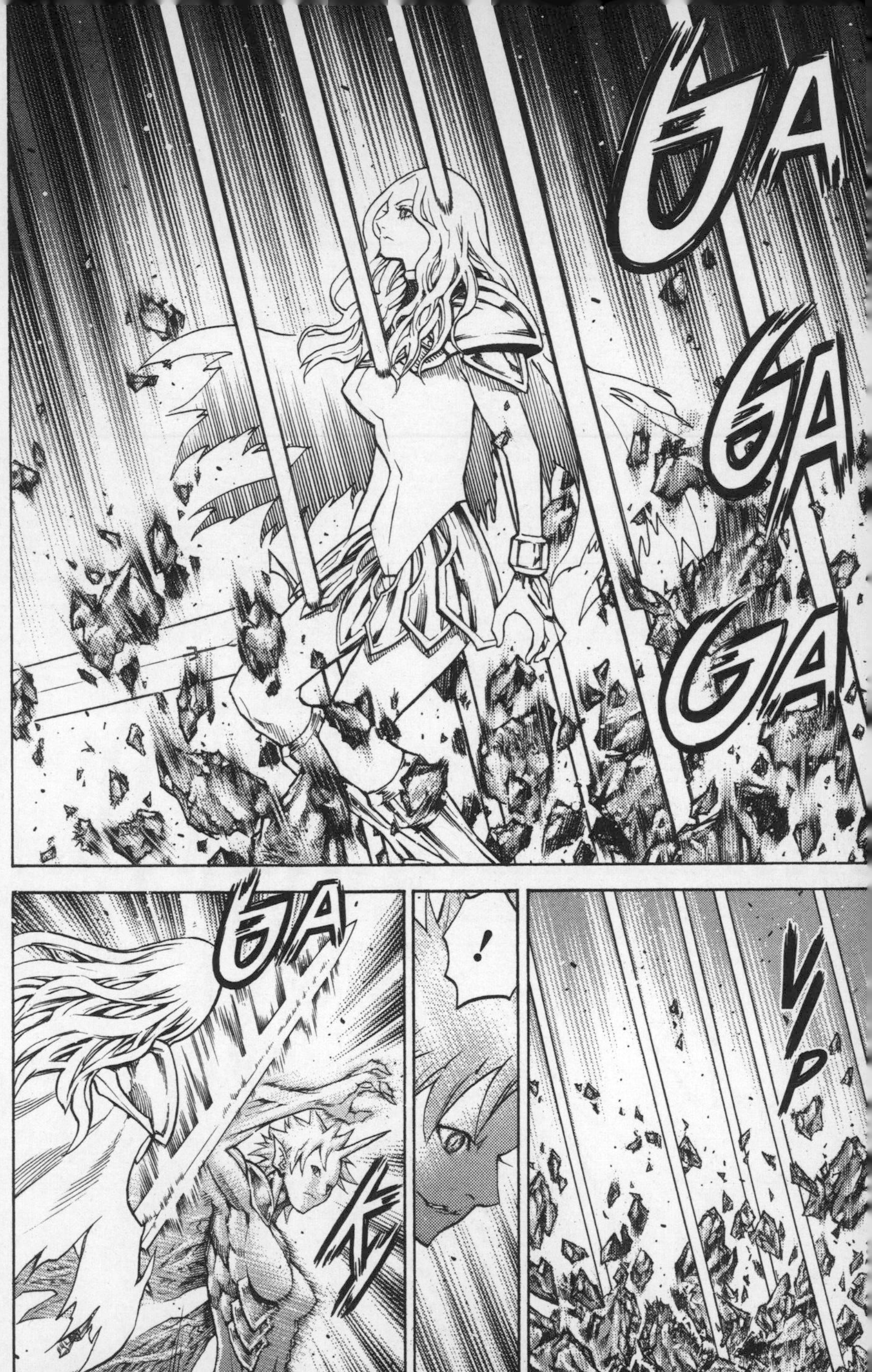
GA
GA
GA
VIP
!
GA
KK

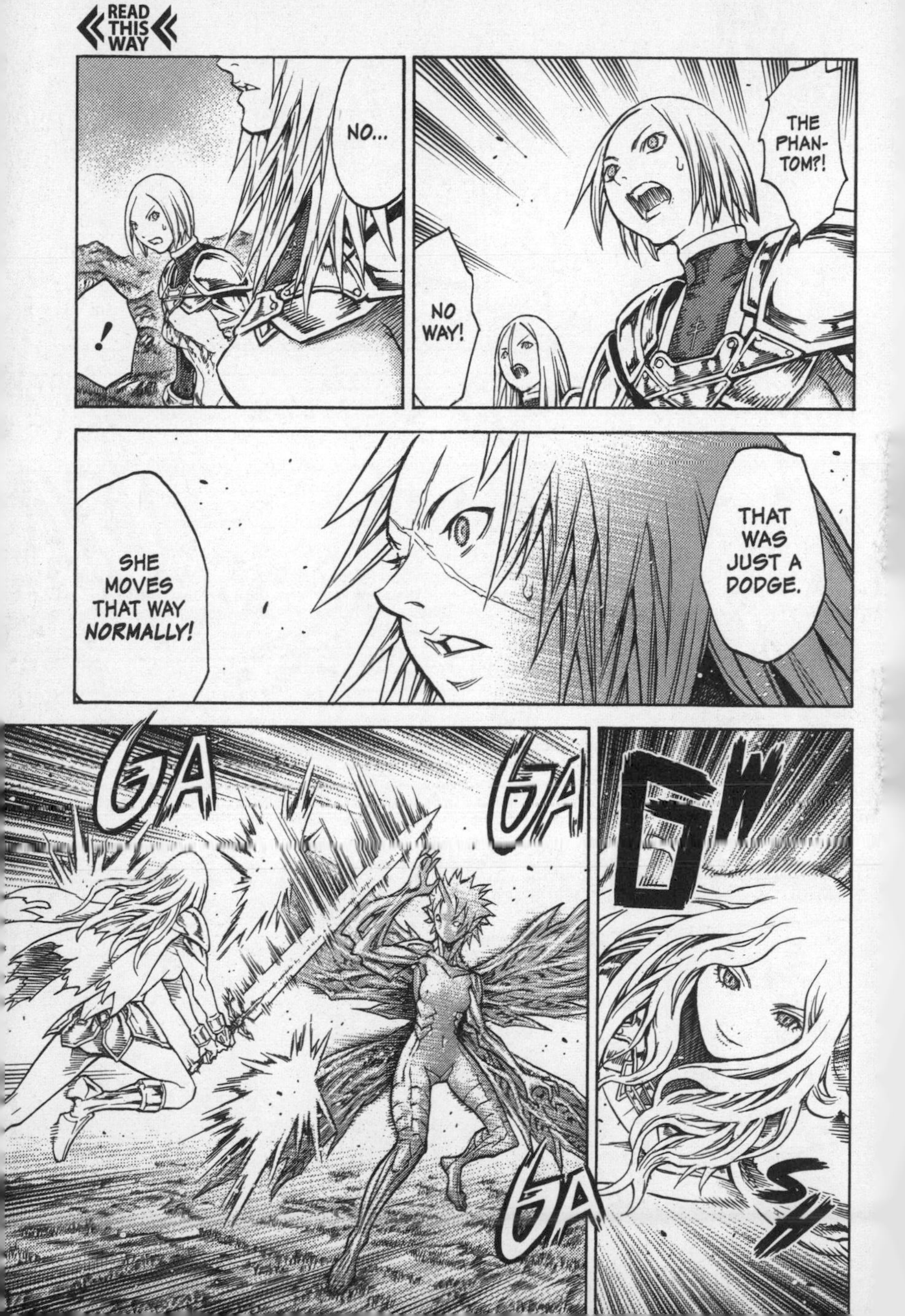
READ THIS WAY
THE PHAN-TOM?!
NO WAY!
NO...
!
THAT WAS JUST A DODGE.
SHE MOVES THAT WAY NORMALLY!
GW
GA
SH
GA
GA

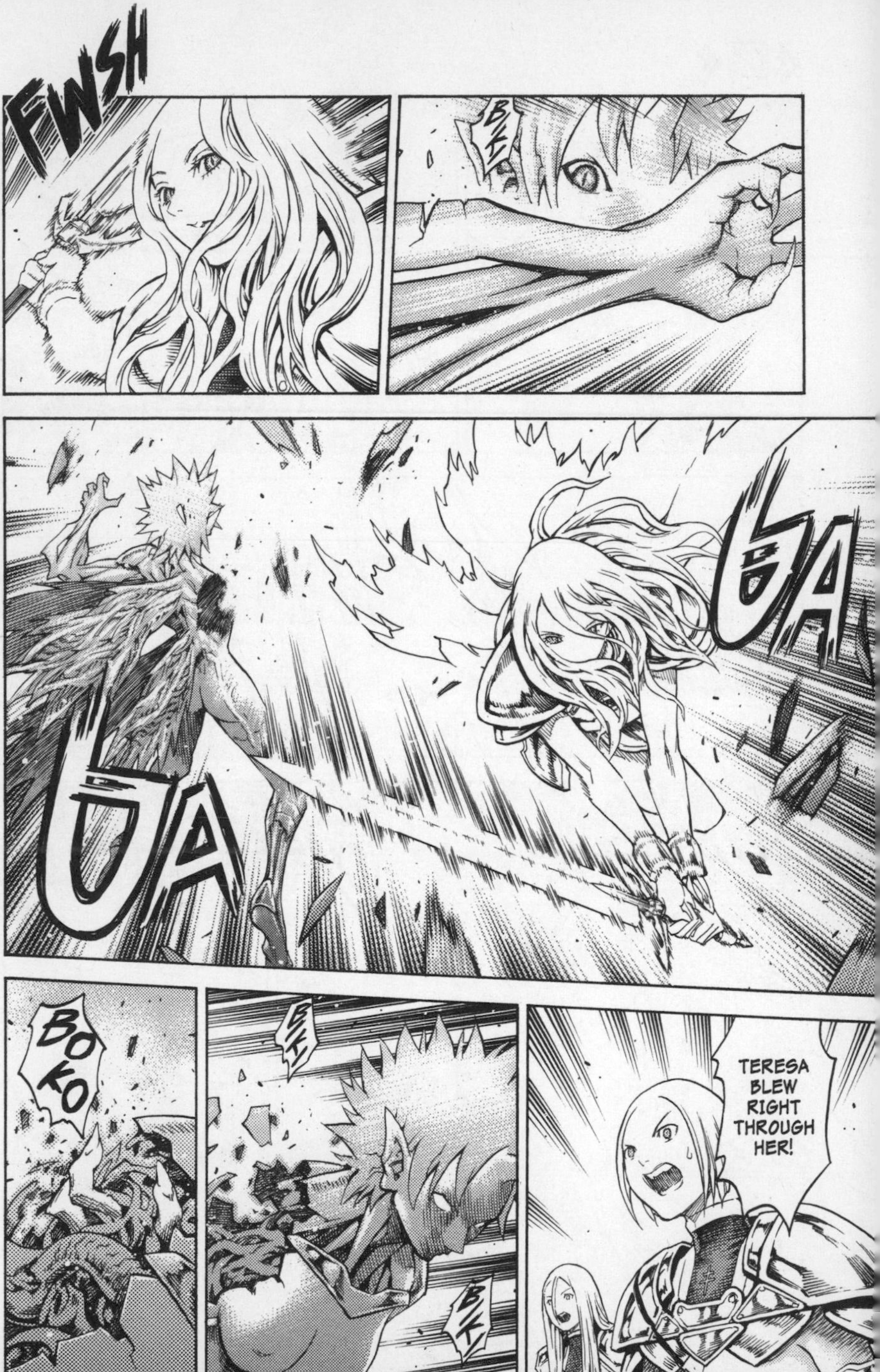

BKI
FWSH
GA
GA
TERESA BLEW RIGHT THROUGH HER!
BKI
BK
BOKO

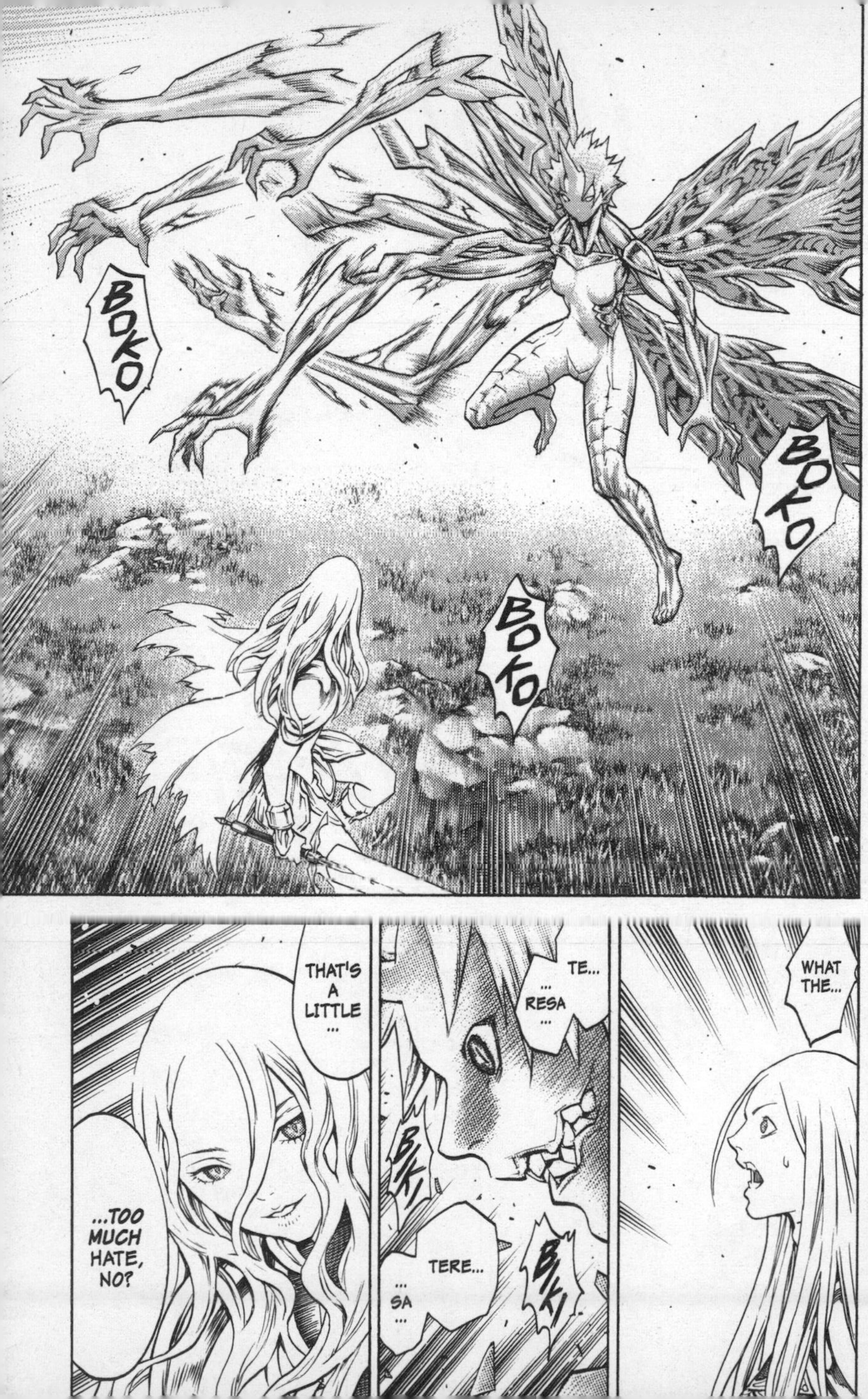
BOKO
BOKO
BOKO
WHAT THE...
TE... ...RESA...
BIKI
BIKI
TERE... ...SA...
THAT'S A LITTLE...
...TOO MUCH HATE, NO?

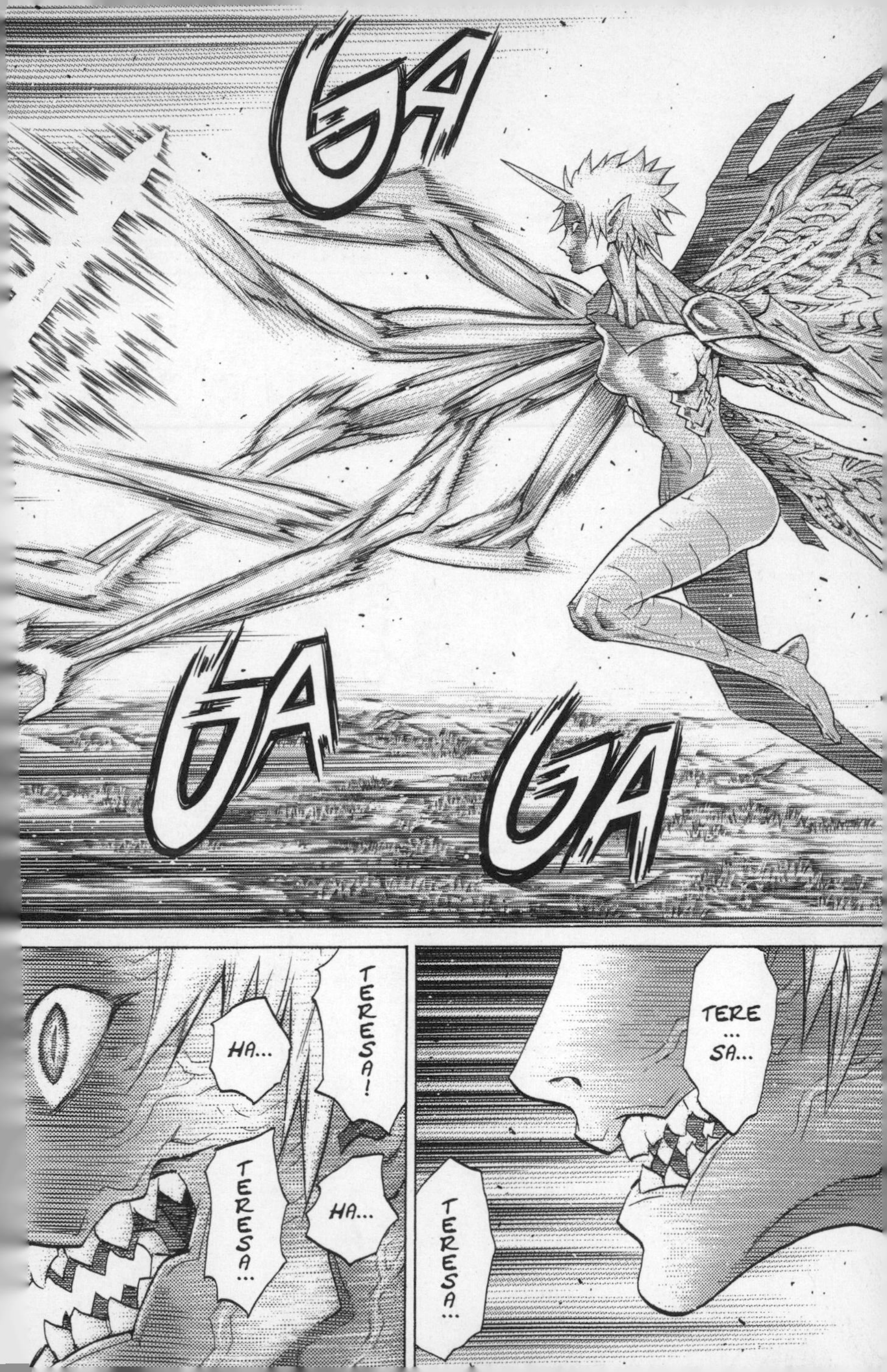
GA
GA
GA
TERE ... SA...
TERESA...
TERESA!
HA...
HA...
TERESA...

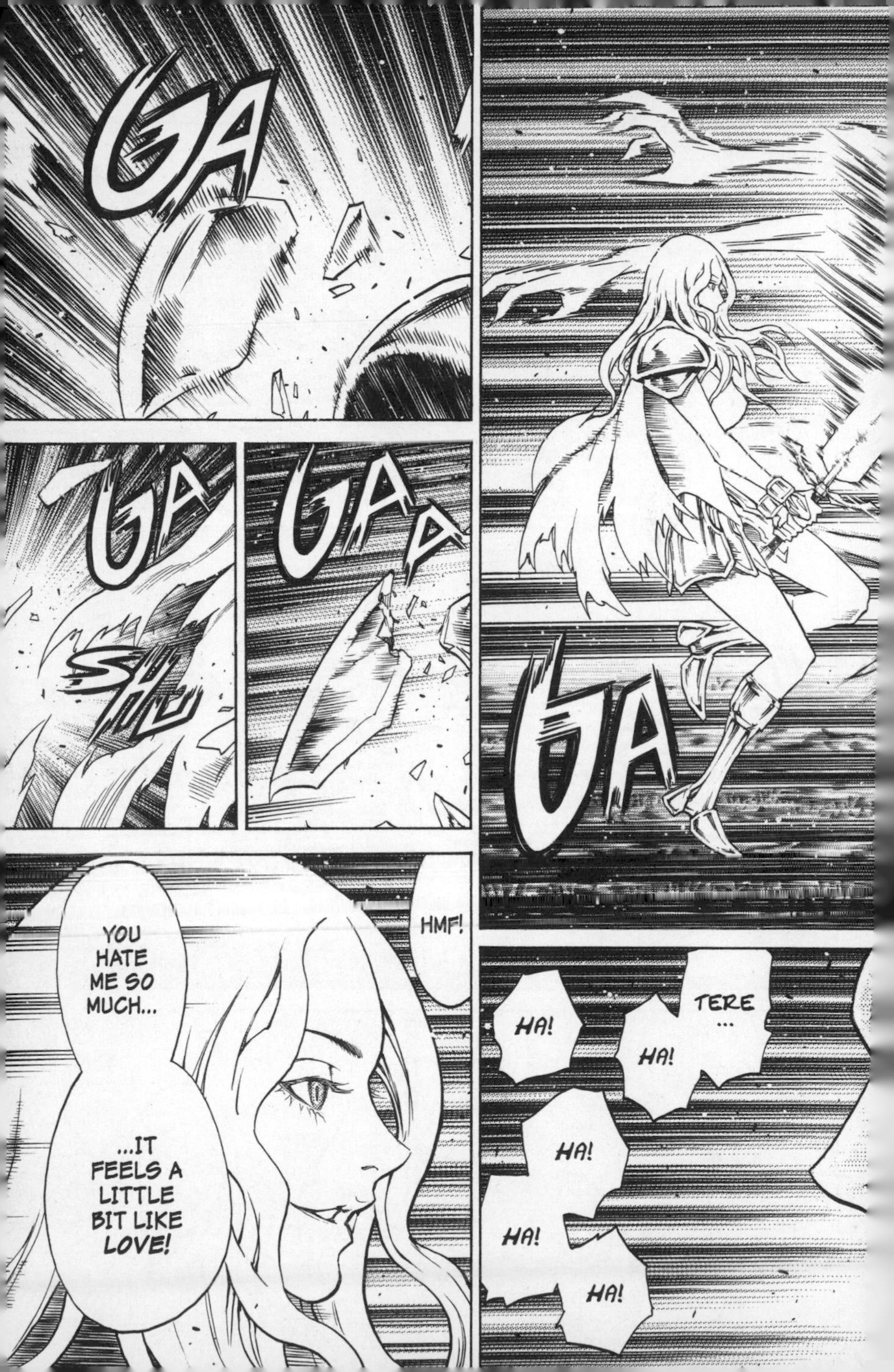
GA
GA
GAA
GA
SHU
TERE...
HA!
HA!
HA!
HA!
HA!
HMF!
YOU HATE ME SO MUCH...
...IT FEELS A LITTLE BIT LIKE LOVE!

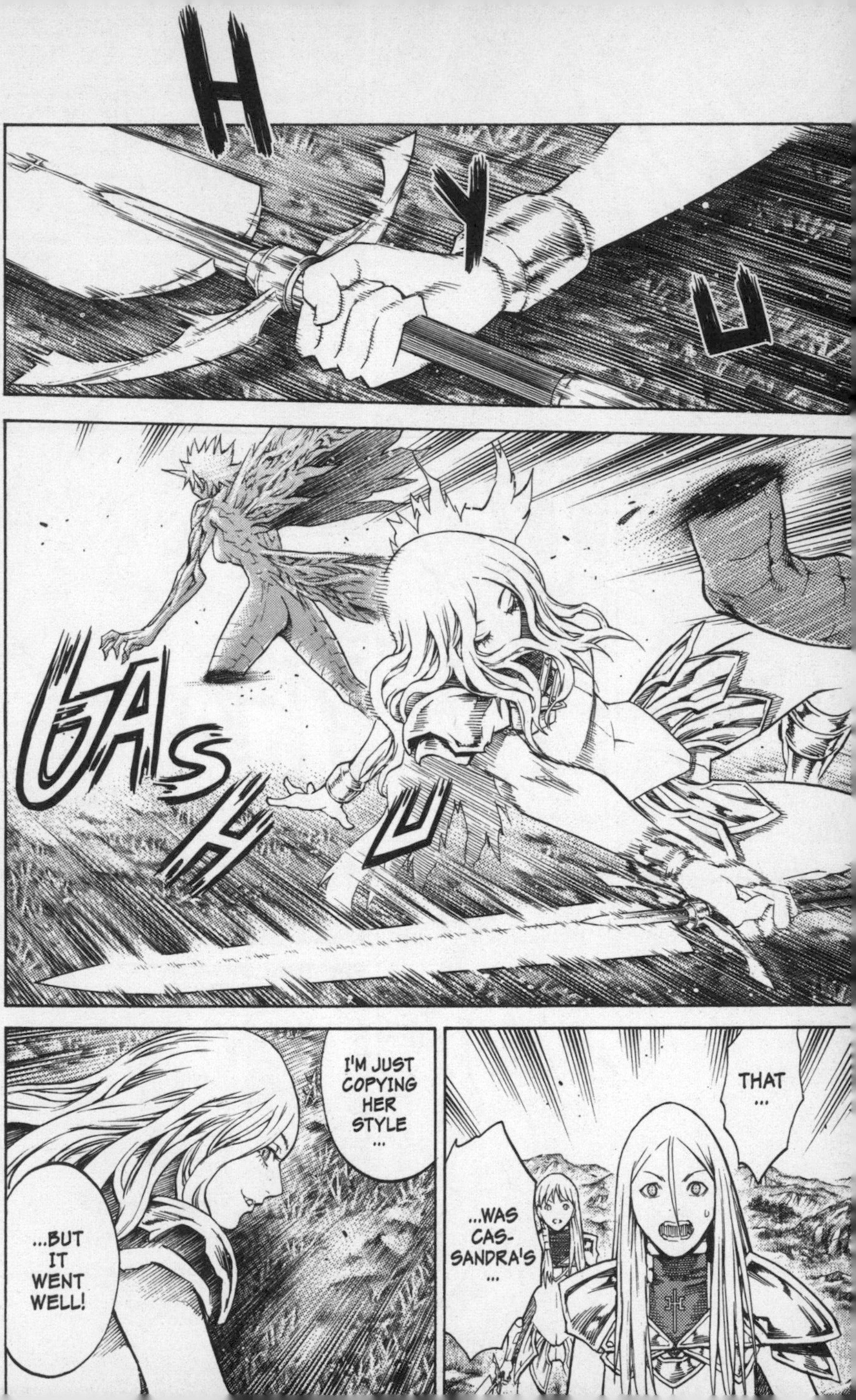
HYU
GASHU
THAT ...
...WAS CAS-SANDRA'S ...
I'M JUST COPYING HER STYLE ...
...BUT IT WENT WELL!

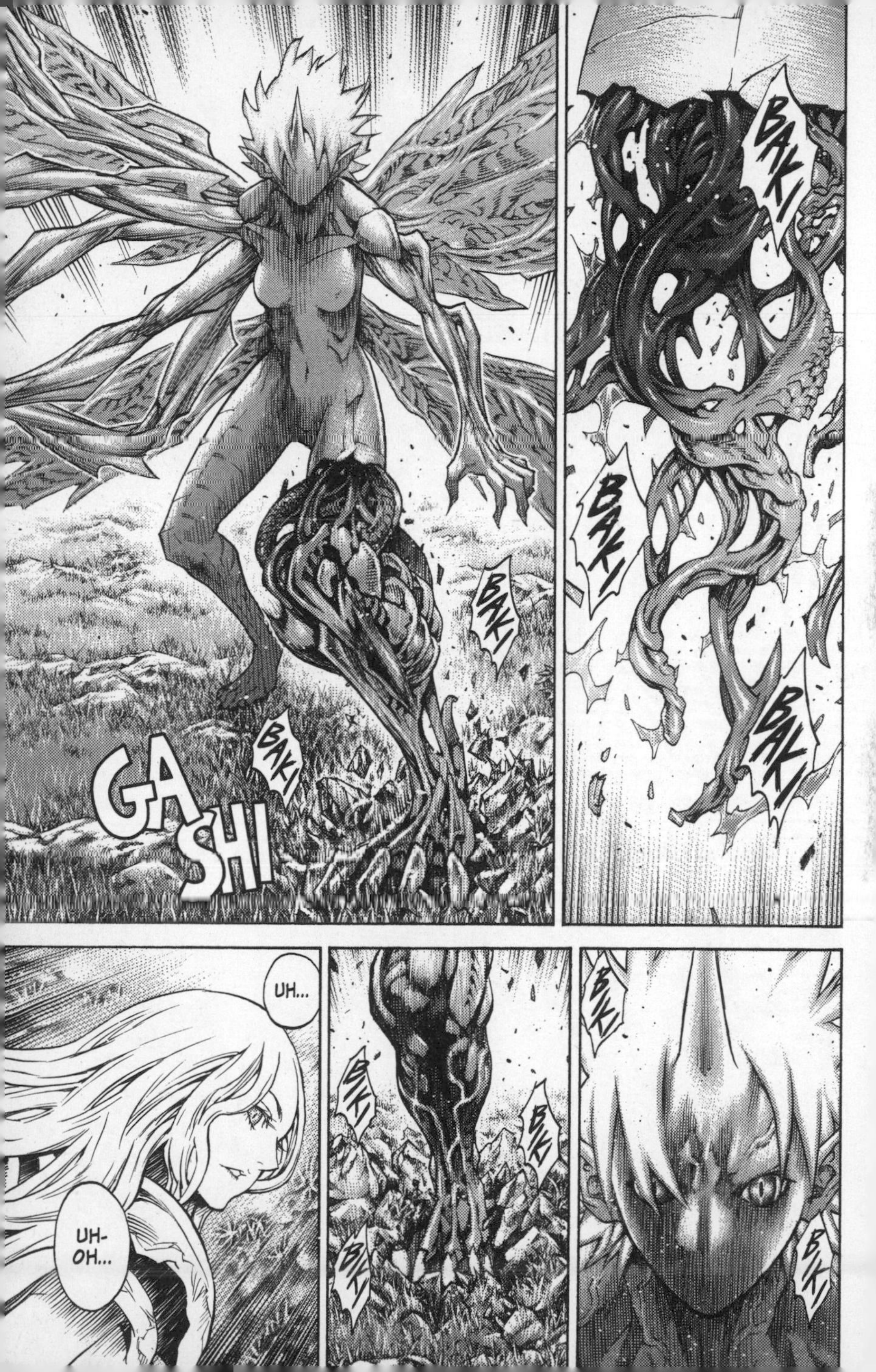
BAKI
BAKI
BAKI
BAKI
BAKI
GA SHI
BIKI
BIKI
BIKI
BIKI
BIKI
UH...
UH-OH...

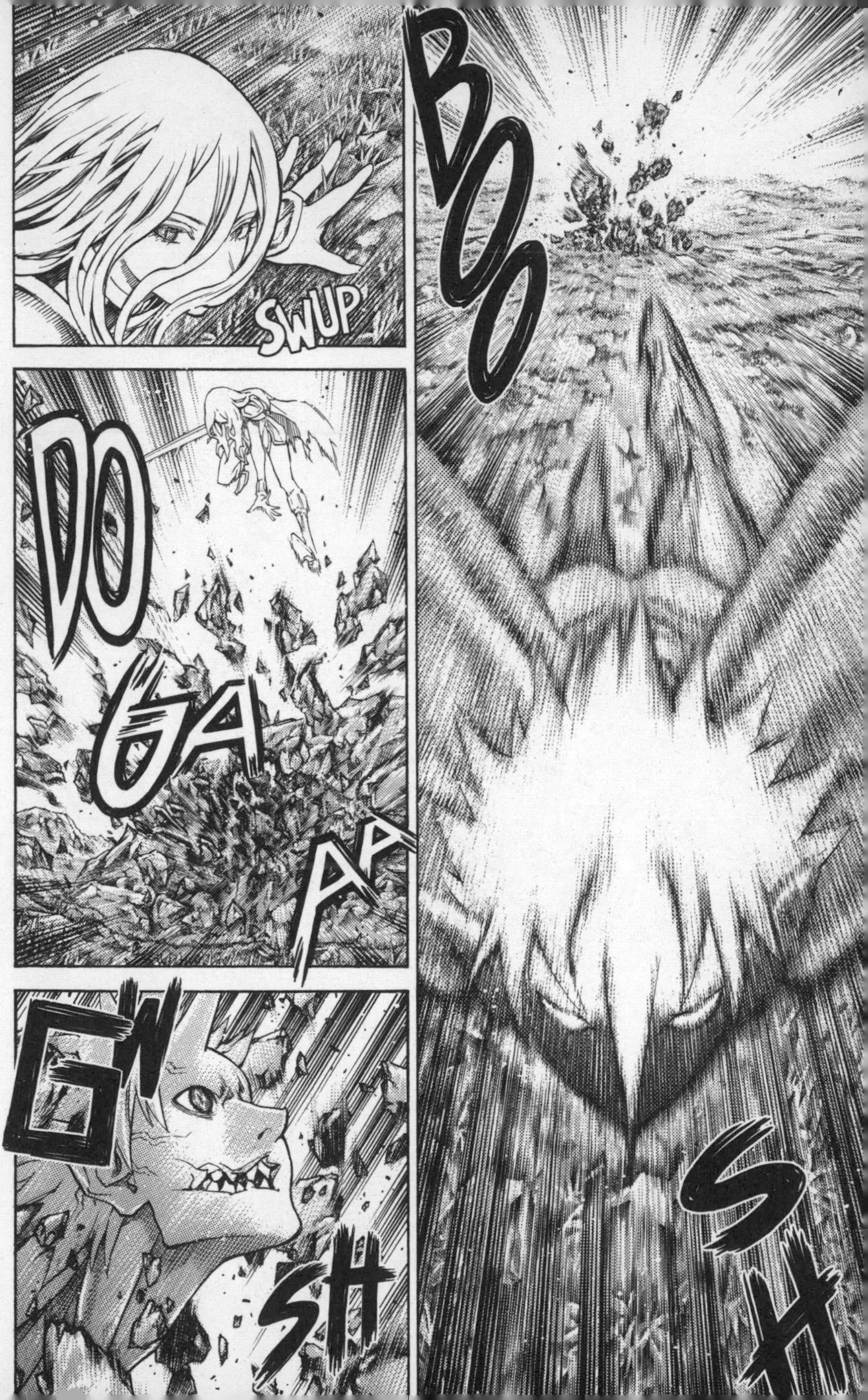
BOOO
SH
SWUP
DOGAAP
GW
SH

READ THIS WAY

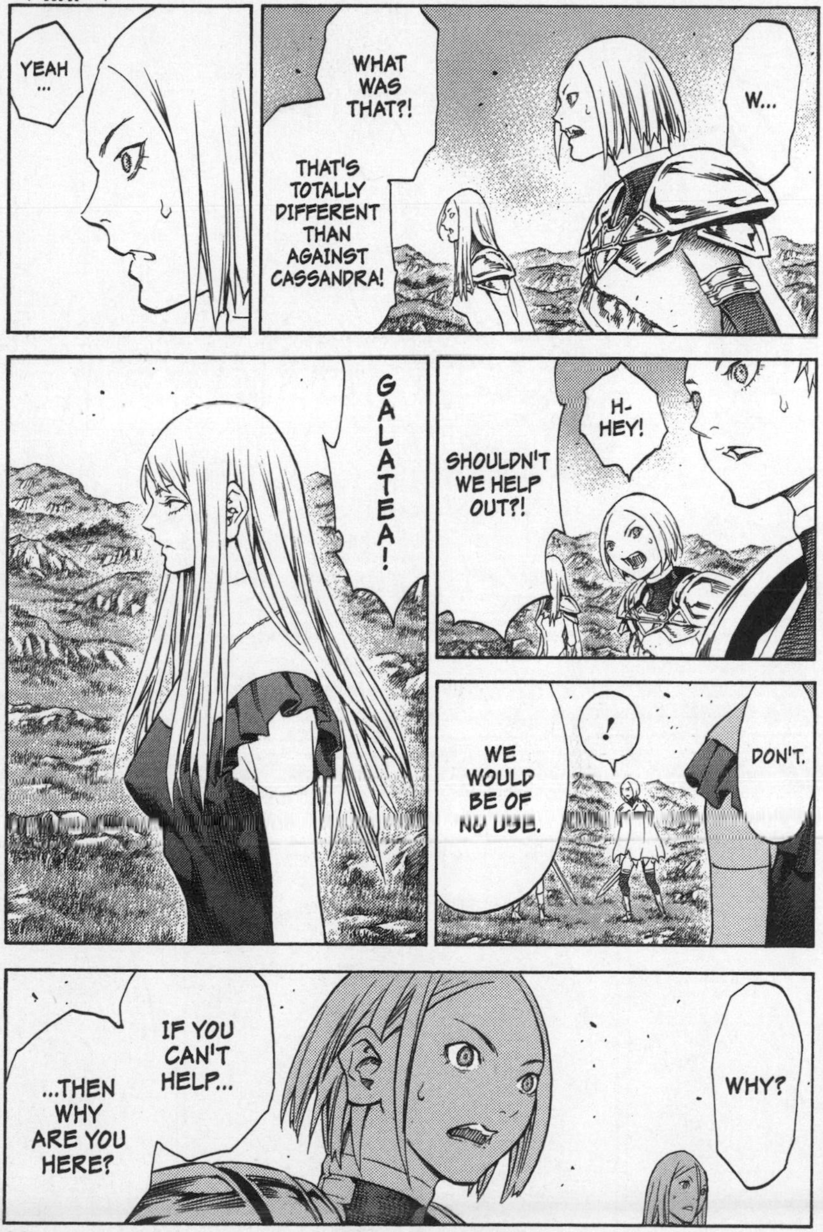

W...
WHAT WAS THAT?!
THAT'S TOTALLY DIFFERENT THAN AGAINST CASSANDRA!
YEAH ...
H-HEY!
SHOULDN'T WE HELP OUT?!
DON'T.
!
WE WOULD BE OF NO USE.
GALATEA!
WHY?
IF YOU CAN'T HELP...
...THEN WHY ARE YOU HERE?

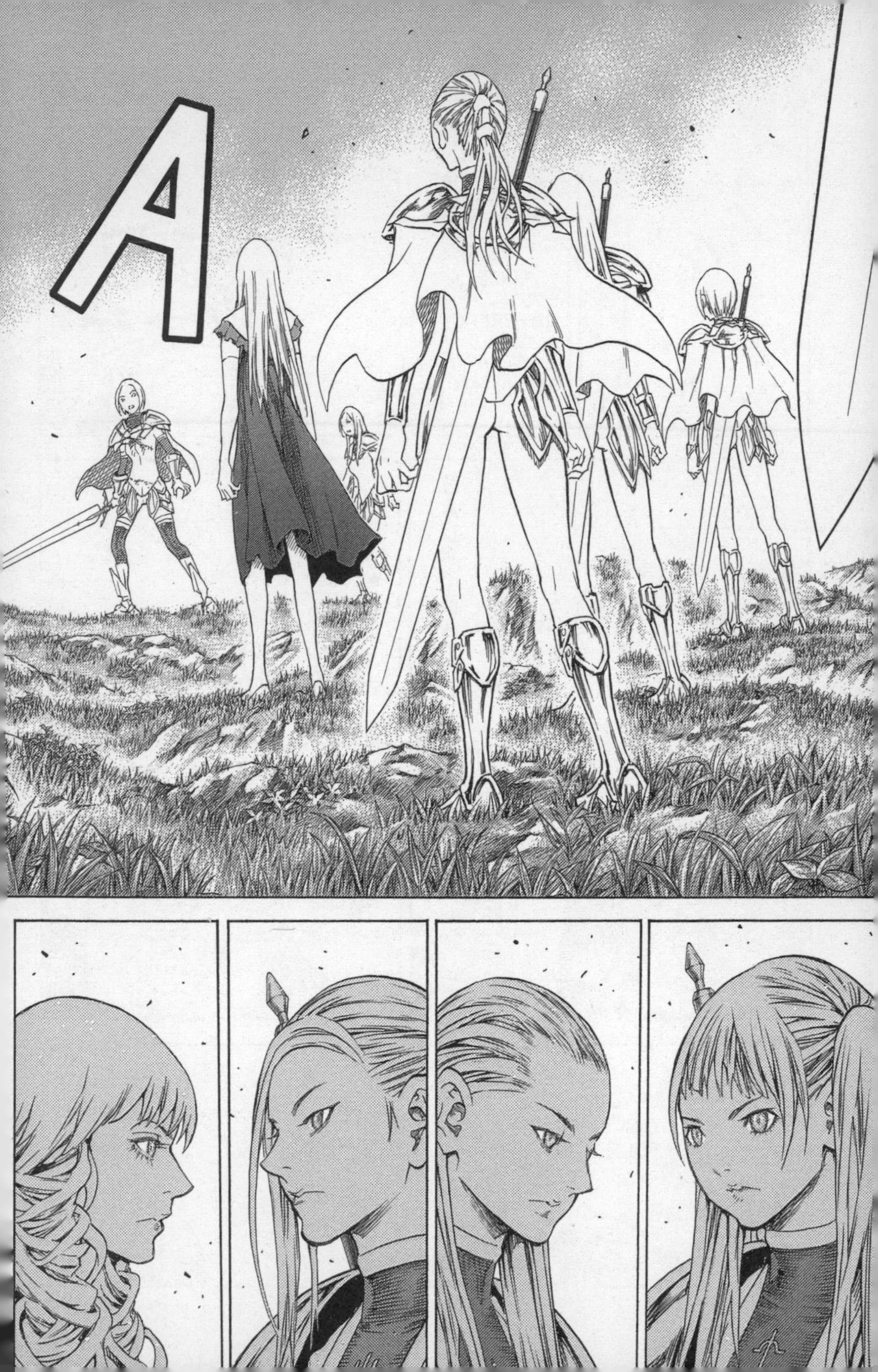
A

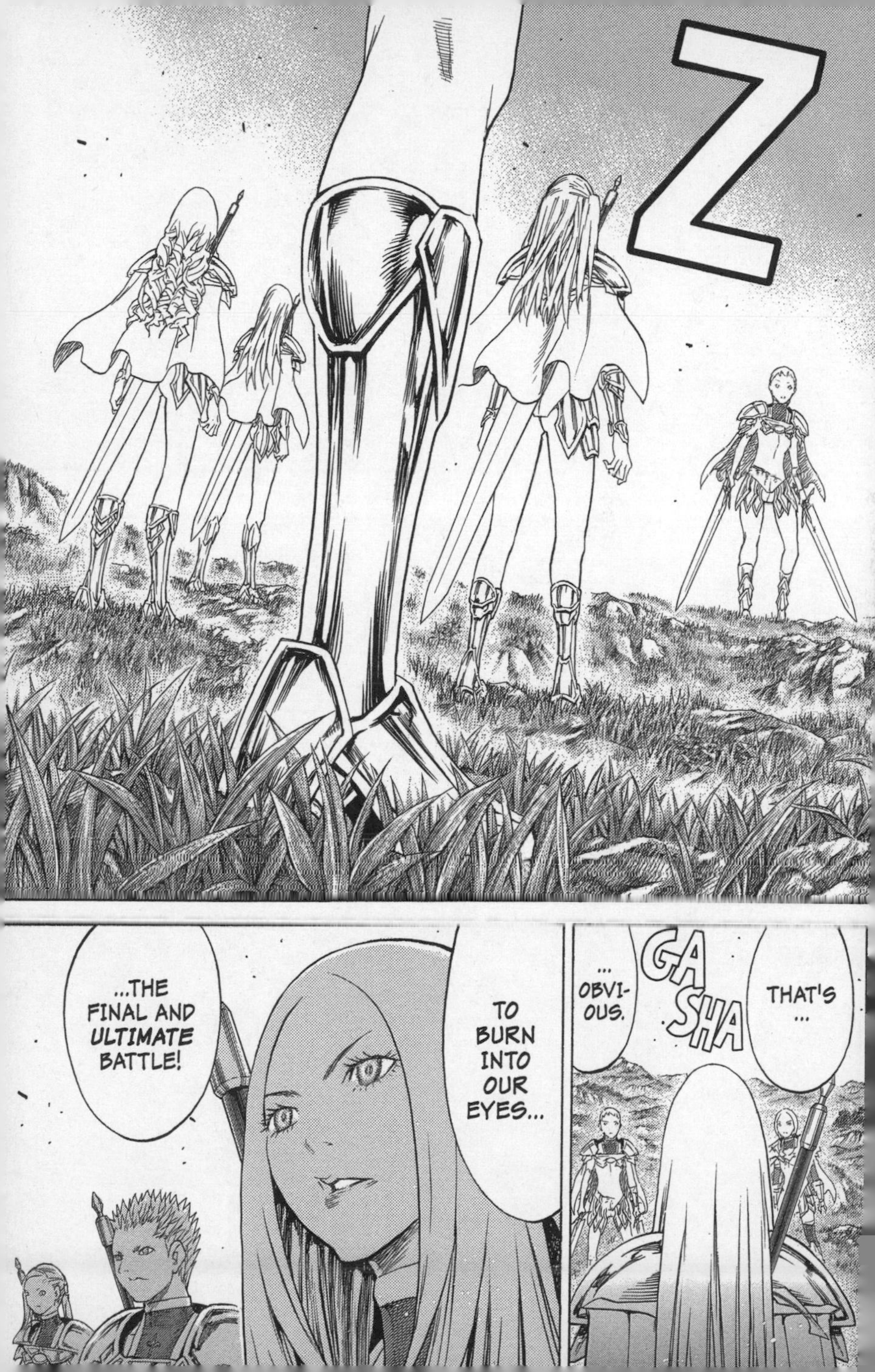
Z
THAT'S ...
GA SHA
... OBVIOUS.
TO BURN INTO OUR EYES...
...THE FINAL AND ULTIMATE BATTLE!

クレイモア
Claymore

Scene 153: Silver-Eyed Warriors, Part 4

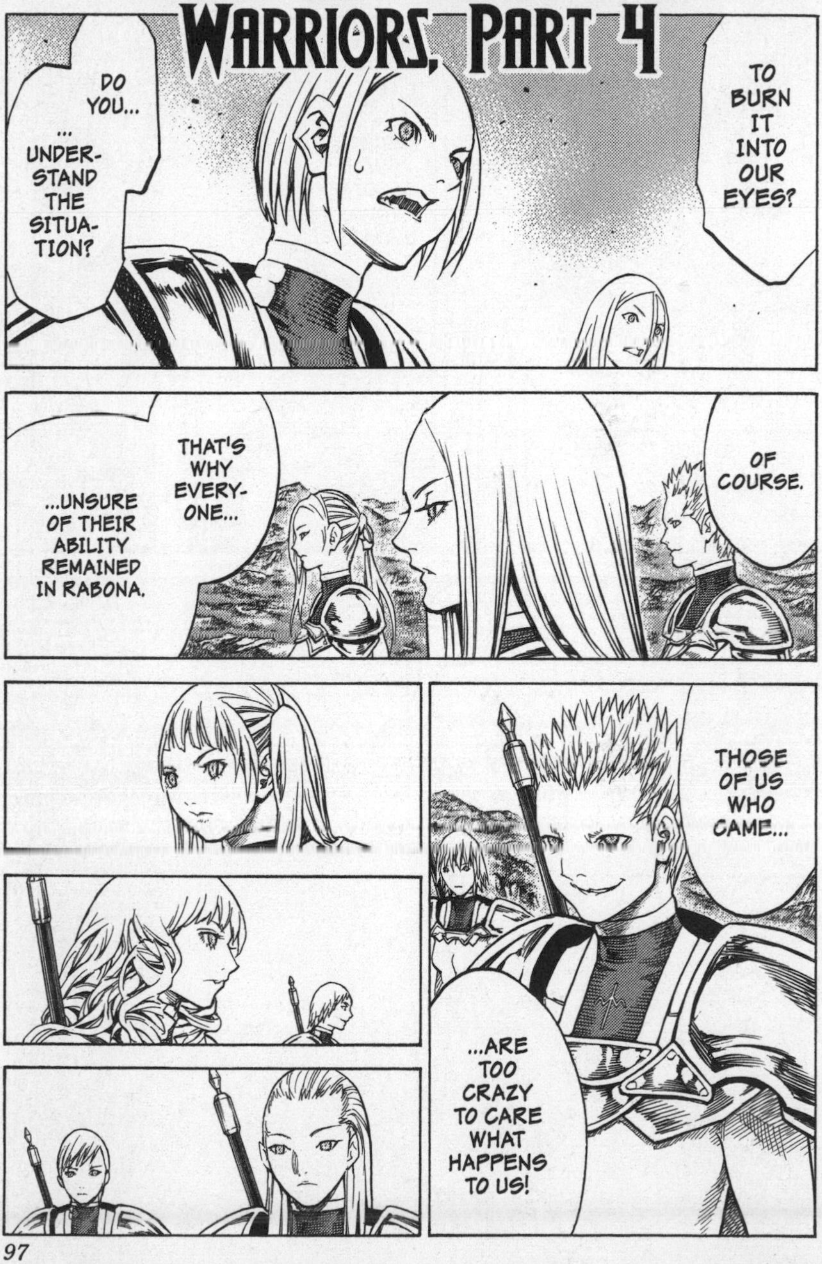

TO BURN IT INTO OUR EYES?
DO YOU... ...UNDERSTAND THE SITUATION?
OF COURSE.
THAT'S WHY EVERYONE...
...UNSURE OF THEIR ABILITY REMAINED IN RABONA.
THOSE OF US WHO CAME...
...ARE TOO CRAZY TO CARE WHAT HAPPENS TO US!

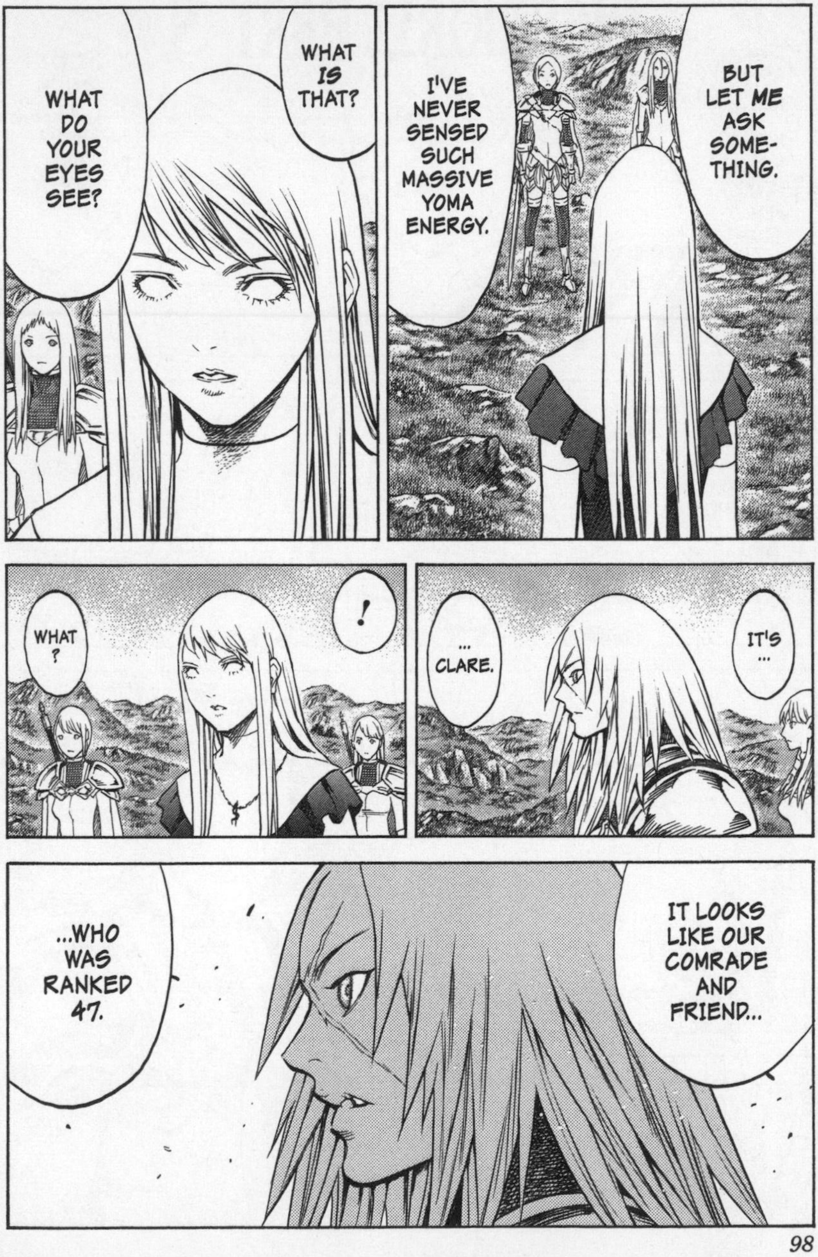
BUT LET ME ASK SOME-THING.
I'VE NEVER SENSED SUCH MASSIVE YOMA ENERGY.
WHAT IS THAT?
WHAT DO YOUR EYES SEE?
!
WHAT?
IT'S ...
... CLARE.
IT LOOKS LIKE OUR COMRADE AND FRIEND...
...WHO WAS RANKED 47.

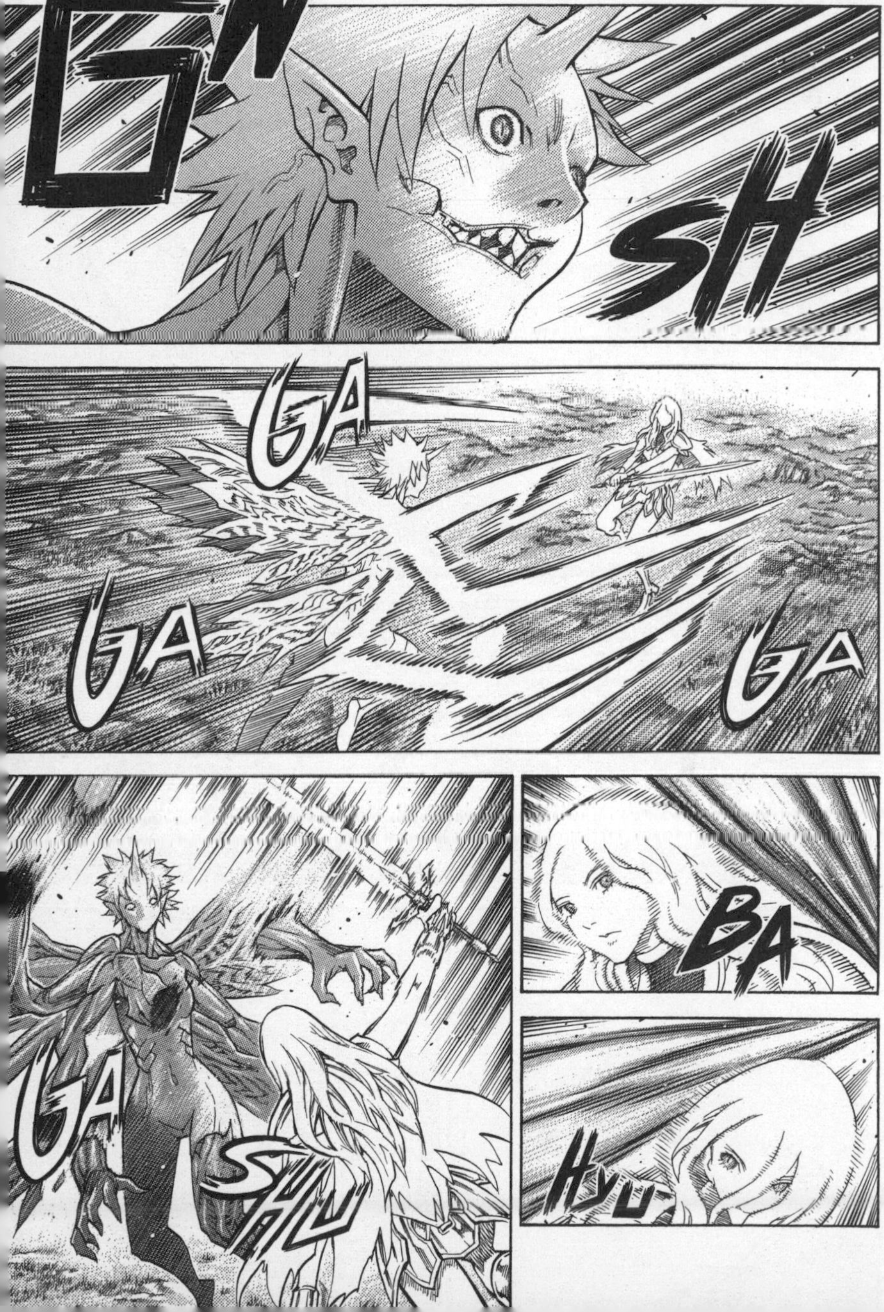
GOW
SH
GA
GA
GA
BA
HYU
GA
SHU

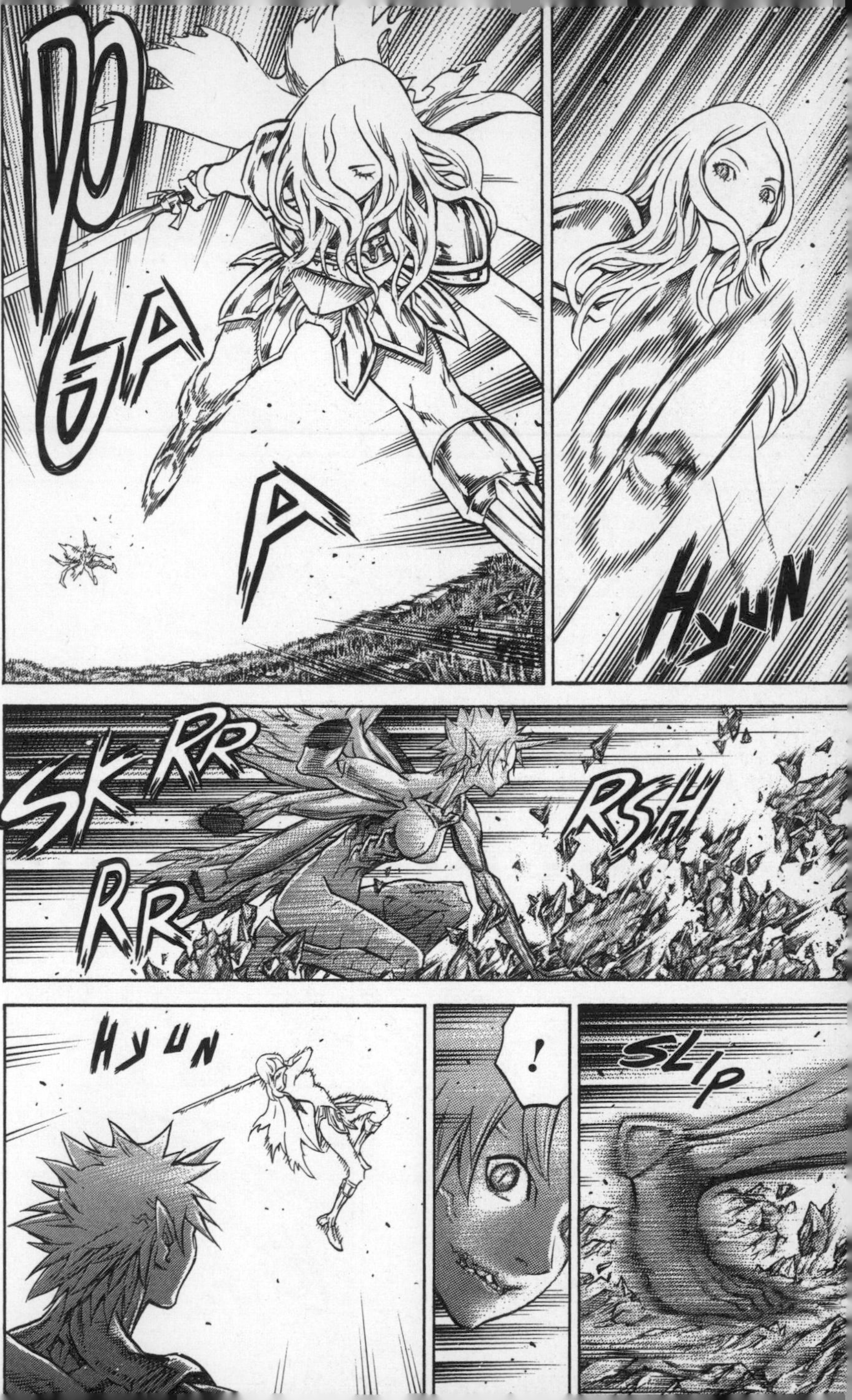
HYUN
DOGAA
RSH
SKRRRR
SLIP
!
HYUN

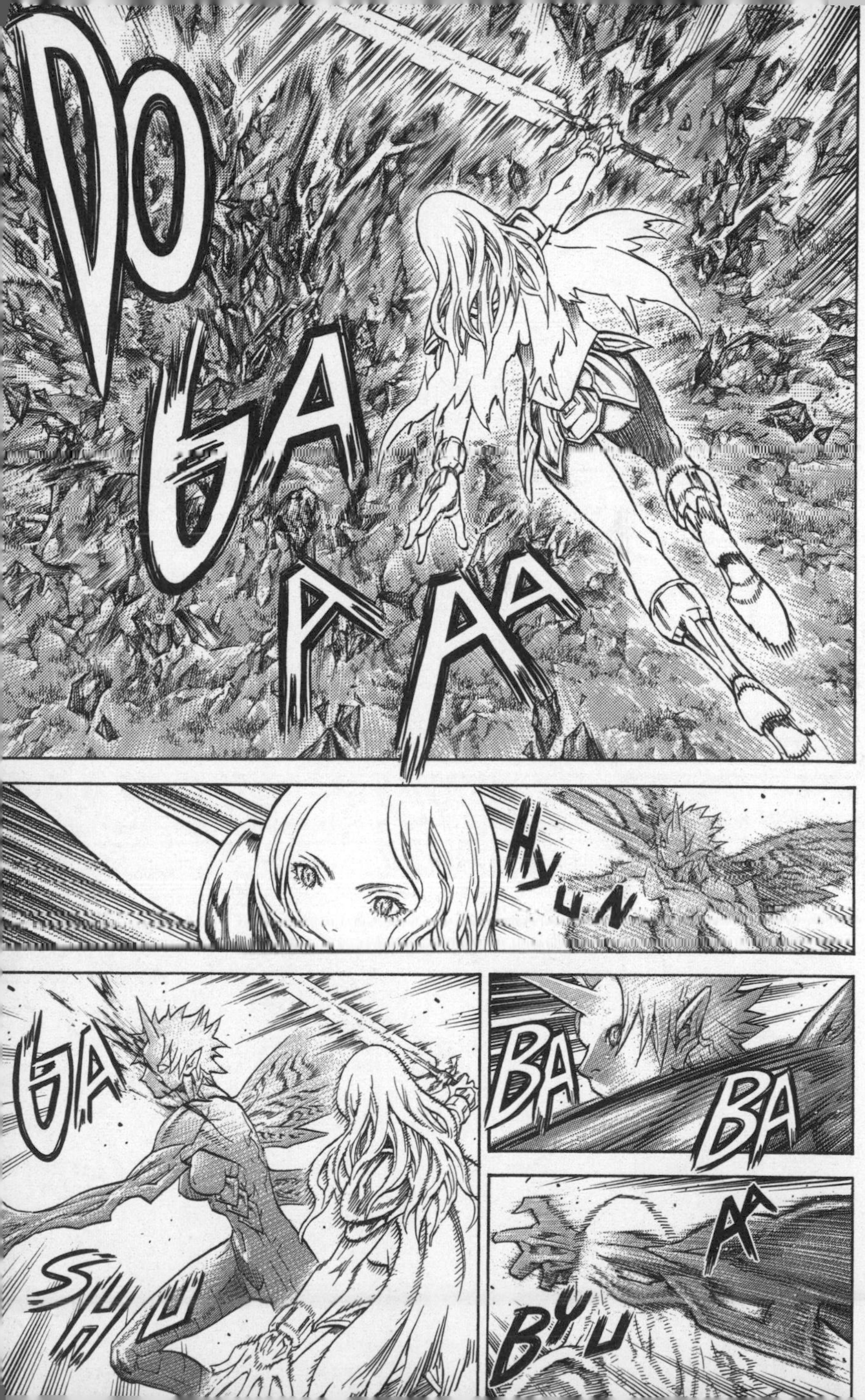
DOGAAA
HYUN
BA
BAA
BYU
GA
SHU

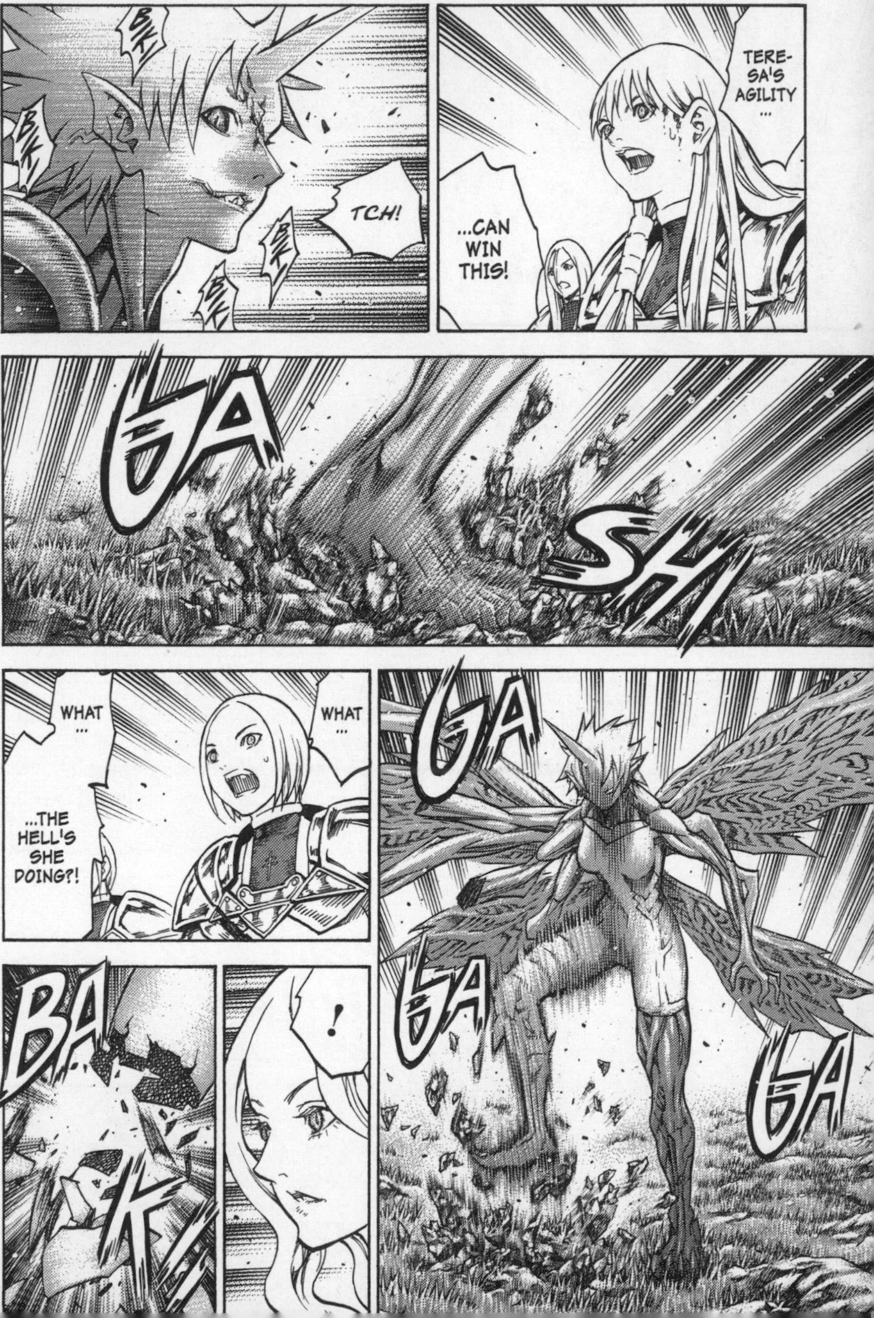
TERE-SA'S AGILITY ...
...CAN WIN THIS!
BKI
BKI
TCH!
BKI
BKI
GA
SHI
GA
GA
GA
WHAT ...
WHAT ...
...THE HELL'S SHE DOING?!
!
BA
KI

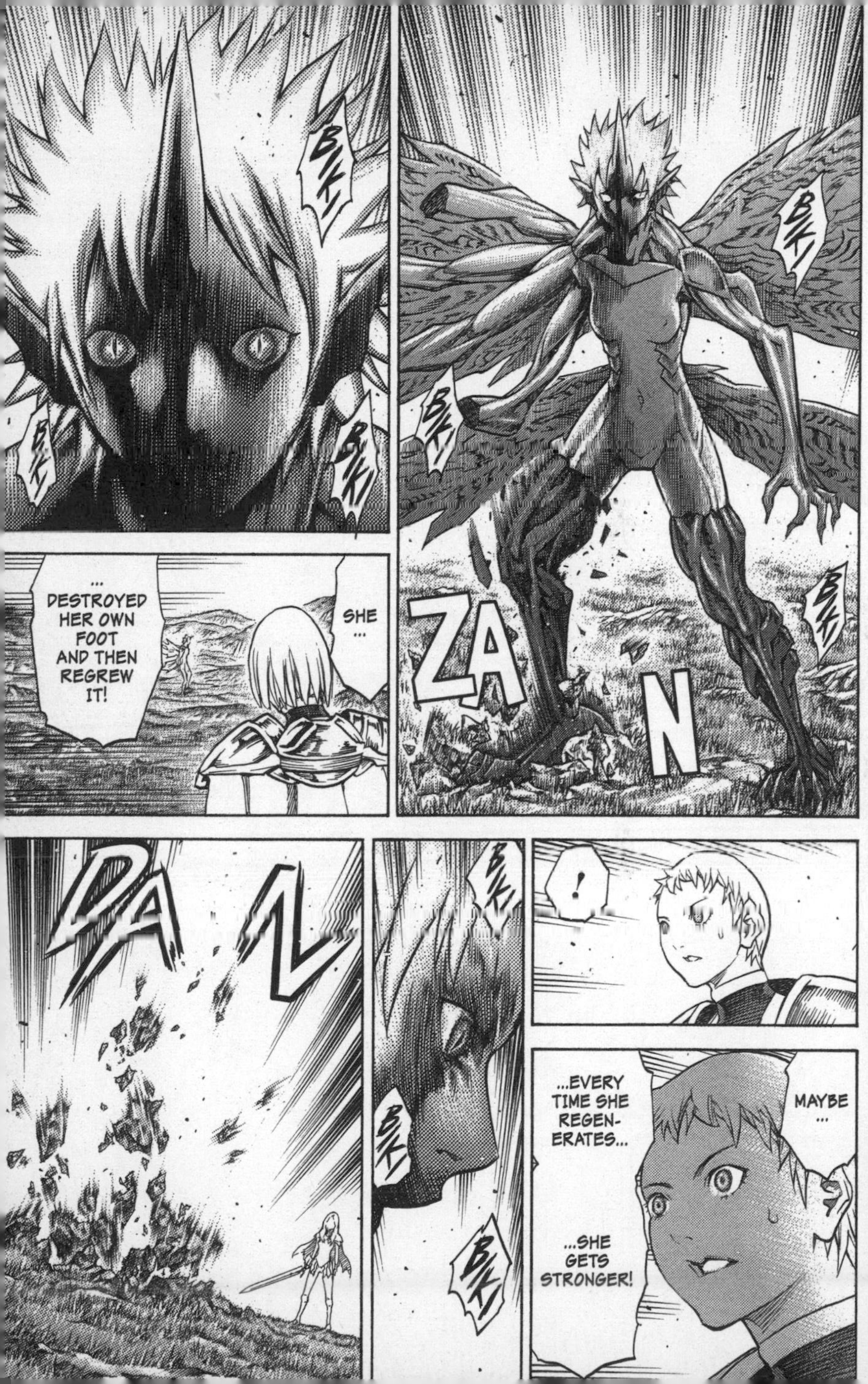
BIKI
BIKI
ZA
N
BIKI
BIKI
BIKI
BIKI
SHE ...
... DESTROYED HER OWN FOOT AND THEN REGREW IT!
!
MAYBE ...
...EVERY TIME SHE REGENERATES...
...SHE GETS STRONGER!
BIKI
BIKI
BIKI
DA N

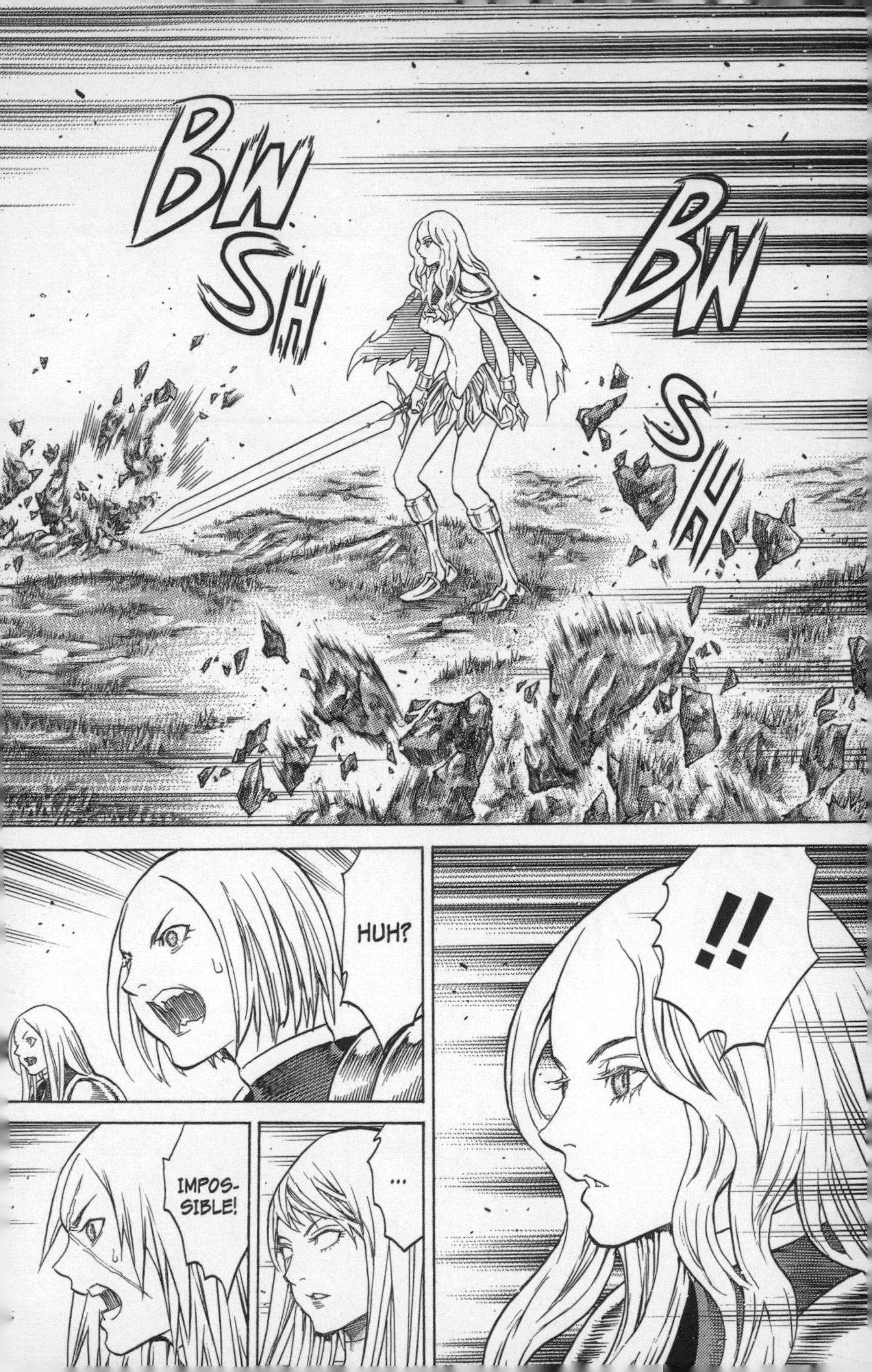
BWSH
BWSH
!!
HUH?
...
IMPOS-
SIBLE!

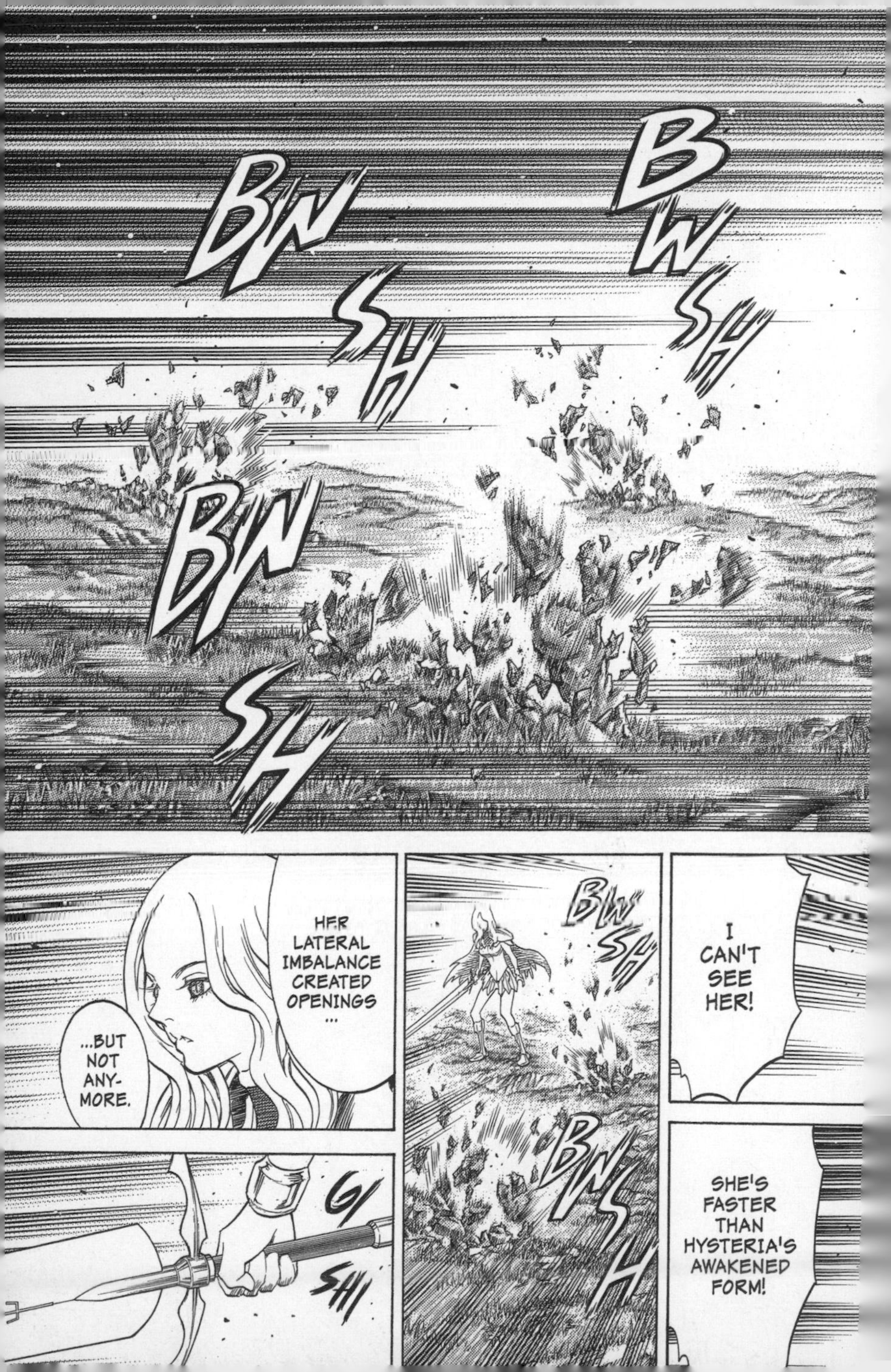
BWSH
BWSH
BWSH
I CAN'T SEE HER!
SHE'S FASTER THAN HYSTERIA'S AWAKENED FORM!
BWSH
BWSH
HER LATERAL IMBALANCE CREATED OPENINGS...
...BUT NOT ANYMORE.
GISHI

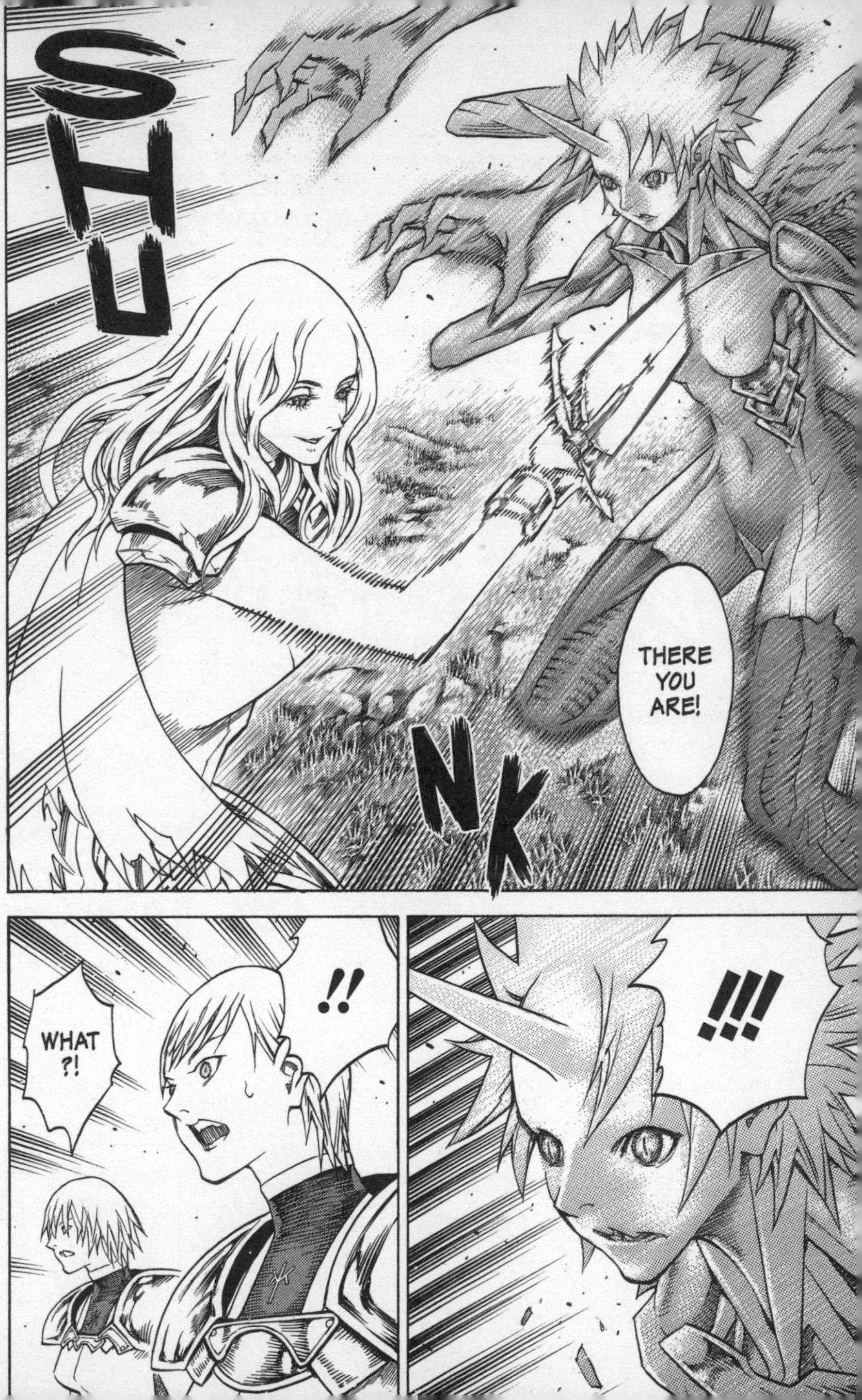
SHU
NK
THERE YOU ARE!
!!!
!!
WHAT ?!

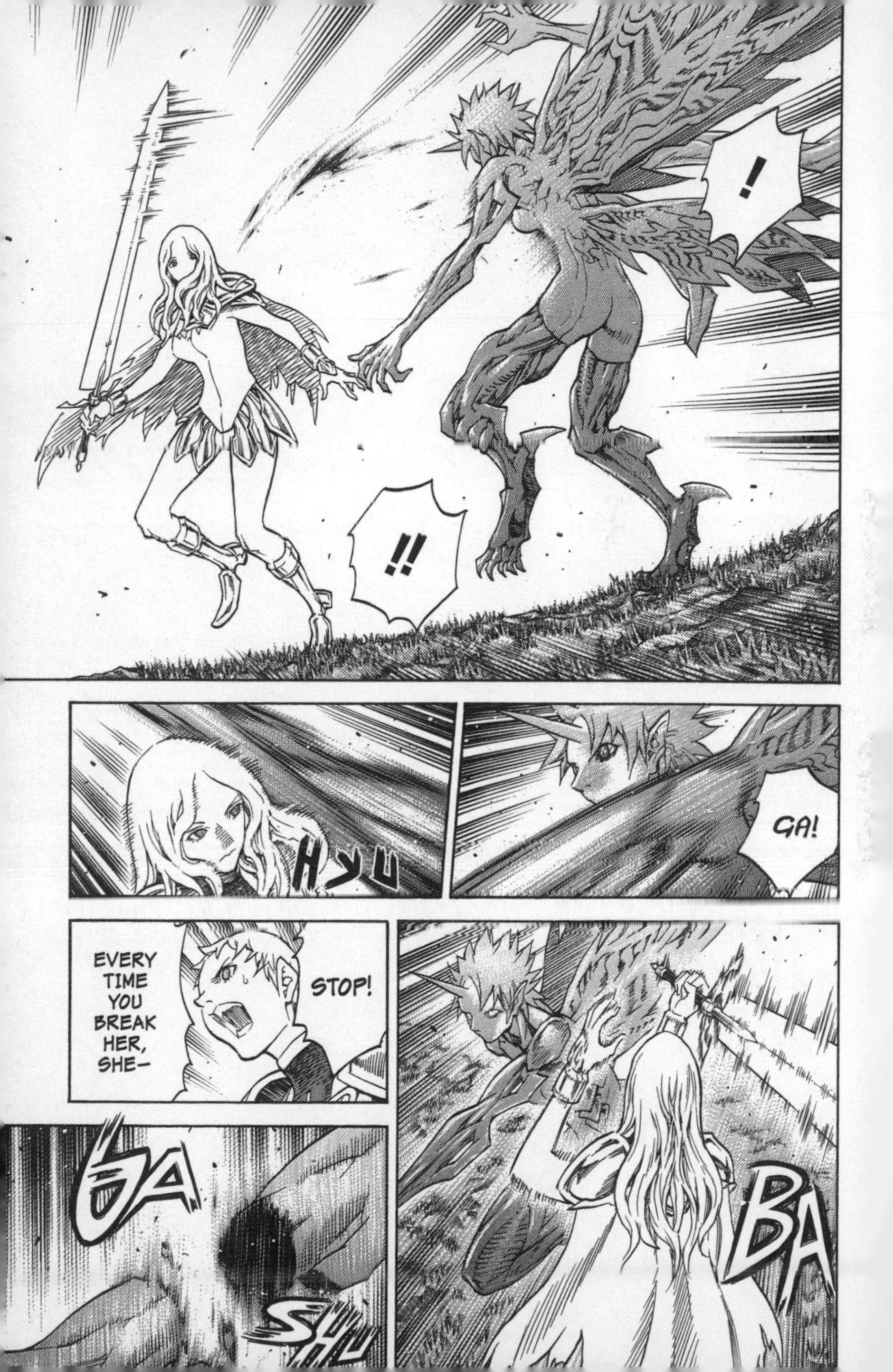
!
!!
GA!
HYU
STOP!
EVERY TIME YOU BREAK HER, SHE—
BA
GA
SHU

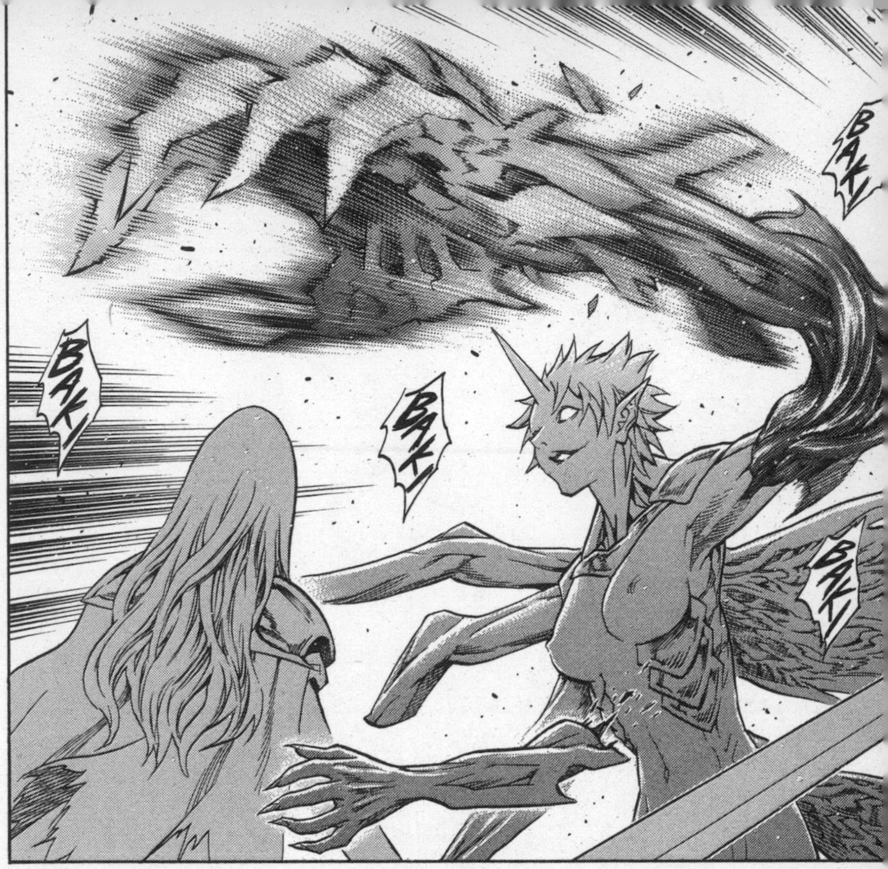
BAKI
BAKI
BAKI
BAKI
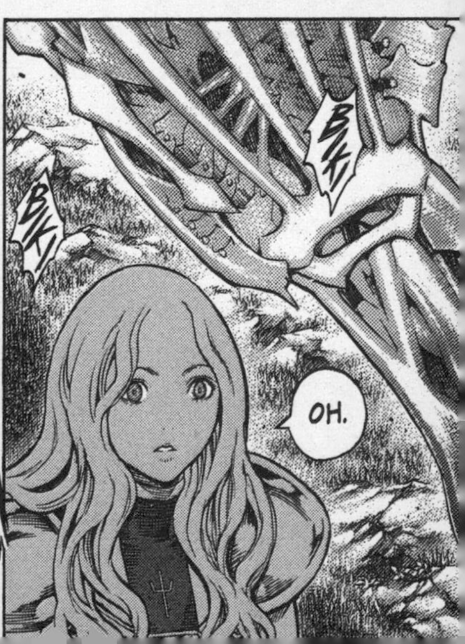
BAKI
BAKI
OH.
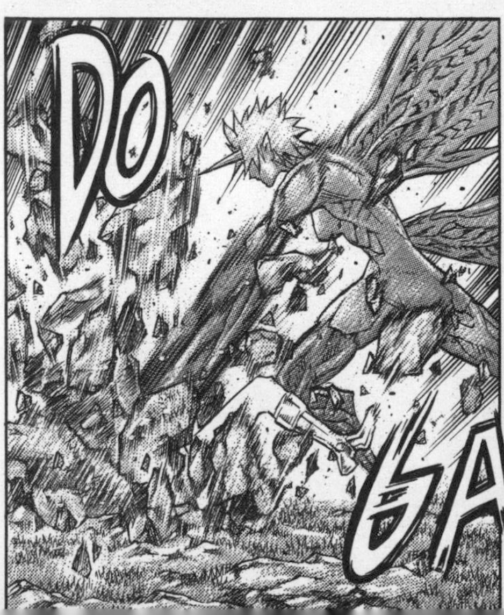
DO
GA

READ THIS WAY

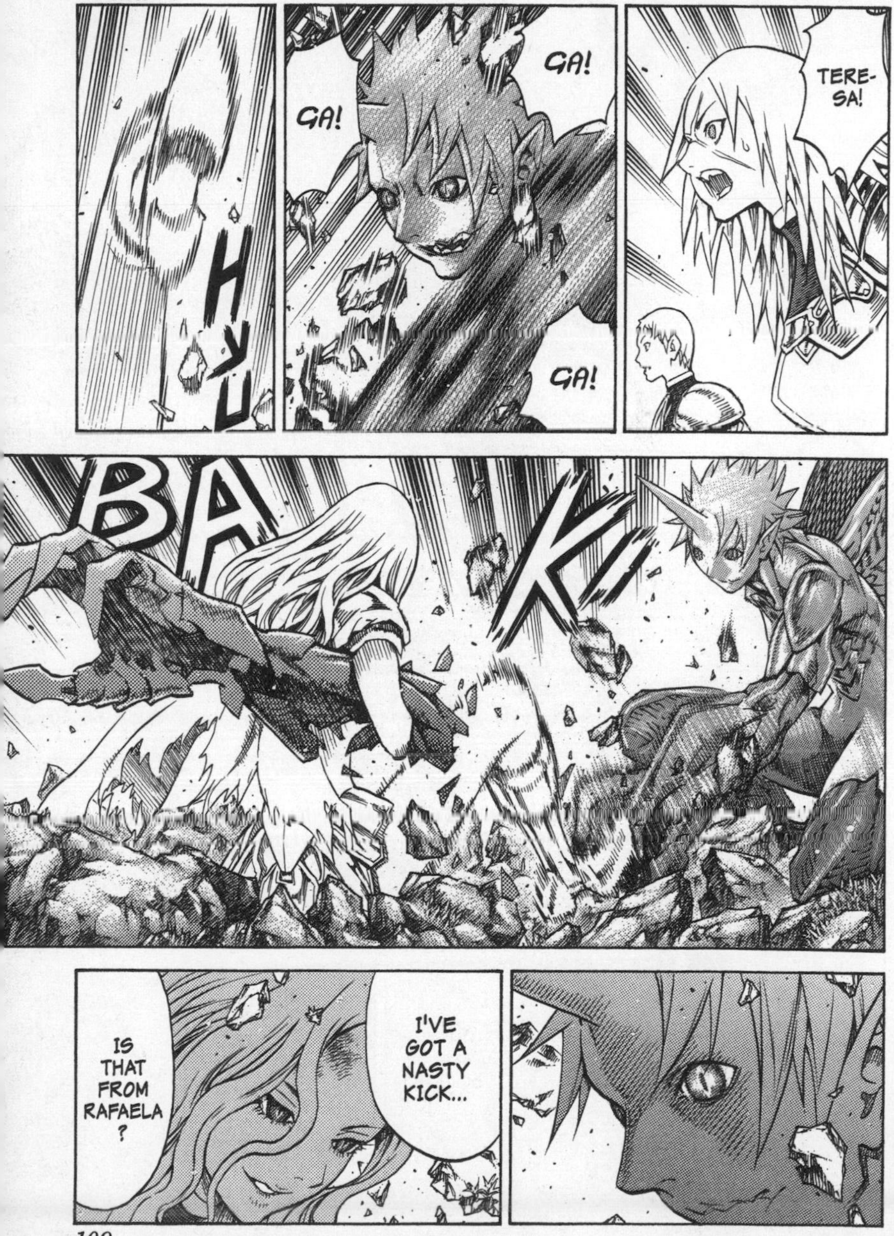
TERE-SA!
GA!
GA!
GA!
HYU
BAKI
I'VE GOT A NASTY KICK...
IS THAT FROM RAFAELA?

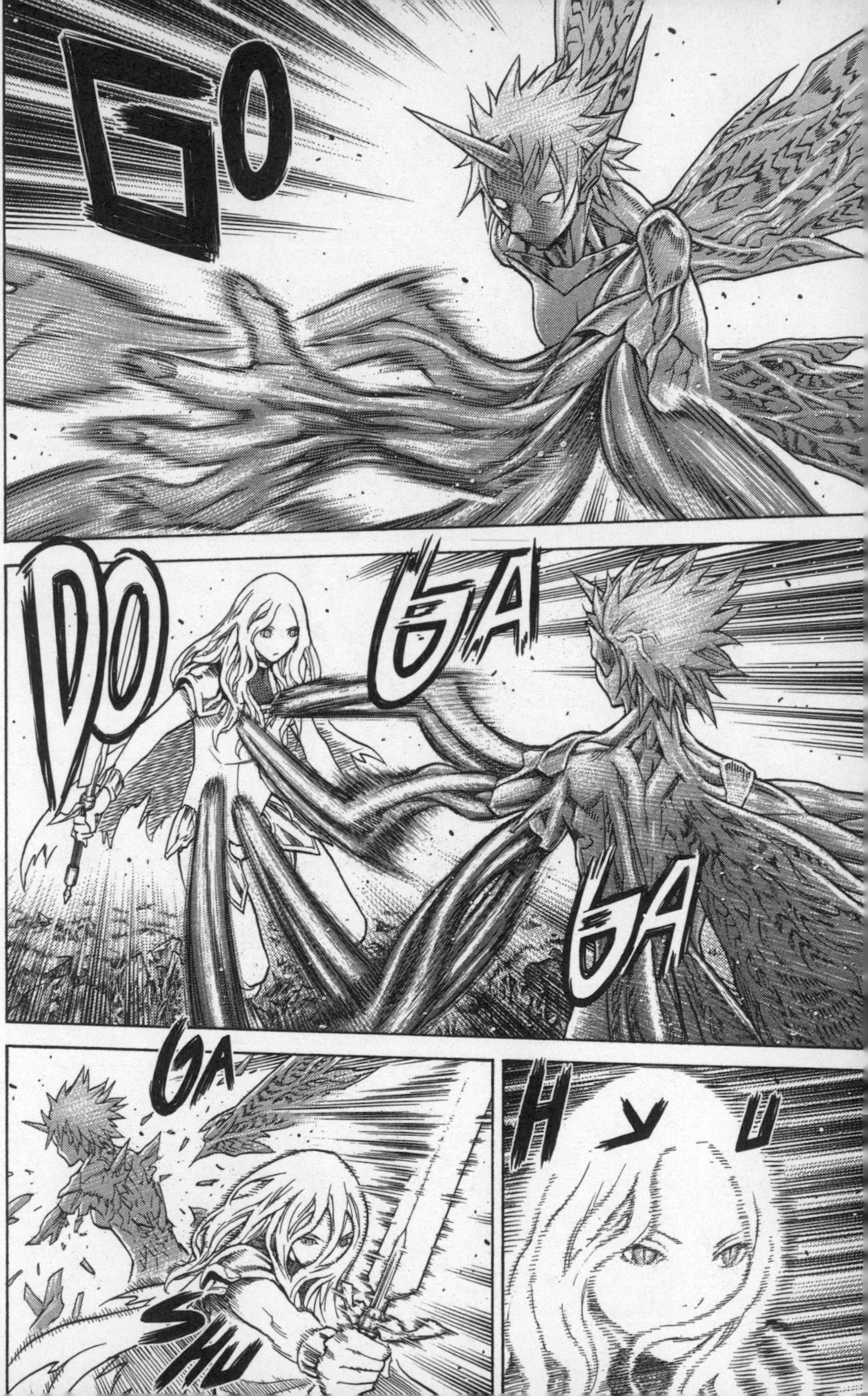
GO
GA
DO
GA
HYU
GA
SHU

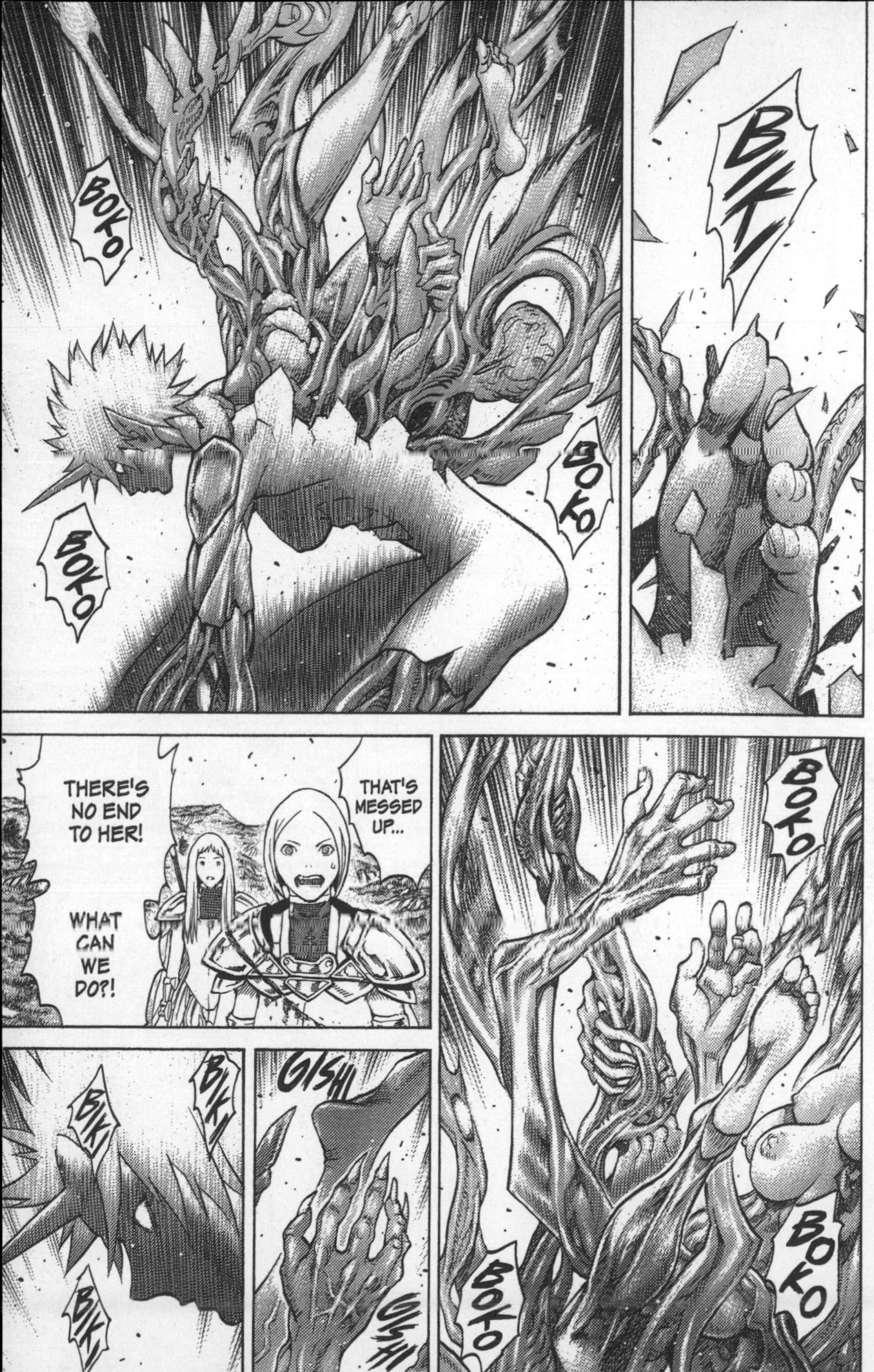
BIKI
BOKO
BOKO
BOKO
BOKO
BOKO
BOKO
THAT'S MESSED UP...
THERE'S NO END TO HER!
WHAT CAN WE DO?!
GISHI
GISHI
BIKI
BIKI
BIKI

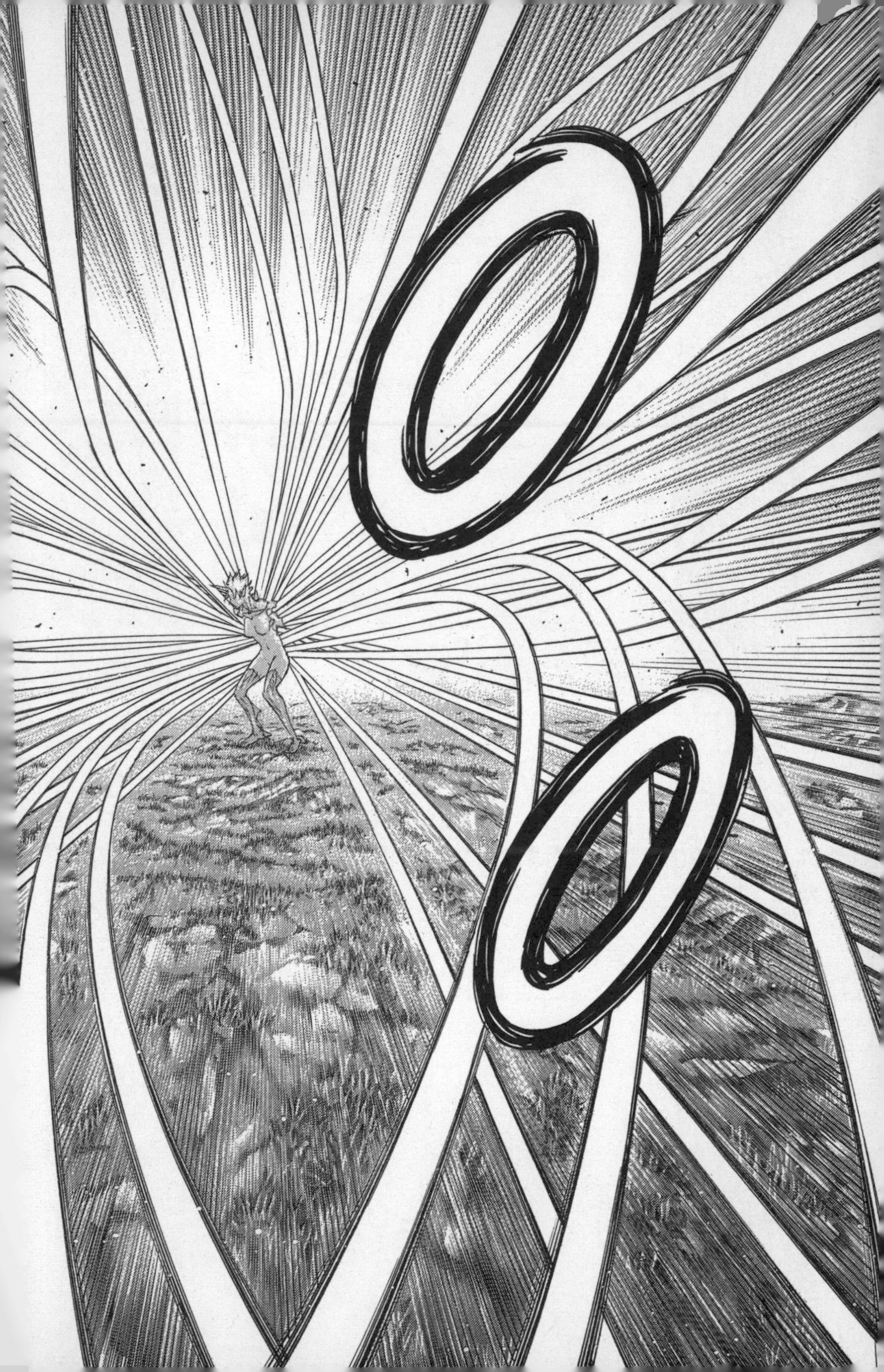

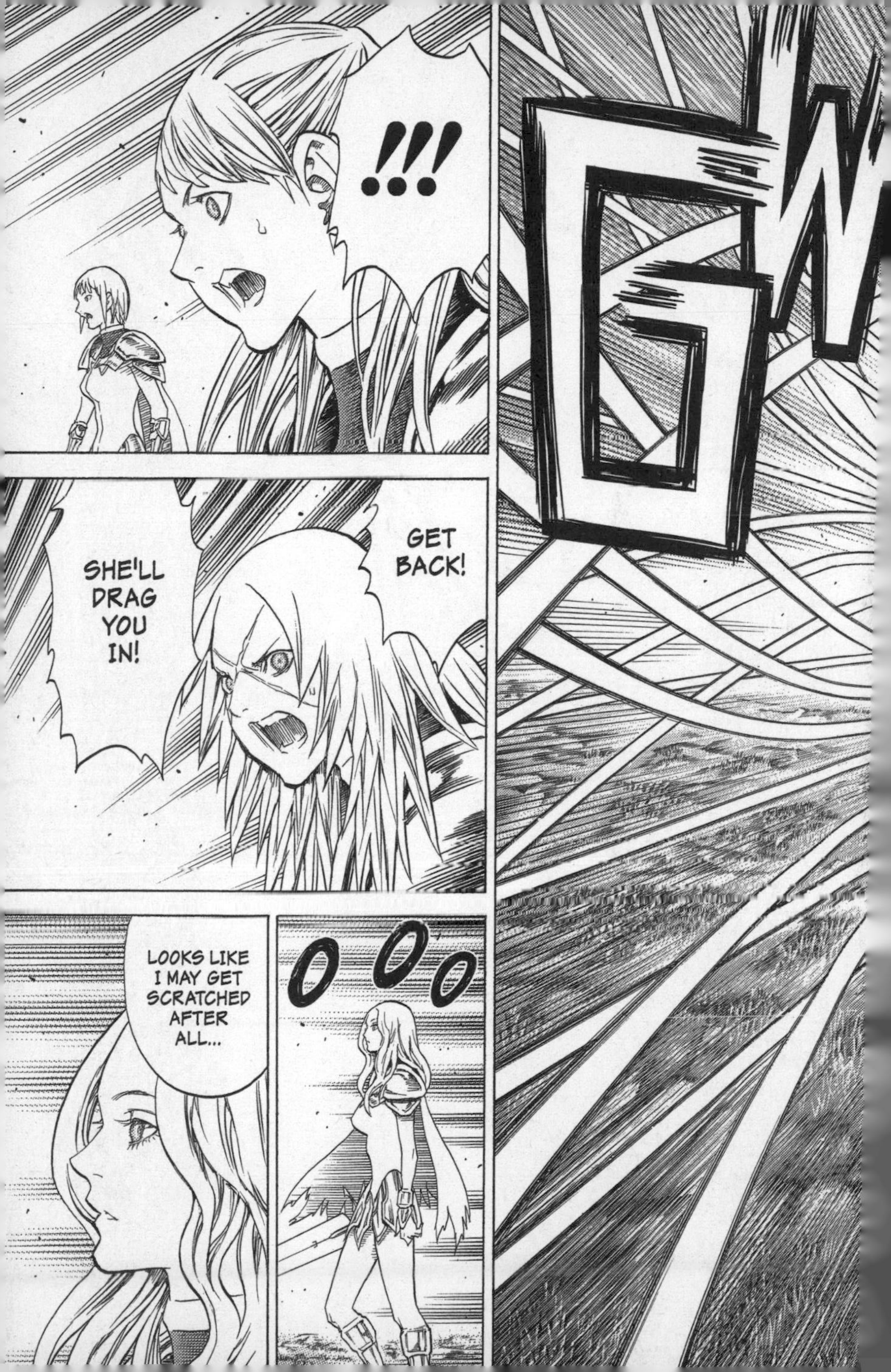
!!!
GET BACK!
SHE'LL DRAG YOU IN!
OOO
LOOKS LIKE I MAY GET SCRATCHED AFTER ALL...

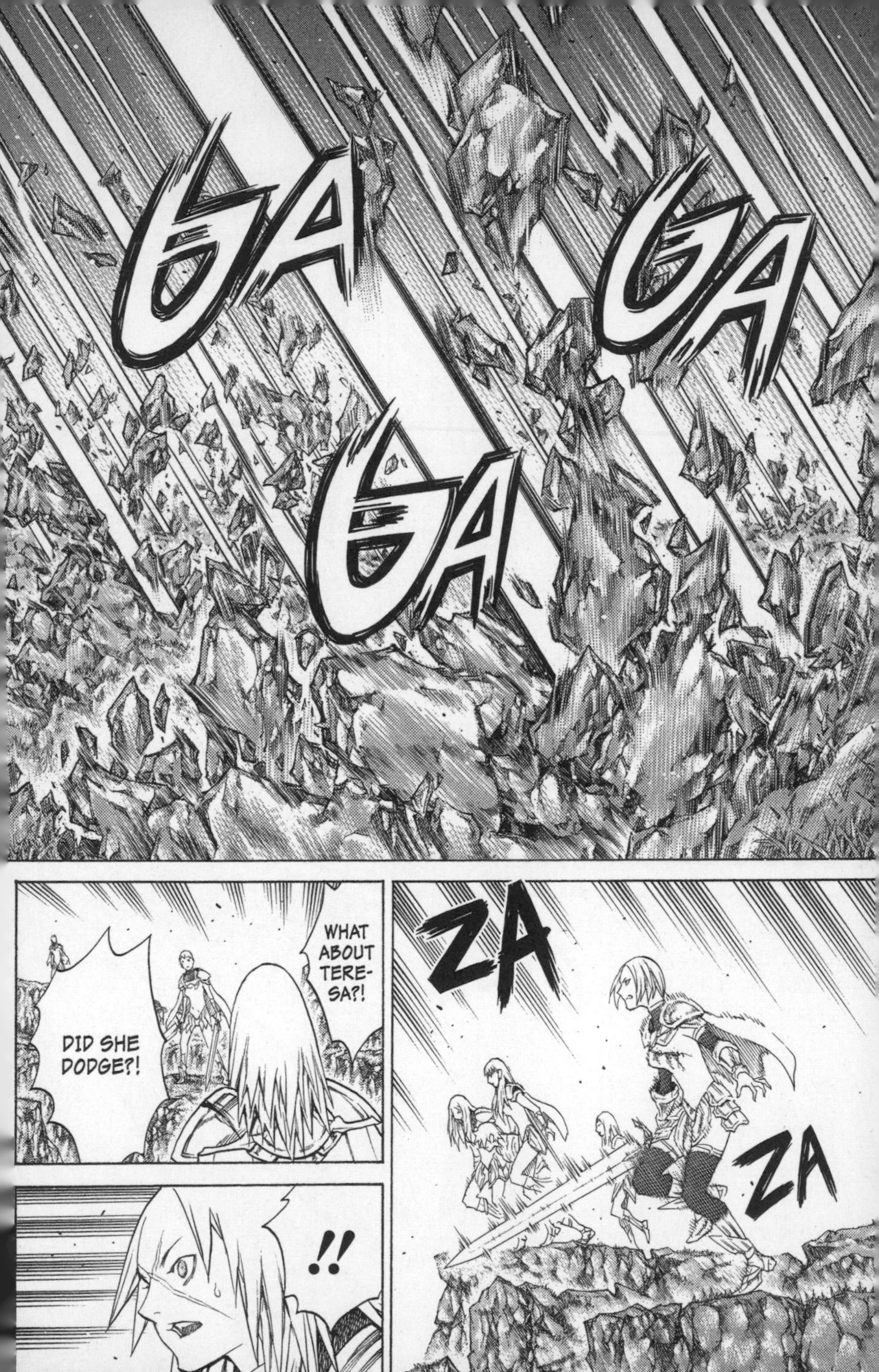
GA
GA
GA
ZA
ZA
WHAT ABOUT TERE-SA?!
DID SHE DODGE?!
!!

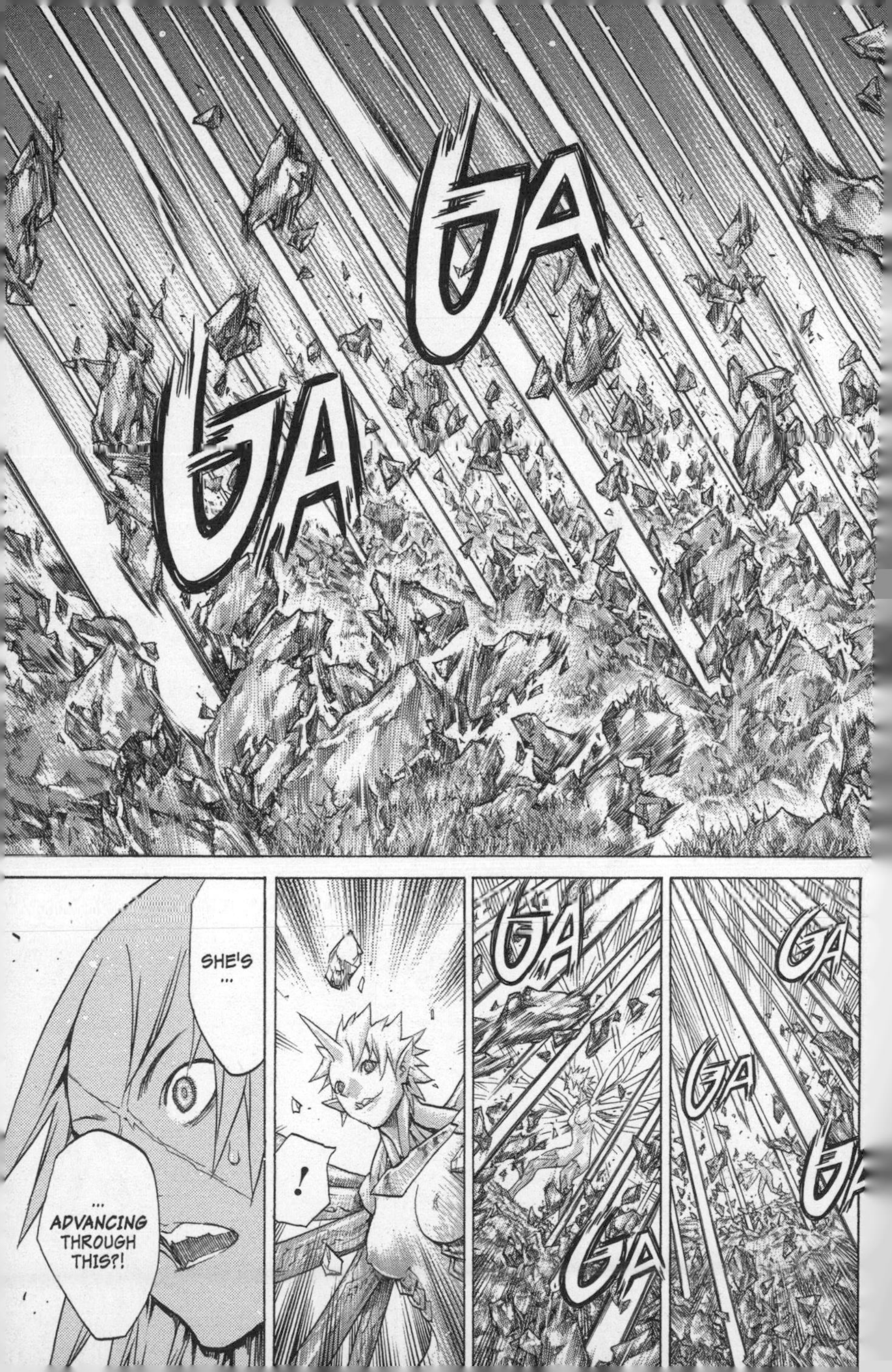
GA GA
GA
GA
GA
GA
GA
!
SHE'S ...
... ADVANCING THROUGH THIS?!

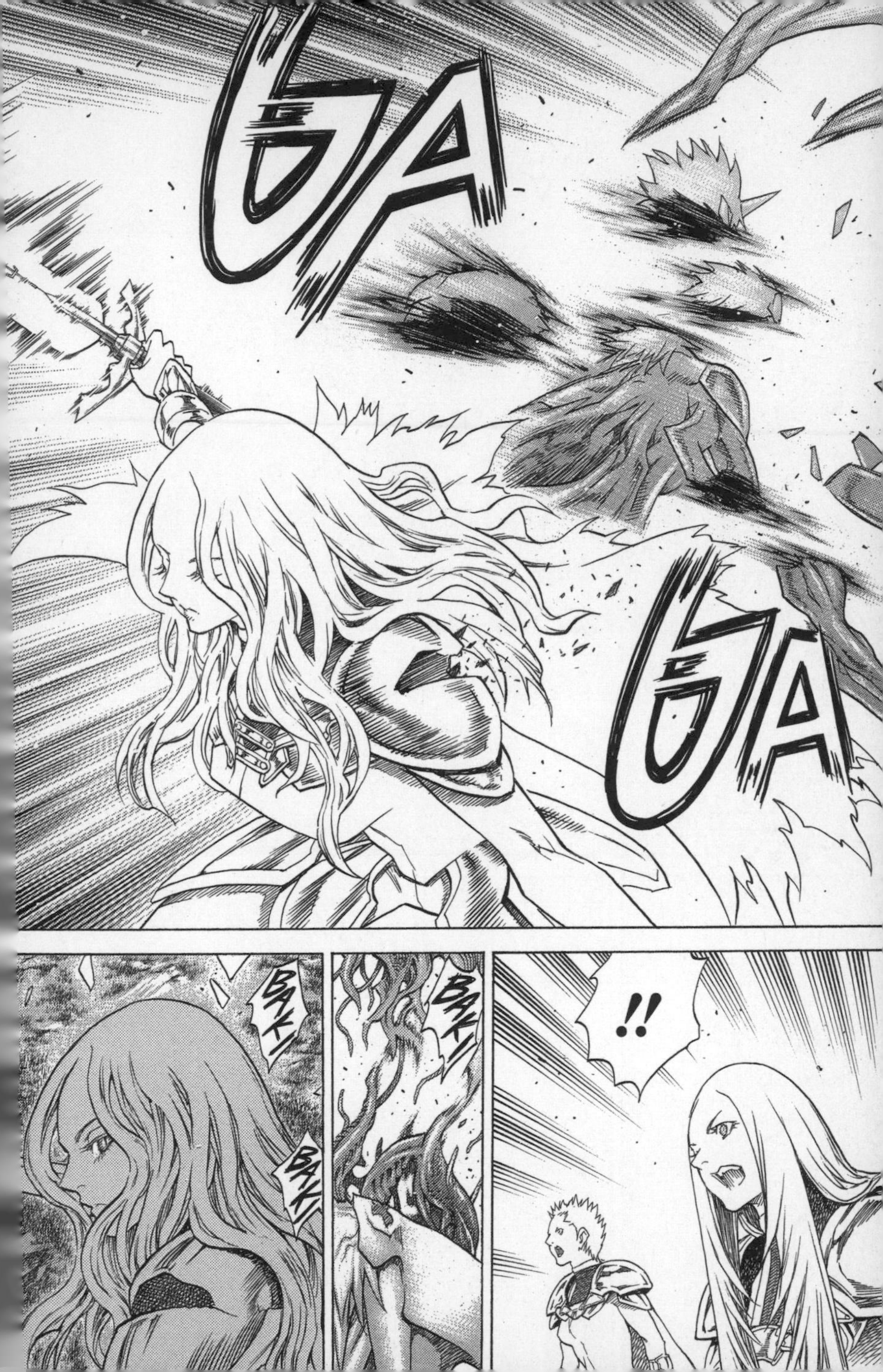
GA
GA
!!
BAKI
BAKI
BAKI

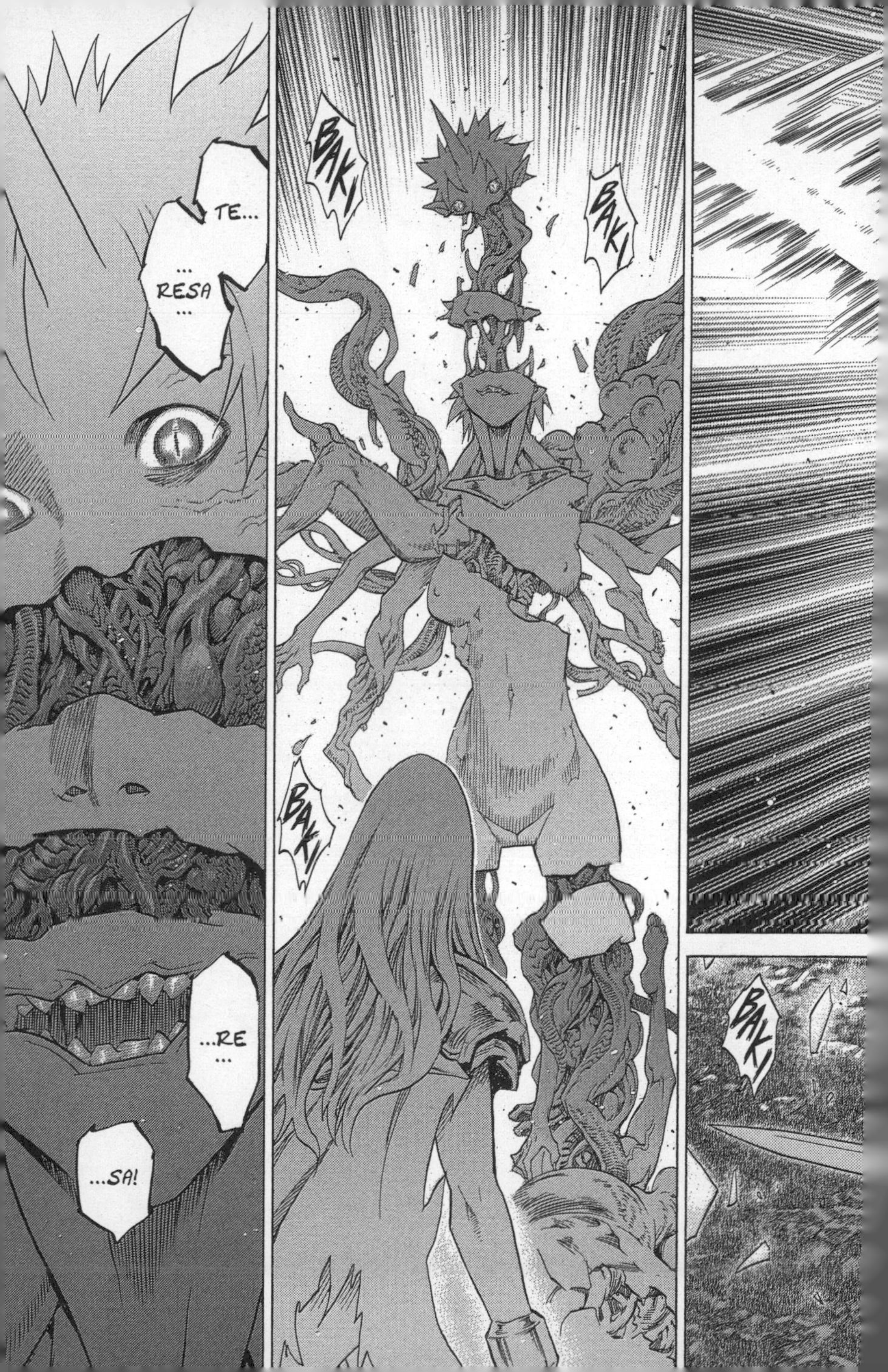
BAKI
BAKI
BAKI
BAKI
TE...
... RESA ...
...RE ...
...SA!

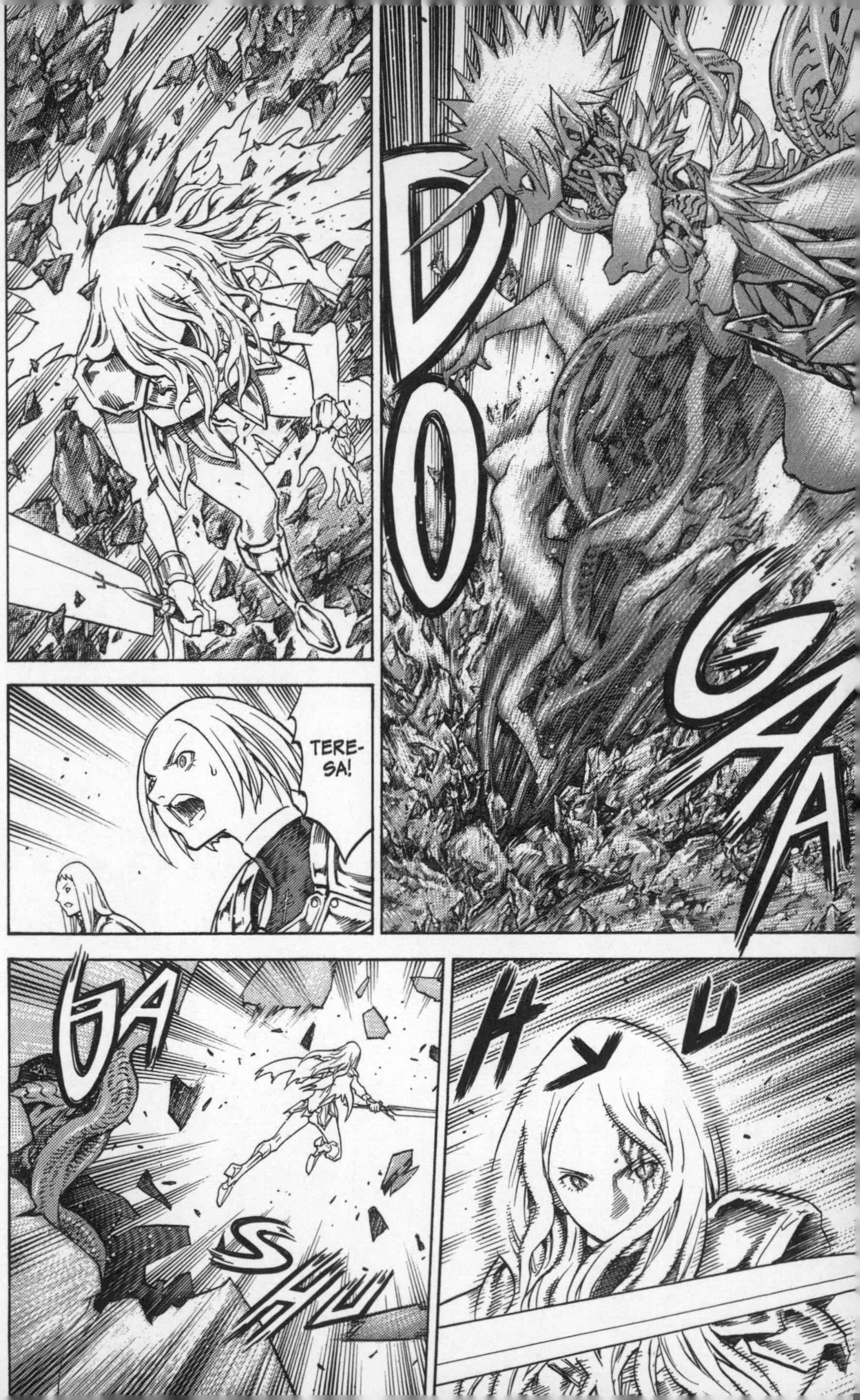
DO
GA
TERE-
SA!
HYU
GA
SHU

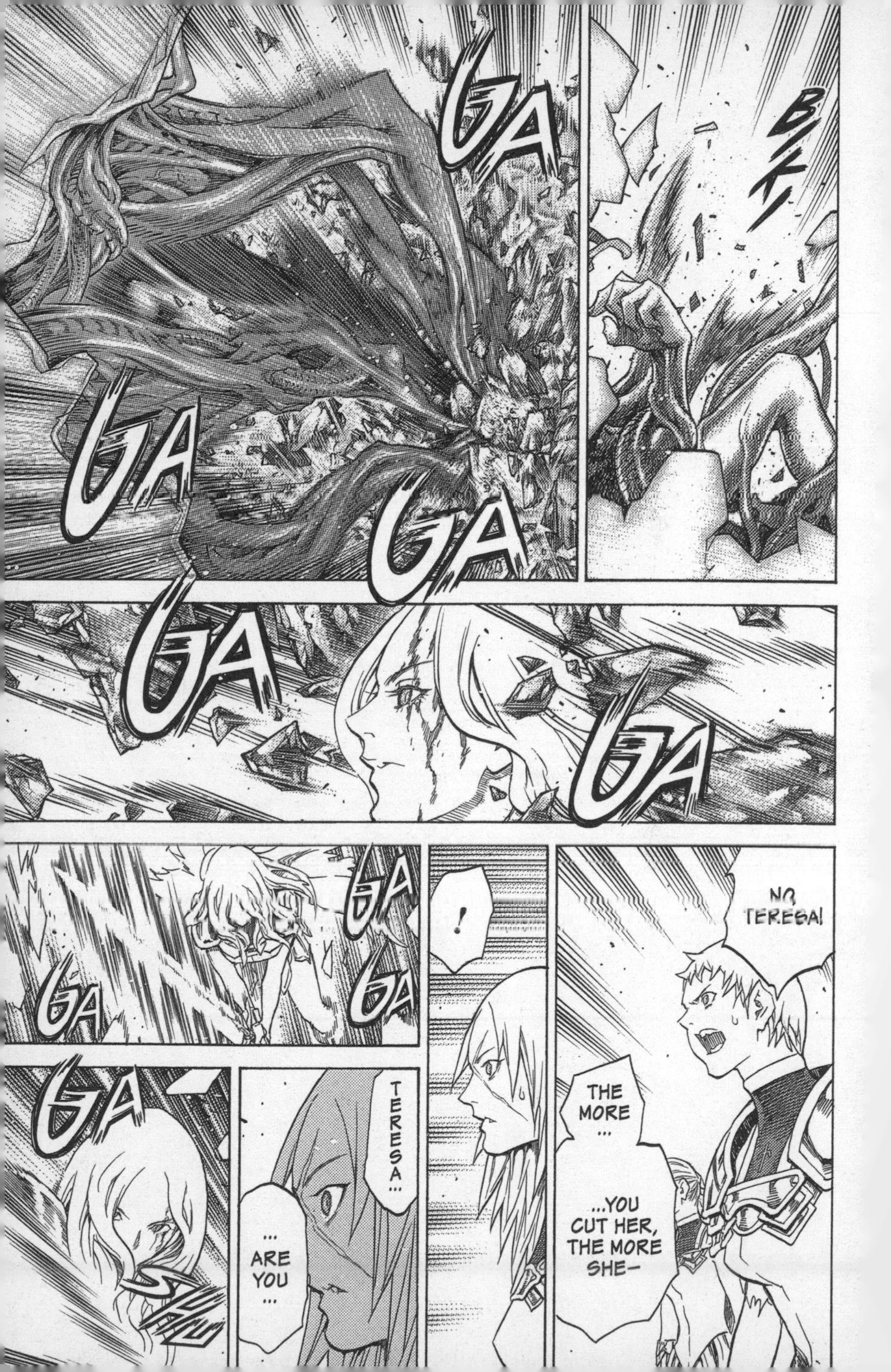

BIKI
GA
GA
GA
GA
GA
NO, TERESA!
THE MORE ...
...YOU CUT HER, THE MORE SHE—
!
GA
GA
GA
TERESA...
... ARE YOU ...
GA
SHU

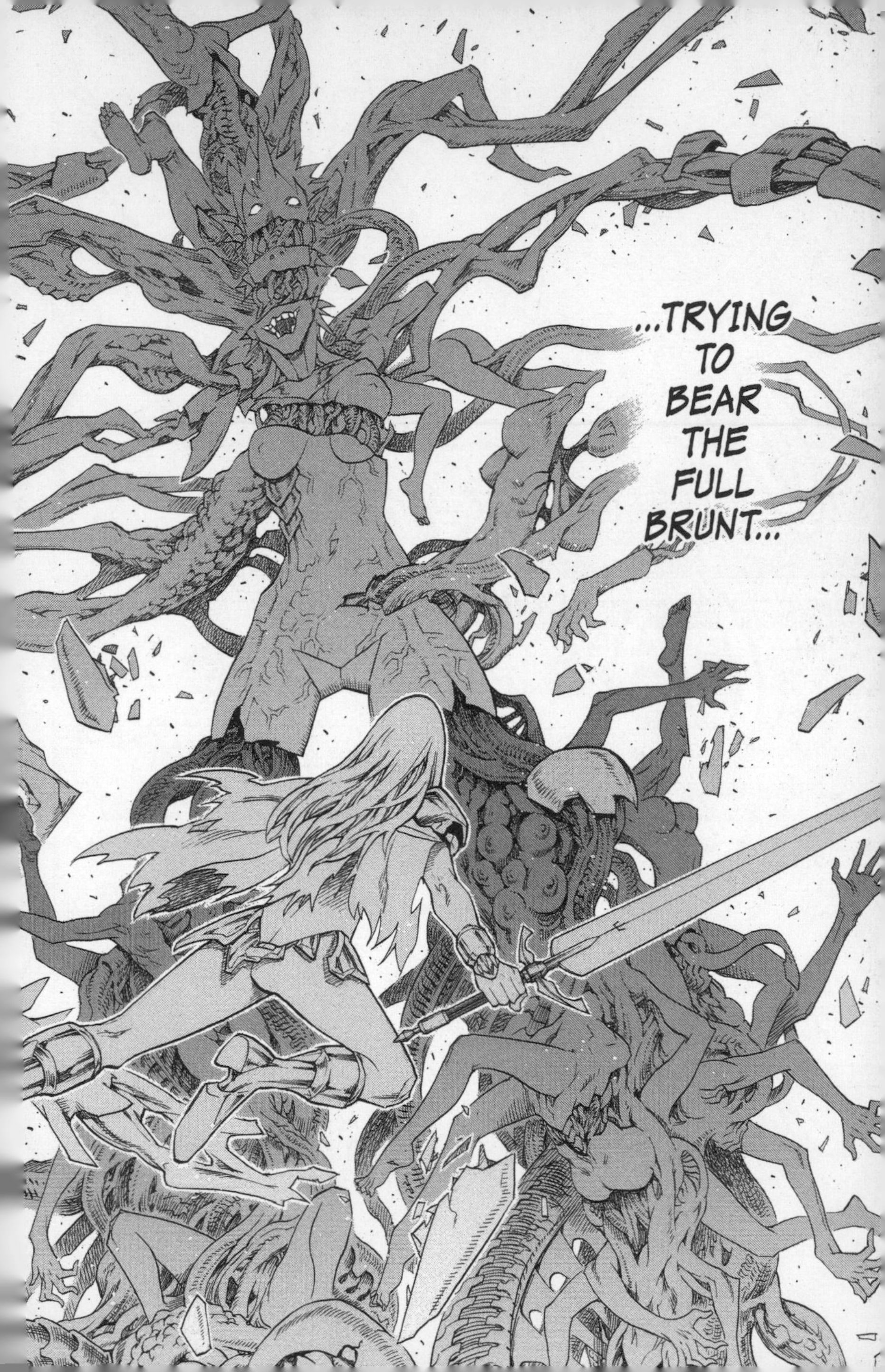
...TRYING TO BEAR THE FULL BRUNT...

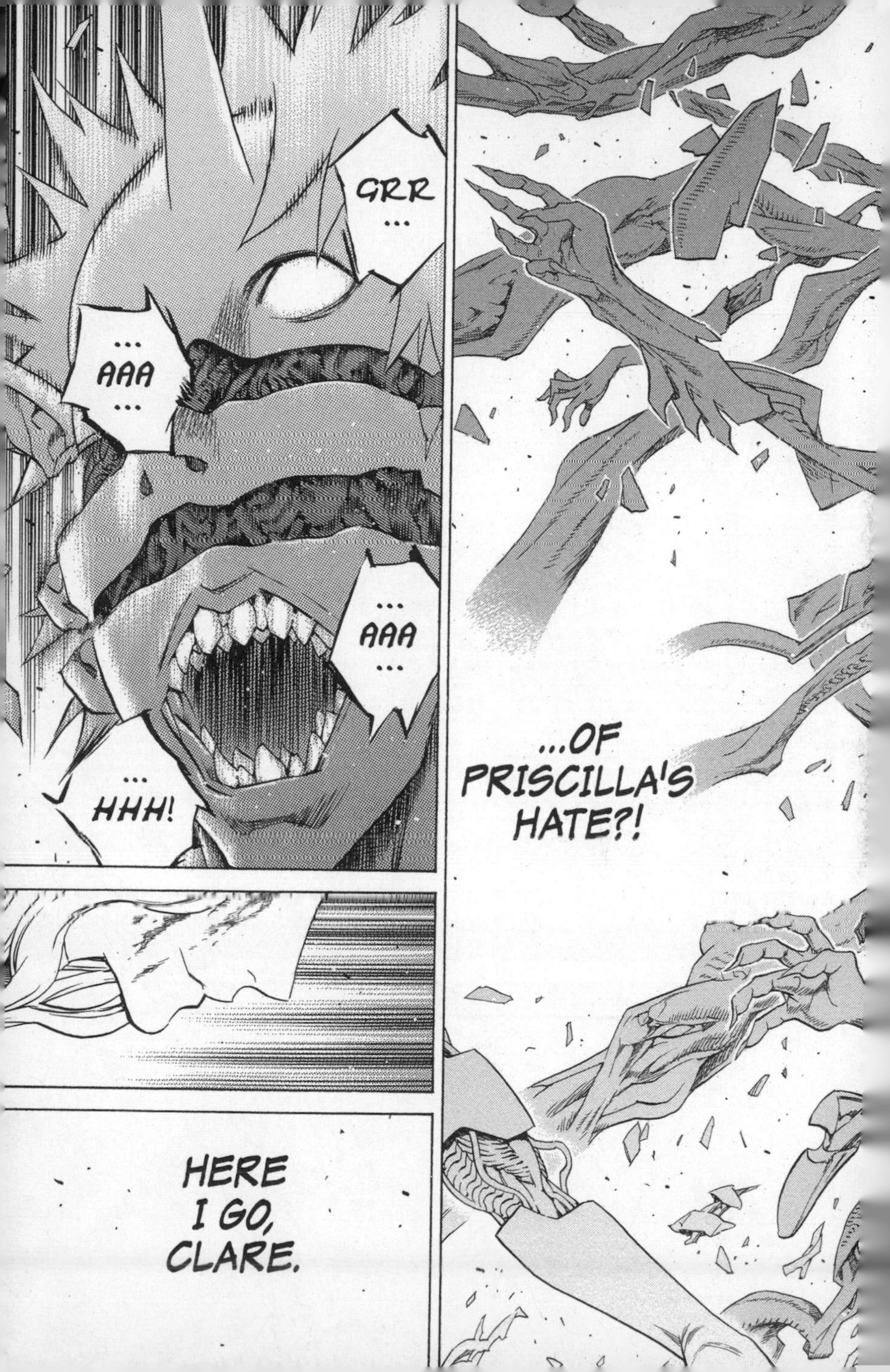
...OF PRISCILLA'S HATE?!
GRR ...
... AAA ...
... AAA ...
... HHH!
HERE I GO, CLARE.

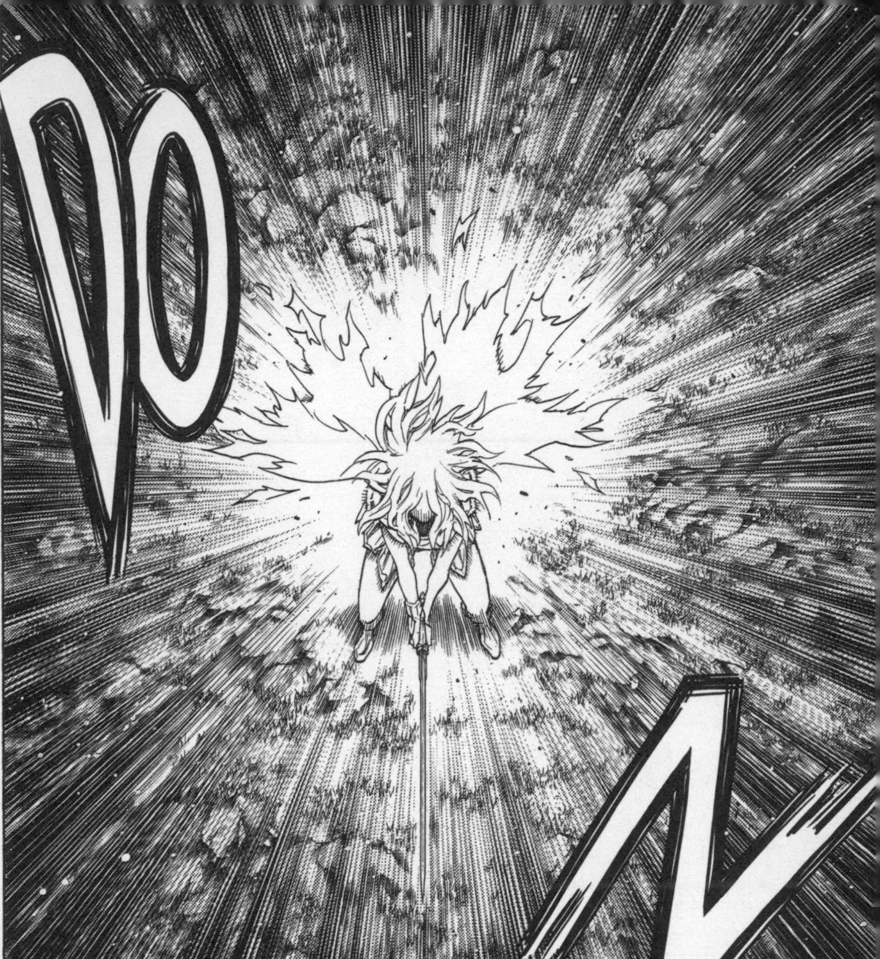
DO
N
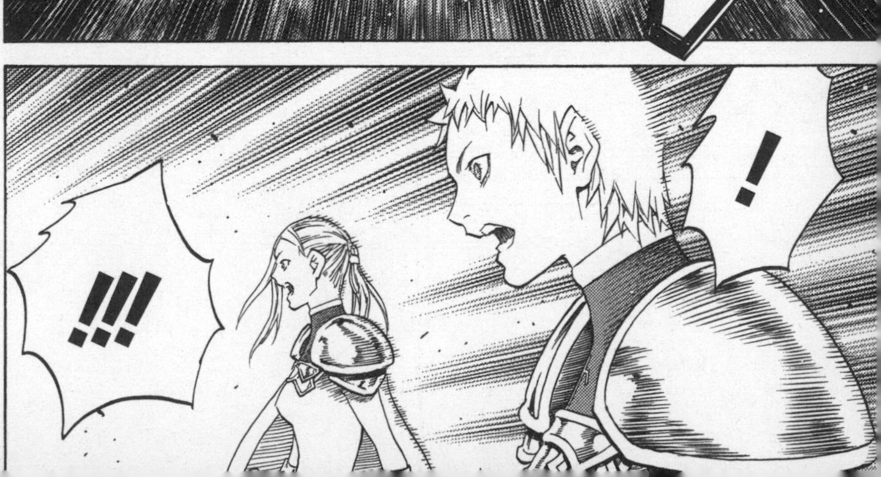
!
!!!

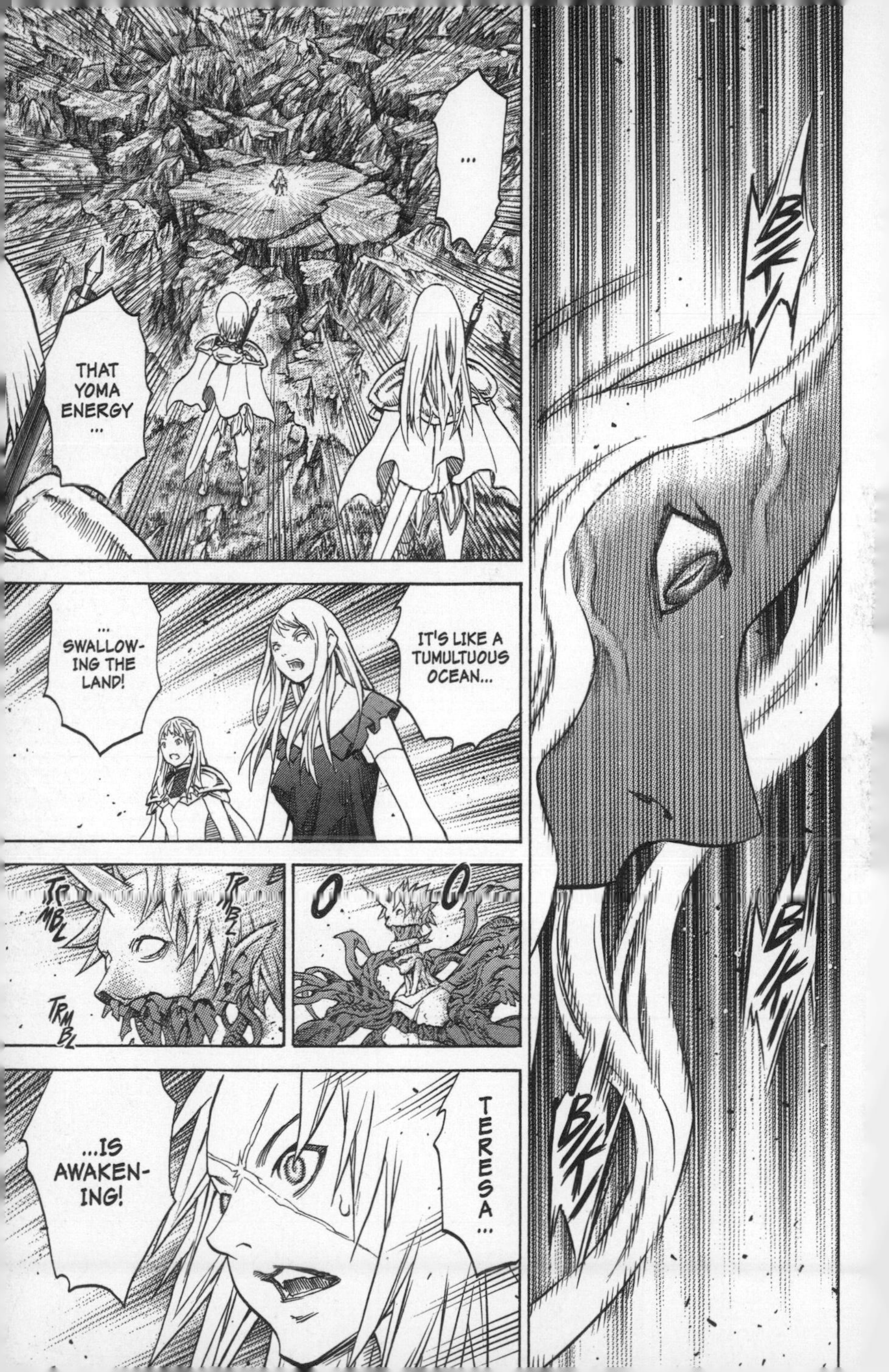
BKKK
BKKK
BK
...
THAT YOMA ENERGY ...
IT'S LIKE A TUMULTUOUS OCEAN...
... SWALLOW-ING THE LAND!
O O
TRMBL
TRMBL
TRMBL
TERESA ...
...IS AWAKEN-ING!

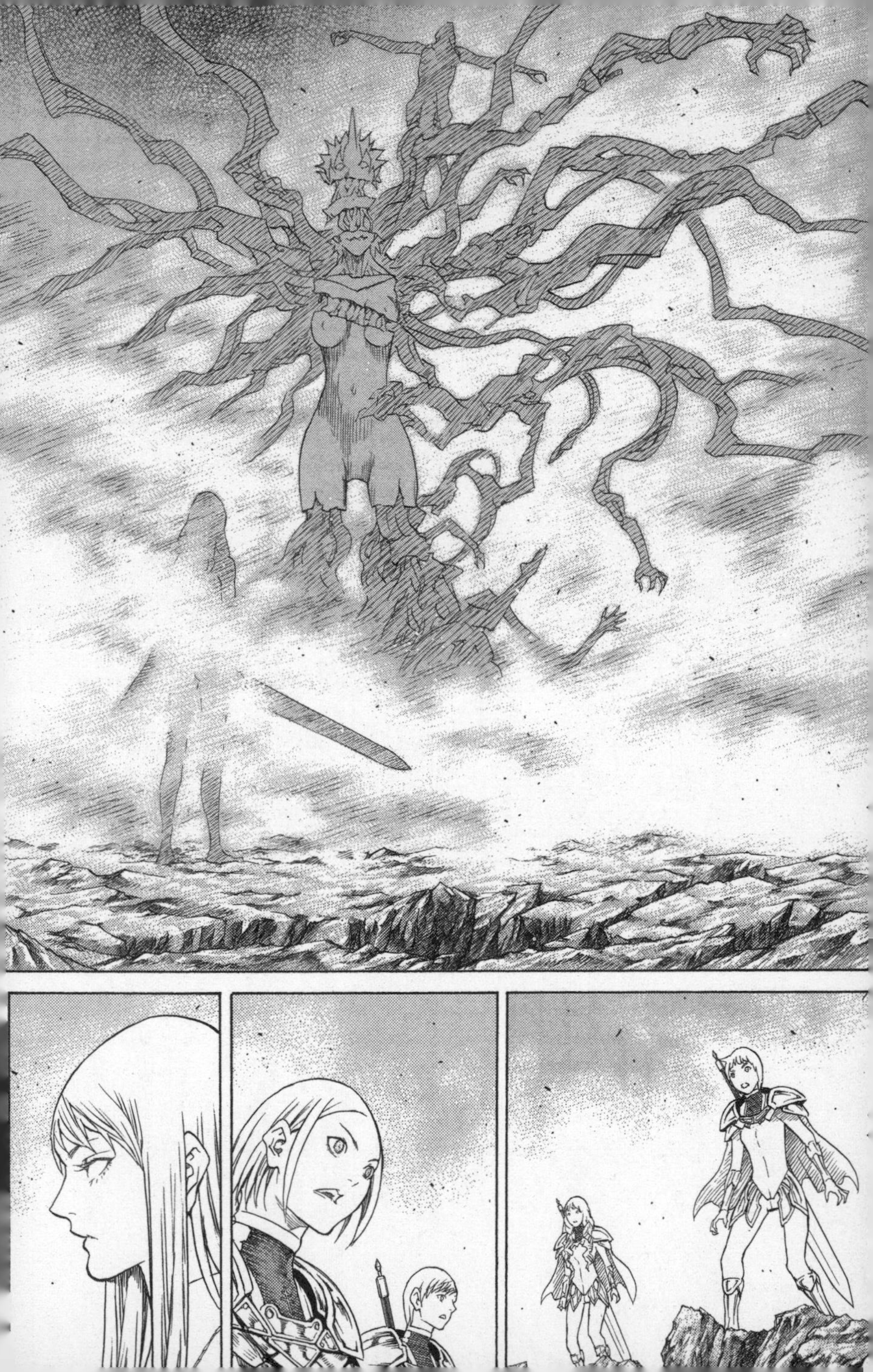

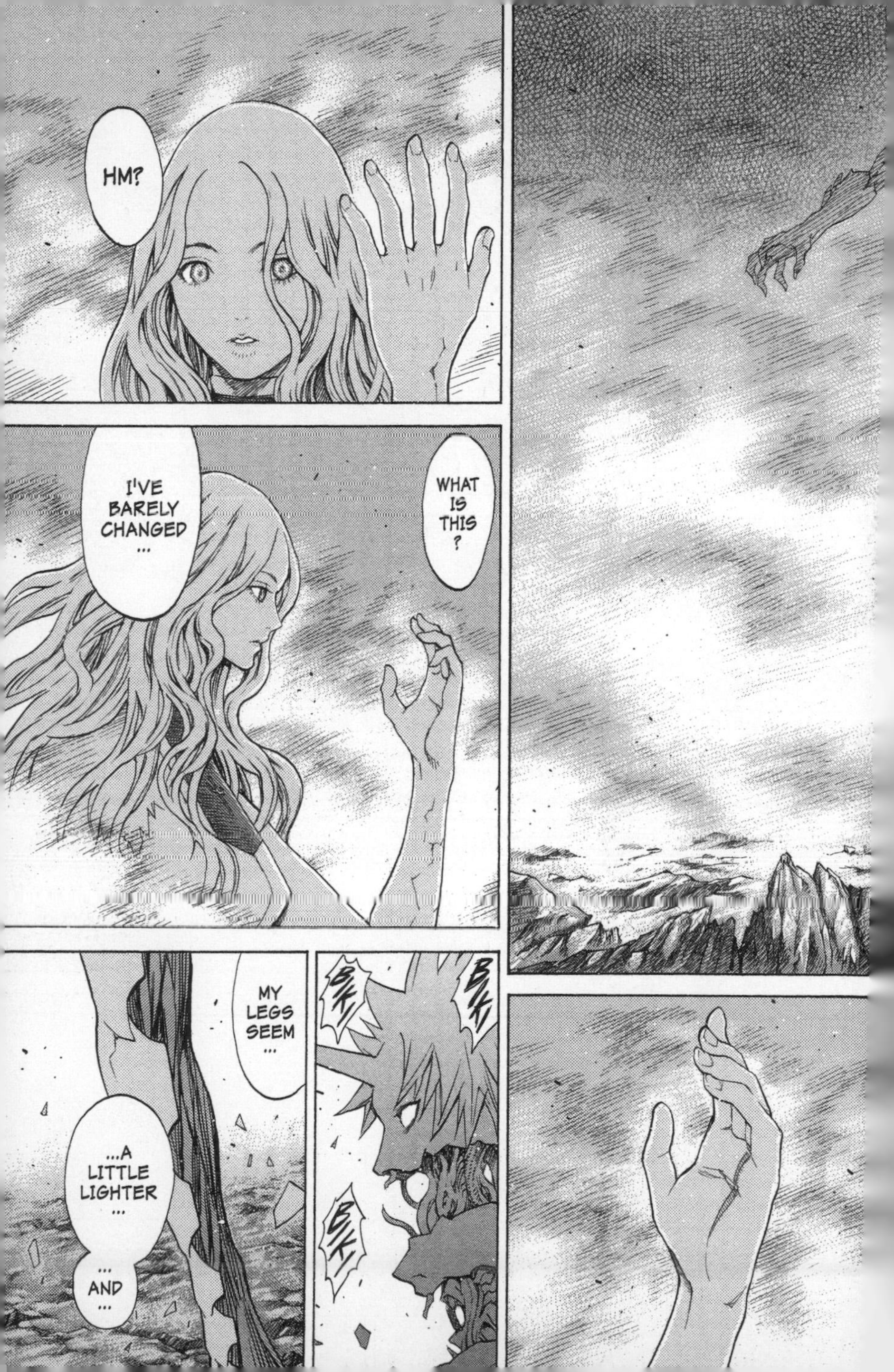
HM?
WHAT IS THIS?
I'VE BARELY CHANGED ...
BKI
BKI
BKI
MY LEGS SEEM ...
...A LITTLE LIGHTER ...
... AND ...

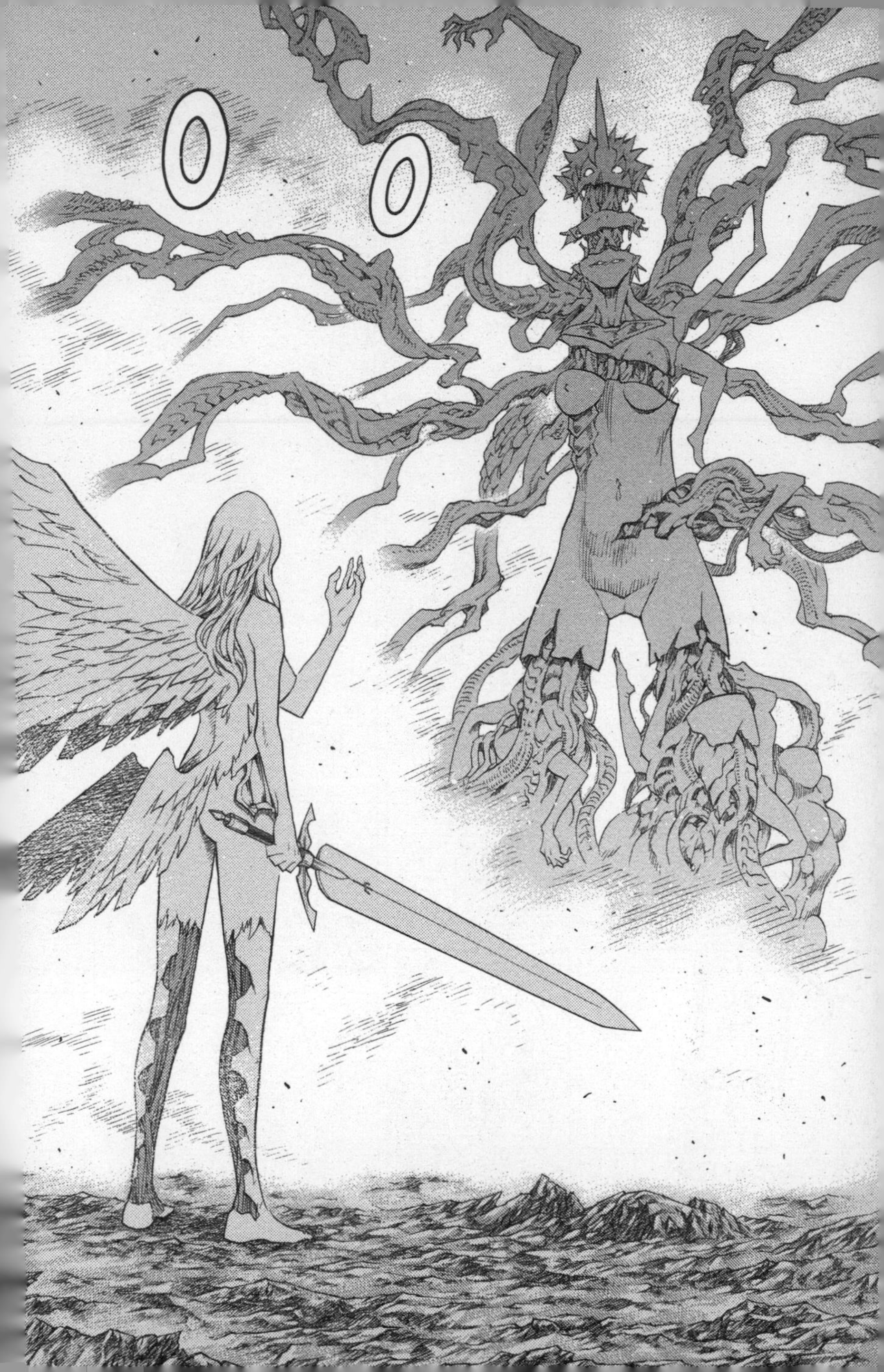

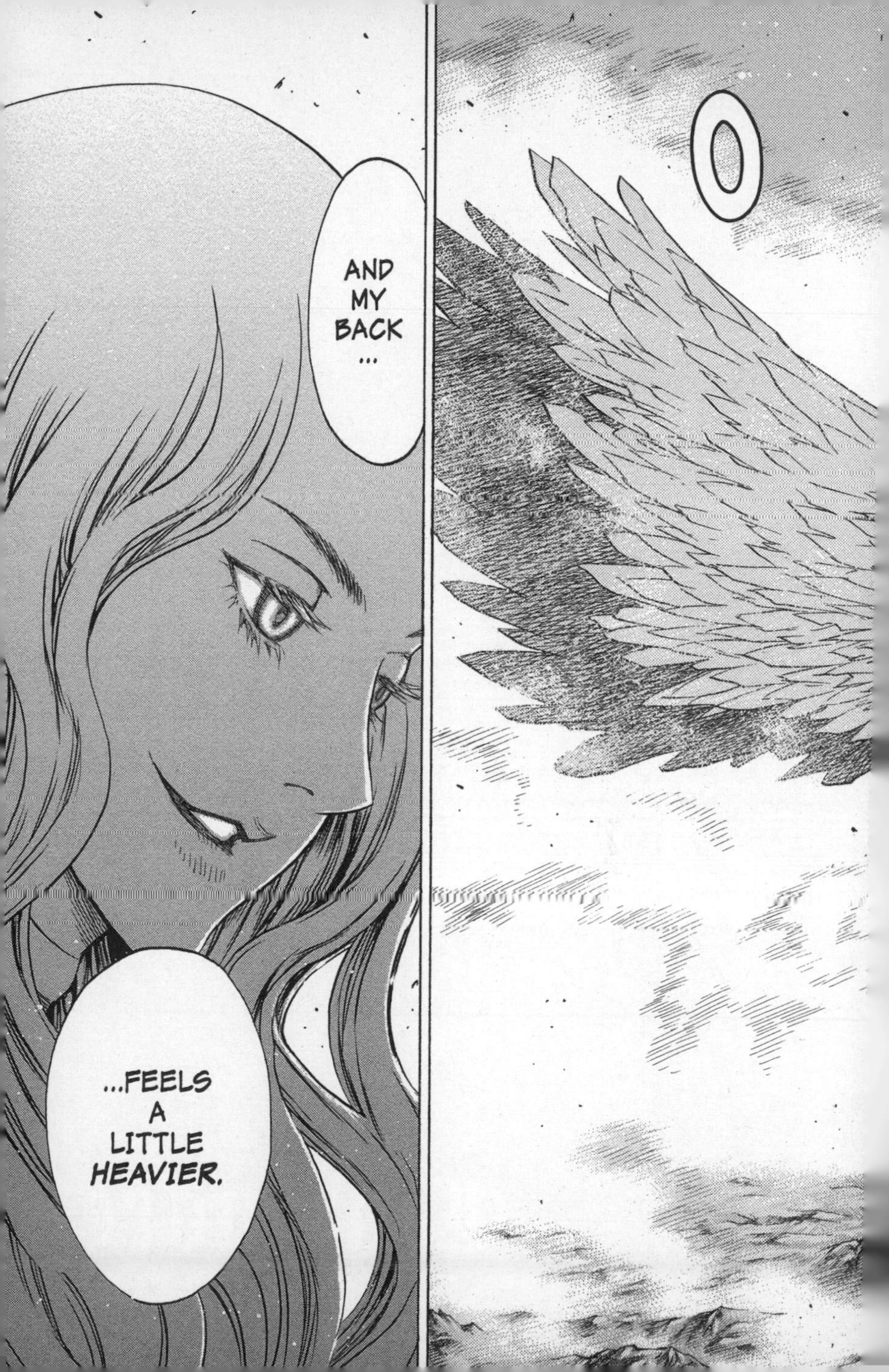
AND MY BACK ...
...FEELS A LITTLE HEAVIER.

クレイモア
Claymore

Scene 154: Silver-Eyed Warriors, Part 5

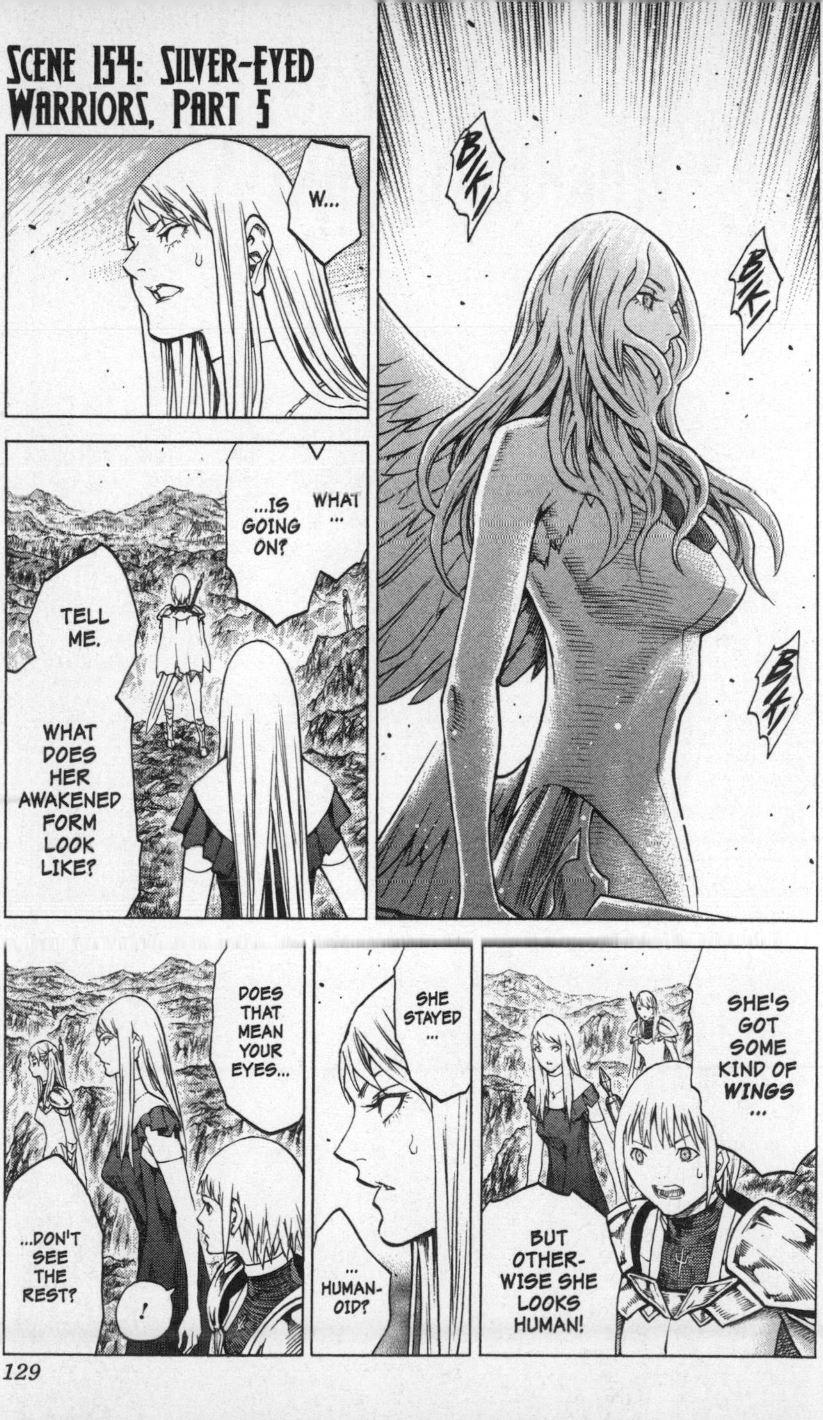
BIKI
BIKI
BIKI
W...
WHAT...
...IS GOING ON?
TELL ME.
WHAT DOES HER AWAKENED FORM LOOK LIKE?
SHE'S GOT SOME KIND OF WINGS...
BUT OTHERWISE SHE LOOKS HUMAN!
SHE STAYED...
...HUMANOID?
DOES THAT MEAN YOUR EYES...
...DON'T SEE THE REST?
!

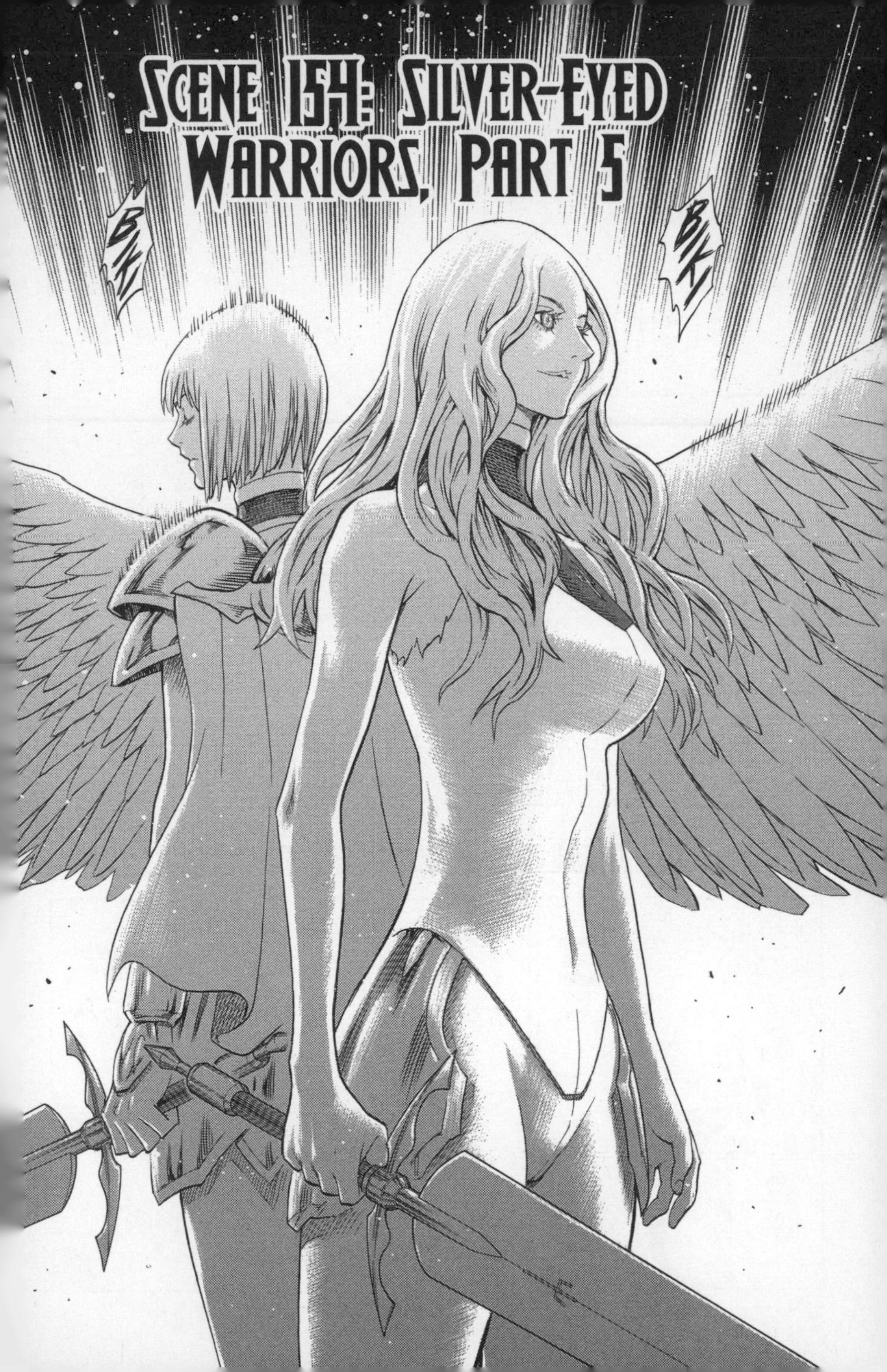

SCENE 154: SILVER-EYED WARRIORS, PART 5
BIKI
BIKI

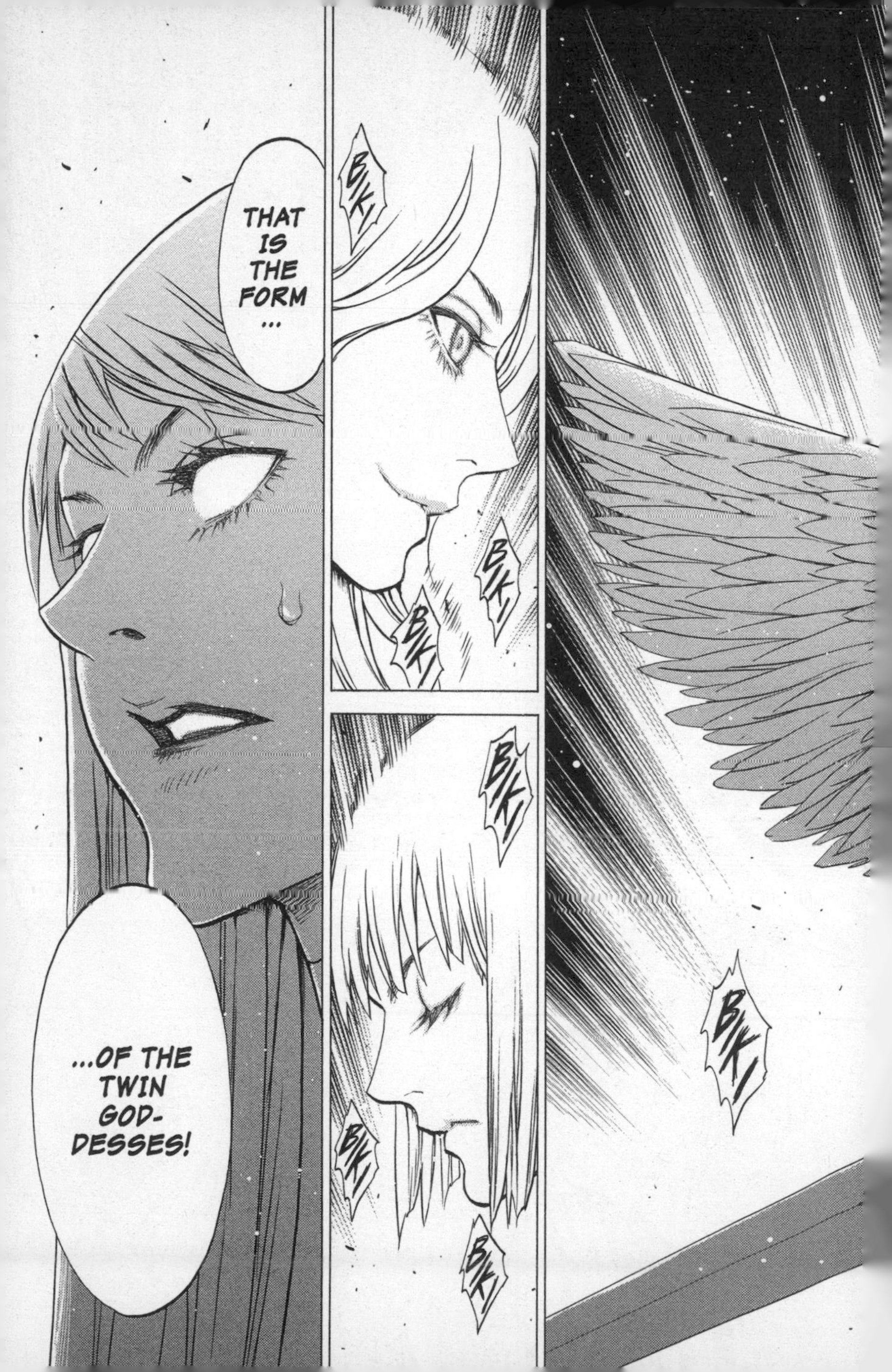
BIKI
BIKI
BIKI
BIKI
BIKI
BIKI
BIKI
THAT IS THE FORM ...
...OF THE TWIN GOD-DESSES!

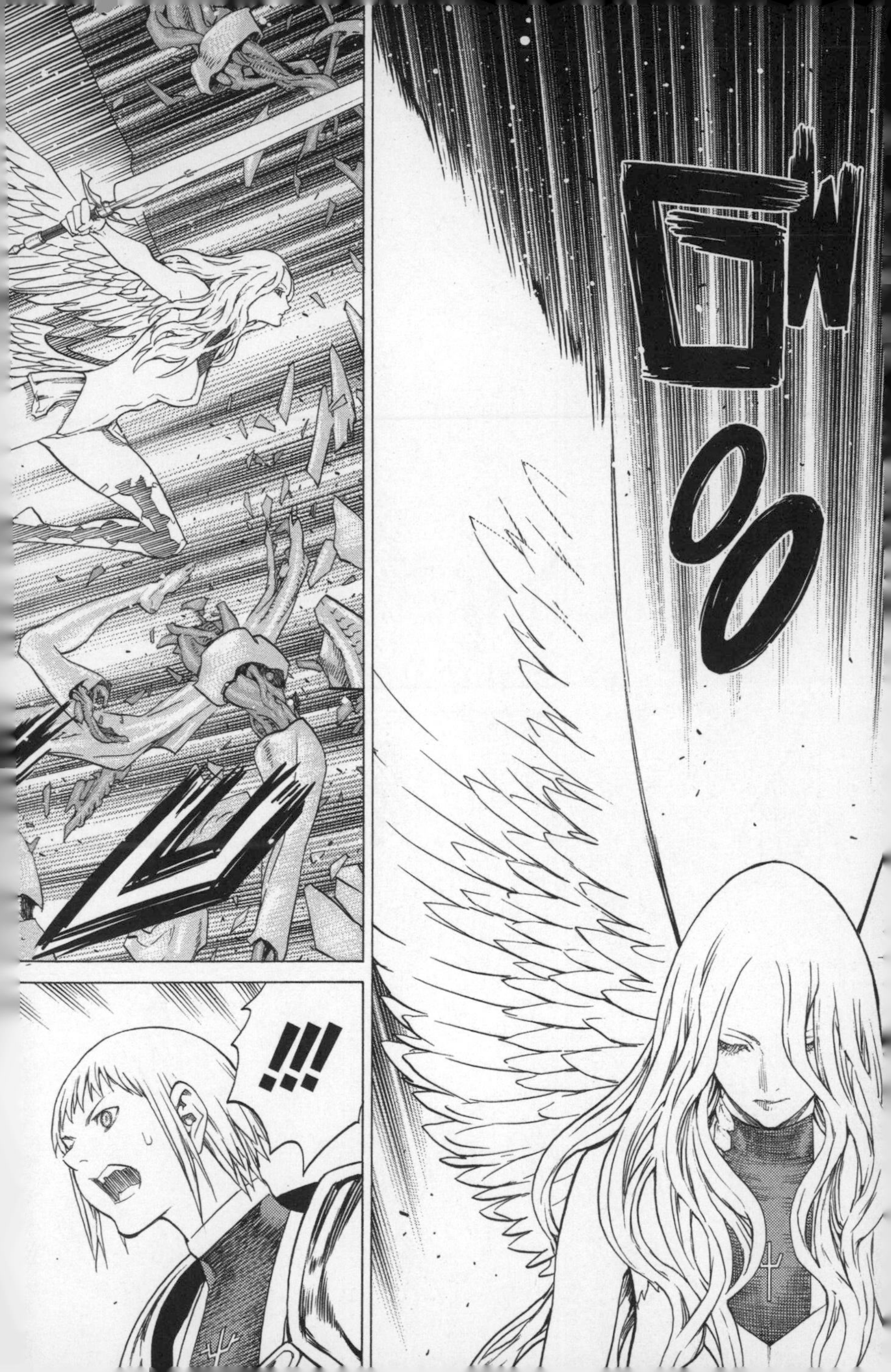
!!!

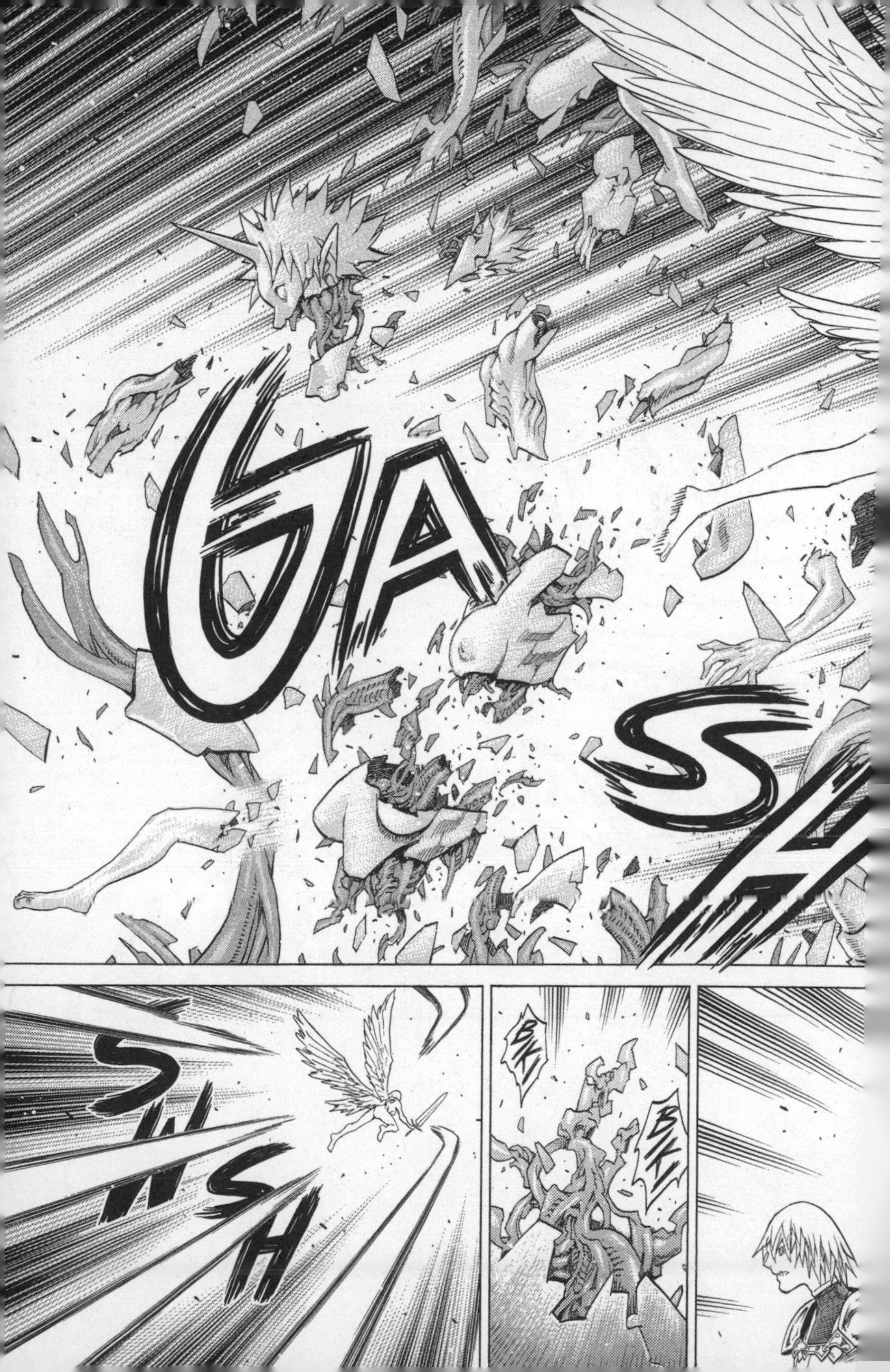
GASH
BKI
BKI
SWSH

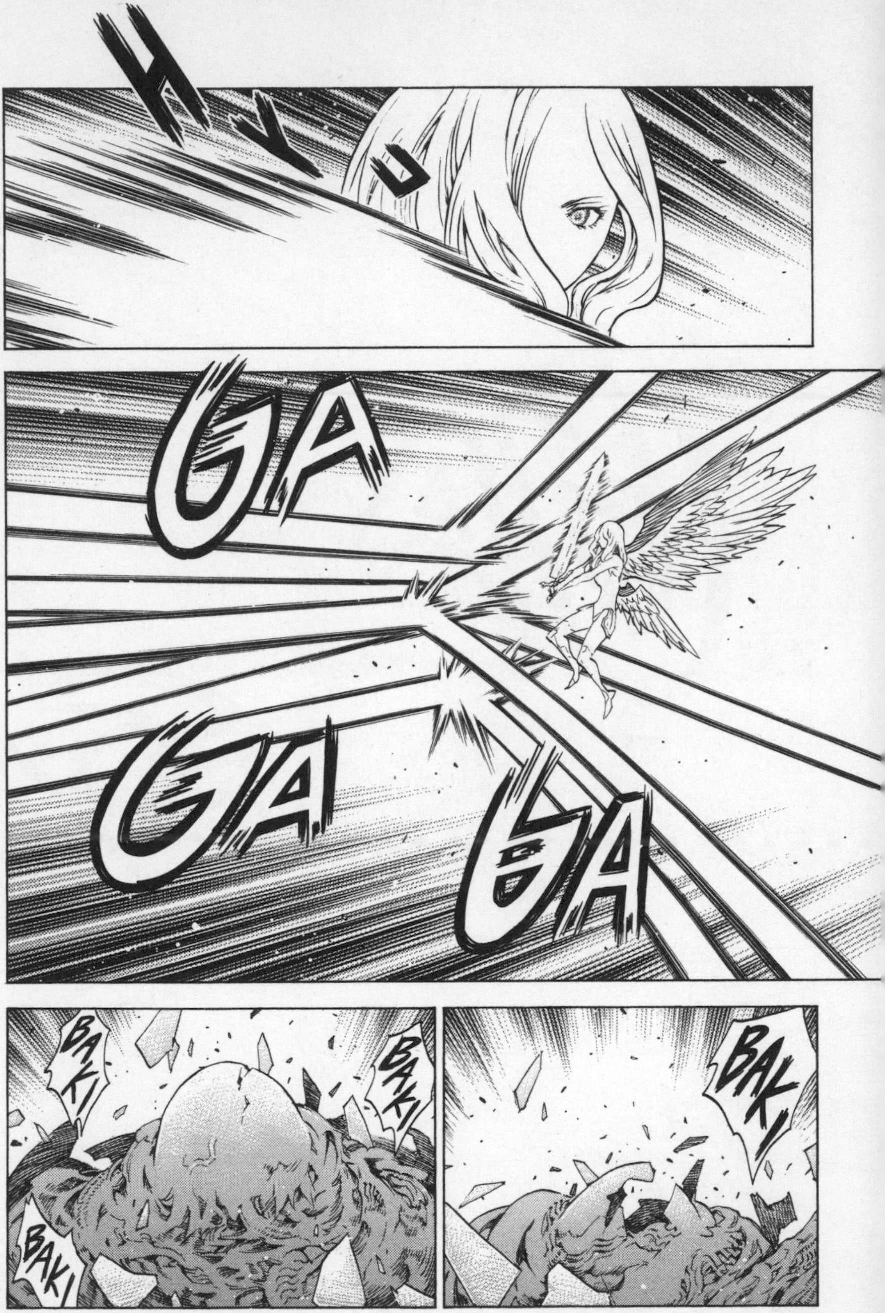
HYU
GA
GA
GA
BAKI
BAKI
BAKI
BAKI

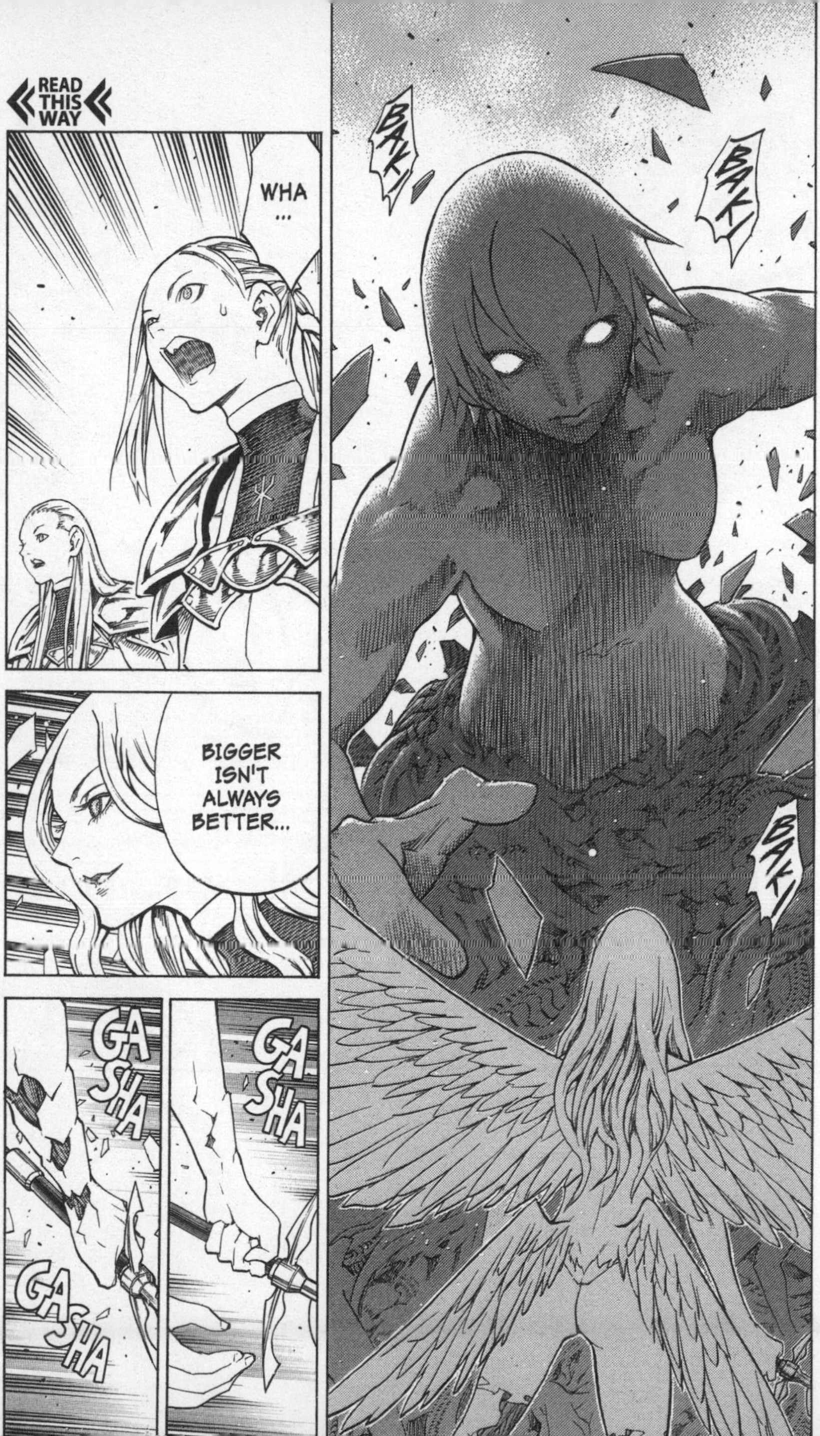
READ THIS WAY
BAKI
BAKI
BAKI
WHA ...
BIGGER ISN'T ALWAYS BETTER...
GASHA
GASHA
GASHA
GASHA

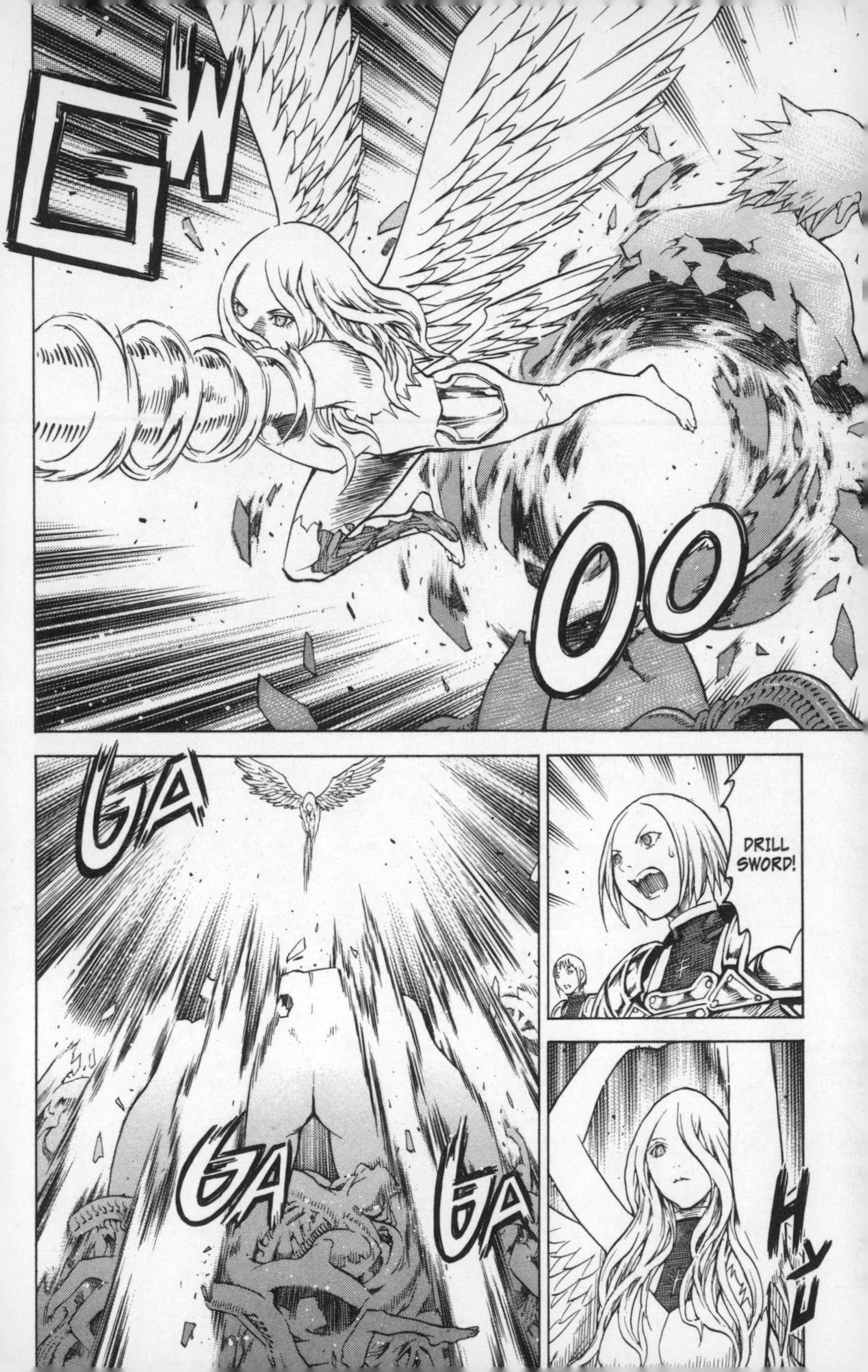
GW
OO
DRILL SWORD!
HYU
GA
GA
GA

READ THIS WAY

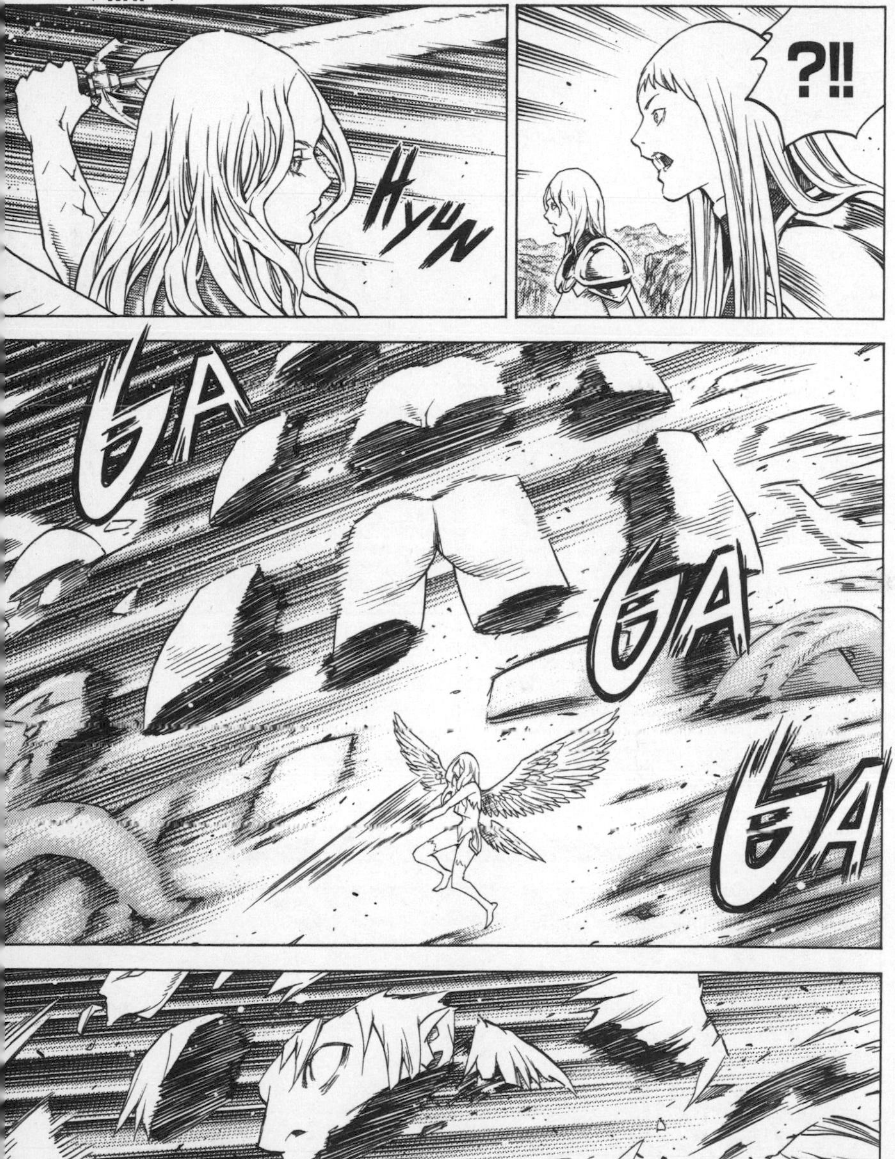
?!!
HYUN
GA
GA
GA

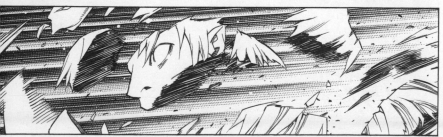

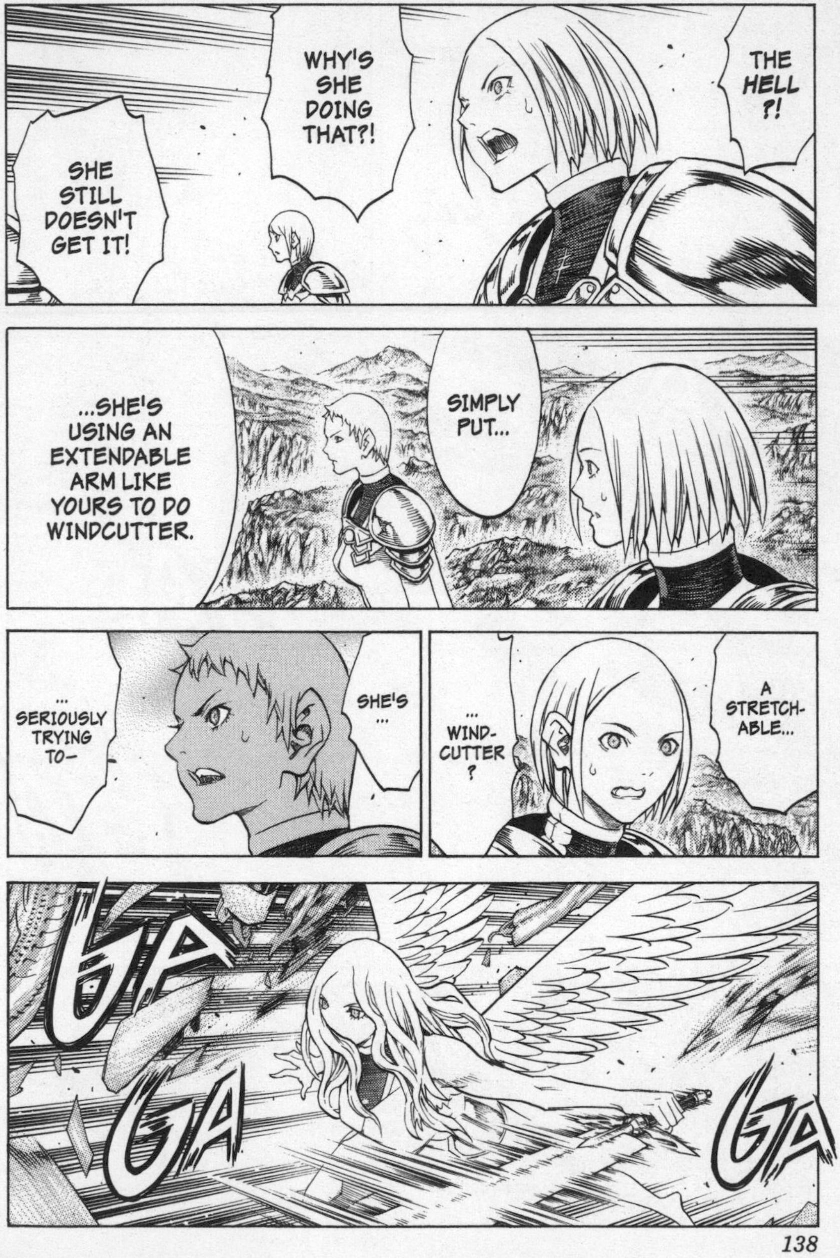
THE HELL ?!
WHY'S SHE DOING THAT?!
SHE STILL DOESN'T GET IT!
SIMPLY PUT...
...SHE'S USING AN EXTENDABLE ARM LIKE YOURS TO DO WINDCUTTER.
A STRETCH-ABLE...
... WIND-CUTTER ?
SHE'S ...
... SERIOUSLY TRYING TO—
GA
GA
GA

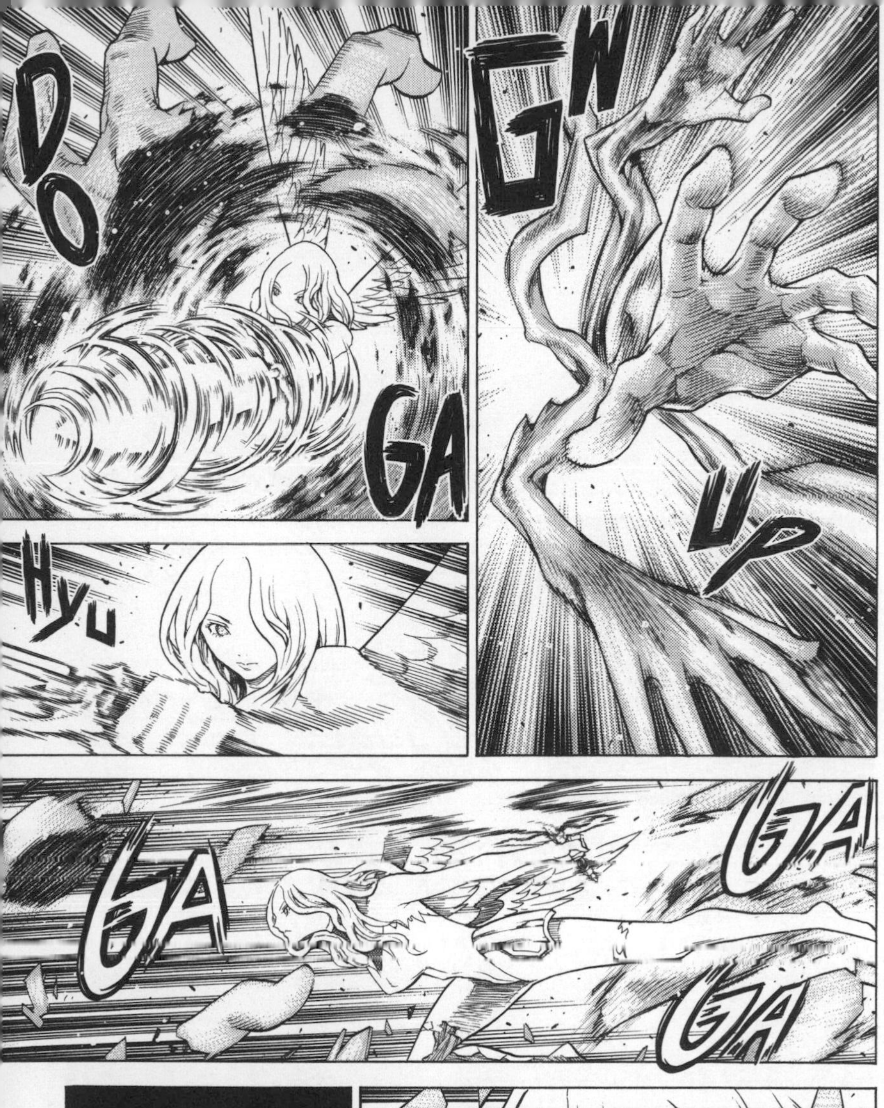
GW
UP
DO
GA
Hyu
GA
GA
GA
IMPRESSIVE, CLARE.

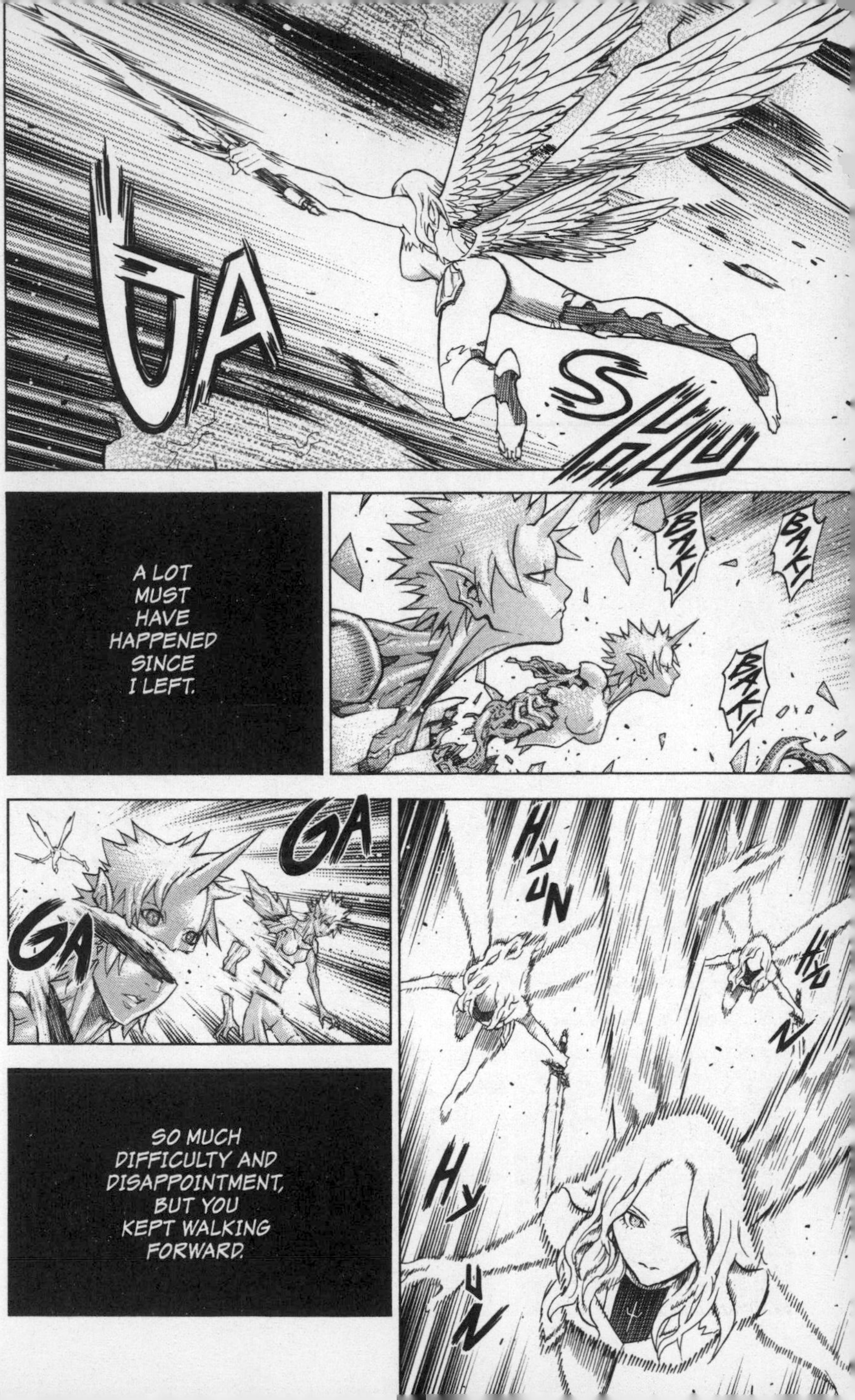
GA
SHUU
BAKI
BAKI
BAKI
A LOT MUST HAVE HAPPENED SINCE I LEFT.
HYUN
HYUN
HYUN
GA
GA
SO MUCH DIFFICULTY AND DISAPPOINTMENT, BUT YOU KEPT WALKING FORWARD.

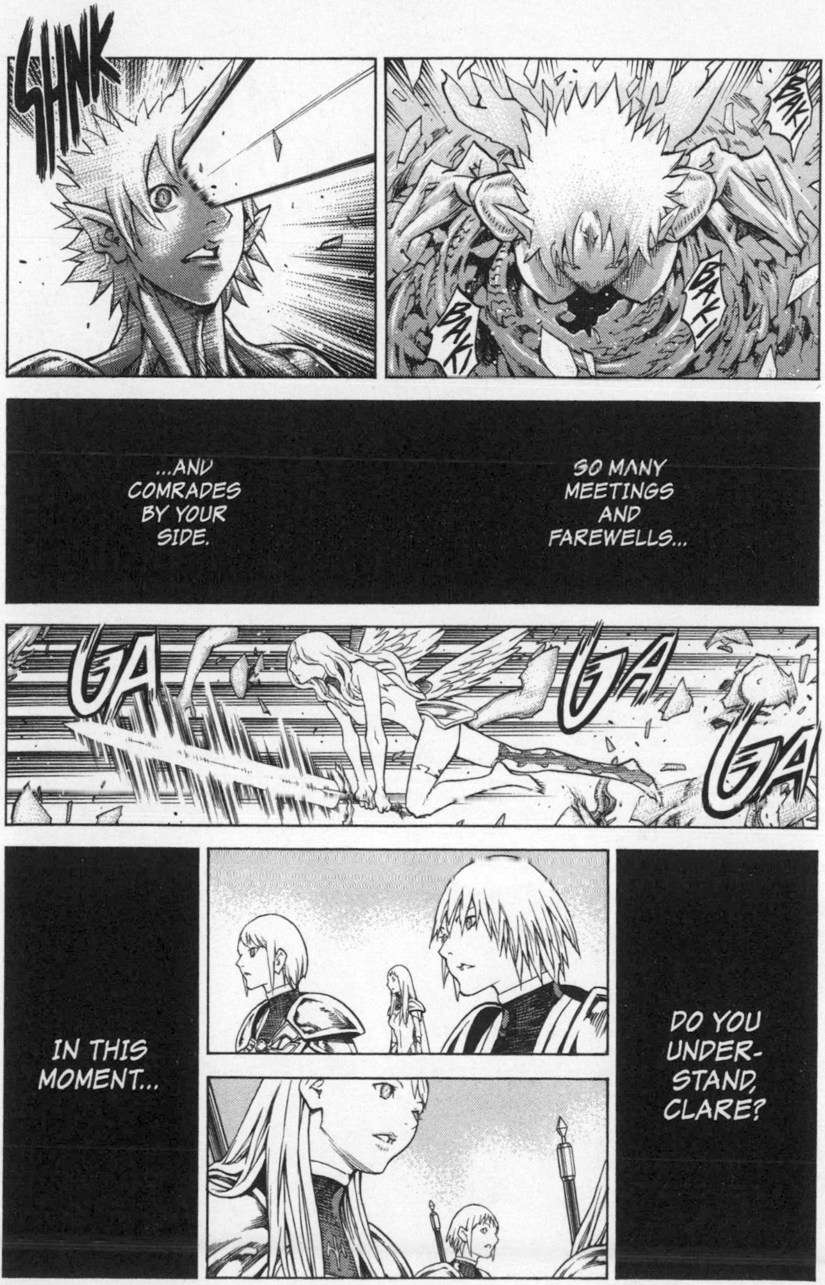
BAKI
BAKI
BAKI
SHNK
SO MANY MEETINGS AND FAREWELLS...
...AND COMRADES BY YOUR SIDE.
GA
GA
GA
DO YOU UNDER-STAND, CLARE?
IN THIS MOMENT...

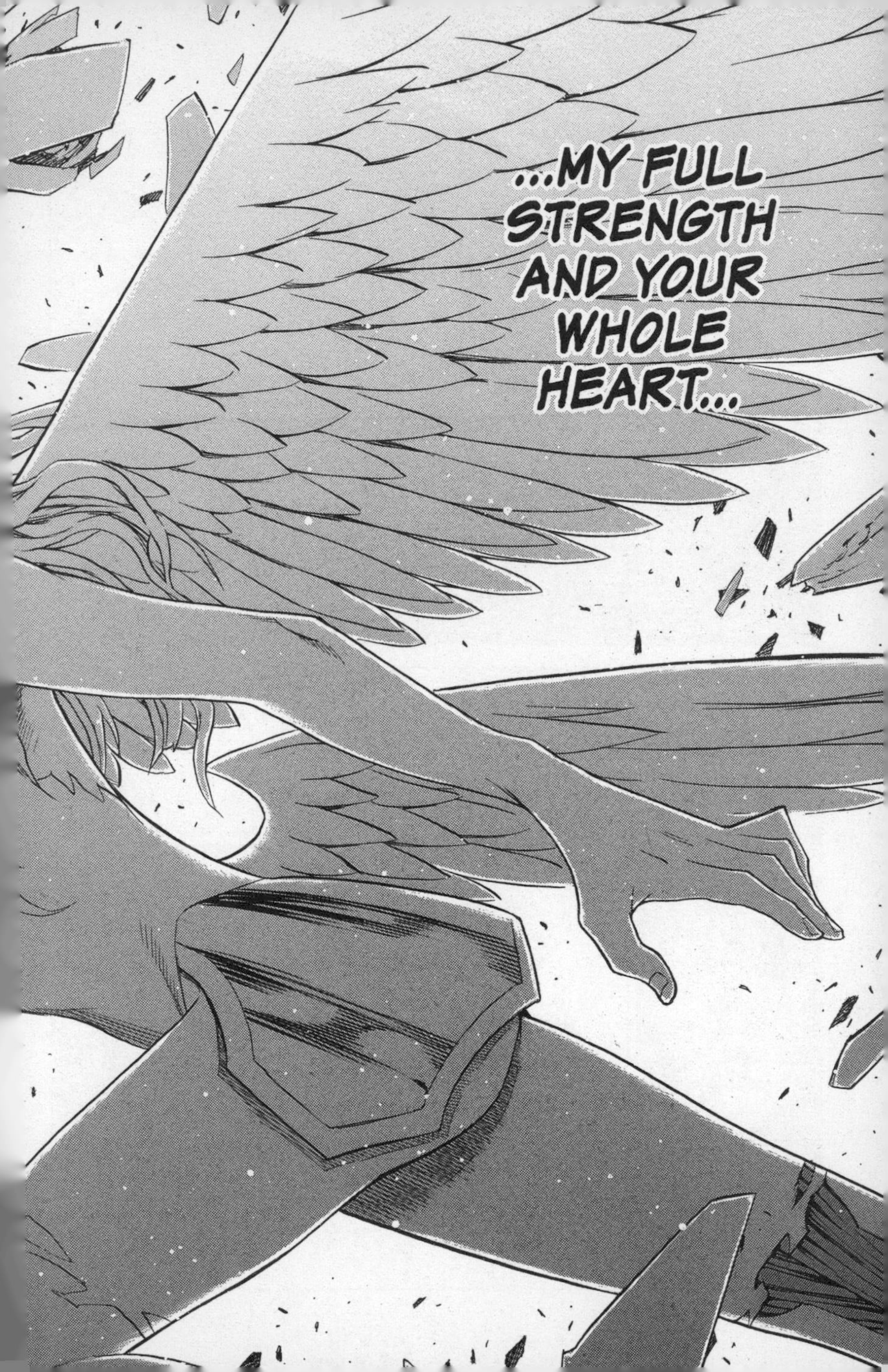
...MY FULL STRENGTH AND YOUR WHOLE HEART...

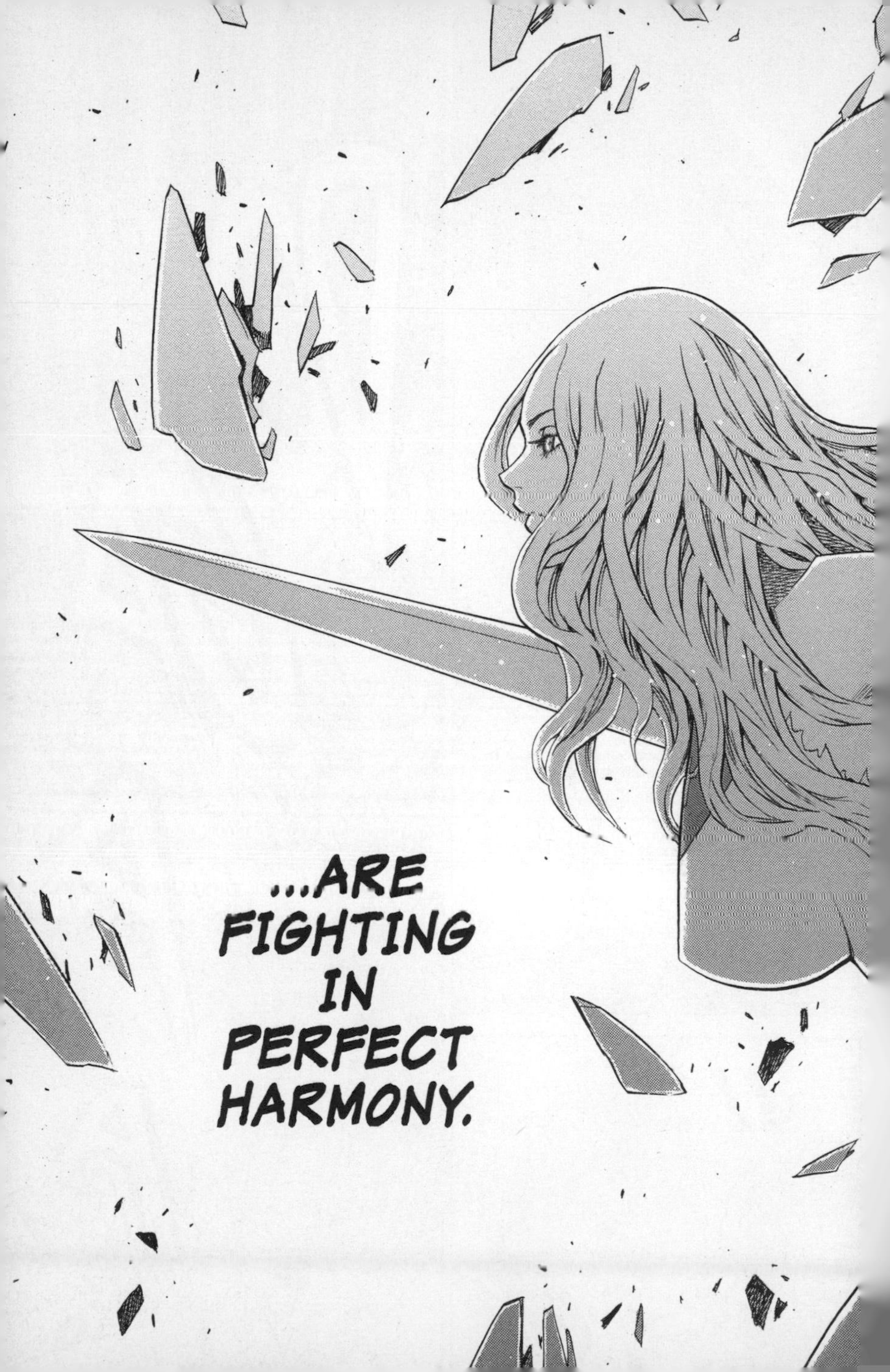
...ARE FIGHTING IN PERFECT HARMONY.

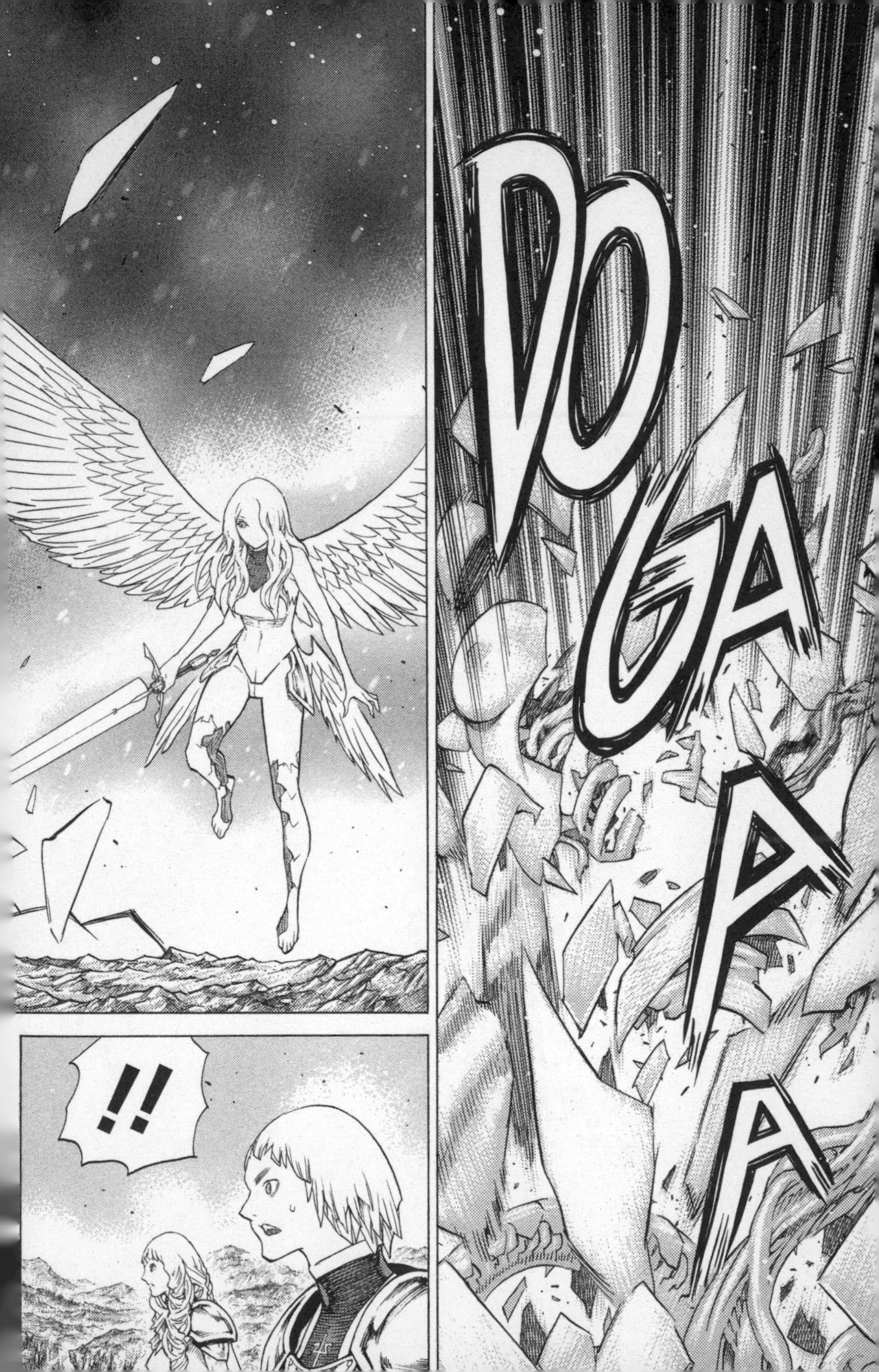
DOGAAA
!!

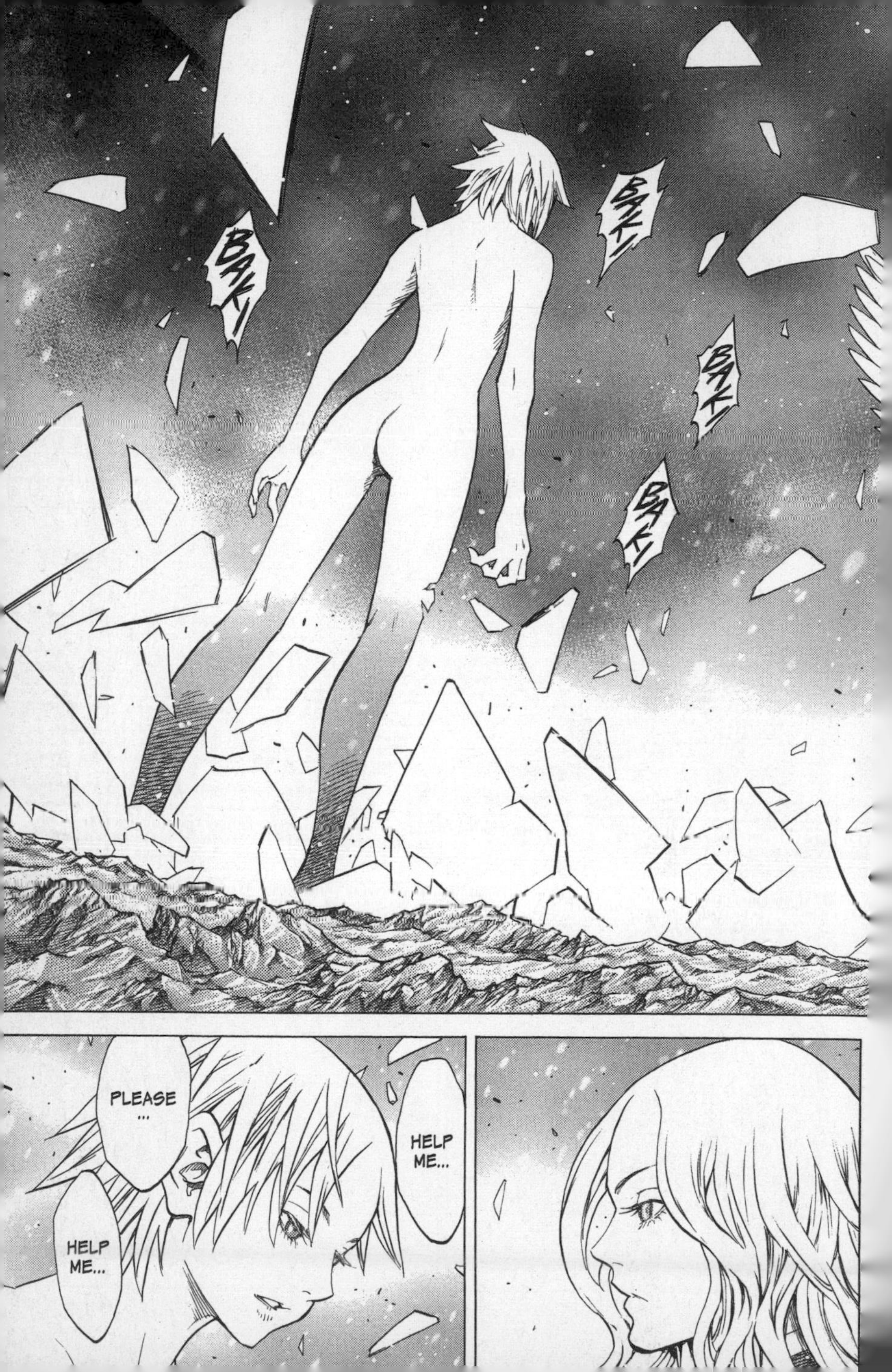
BAKI
BAKI
BAKI
BAKI
PLEASE ...
HELP ME...
HELP ME...

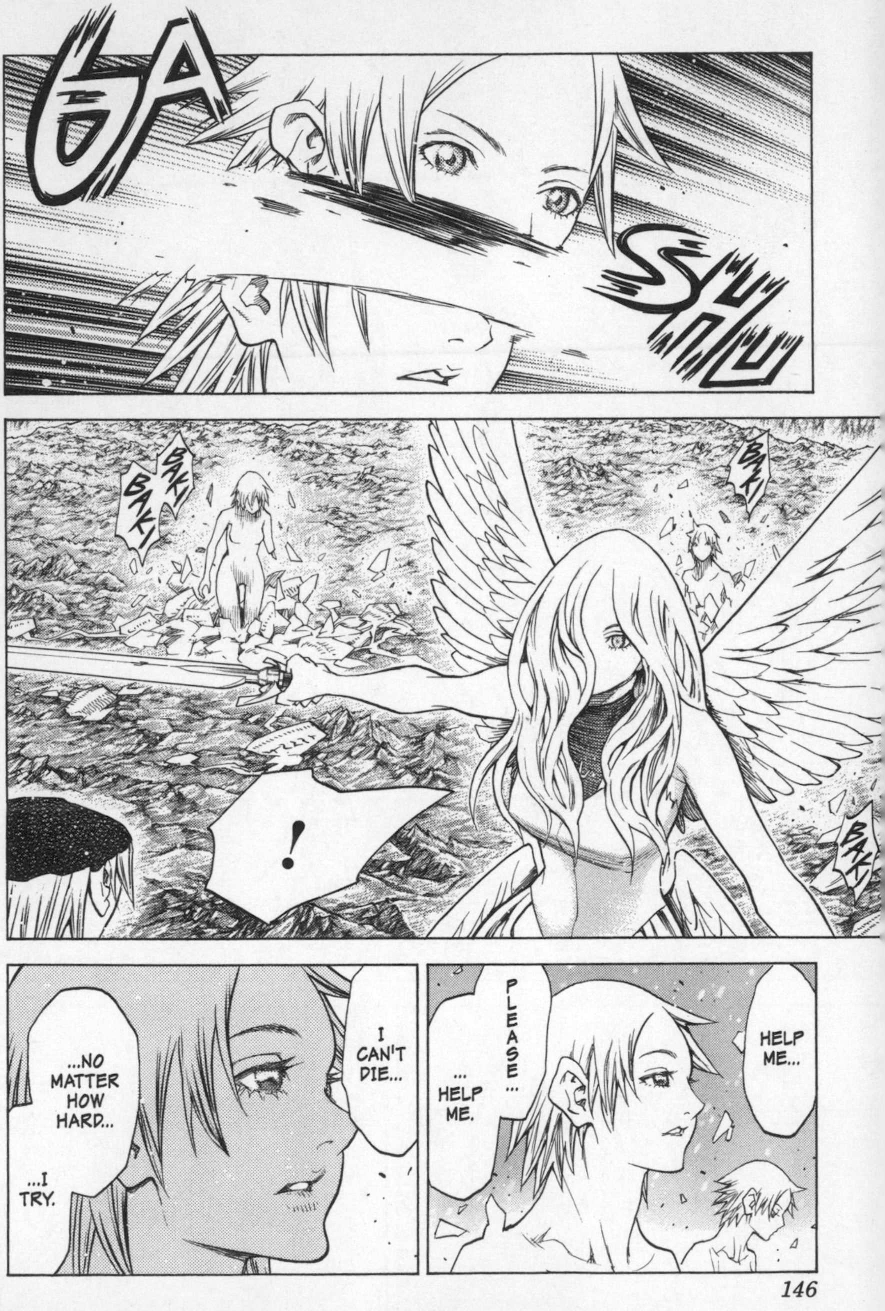
GA
SHU
BAKI
BAKI
BAKI BAKI
!
HELP ME...
PLEASE...
...HELP ME.
I CAN'T DIE...
...NO MATTER HOW HARD...
...I TRY.

READ THIS WAY

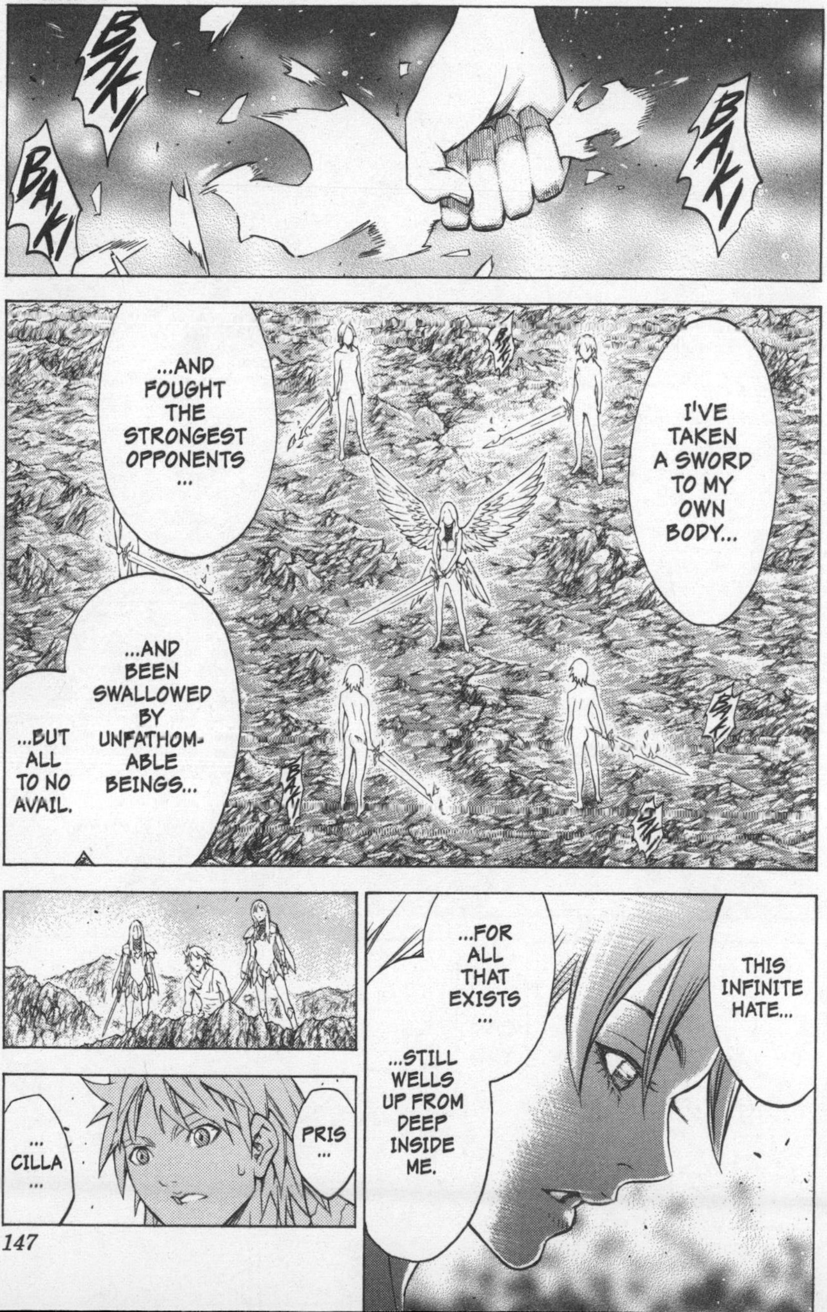
BAKI
BAKI
BAKI
I'VE TAKEN A SWORD TO MY OWN BODY...
...AND FOUGHT THE STRONGEST OPPONENTS...
...AND BEEN SWALLOWED BY UNFATHOMABLE BEINGS...
...BUT ALL TO NO AVAIL.
THIS INFINITE HATE...
...FOR ALL THAT EXISTS...
...STILL WELLS UP FROM DEEP INSIDE ME.
PRIS...
...CILLA...

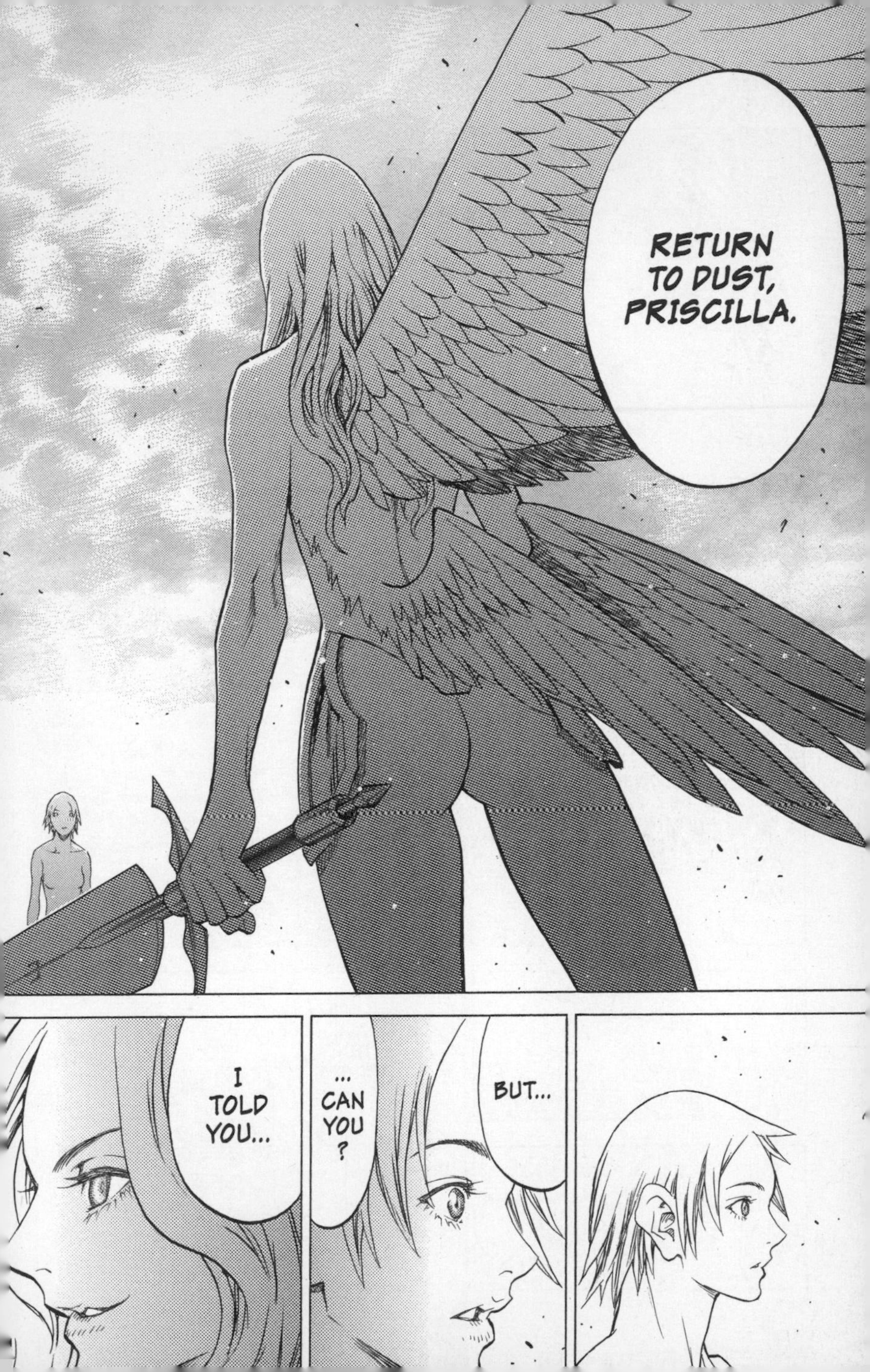
RETURN TO DUST, PRISCILLA.
BUT...
... CAN YOU ?
I TOLD YOU...

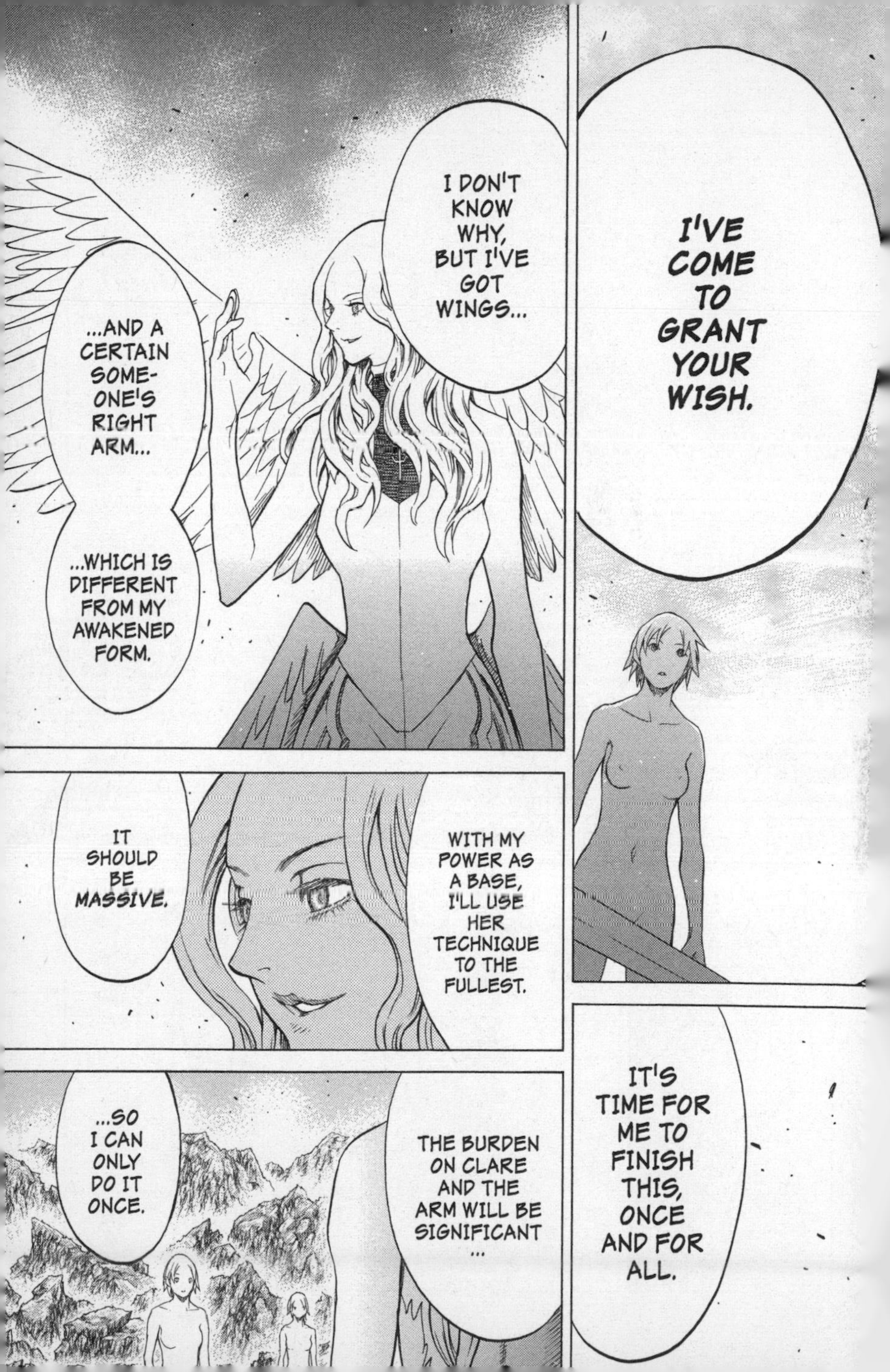
I'VE COME TO GRANT YOUR WISH.
I DON'T KNOW WHY, BUT I'VE GOT WINGS...
...AND A CERTAIN SOME-ONE'S RIGHT ARM...
...WHICH IS DIFFERENT FROM MY AWAKENED FORM.
WITH MY POWER AS A BASE, I'LL USE HER TECHNIQUE TO THE FULLEST.
IT SHOULD BE MASSIVE.
IT'S TIME FOR ME TO FINISH THIS, ONCE AND FOR ALL.
THE BURDEN ON CLARE AND THE ARM WILL BE SIGNIFICANT...
...SO I CAN ONLY DO IT ONCE.

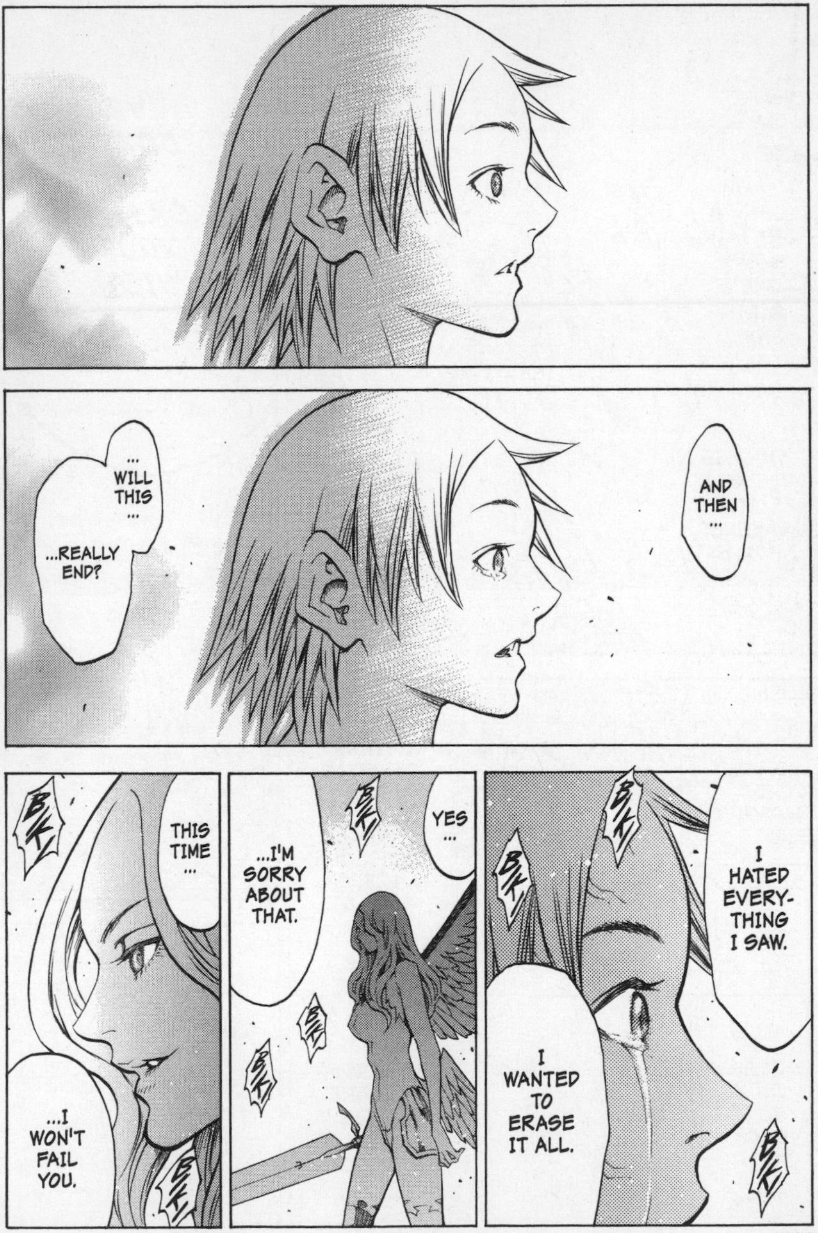
AND THEN ...
... WILL THIS ... ...REALLY END?
BKI
BKI
I HATED EVERY-THING I SAW.
I WANTED TO ERASE IT ALL.
BKI
YES ...
BKI
...I'M SORRY ABOUT THAT.
BKI
BKI
BKI
THIS TIME ...
...I WON'T FAIL YOU.
BKI

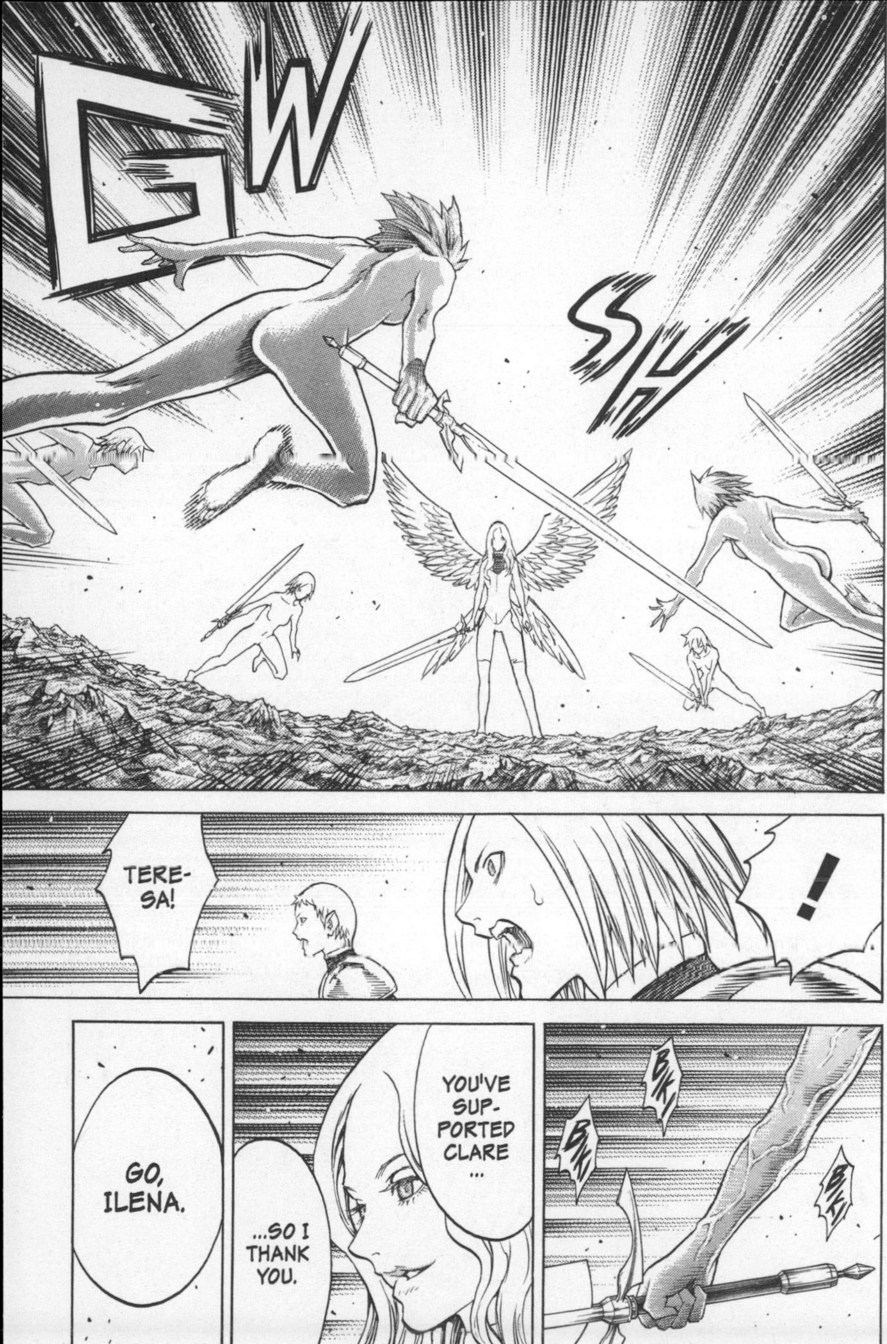
SHH
GW
!
TERE-SA!
BKI
BKI
BKI
YOU'VE SUP-PORTED CLARE ...
...SO I THANK YOU.
GO, ILENA.

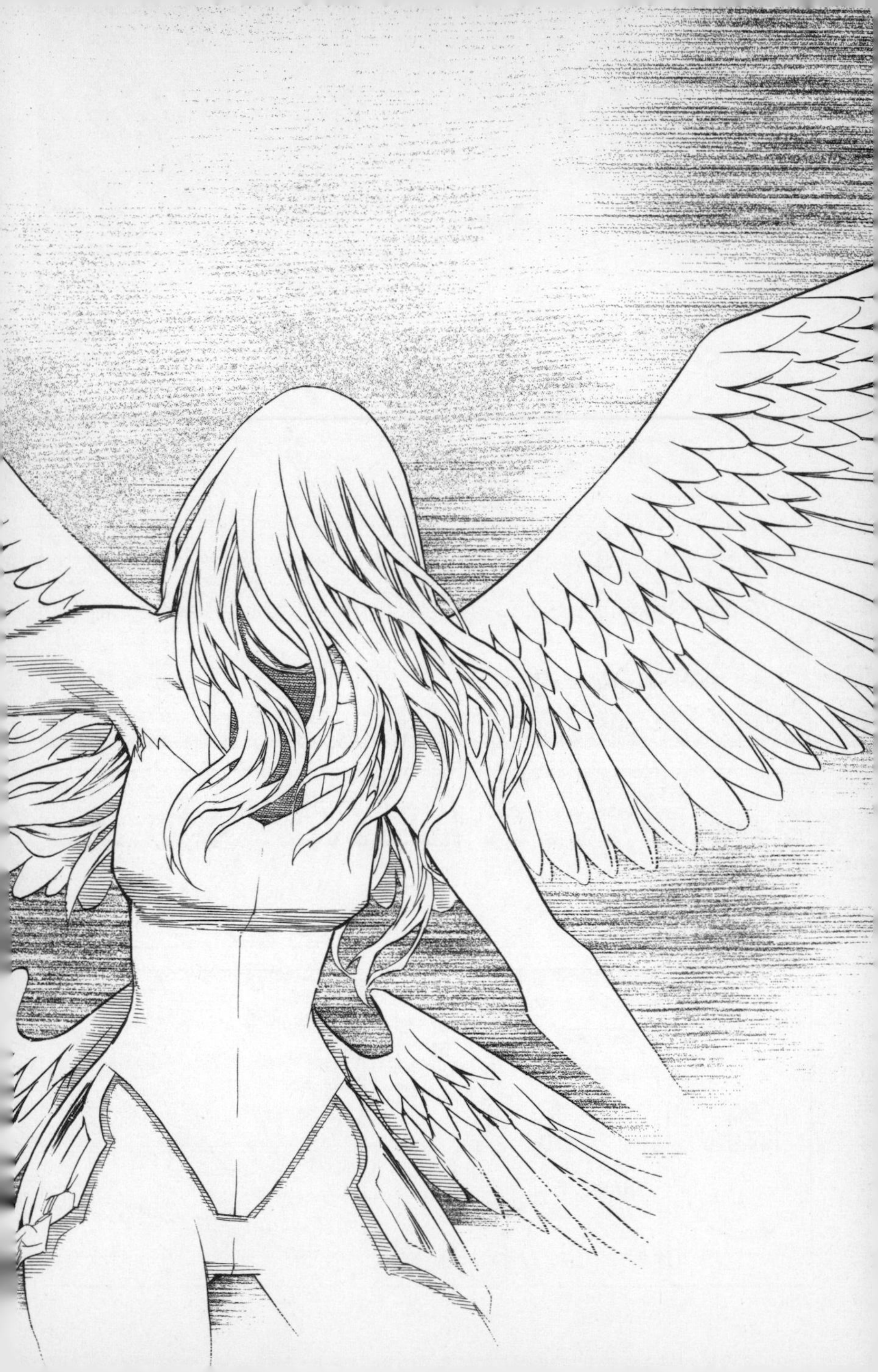

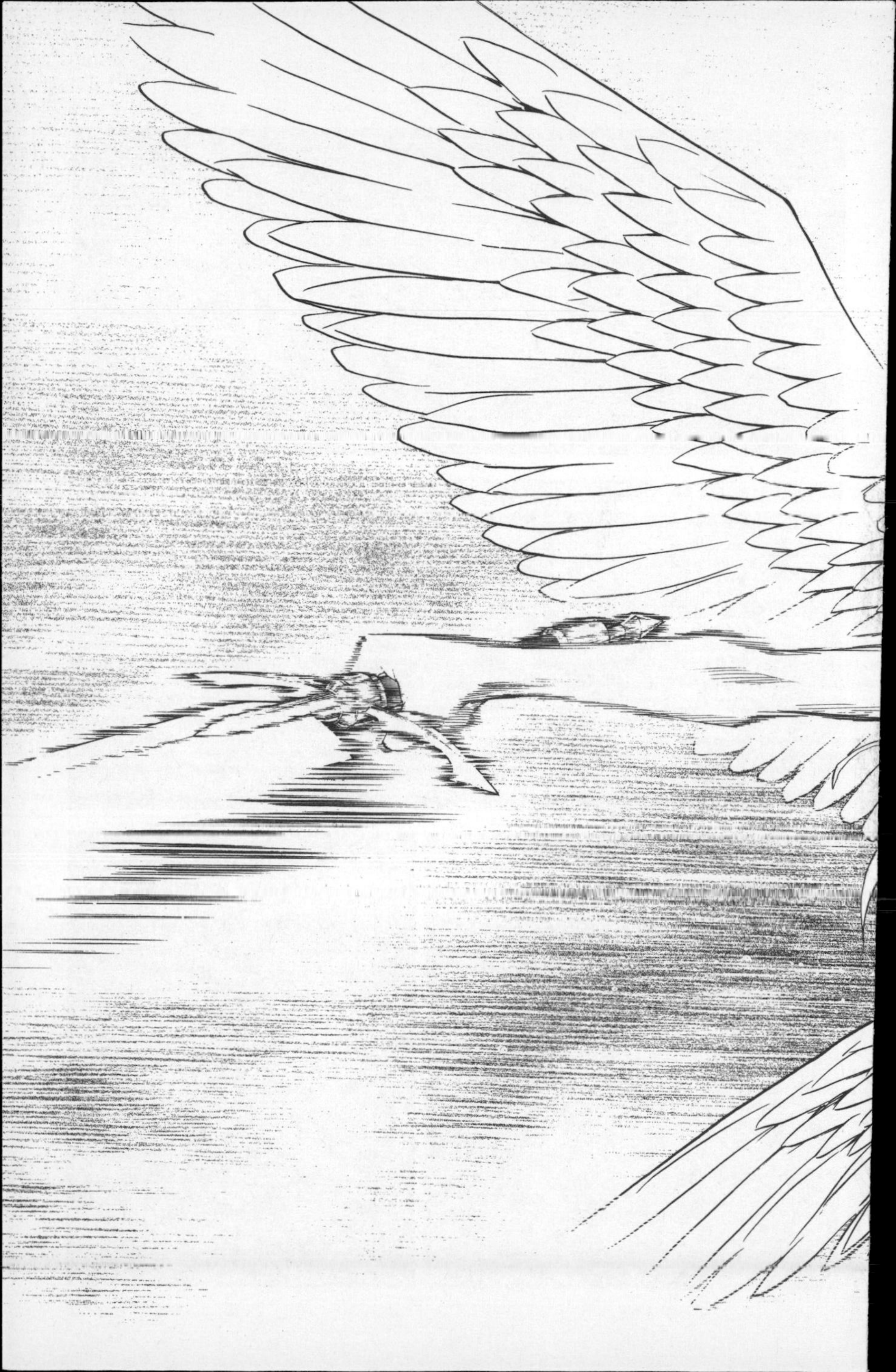

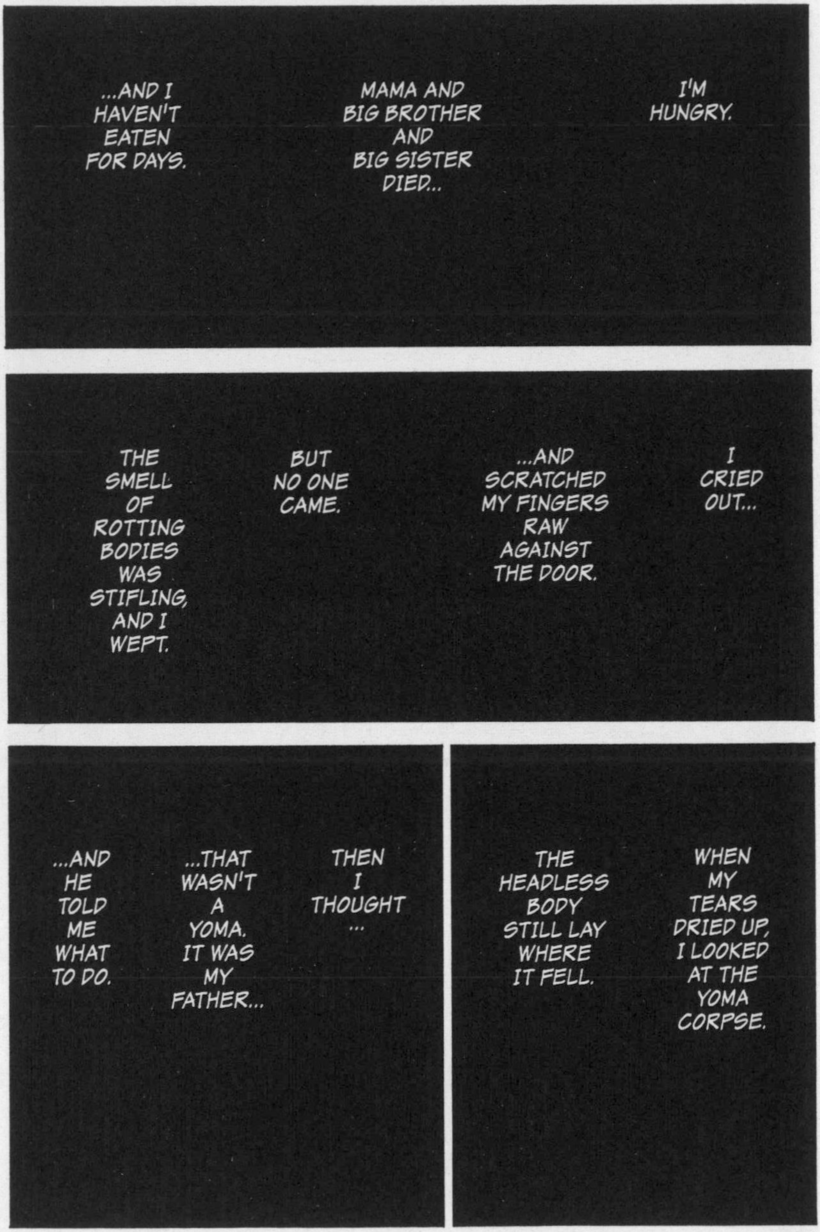
I'M HUNGRY.
MAMA AND BIG BROTHER AND BIG SISTER DIED...
...AND I HAVEN'T EATEN FOR DAYS.
I CRIED OUT...
...AND SCRATCHED MY FINGERS RAW AGAINST THE DOOR.
BUT NO ONE CAME.
THE SMELL OF ROTTING BODIES WAS STIFLING, AND I WEPT.
WHEN MY TEARS DRIED UP, I LOOKED AT THE YOMA CORPSE.
THE HEADLESS BODY STILL LAY WHERE IT FELL.
THEN I THOUGHT...
...THAT WASN'T A YOMA. IT WAS MY FATHER...
...AND HE TOLD ME WHAT TO DO.

READ THIS WAY

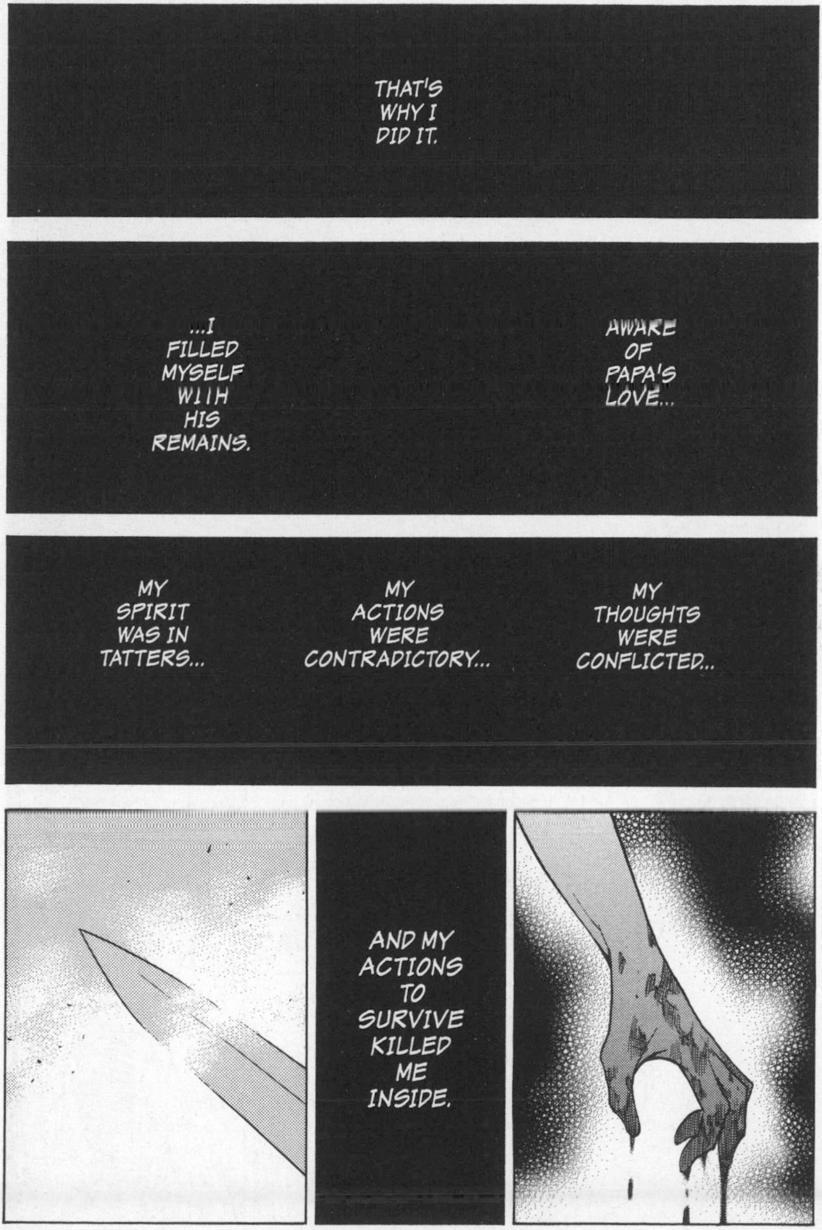
THAT'S WHY I DID IT.
AWARE OF PAPA'S LOVE...
...I FILLED MYSELF WITH HIS REMAINS.
MY THOUGHTS WERE CONFLICTED...
MY ACTIONS WERE CONTRADICTORY...
MY SPIRIT WAS IN TATTERS...
AND MY ACTIONS TO SURVIVE KILLED ME INSIDE.

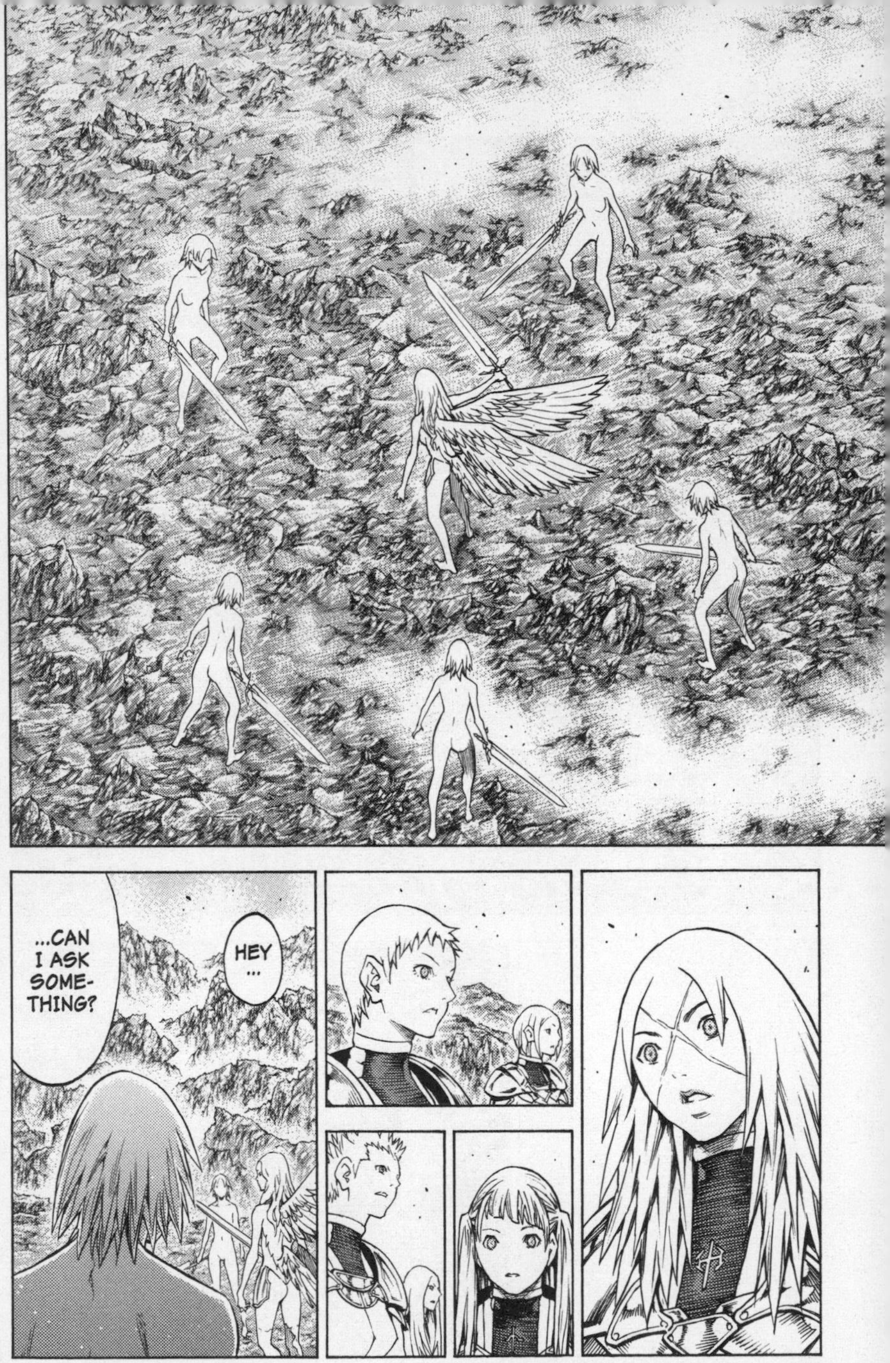
HEY ...
...CAN I ASK SOMETHING?

READ THIS WAY

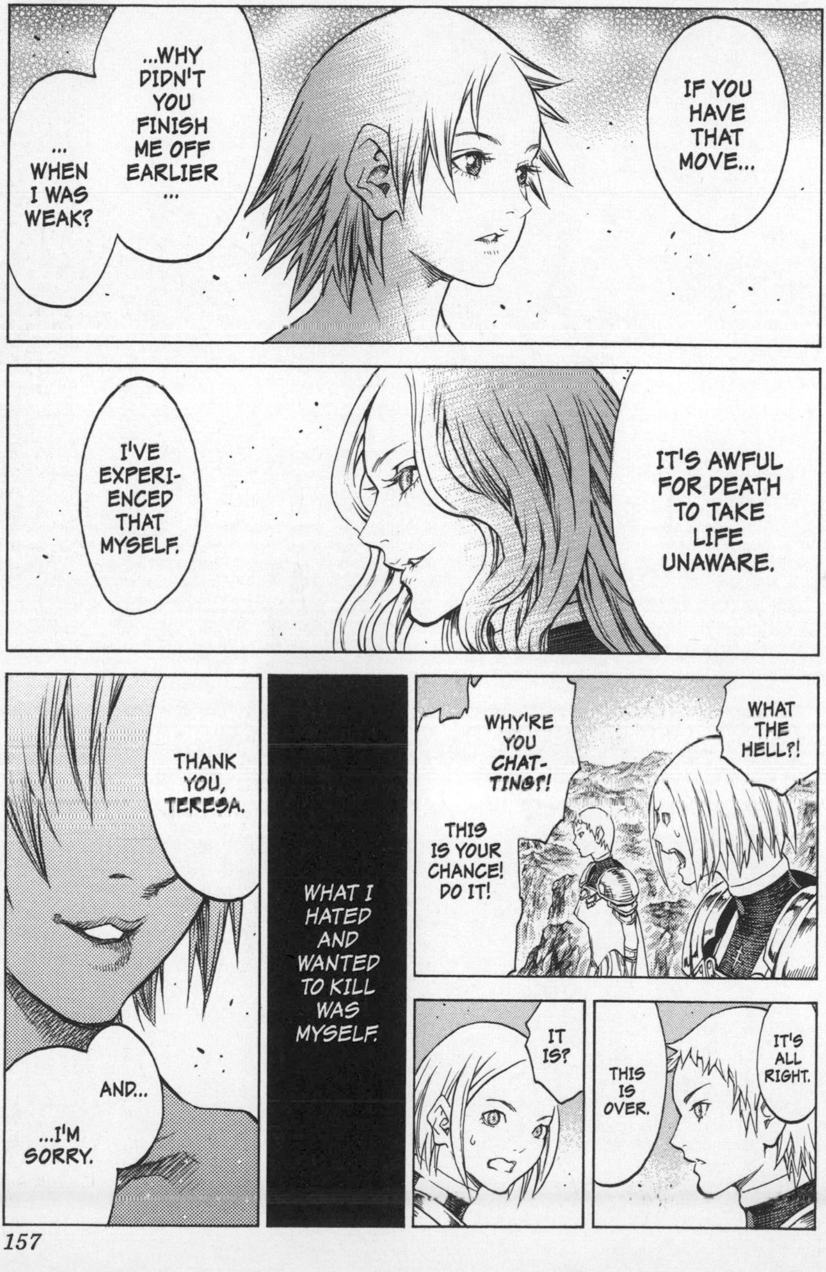
IF YOU HAVE THAT MOVE...
...WHY DIDN'T YOU FINISH ME OFF EARLIER ...
... WHEN I WAS WEAK?
IT'S AWFUL FOR DEATH TO TAKE LIFE UNAWARE.
I'VE EXPERI-ENCED THAT MYSELF.
WHAT THE HELL?!
WHY'RE YOU CHAT-TING?!
THIS IS YOUR CHANCE! DO IT!
IT'S ALL RIGHT.
THIS IS OVER.
IT IS?
WHAT I HATED AND WANTED TO KILL WAS MYSELF.
THANK YOU, TERESA.
AND...
...I'M SORRY.

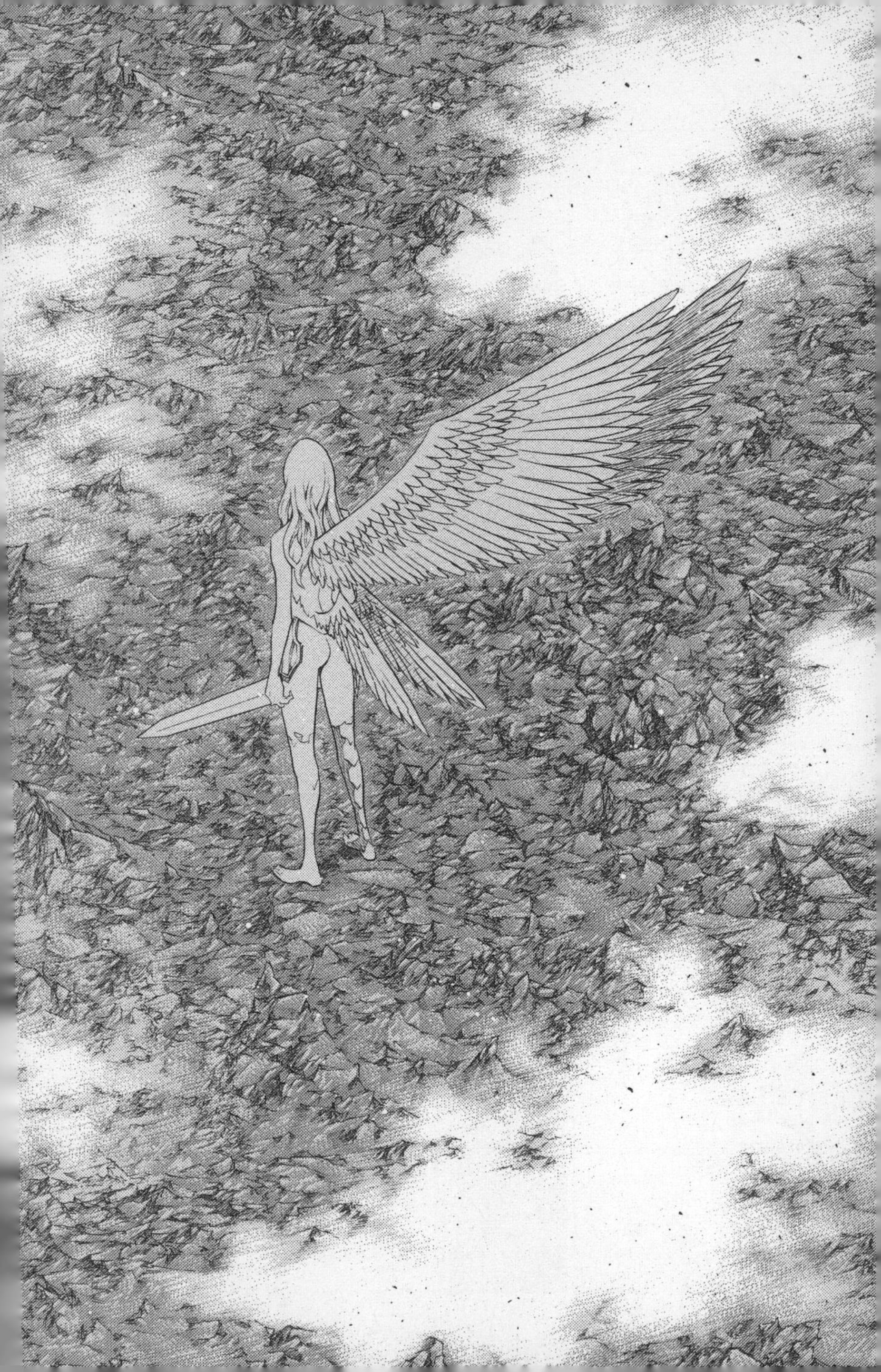

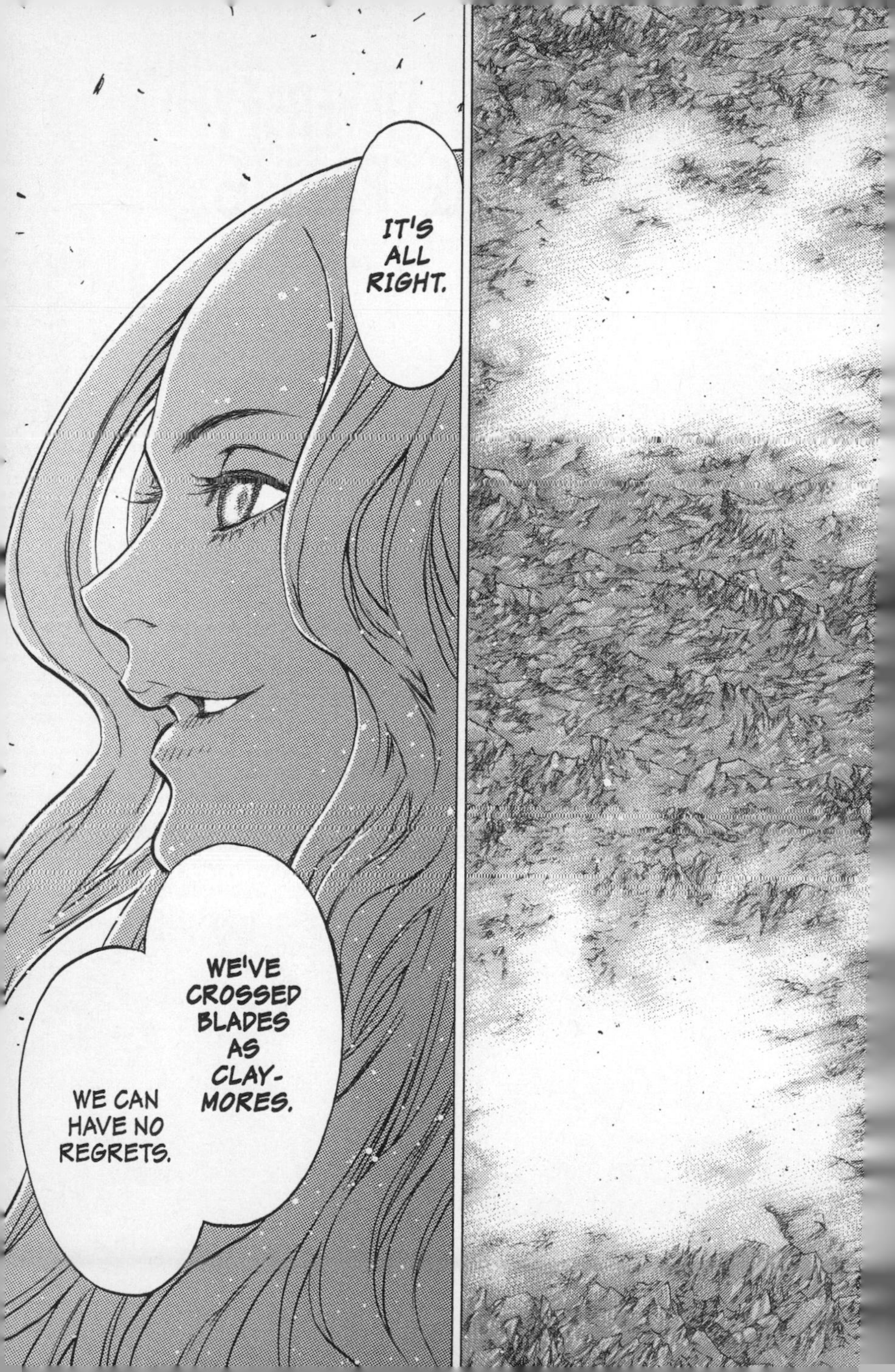
IT'S ALL RIGHT.
WE'VE CROSSED BLADES AS CLAY-MORES.
WE CAN HAVE NO REGRETS.

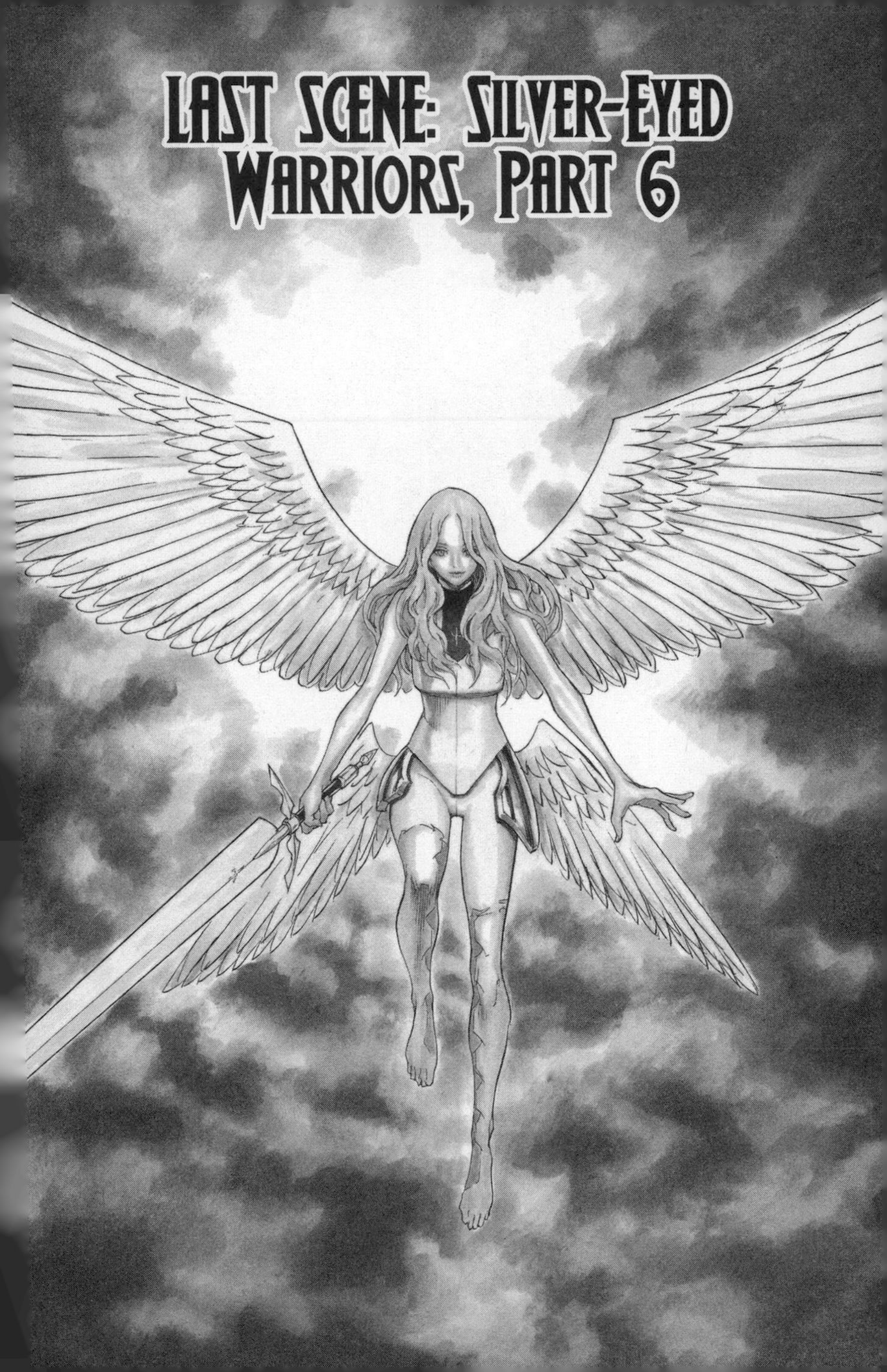
LAST SCENE: SILVER-EYED WARRIORS, PART 6

READ THIS WAY

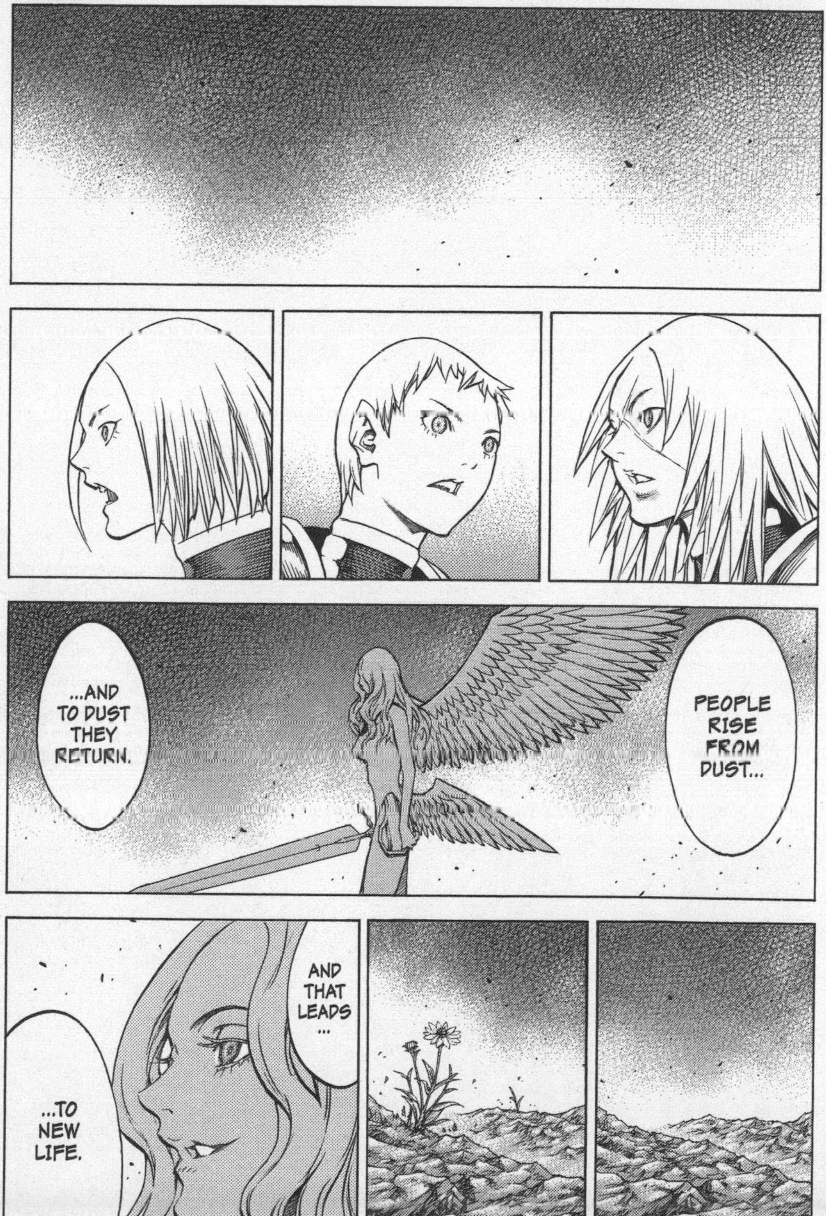
PEOPLE RISE FROM DUST...
...AND TO DUST THEY RETURN.
AND THAT LEADS ...
...TO NEW LIFE.

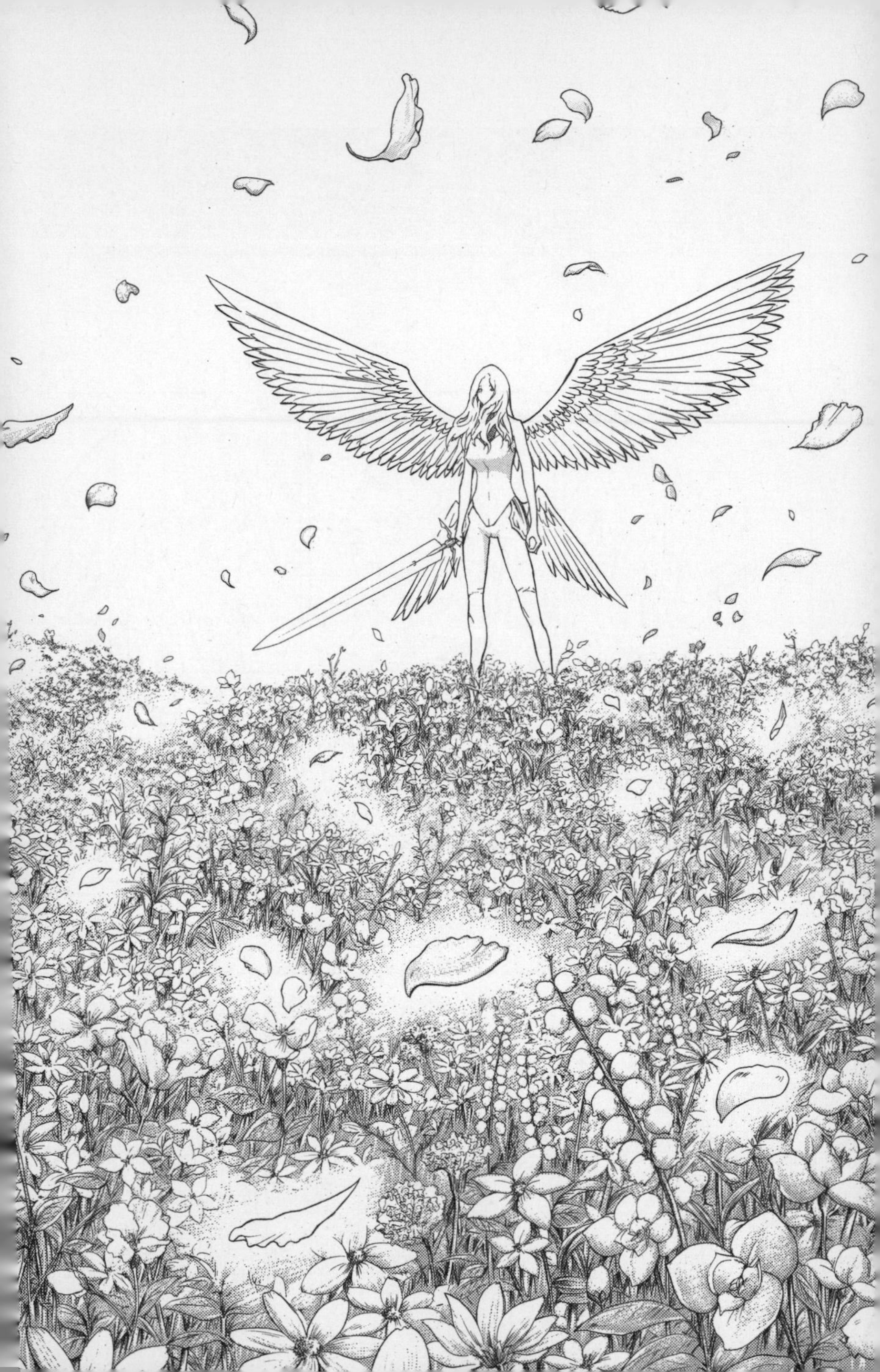

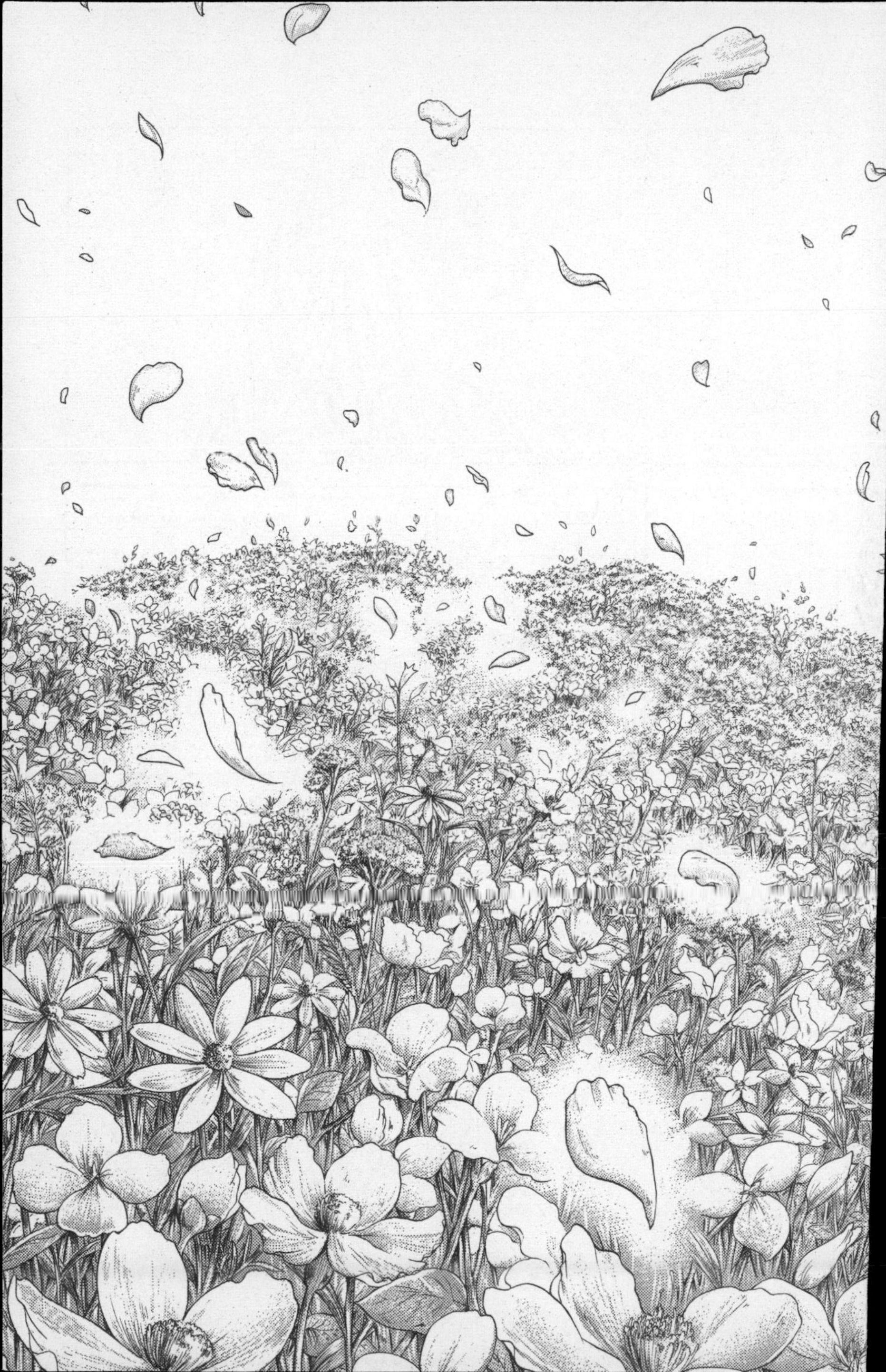

...
SOB
SOB
!
GASHI
CRY WHILE YOU CAN.
BE-CAUSE...
...YOU MUSTN'T CRY IN FRONT OF CLARE.

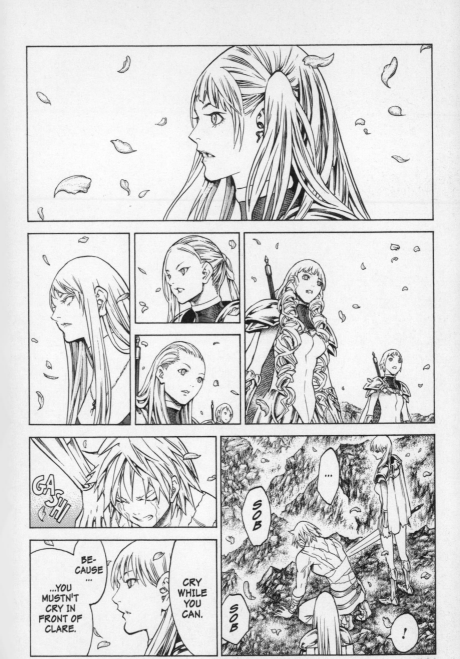

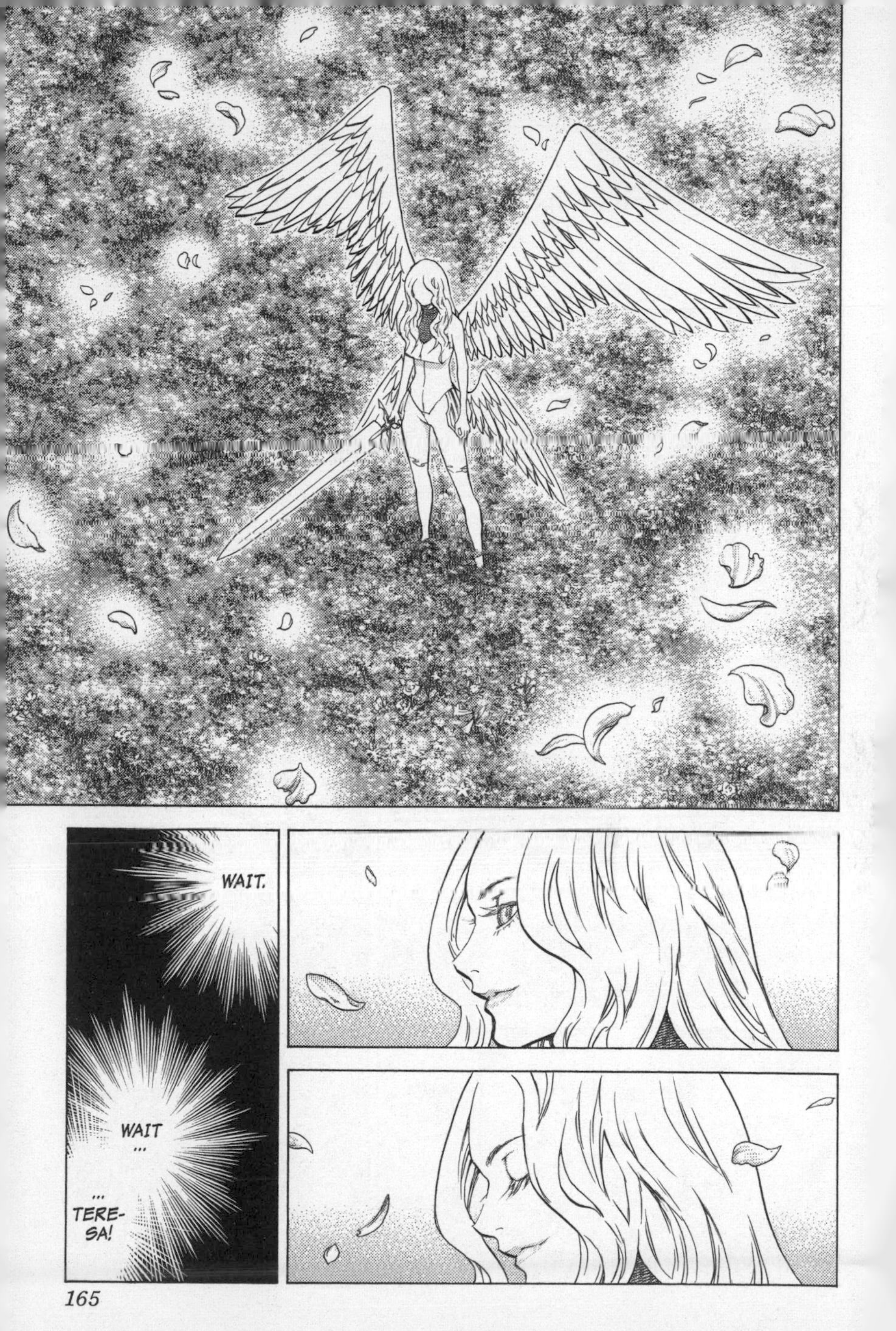
WAIT.
WAIT
...
...
TERE-
SA!

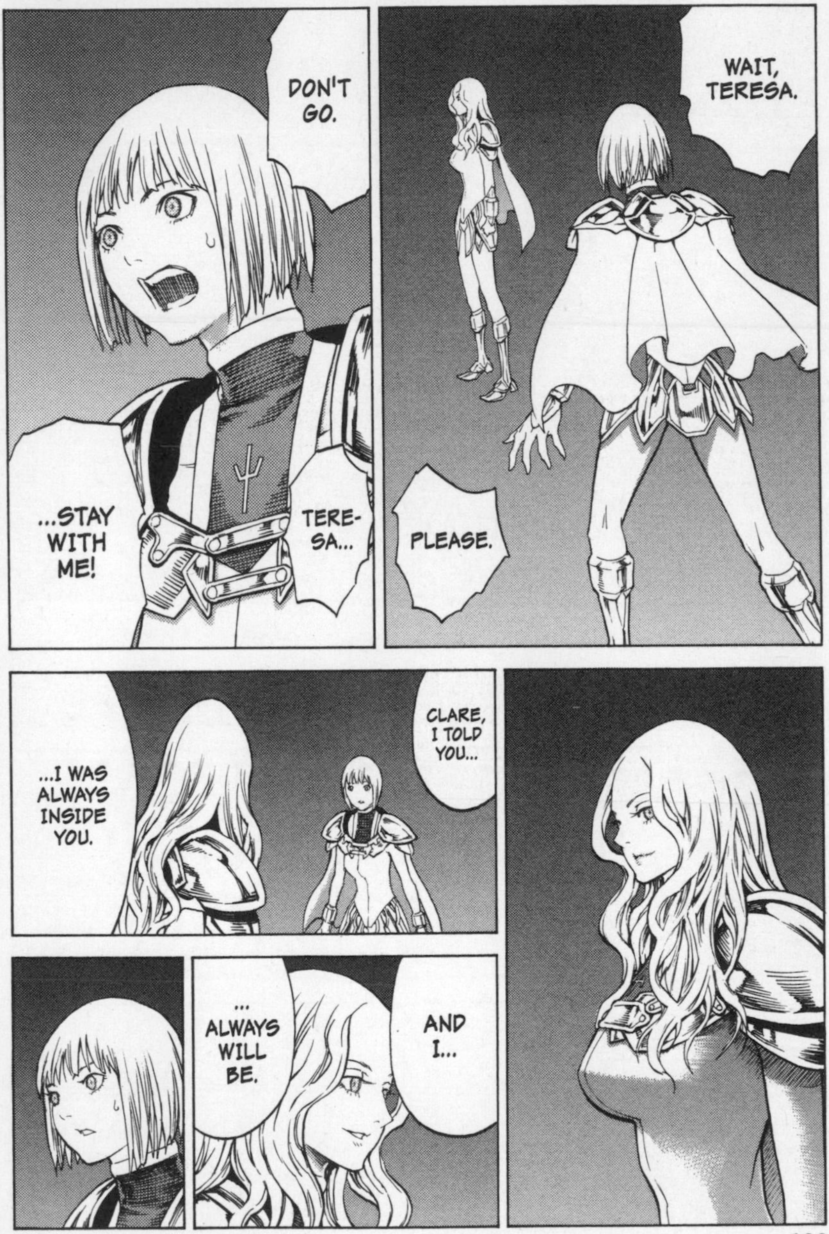
WAIT, TERESA.
PLEASE.
DON'T GO.
TERE-SA...
...STAY WITH ME!
CLARE, I TOLD YOU...
...I WAS ALWAYS INSIDE YOU.
AND I...
...ALWAYS WILL BE.

READ THIS WAY

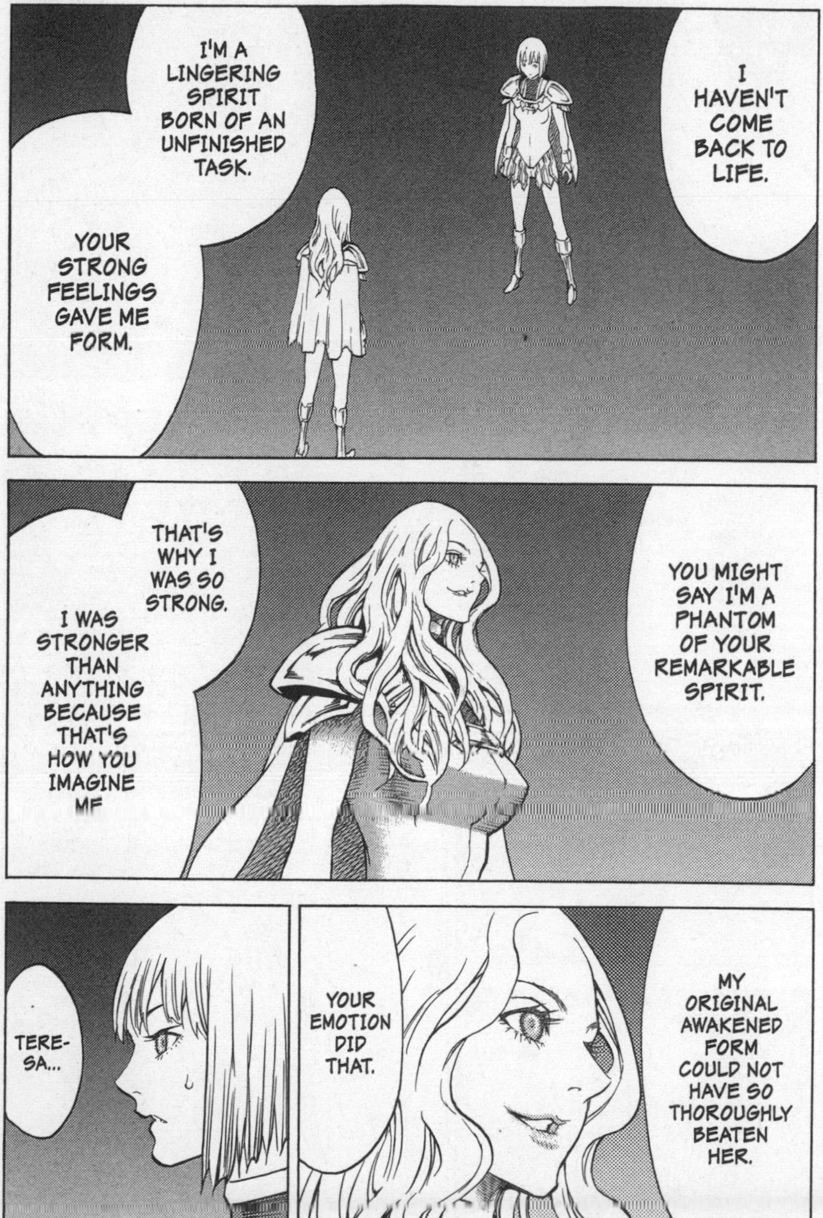

I HAVEN'T COME BACK TO LIFE.
I'M A LINGERING SPIRIT BORN OF AN UNFINISHED TASK.
YOUR STRONG FEELINGS GAVE ME FORM.
YOU MIGHT SAY I'M A PHANTOM OF YOUR REMARKABLE SPIRIT.
THAT'S WHY I WAS SO STRONG.
I WAS STRONGER THAN ANYTHING BECAUSE THAT'S HOW YOU IMAGINE ME
MY ORIGINAL AWAKENED FORM COULD NOT HAVE SO THOROUGHLY BEATEN HER.
YOUR EMOTION DID THAT.
TERE-SA...

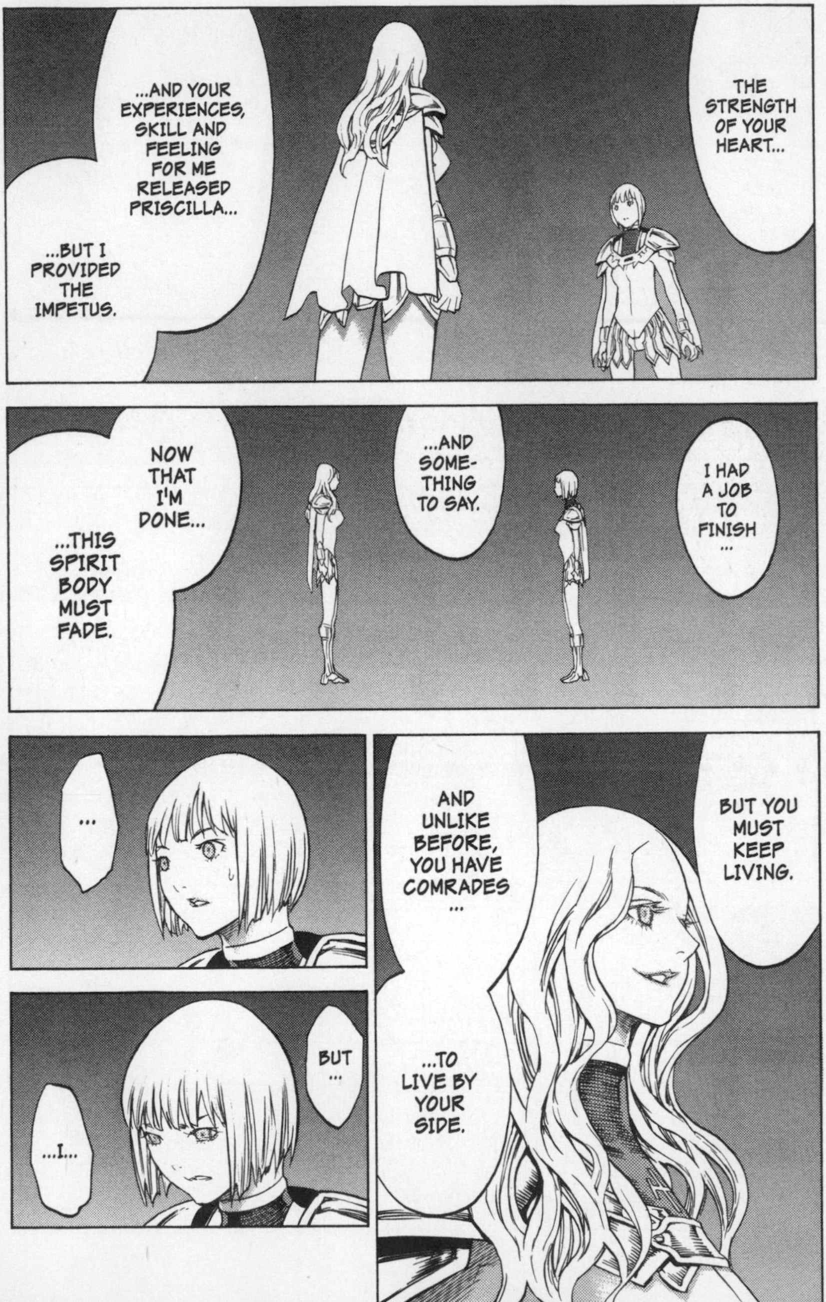
THE STRENGTH OF YOUR HEART...
...AND YOUR EXPERIENCES, SKILL AND FEELING FOR ME RELEASED PRISCILLA...
...BUT I PROVIDED THE IMPETUS.
I HAD A JOB TO FINISH ...
...AND SOME-THING TO SAY.
NOW THAT I'M DONE...
...THIS SPIRIT BODY MUST FADE.
BUT YOU MUST KEEP LIVING.
AND UNLIKE BEFORE, YOU HAVE COMRADES ...
...TO LIVE BY YOUR SIDE.
...
BUT ...
...I...

READ THIS WAY

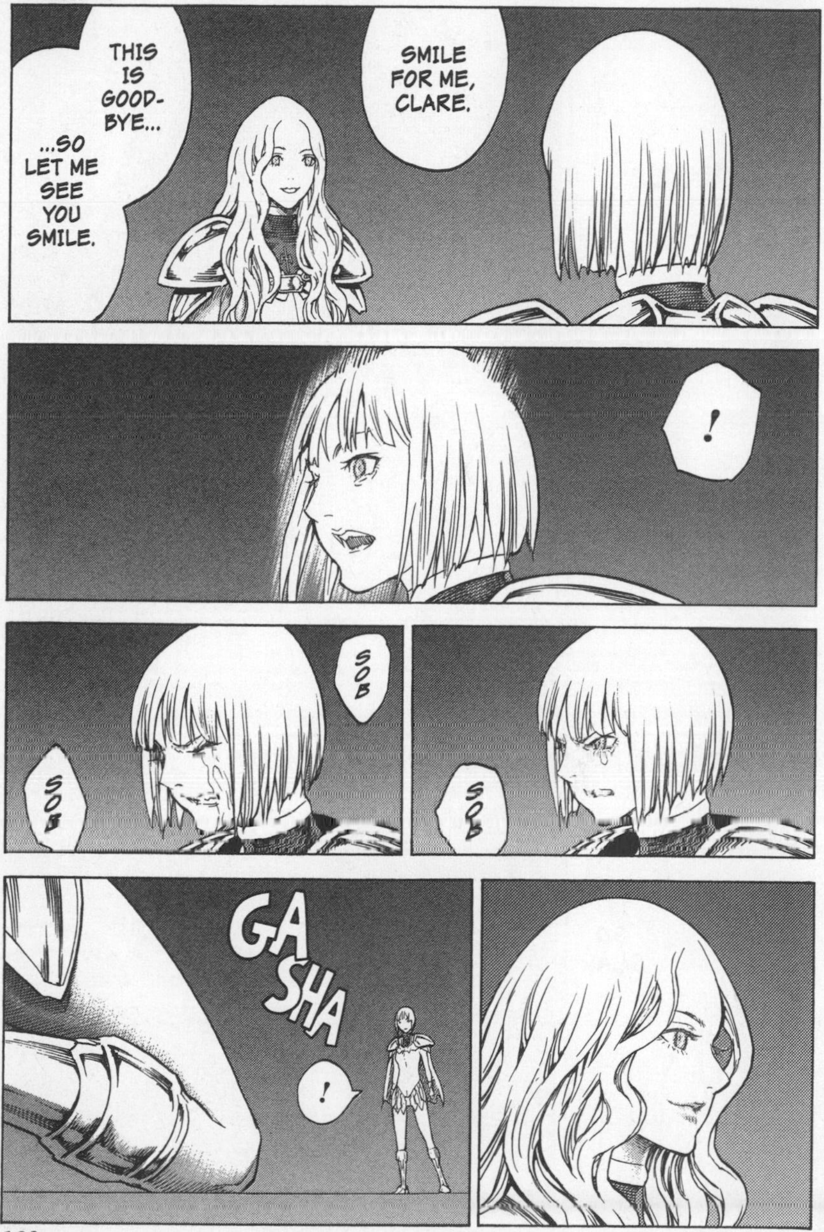
SMILE FOR ME, CLARE.
THIS IS GOOD-BYE...
...SO LET ME SEE YOU SMILE.
!
SOB
SOB
SOB
SOB
GA SHA
!

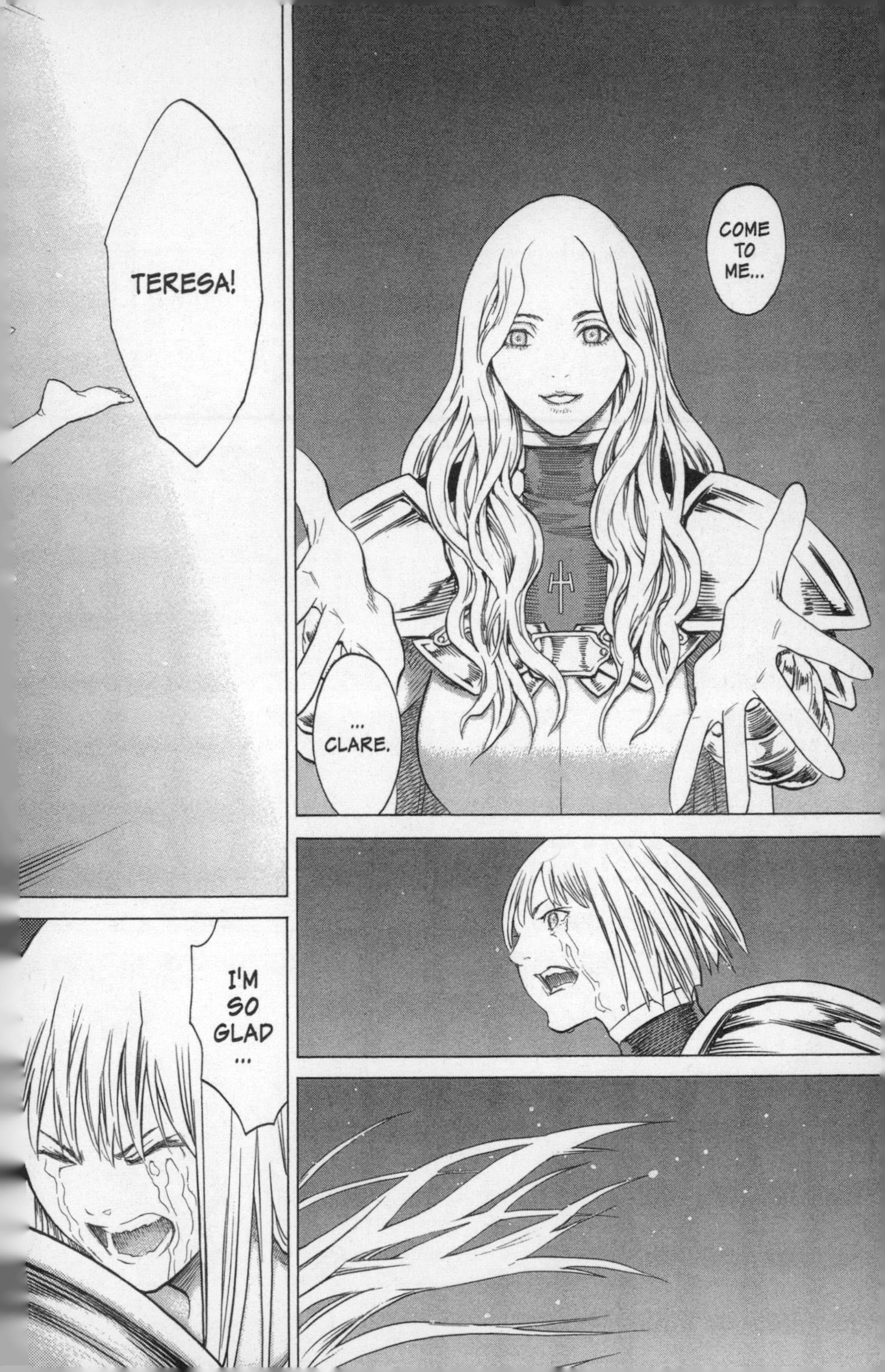
COME TO ME...
... CLARE.
TERESA!
I'M SO GLAD ...

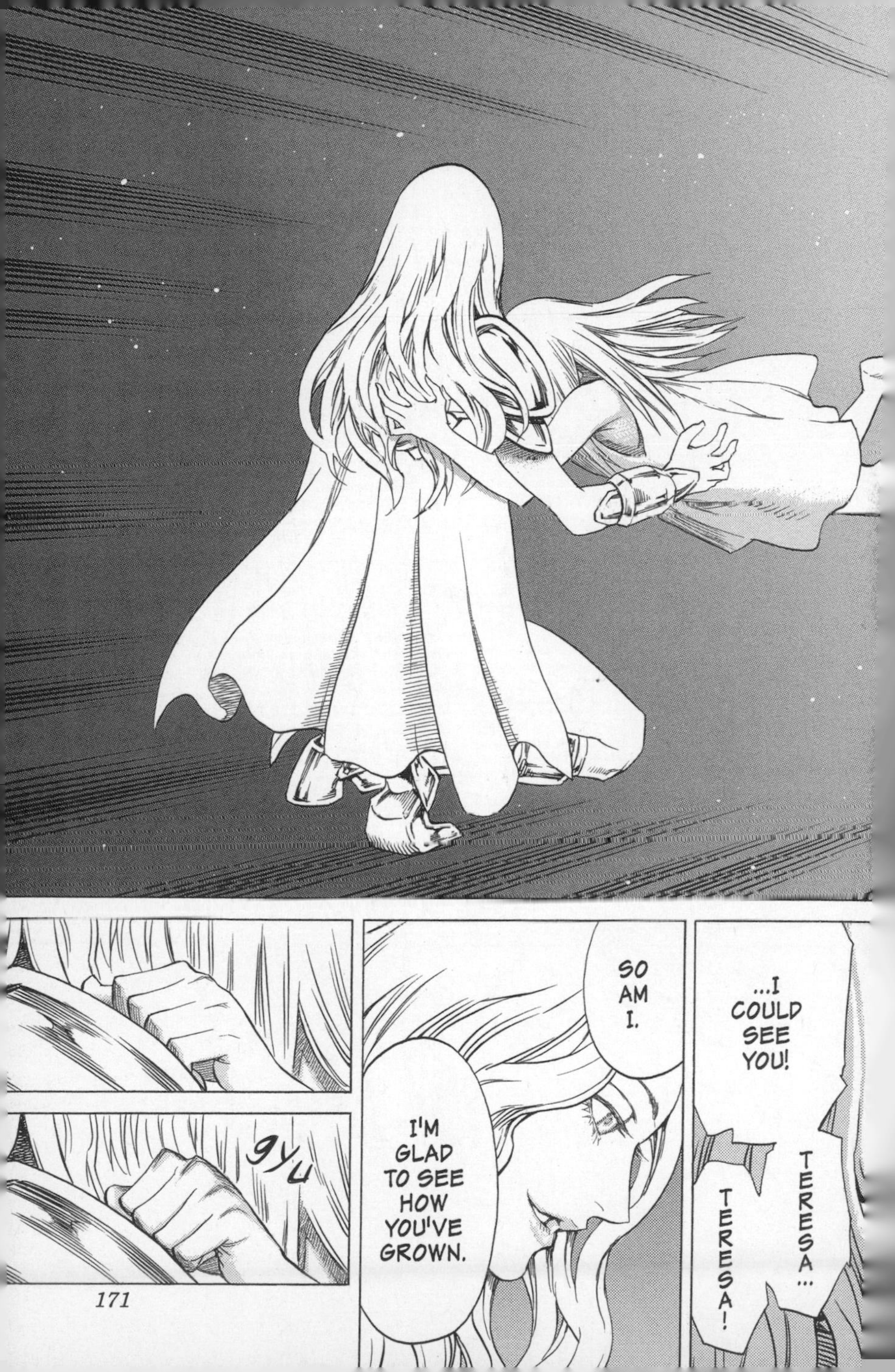
...I COULD SEE YOU!
TERESA...
TERESA!
SO AM I.
I'M GLAD TO SEE HOW YOU'VE GROWN.
gyu

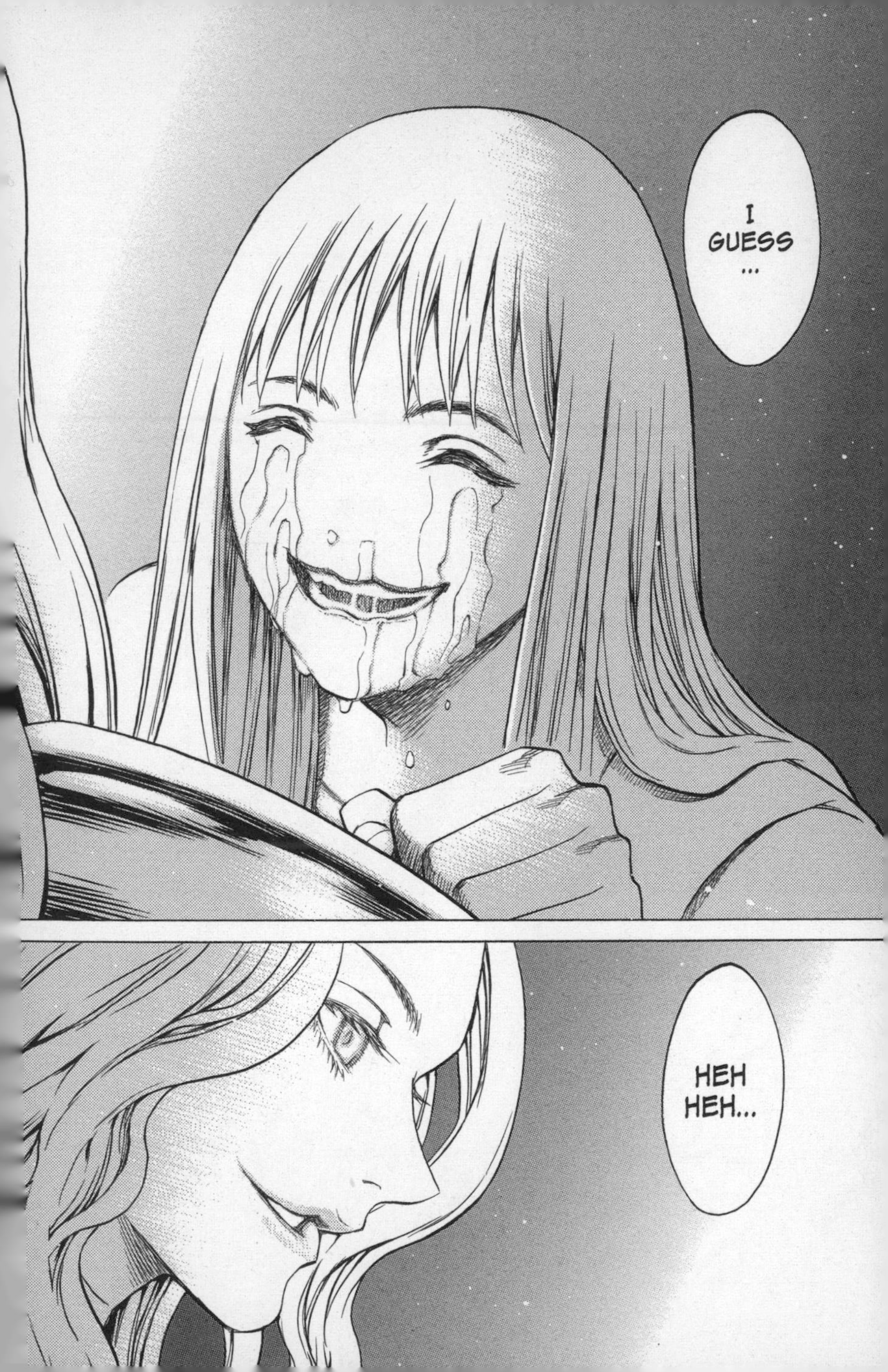
I GUESS ...
HEH HEH...

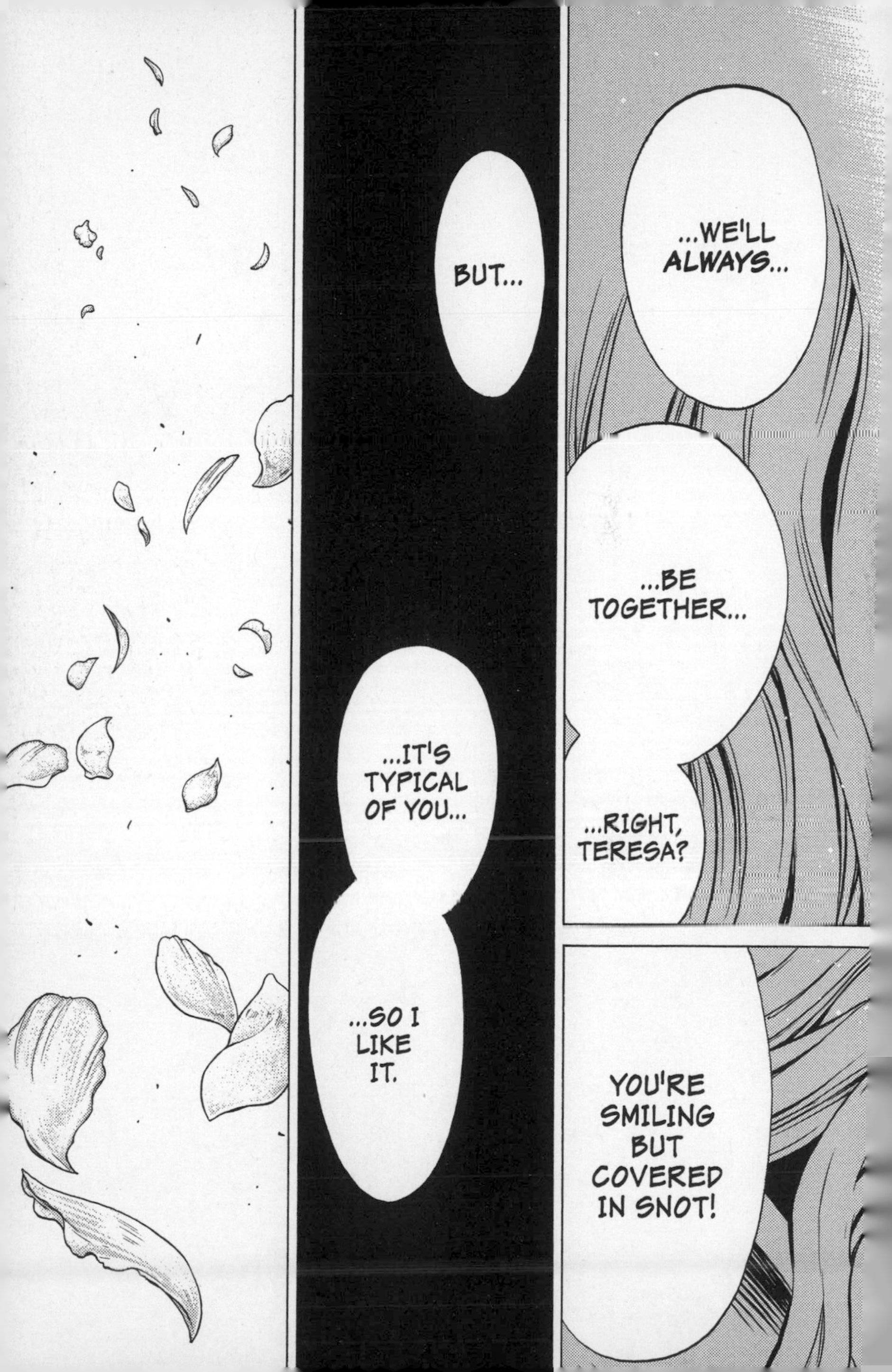
...WE'LL ALWAYS...
...BE TOGETHER...
...RIGHT, TERESA?
YOU'RE SMILING BUT COVERED IN SNOT!
BUT...
...IT'S TYPICAL OF YOU...
...SO I LIKE IT.

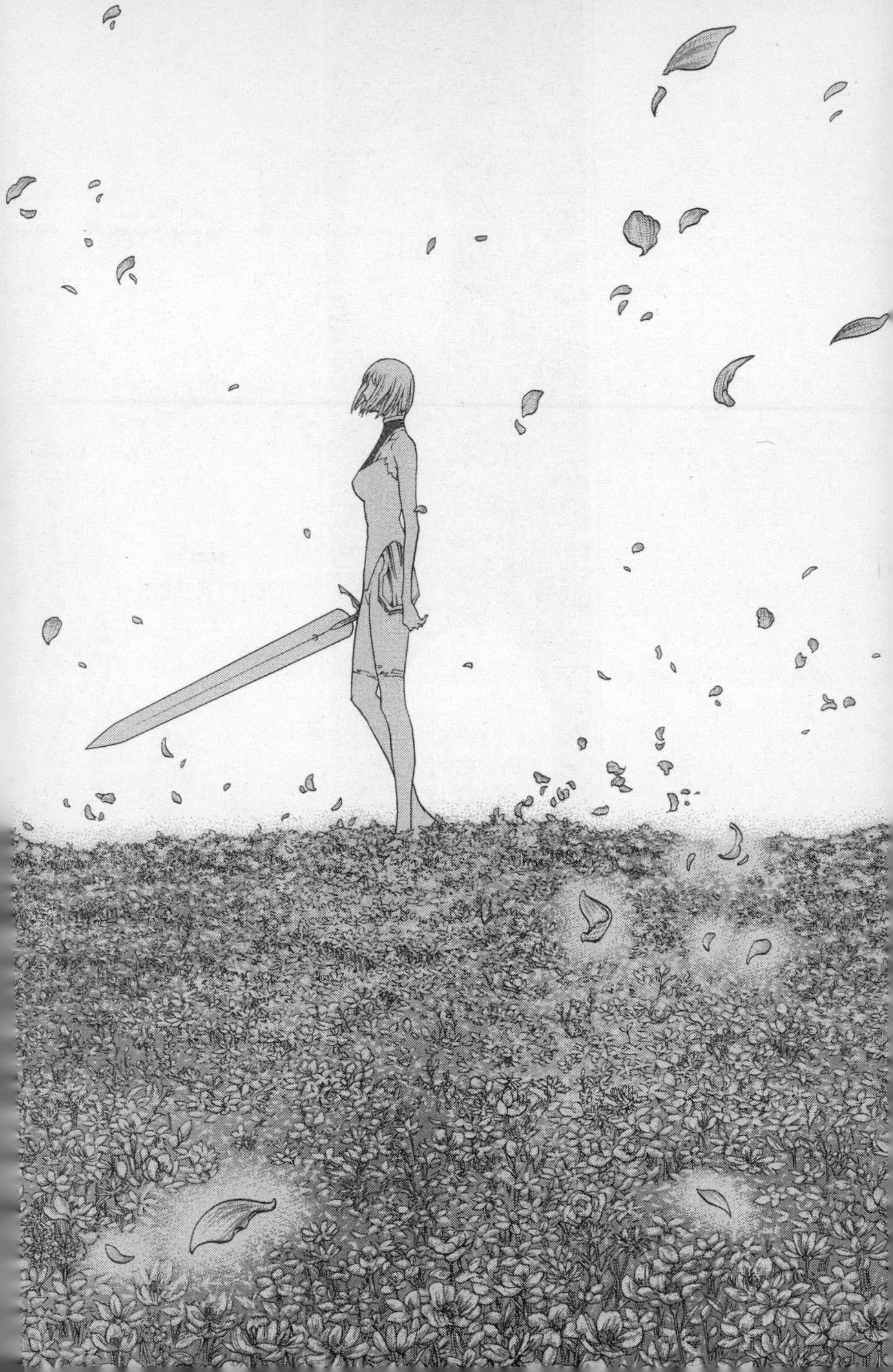

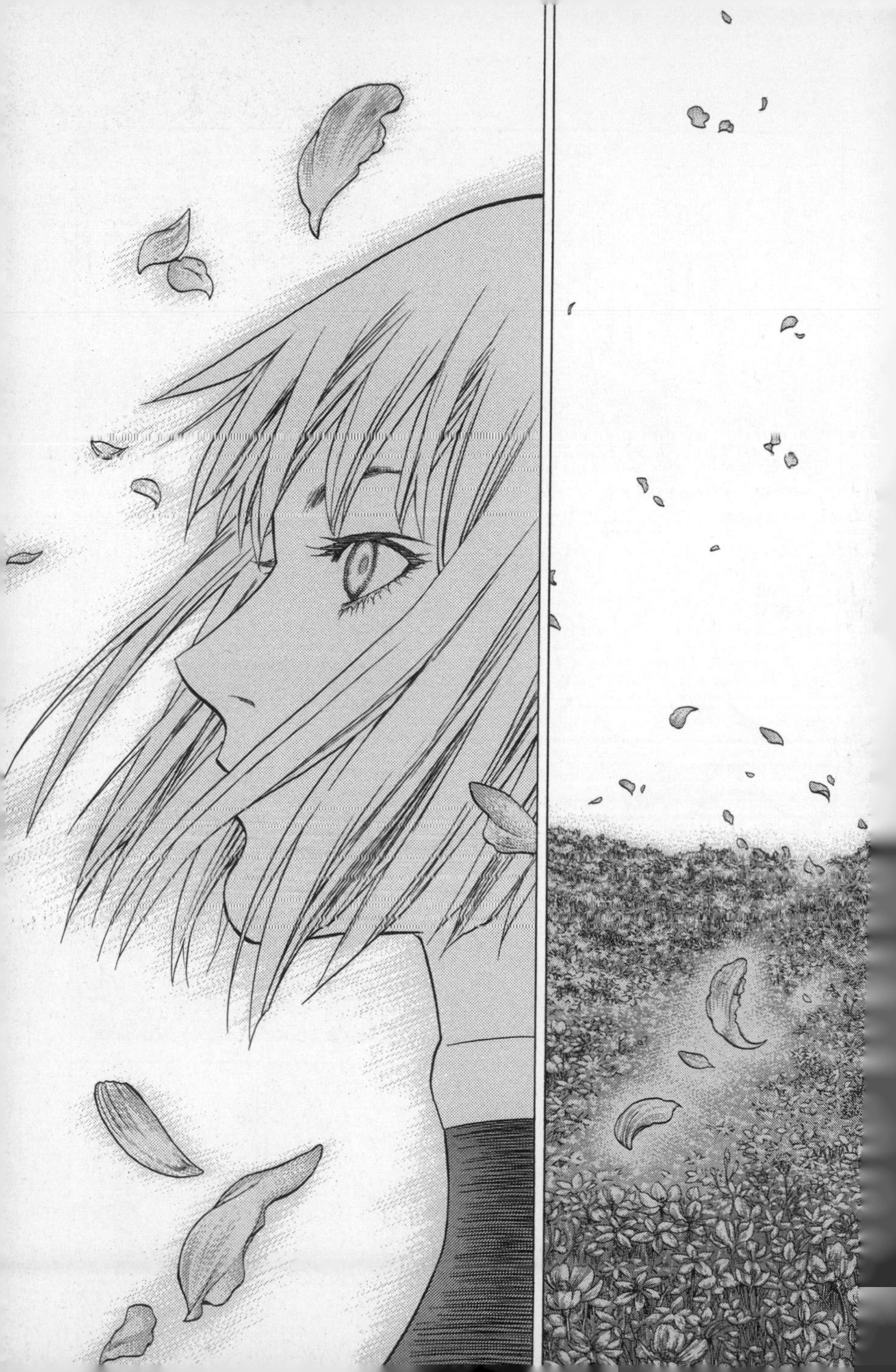

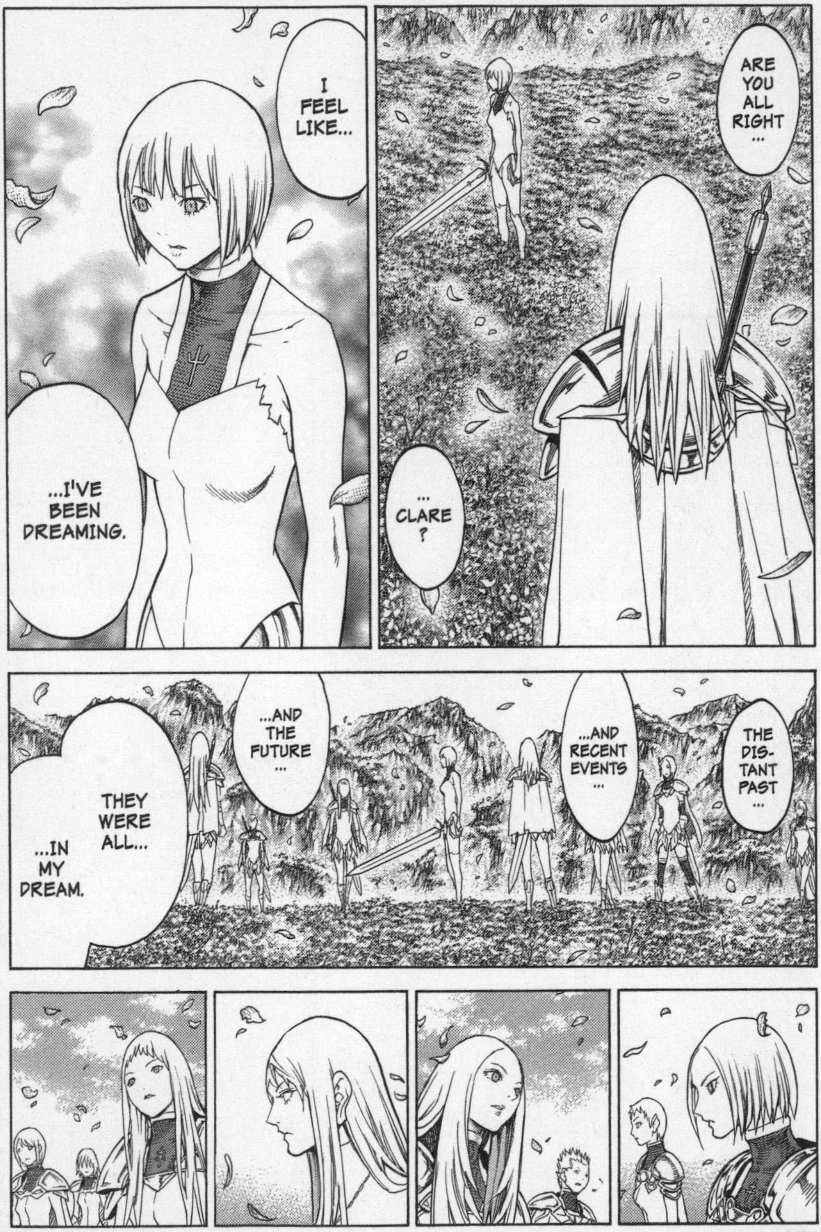

ARE YOU ALL RIGHT ...
... CLARE ?
I FEEL LIKE...
...I'VE BEEN DREAMING.
THE DIS-TANT PAST ...
...AND RECENT EVENTS ...
...AND THE FUTURE ...
THEY WERE ALL...
...IN MY DREAM.

READ THIS WAY

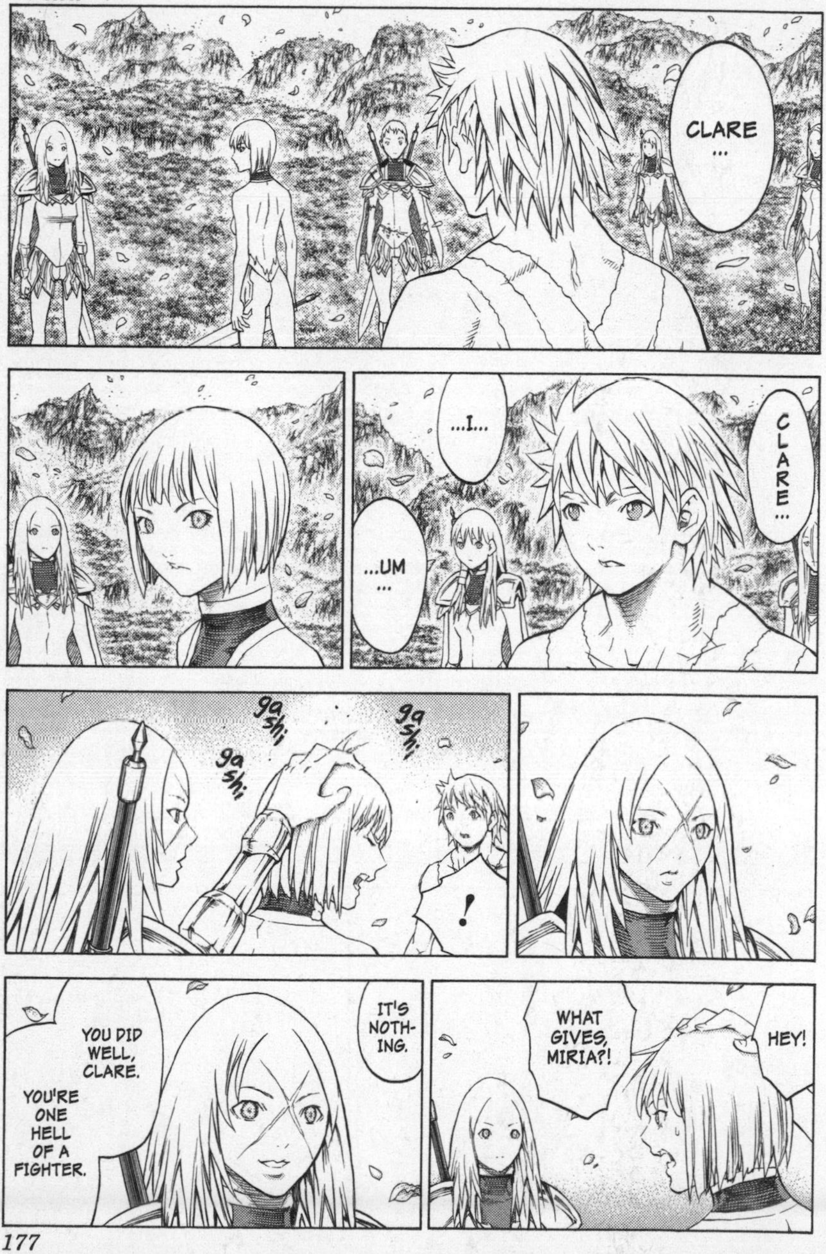

CLARE ...
CLARE ...
...I...
...UM ...
gashi
gashi
gashi
!
HEY!
WHAT GIVES, MIRIA?!
IT'S NOTHING.
YOU DID WELL, CLARE.
YOU'RE ONE HELL OF A FIGHTER.

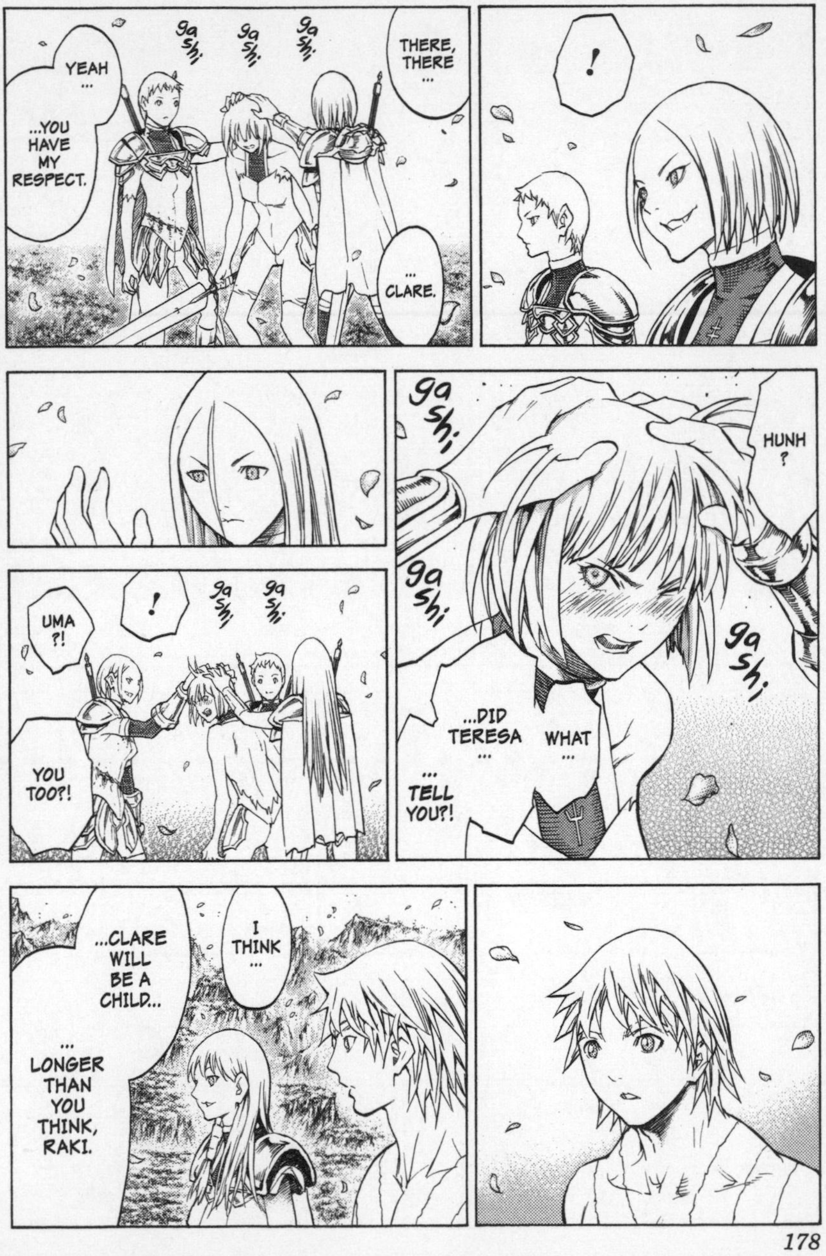
!
THERE, THERE ...
... CLARE.
ga shi
ga shi
ga shi
YEAH ...
...YOU HAVE MY RESPECT.
HUNH ?
ga shi
ga shi
ga shi
WHAT ...
...DID TERESA ...
... TELL YOU?!
ga shi
ga shi
!
UMA ?!
YOU TOO?!
I THINK ...
...CLARE WILL BE A CHILD...
... LONGER THAN YOU THINK, RAKI.

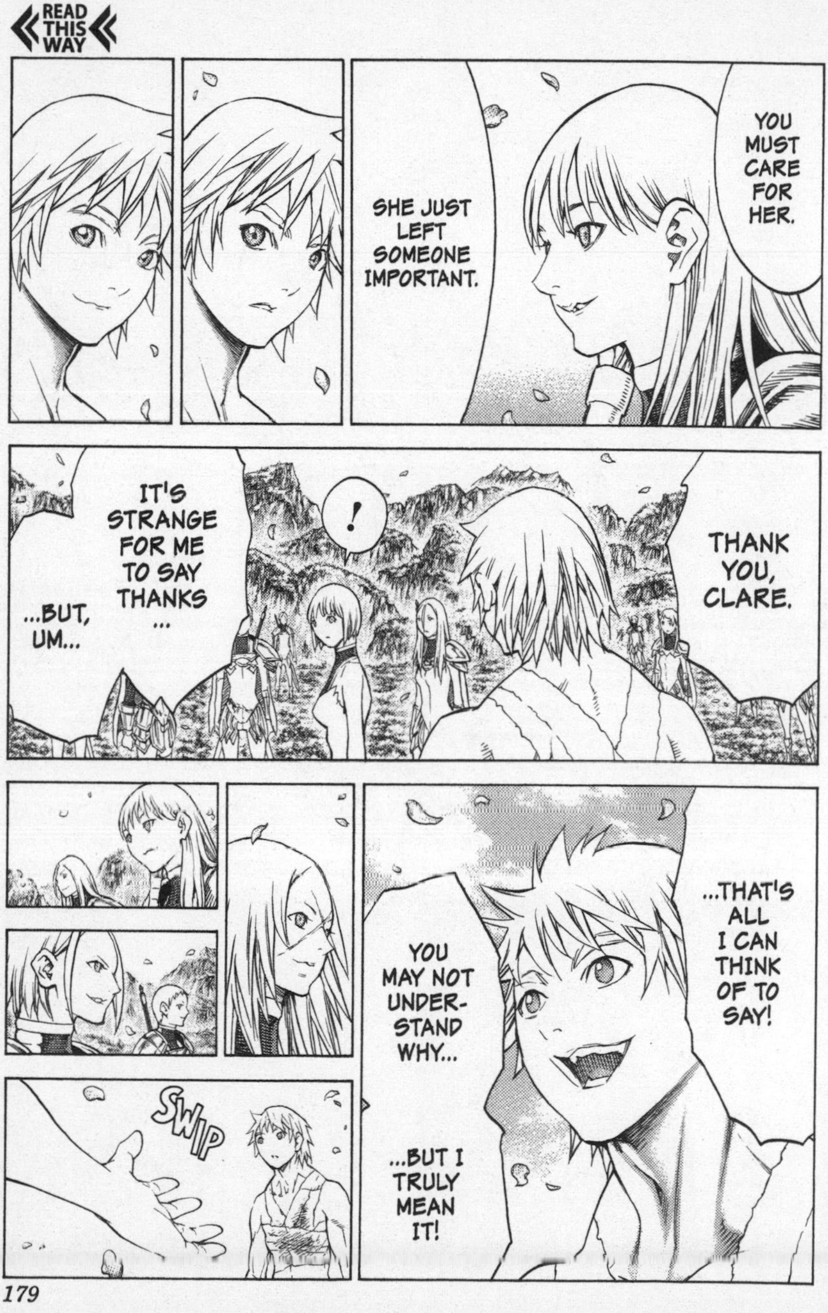
READ THIS WAY
YOU MUST CARE FOR HER.
SHE JUST LEFT SOMEONE IMPORTANT.
THANK YOU, CLARE.
!
IT'S STRANGE FOR ME TO SAY THANKS ...
...BUT, UM...
...THAT'S ALL I CAN THINK OF TO SAY!
YOU MAY NOT UNDER-STAND WHY...
...BUT I TRULY MEAN IT!
SWIP

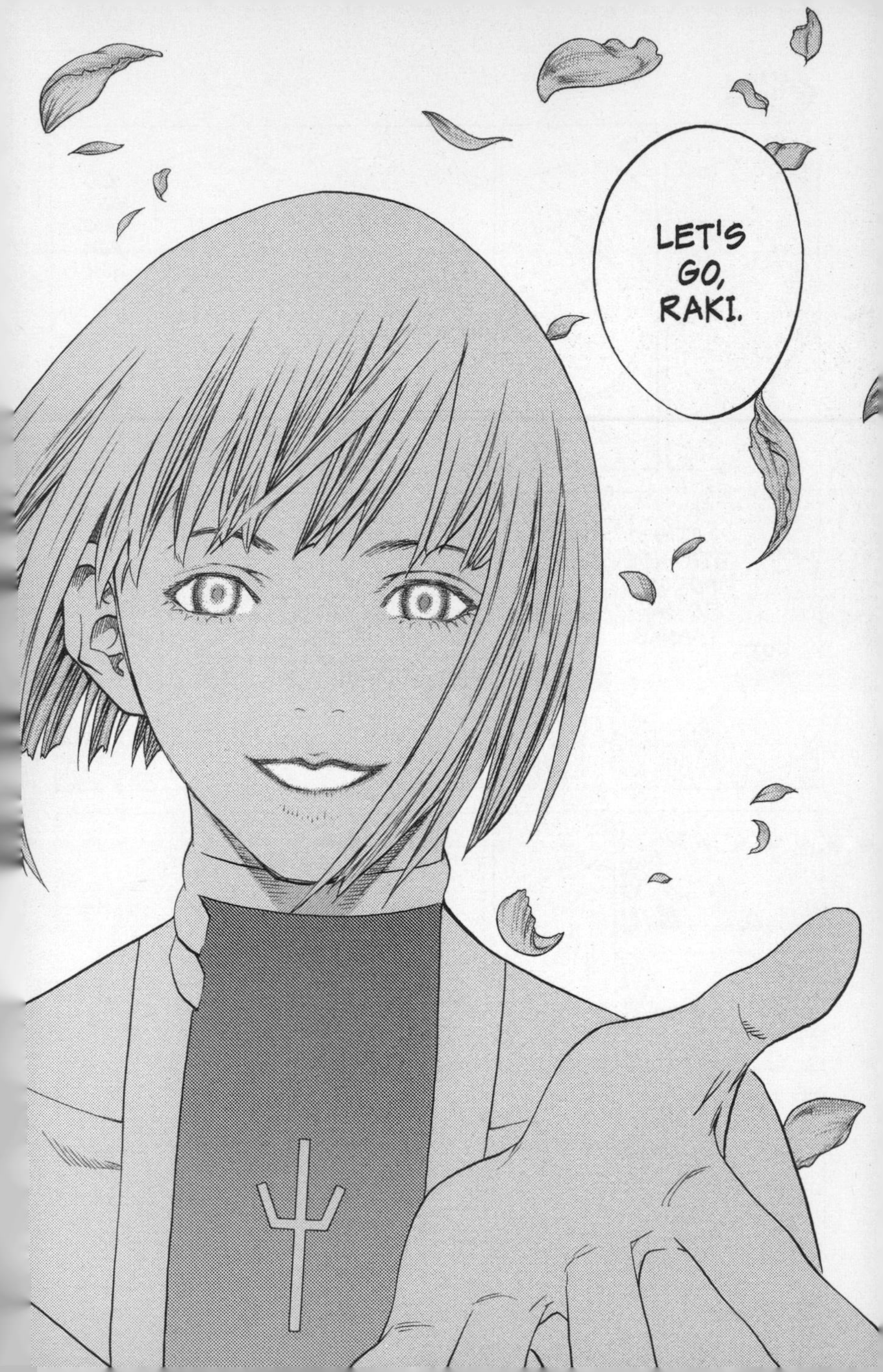
LET'S GO, RAKI.

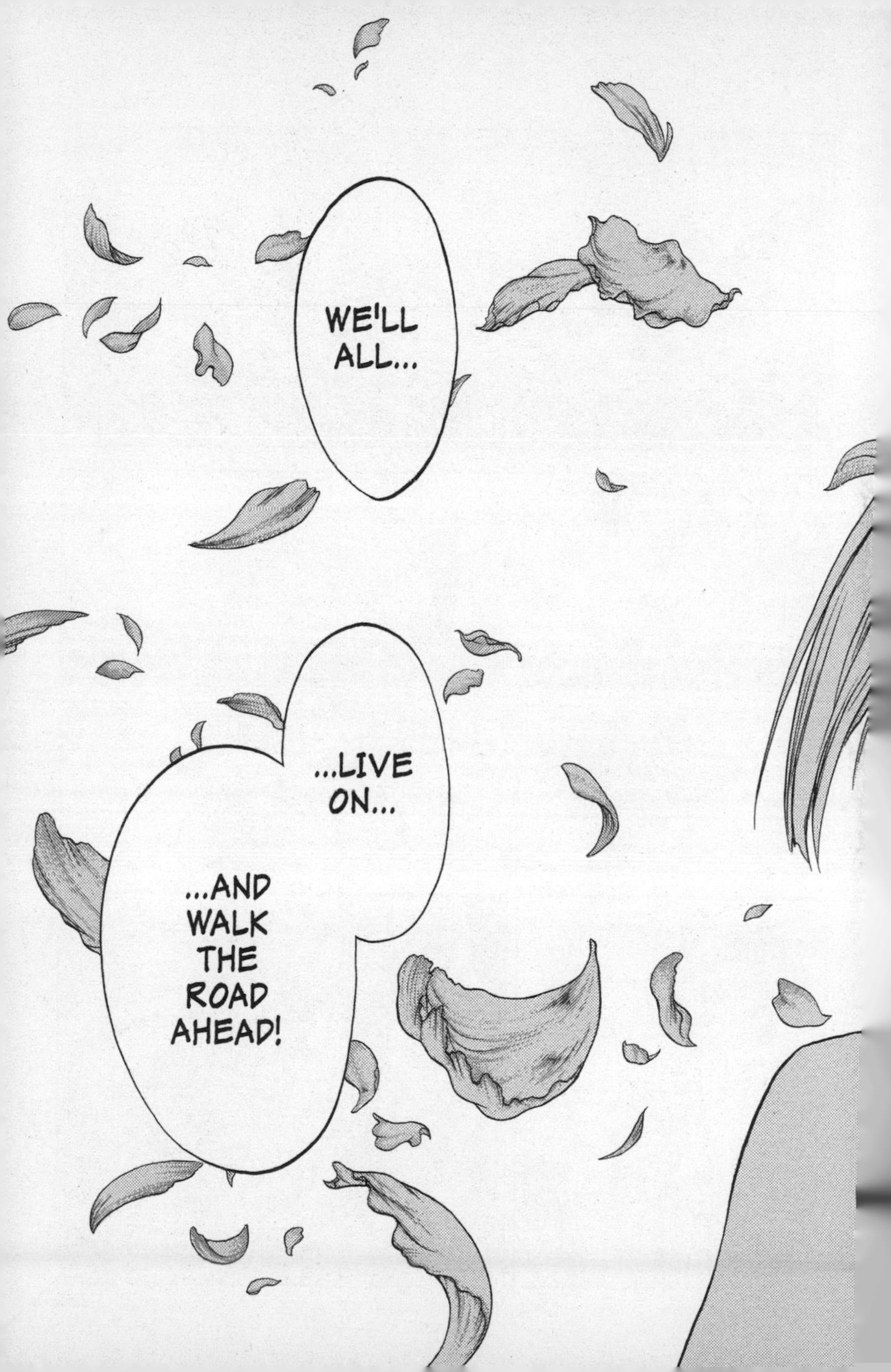
WE'LL ALL...
...LIVE ON...
...AND WALK THE ROAD AHEAD!

...ENDS HERE.

I GUESS MY ROAD...

!

GA

KA

KA

GA

KA

KA

READ THIS WAY

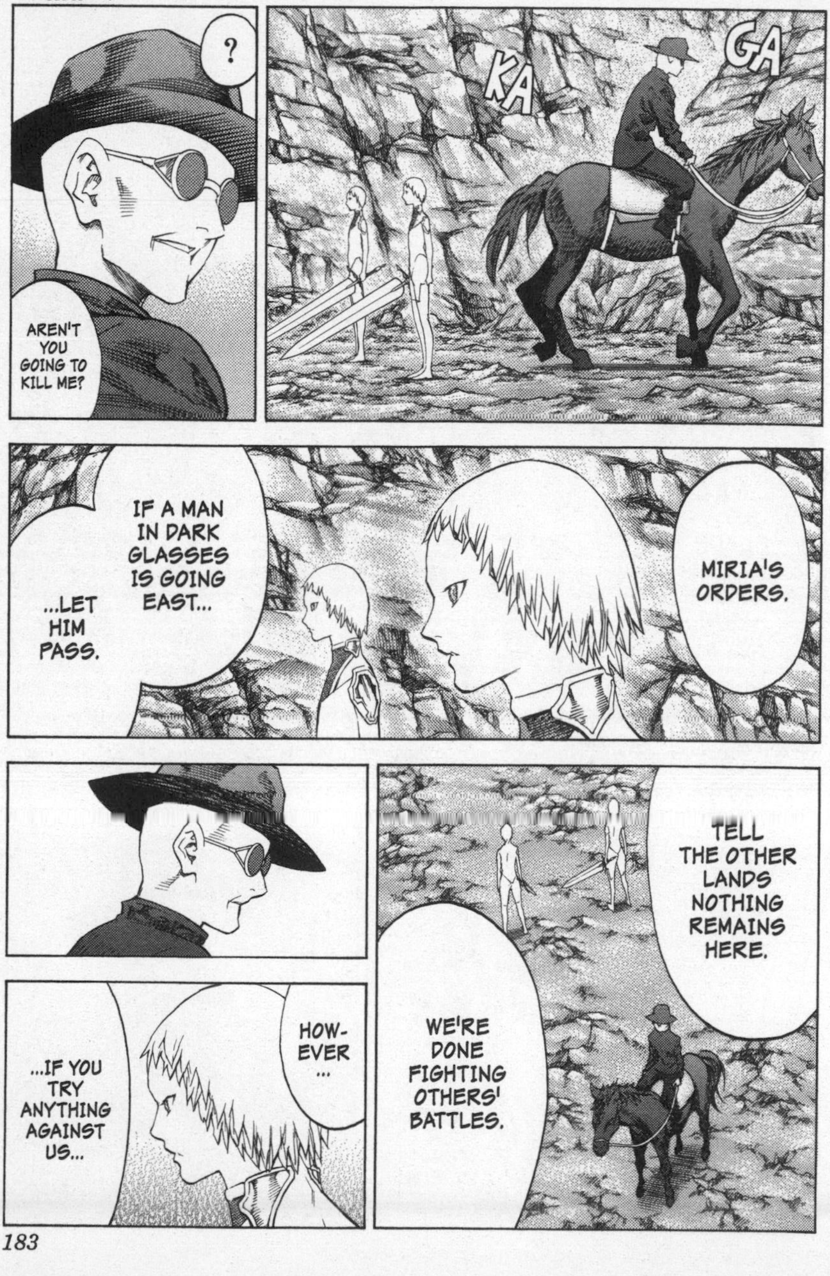
KA
GA
?
AREN'T YOU GOING TO KILL ME?
MIRIA'S ORDERS.
IF A MAN IN DARK GLASSES IS GOING EAST...
...LET HIM PASS.
TELL THE OTHER LANDS NOTHING REMAINS HERE.
WE'RE DONE FIGHTING OTHERS' BATTLES.
HOW-EVER...
...IF YOU TRY ANYTHING AGAINST US...

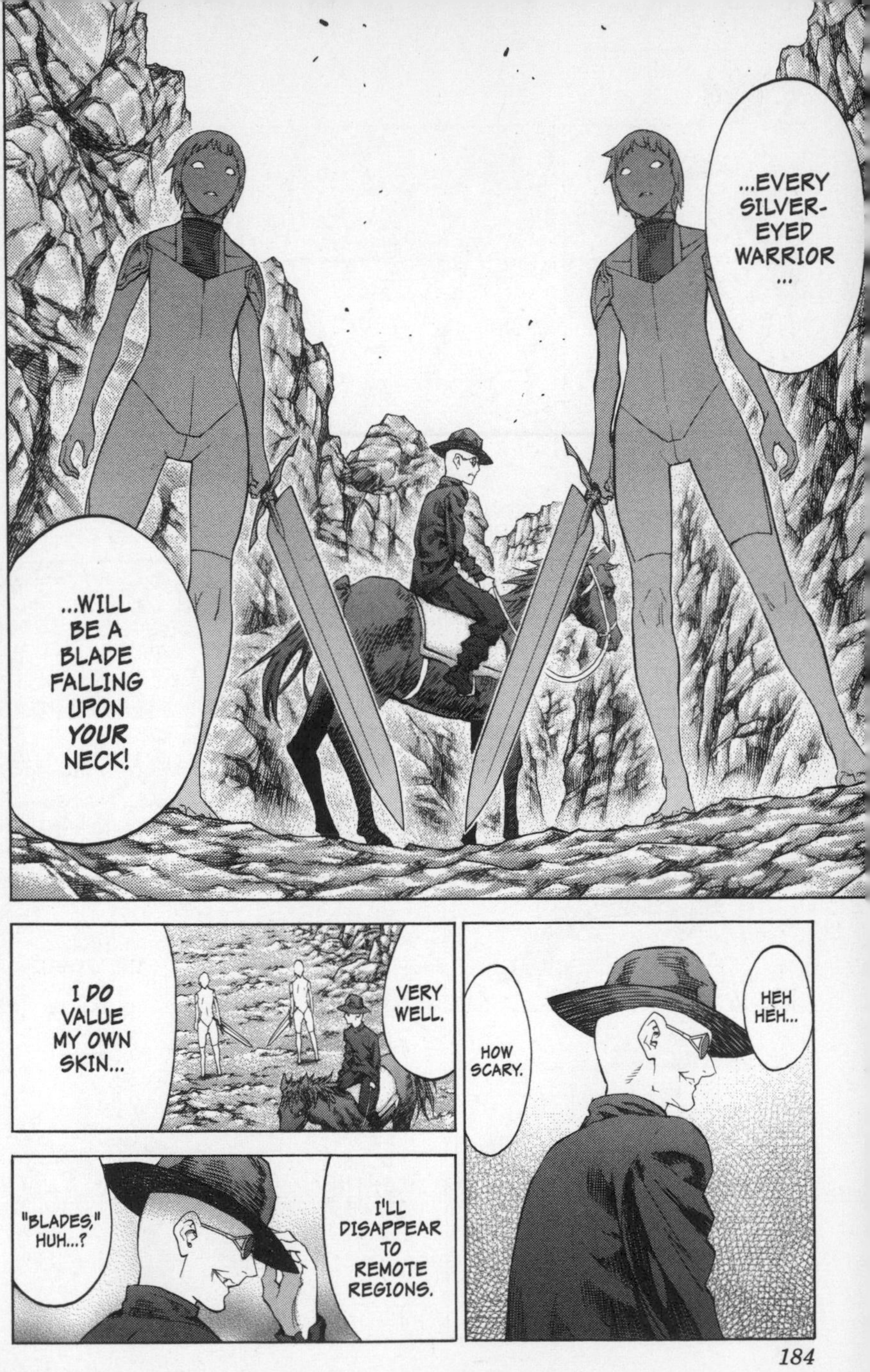
...EVERY SILVER-EYED WARRIOR ...
...WILL BE A BLADE FALLING UPON YOUR NECK!
HEH HEH...
HOW SCARY.
VERY WELL.
I DO VALUE MY OWN SKIN...
I'LL DISAPPEAR TO REMOTE REGIONS.
"BLADES," HUH...?

READ THIS WAY

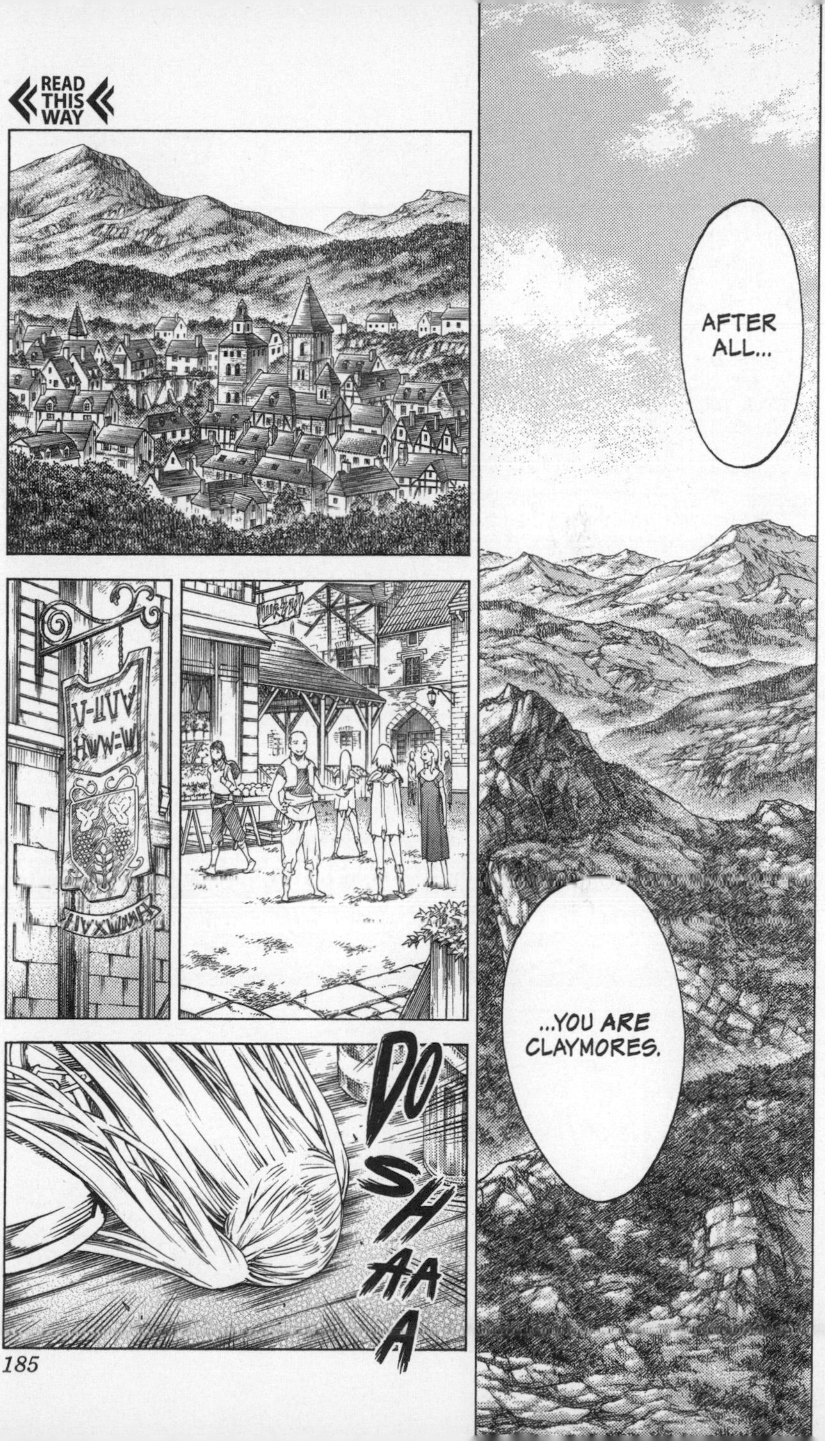
AFTER ALL...
...YOU ARE CLAYMORES.
DOSHAAAA

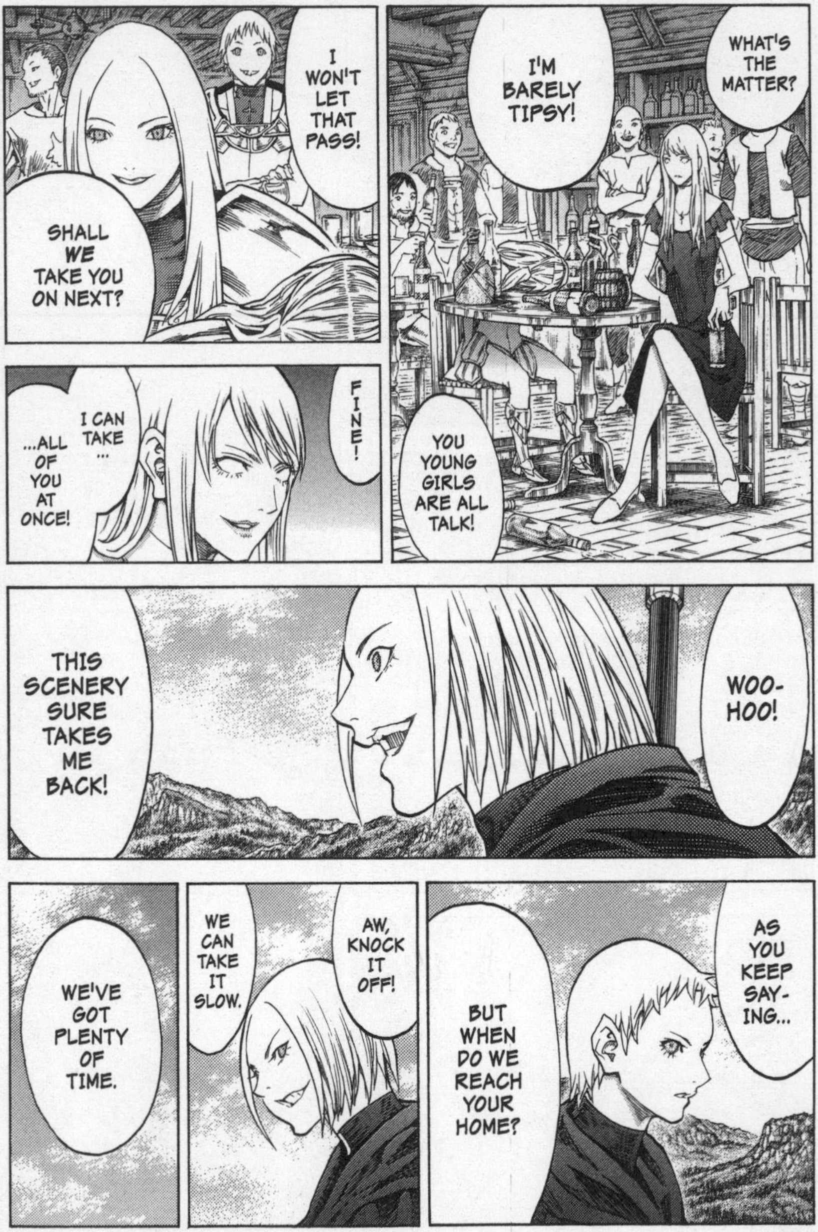
WHAT'S THE MATTER?
I'M BARELY TIPSY!
YOU YOUNG GIRLS ARE ALL TALK!
I WON'T LET THAT PASS!
SHALL WE TAKE YOU ON NEXT?
FINE!
I CAN TAKE...
...ALL OF YOU AT ONCE!
WOO-HOO!
THIS SCENERY SURE TAKES ME BACK!
AS YOU KEEP SAY-ING...
BUT WHEN DO WE REACH YOUR HOME?
AW, KNOCK IT OFF!
WE CAN TAKE IT SLOW.
WE'VE GOT PLENTY OF TIME.

READ THIS WAY

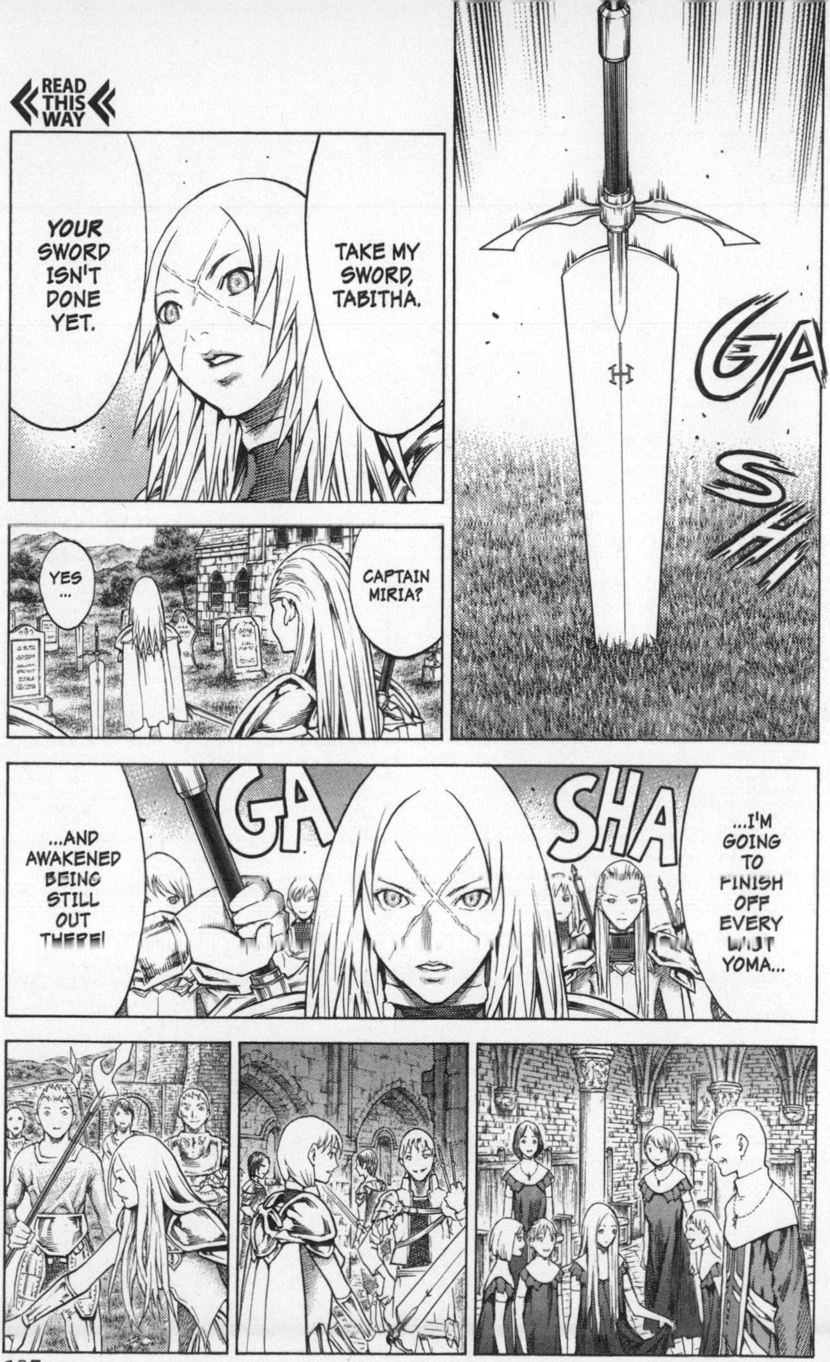
GA SHI
TAKE MY SWORD, TABITHA.
YOUR SWORD ISN'T DONE YET.
CAPTAIN MIRIA?
YES ...
GA SHA
...I'M GOING TO FINISH OFF EVERY LAST YOMA...
...AND AWAKENED BEING STILL OUT THERE!

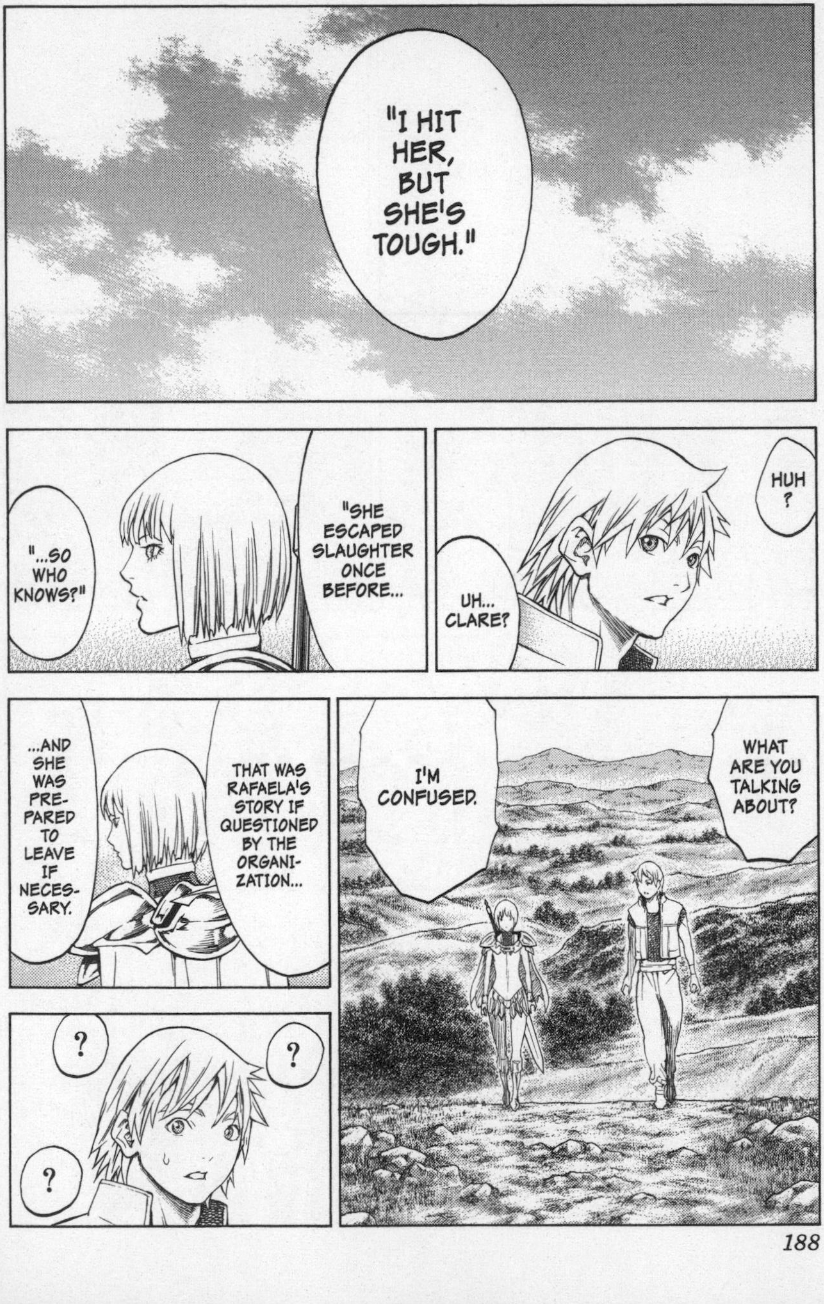
"I HIT HER, BUT SHE'S TOUGH."
HUH?
UH... CLARE?
"SHE ESCAPED SLAUGHTER ONCE BEFORE...
"...SO WHO KNOWS?"
WHAT ARE YOU TALKING ABOUT?
I'M CONFUSED.
THAT WAS RAFAELA'S STORY IF QUESTIONED BY THE ORGANI-ZATION...
...AND SHE WAS PRE-PARED TO LEAVE IF NECES-SARY.
?
?
?

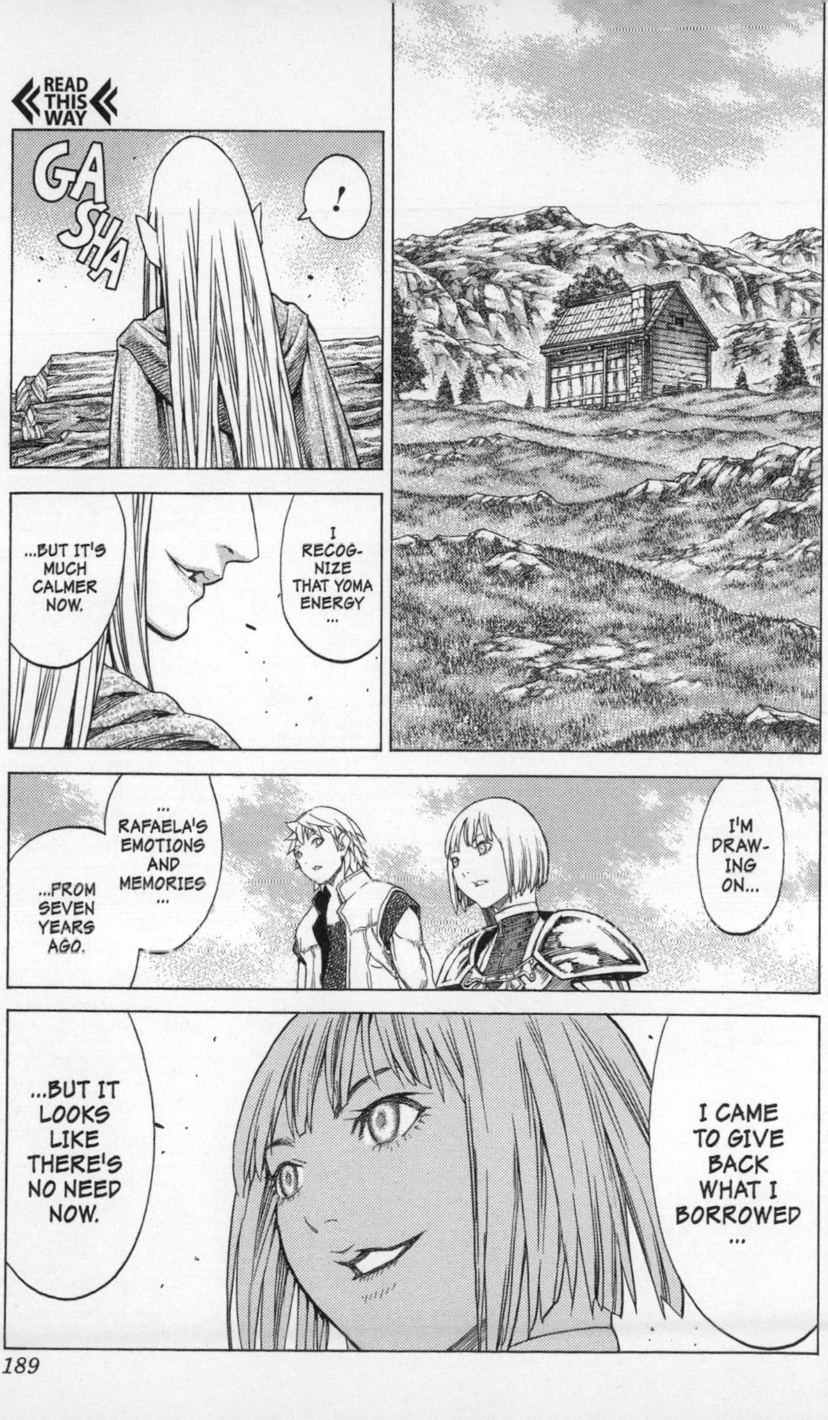
READ THIS WAY
GASHA
!
I RECOGNIZE THAT YOMA ENERGY...
...BUT IT'S MUCH CALMER NOW.
I'M DRAWING ON...
...RAFAELA'S EMOTIONS AND MEMORIES...
...FROM SEVEN YEARS AGO.
I CAME TO GIVE BACK WHAT I BORROWED...
...BUT IT LOOKS LIKE THERE'S NO NEED NOW.

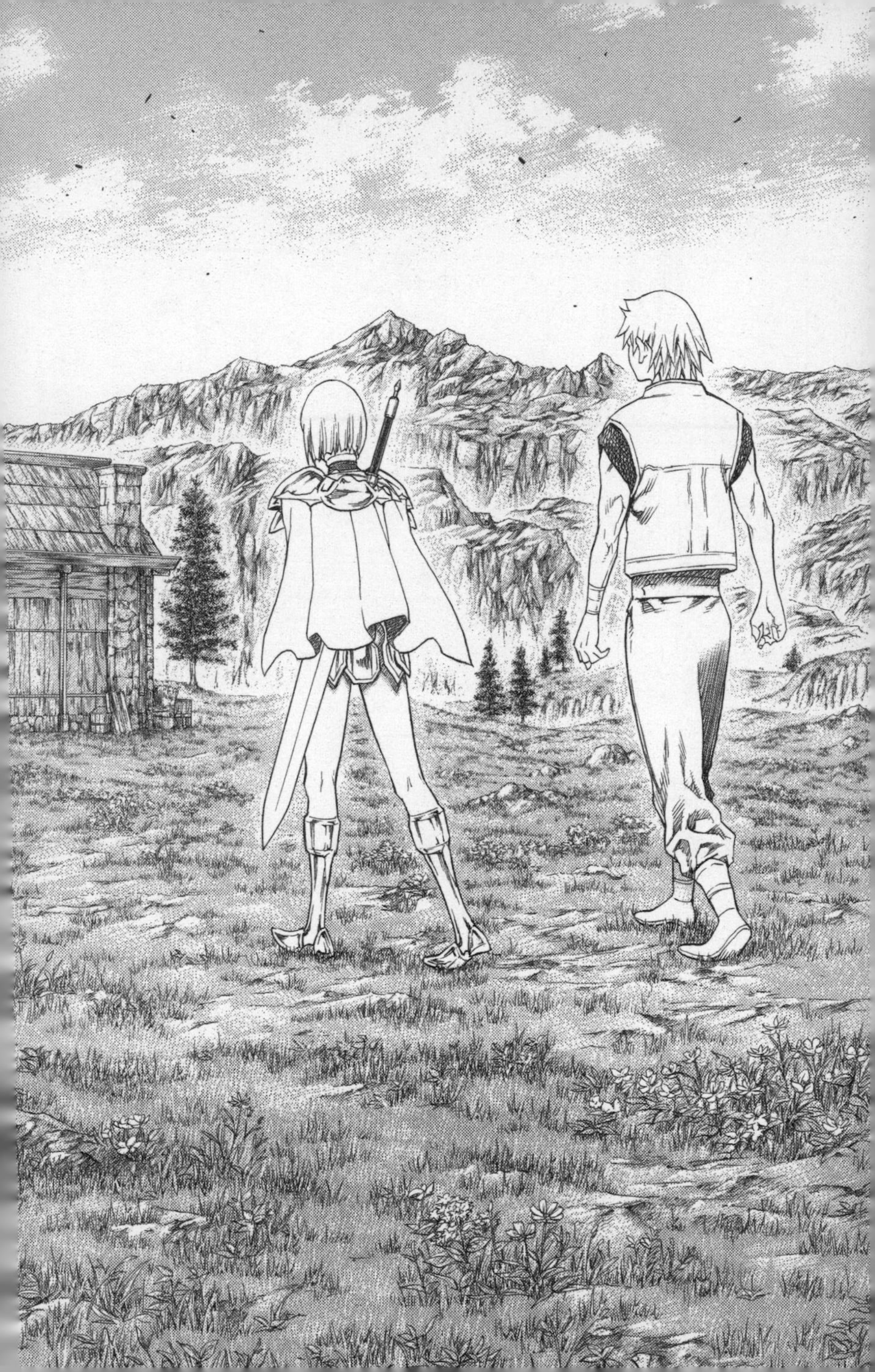

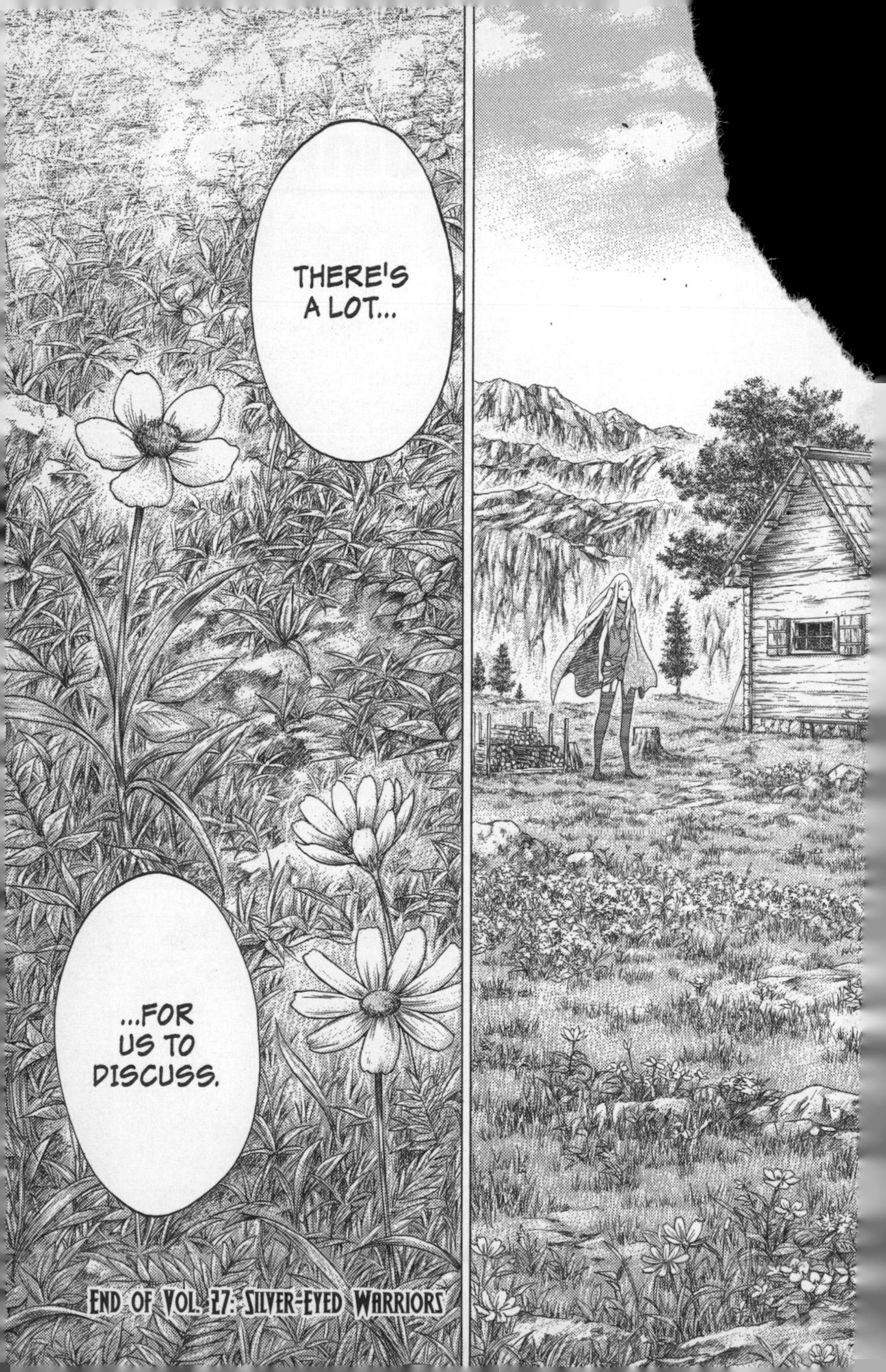
THERE'S A LOT...
...FOR US TO DISCUSS.
END OF VOL. 27: SILVER-EYED WARRIORS

ou're ~~Reading~~ in
e Wrong Direction!!

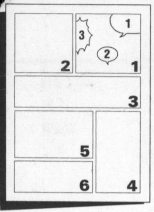

Whoops! Guess what? You're starting at the wrong end of the comic!

...It's true! In keeping with the original Japanese format, **Claymore** is meant to be read from right to left, starting in the upper-right corner.

Unlike English, which is read from left to right, Japanese is read from right to left, meaning that action, sound effects and word-balloon order are completely reversed... something which can make readers unfamiliar with Japanese feel pretty backwards themselves. For this reason, manga or Japanese comics published in the U.S. in English have sometimes been published "flopped"—that is, printed in exact reverse order, as though seen from the other side of a mirror.

By flopping pages, U.S. publishers can avoid confusing readers, but the compromise is not without its downside. For one thing, a character in a flopped manga series who once wore in the original Japanese version a T-shirt emblazoned with "M A Y" (as in "the merry month of") now wears one which reads "Y A M"! Additionally, many manga creators in Japan are themselves unhappy with the process, as some feel the mirror-imaging of their art skews their original intentions.

N
o   ow,
t   the
b   n...!

—Editor